.NET MAUI Cross-Platform Application Development

Second Edition

Build high-performance apps for Android, iOS, macOS, and Windows using XAML and Blazor with .NET 8

Roger Ye

BIRMINGHAM—MUMBAI

.NET MAUI Cross-Platform Application Development
Second Edition

Senior Publishing Product Manager: Larissa Pinto

Acquisition Editor – Peer Reviews: Jane D'Souza

Project Editor: Yamini Bhandari

Content Development Editor: Matthew Davies

Copy Editor: Safis Editing

Technical Editor: Tejas Mhasvekar

Proofreader: Safis Editing

Indexer: Hemangini Bari

Presentation Designer: Pranit Padwal

Developer Relations Marketing Executive: Sohini Ghosh

First published: January 2023

Second edition: March 2024

Production reference: 1190324

Published by Packt Publishing Ltd.

Grosvenor House

11 St Paul's Square

Birmingham

B3 1RB, UK.

ISBN 978-1-83508-059-7

www.packt.com

Contributors

About the author

Roger Ye is a seasoned software engineering manager with expansive experience in the software industry. He began his professional journey working on embedded system development for notable companies such as Motorola, Emerson, and Intersil, during which he authored two books on the subject: **Embedded Programming with Android** and **Android System Programming**.

In 2013, Roger moved to McAfee, where he assumed the role of software engineering manager. More recently, he served in a similar capacity at EPAM Systems, transitioning from system programming to application programming. His current interests revolve around .NET programming and Microsoft technologies; he dedicates himself to continuous learning and mastery in these areas.

I would like to express my profound gratitude to the diligent team at Packt, who worked tirelessly alongside me to maintain our demanding schedule. I am deeply appreciative of my wife and daughter, whose unwavering support has been a beacon of strength for me throughout every endeavor.

About the reviewers

Rohit Vinod Kelkar is a software professional with over six years of experience working in various domains, with a focus on multi-stack development in cross-platform domains. He currently works for Globant as an engineer. His expertise includes full stack .NET development focused on Xamarin and MAUI, multiplatform application development using Flutter, and native iOS development with Swift and SwiftUI. On top of front-end development, he is enthusiastic about back-end technologies like Node .js and express stacks with MongoDB.

I would like to thank Packt for reaching out and providing this opportunity to be a part of this book.

Almir Vuk is an active Microsoft MVP and a senior software engineer with a primary focus on the .NET platform. He excels in crafting applications using C# and ASP.NET Core for back-end systems and .NET MAUI for mobile development. Some of the titles and awards that illustrate his career are Microsoft MVP, Xamarin Certified Mobile Developer, Microsoft Certified Solution Associate, and Microsoft Certified Trainer.

A frequent speaker at Microsoft-related events and user group meetings, both regionally and internationally, he finds enjoyment in various pursuits during his free time. These include playing chess, reviewing technical books, writing blog posts, offering help on StackOverflow, contributing to open-source projects, and taking the role of an instructor at NGO programming-related events.

Learn more on Discord

Join our community's Discord space for discussions with the author and other readers:

```
https://packt.link/cross-platform-app
```

Table of Contents

Chapter 7: Using Platform-Specific Features   227

Part 2: Implementing .NET MAUI Blazor   259

Chapter 8: Introducing Blazor Hybrid App Development   261

Chapter 10: Implementing Razor Components 327

Preface

.NET MAUI is a cross-platform technology developed by Microsoft. The inaugural edition of this book was authored using .NET 6. However, this second edition coincides with the diverse improvements initiated with the release of .NET 8. The latest .NET MAUI release predominantly seeks to enhance code quality. Simultaneously, updates have been made to the development environment that supports iOS and Android, upgrading to Xcode 15 and Android API 34 respectively.

The improvements targeted are concentrated on a range of vital aspects, such as rectifying memory leaks, refining UI controls, instituting platform-specific fixes, and optimizing performance. The goal of these enhancements is to fortify memory management, escalate application stability, and polish the consistency of user experiences across varying platforms, thereby augmenting the overall application performance and responsiveness. With a focus on these components, I strive to provide you with an exhaustive understanding of the latest advancements in .NET MAUI technology.

Despite the broad array of cross-platform programming options available today, including Flutter and React Native, .NET MAUI stands out due to its unique features that should be considered when opting for a cross-platform solution.

One significant advantage of .NET MAUI is its single project structure, a marked improvement over Xamarin.Forms. This streamlined structure enhances various areas, such as:

- **Improving debugging and testing**: With a single project structure, it's possible to select and debug multiple targets within the same project, eliminating the need to switch between different projects for varied targets.
- **Sharing resources**: Traditionally, in Xamarin, resources had to be managed individually for each platform. However, .NET MAUI has improved this aspect by enabling the sharing of the majority of resources across platforms, including fonts, images, icons, etc.

- **Simplified configuration:** By utilizing a singular app manifest for most tasks, it is no longer necessary to separately manage platform configuration files such as `AndroidManifest.xml`, `Info.plist` or `Package.appxmanifest`.

In contrast, to access native device features in Flutter or React Native, you must rely on Flutter plugins or React Native Modules, which in turn rely on the developer community or require personal development. Furthermore, these interfaces are developer-designed and thus lack standardization. Thankfully, Microsoft has standardized APIs for most often used native device features as part of .NET MAUI's release.

.NET MAUI facilitates application development using a traditional XAML-based UI or a Blazor-based UI in Blazor Hybrid apps, furthering opportunities for advanced code reuse. This advantage is particularly valuable for projects encompassing web and mobile apps, as it allows the sharing of user interface design and source code.

As .NET MAUI is now part of the .NET platform releases, we can always have access to the latest .NET platform and C# language features with every .NET release. This inclusion enables the use of advanced features like .NET generic hosting, dependency injection, and the MVVM Toolkit, among others.

In this book, I will guide you through my journey in .NET MAUI development using an open-source app I engineered. Both .NET MAUI and .NET platform features will be thoroughly explored throughout this edition.

Who this book is for

This book is primarily intended for front-end developers or native app developers who are interested in delving into cross-platform programming technology. It assumes that readers possess knowledge of C# programming or any object-oriented programming language akin to C#.

What this book covers

Part 1, Exploring .NET MAUI

Chapter 1, Getting Started with .NET MAUI, provides an introductory overview of cross-platform technologies. As part of this introduction, .NET MAUI is compared with other cross-platform technologies to highlight its unique features. Additionally, this chapter guides you through the process of setting up a .NET MAUI development environment. By reading this chapter, you'll gain a broad understanding of cross-platform technologies that will assist you in selecting the most suitable option for your project.

Chapter 2, Building Our First .NET MAUI App, walks you through the process of setting up a new project, which will serve as the foundation for the development work presented in this book. Additionally, this chapter expounds upon the .NET MAUI project structure and comprehensively discusses the application lifecycle. By the end of this chapter, you'll have mastered how to create a new project and acquired basic debugging skills pertinent to a .NET MAUI application.

Chapter 3, User Interface Design with XAML, introduces you to the concept of user interface design using XAML. This chapter explores the basic understanding of XAML along with .NET MAUI's UI elements. Upon completion of this chapter, you'll have gained the necessary proficiency to create your own user interface design.

Chapter 4, Exploring MVVM and Data Binding, introduces key topics in .NET MAUI app development, including the MVVM pattern and data binding. We will start with theory and then apply what we learn to the development work of the password management app. You will learn how to use data binding and apply it to the MVVM pattern.

Chapter 5, Navigation using .NET MAUI Shell and NavigationPage, explores the essential aspects of navigation in .NET MAUI app development. This includes topics such as the utilization of .NET MAUI Shell and NavigationPage for efficient navigation. The chapter begins with a theoretical overview and then transitions into practical use cases, specifically focusing on the development of a password management app. By the end of this chapter, you will have a robust understanding of how to effectively implement navigation within your .NET MAUI apps.

Chapter 6, Software Design with Dependency Injection, delves into design principles, specifically providing an overview of SOLID design principles. Subsequently, the chapter elucidates the use of dependency injection in .NET MAUI and incorporates this technique into our app development process. By the end of this chapter, you will not only have a broad understanding of SOLID design principles, but also a detailed understanding of dependency injection.

Chapter 7, Using Platform-Specific Features, covers sophisticated topics related to the utilization of platform-specific functionalities in .NET MAUI development. This chapter will guide you through the fundamental steps involved in implementing platform-specific code. This knowledge will be further cemented as you delve deeper into developing platform-specific features in our application.

Part 2, Implementing .NET MAUI Blazor

Chapter 8, Introducing Blazor Hybrid App Development, introduces the concept of developing applications using .NET MAUI Blazor. This chapter guides you through creating a new Blazor Hybrid app and provides instructions on converting a .NET MAUI XAML app to a .NET MAUI Blazor Hybrid app.

The knowledge you'll acquire includes understanding the basic environment setup and Razor syntax that's fundamental to .NET MAUI Blazor application development.

Chapter 9, Understanding Blazor Routing and Layout, focuses on the layout and routing aspects of a Blazor Hybrid app. This chapter provides insight into the setup process of the router and usage of layout components. By the end of this chapter, you'll understand how to design a layout and set up routing for your application.

Chapter 10, Implementing Razor Components, delves into the concept of Razor components and the usage of data binding within them. This chapter will teach you how to create a Razor class library and guide you in refining existing Razor code to craft reusable Razor components. By the end of this chapter, you'll have a practical understanding of how to effectively implement Razor components.

Part 3, Testing and Deployment

Chapter 11, Developing Unit Tests, introduces you to the unit test framework available for .NET MAUI. This chapter will teach you how to utilize xUnit and bUnit to develop effective unit test cases. Additionally, you will learn how to construct unit test cases for .NET classes as well as how to create unit test cases specifically for Razor components using bUnit.

Chapter 12, Deploying and Publishing in App Stores, discusses the procedure for preparing application packages for app stores and setting up a CI/CD workflow using GitHub Actions. This chapter provides insight into creating packages suitable for Google Play, Apple Store, and the Microsoft Store. Additionally, you will learn how to automate the package creation process using GitHub Actions, streamlining your publication efforts.

To get the most out of this book

After completing the first chapter, you can choose to proceed with *Part 1* or jump to *Part 2*. The first part of this book delves into the development of a classic .NET MAUI app utilizing XAML UI. In contrast, the second part introduces Blazor Hybrid app development, a new concept in .NET MAUI. The last part of the book focuses on unit test and deployment strategies.

Please note that both Windows and macOS computers are required to build the projects discussed in this book. We'll be using Visual Studio 2022 and .NET 8 SDK throughout. To build iOS and macOS targets on Windows, it is necessary to connect to a network-accessible Mac, as outlined in the Microsoft documentation provided: `https://learn.microsoft.com/en-us/dotnet/maui/ios/pair-to-mac`.

Since Visual Studio for Mac is scheduled for retirement by August 31, 2024, you may install .NET SDK and Visual Studio Code to replace it on Mac.

Software/hardware covered in the book	OS requirements
Visual Studio 2022	Windows
Visual Studio Code with .NET SDK	macOS

Download the example code files

You can download the example code files for this book from GitHub at `https://github.com/PacktPublishing/.NET-MAUI-Cross-Platform-Application-Development-Second-edition`. If there's an update to the code, it will be updated in the GitHub repository.

My working repository is `https://github.com/shugaoye/PassXYZ.Vault2`.

I will update the source code in my working repository first and then push the commits to Packt repository.

We also have other code bundles from our rich catalog of books and videos available at `https://github.com/PacktPublishing/`. Check them out!

Download the color images

We also provide a PDF file that has color images of the screenshots and diagrams used in this book. You can download it here: `https://packt.link/gbp/9781835080597`.

Conventions used

There are a number of text conventions used throughout this book.

`Code in text`: Indicates code words in text, database table names, folder names, filenames, file extensions, pathnames, dummy URLs, user input, and Twitter handles. Here is an example: "The return value of `CreateMauiApp` is a `MauiApp` instance, which is the entry point of our app."

A block of code is set as follows:

```
private async Task<bool> UpdateItemAsync(string key,
string value)
{
  if (listGroupItem == null) return false;
  if (string.IsNullOrEmpty(key) ||
      string.IsNullOrEmpty(value))
```

```
        return false;
    listGroupItem.Name = key;
    listGroupItem.Notes = value;

    if (_isNewItem) {...}
    else {...}
    StateHasChanged();
    return true;
}
```

When we wish to draw your attention to a particular part of a code block, the relevant lines or items are set in bold:

```
Image image = new Image {
    BackgroundColor = Color.FromHex("#D1D1D1")
};
image.Source = new FontImageSource {
    Glyph = "\uf007",
    FontFamily = "FontAwesomeRegular",
    Size = 32
};
```

Any command-line input or output is written as follows:

```
git clone -b chapter09
https://github.com/PacktPublishing/Modern-Cross-Platform-Application-
Development-with-.NET-MAUI PassXYZ.Vault2
```

Bold: Indicates a new term, an important word, or words that you see onscreen. For instance, words in menus or dialog boxes appear in **bold**. Here is an example: "Launch Visual Studio 2022 and select **Create a new project** on the startup screen."

Tips

Appear like this.

Important notes

Appear like this.

Get in touch

Feedback from our readers is always welcome.

General feedback: Email feedback@packtpub.com, and mention the book's title in the subject of your message. If you have questions about any aspect of this book, please email us at questions@packtpub.com.

Errata: Although we have taken every care to ensure the accuracy of our content, mistakes do happen. If you have found a mistake in this book we would be grateful if you would report this to us. Please visit, http://www.packtpub.com/submit-errata, selecting your book, clicking on the Errata Submission Form link, and entering the details.

Piracy: If you come across any illegal copies of our works in any form on the Internet, we would be grateful if you would provide us with the location address or website name. Please contact us at copyright@packtpub.com with a link to the material.

If you are interested in becoming an author: If there is a topic that you have expertise in and you are interested in either writing or contributing to a book, please visit http://authors.packtpub.com.

Share your thoughts

Once you've read *.NET MAUI Cross-Platform Application Development, Second Edition*, we'd love to hear your thoughts! Scan the QR code below to go straight to the Amazon review page for this book and share your feedback.

https://packt.link/r/1835080596

Your review is important to us and the tech community and will help us make sure we're delivering excellent quality content.

Download a free PDF copy of this book

Thanks for purchasing this book!

Do you like to read on the go but are unable to carry your print books everywhere?

Is your eBook purchase not compatible with the device of your choice?

Don't worry, now with every Packt book you get a DRM-free PDF version of that book at no cost.

Read anywhere, any place, on any device. Search, copy, and paste code from your favorite technical books directly into your application.

The perks don't stop there, you can get exclusive access to discounts, newsletters, and great free content in your inbox daily

Follow these simple steps to get the benefits:

1. Scan the QR code or visit the link below

https://packt.link/free-ebook/9781835080597

2. Submit your proof of purchase
3. That's it! We'll send your free PDF and other benefits to your email directly

Part 1

Exploring .NET MAUI

In the first part of this book, we will delve into .NET MAUI programming. We will begin with an introduction to .NET MAUI and its predecessor, Xamarin.Forms. Following that, we will create a code base using the Visual Studio template for our application. Throughout this book, we will develop a password manager app called PassXYZ.Vault, building it step by step. During the app's development, we will cover user interface design using XAML, the MVVM pattern, data binding, Shell, and dependency injection, among other topics.

By the end of *Part 1*, we will have completed a fully functional password manager application. In this part, we'll explore some of the important groundwork for this application, such as using the .NET Community Toolkit in the context of MVVM and data binding. This will enable you to build and implement applications that involve handling high volumes of data effectively.

Part 1 includes the following chapters:

- *Chapter 1, Getting Started with .NET MAUI*
- *Chapter 2, Building Our First .NET MAUI App*
- *Chapter 3, User Interface Design with XAML*
- *Chapter 4, Exploring MVVM and Data Binding*
- *Chapter 5, Navigation Using .NET MAUI Shell and NavigationPage*
- *Chapter 6, Software Design with Dependency Injection*
- *Chapter 7, Using Platform-Specific Features*

1

Getting Started with .NET MAUI

Since the release of .NET 5, Microsoft has been trying to unify different .NET implementations into one .NET release. .NET Multi-platform App UI (or .NET MAUI) is the effort to provide a unified cross-platform UI framework. We will learn how to use .NET MAUI to develop cross-platform applications in this book.

The following is what we will cover in this chapter:

- Overview of cross-platform technologies
- Comparison of cross-platform technologies (.NET, Java, and JavaScript)
- .NET landscape and the history of Xamarin
- .NET MAUI features
- .NET MAUI Blazor apps
- What's new in .NET 8 for .NET MAUI?
- Development environment setup

If you're new to .NET development, this chapter will help you to understand the .NET landscape. For Xamarin developers, many topics in this book may sound familiar; this chapter will give you an overview of what we will discuss in this book.

Overview of cross-platform and full stack technologies

.NET Multi-platform App UI, or .NET MAUI, is a cross-platform development framework from Microsoft for building apps that targets both mobile and desktop form factors on Android, iOS, macOS, Windows, and Tizen. It is one of a number of cross-platform frameworks available on the market.

Before discussing cross-platform technologies, let's review the scope of application development first. This review will help us to understand the various cross-platform frameworks better.

Generally, software development can be divided into two categories – **systems programming** and **application programming**. Application programming aims to produce software that provides services to the user directly, whereas systems programming aims to produce software and software platforms that provide services to other software. In the .NET domain, the development of the .NET platform itself belongs to systems programming, whereas application development on top of the .NET platform belongs to application programming.

Compared to systems programming, most software development demands are from application programming.

Many business solutions fall under the category of application development. To understand why we choose a specific technology stack for a solution, it is essential to have an overview of all the technologies used in the entire solution. Once we have a clear understanding of the role cross-platform technologies play within the entire solution, we can better comprehend the technology we wish to select.

Most of the development effort for business solutions consists of frontend and backend components. Frontend developers are responsible for the visible and interactive part of an application that users directly see, touch, and interact with. Typically, the frontend team focuses on developing web and native applications. On the other hand, backend development deals with server-side processing, data management, and the implementation of business logic within an application.

Frontend and backend development involve different programming languages and frameworks. Sometimes, the same team may work on both frontend and backend development due to various reasons. In this case, we need a team who can work on full stack development.

To classify application development by programming languages and frameworks, we have the below three categories.

Native application

By native application development, we usually refer to application development for a particular operating system. For desktop applications, it could involve Windows applications, macOS applications, or Linux applications. For mobile applications, it could involve Android or iOS.

When we develop a native application, we may need to support multiple platforms (Windows, Linux, Android, macOS/iOS, etc.). To support multiple platforms, we need to use different programming languages, tools, and libraries to develop each of them individually.

Web application

Web application development has gone through several generations of evolution over the past few decades, from the Netscape browser with static web pages to today's **single-page application (SPA)** using JavaScript frameworks (such as React and Angular). In web application development, JavaScript and various JavaScript-based frameworks dominate the market. In the .NET ecosystem, Blazor is trying to catch up in this area. We'll learn more about Blazor in Chapter 8, *Introducing Blazor Hybrid App Development.*

Backend services

Both native applications and web applications typically require backend services to access business logic or a database. For backend development, there are various languages and frameworks available, including Java/Spring, .NET, Node.js, Ruby on Rails, and Python/Django. In many cases, native applications and web applications can share the same backend service. Java/Spring, ASP.NET, and Node.js are among the most popular choices for backend service developments.

The selection of the technical stack for each category can significantly impact the complexity of a solution. In the next section, we will review and analyze solution complexity.

Managing development complexity

Building a complete solution usually requires a web app, a native app, and a backend service. Since web, native, and backend development use different programming languages and frameworks, we have to set up multiple teams to implement one solution. To manage the complexity of the development process, we need to manage the profile of the development team. The team profile can be managed according to two extreme cases/approaches. The simplest one is to set up one team that works on all stacks. The more complex one is to have separate teams for each stack. To successfully develop for all stacks using one team, the team must be a cross-platform full stack development team. Is it possible to have a cross-platform full stack team? Let's review various scenarios for this in the next two sections.

Full stack development

Many people doubt whether it is good, or even possible, to set up a full stack team, but in fact, the earliest web development frameworks were full stack frameworks. If you had a chance to use Java/Thymeleaf or ASP.NET MVC, you will know that they are full stack frameworks. These frameworks use server-side rendering, so the implementation of the UI and business logic are all on the server side.

The separation of frontend and backend came with the emergence of SPAs. To move the UI to the client side, SPA frameworks, such as React, Angular, and Vue.js, are used to implement the client-side logic. Backend services are implemented using frameworks such as Java/Spring and ASP.NET Core.

SPA frameworks use **client-side rendering (CSR)**, while Java/Thymeleaf and ASP.NET MVC use **server-side rendering (SSR)**. Both CSR and SSR have their pros and cons. In modern application development, both CSR and SSR are used by frameworks, as in Next.js and Nuxt.js. In .NET 8, Microsoft introduced server-side Blazor component rendering, or Blazor United. With this feature, the boundary between frontend and backend in ASP.NET has blurred again.

In summary, we should choose technology stacks based on business requirements, so there is not a single, catch-all answer as to whether we should go with full stack development or not.

For end users, SPAs are very similar to native applications, and some SPA frameworks have even evolved into cross-platform frameworks, such as React Native. With React and React Native, it is possible to have one team working on both frontend development and native application development. Furthermore, if a JavaScript-based backend framework is chosen, it is possible to set up one cross-platform full stack team to implement the entire solution.

To understand cross-platform frameworks better, let us analyze the cross-platform frameworks currently available on the market in the next section.

Cross-platform technologies

Cross-platform frameworks are alternative solutions to native application development. Native application development refers to using the programming language and **software development kit (SDK)** provided by the operating system. In native application development, we use native development tools, such as Swift/UIKit for iOS, Java/Kotlin for Android, and C#/WinUI for Windows. Ideally, we should use the tools provided by the operating system vendor to develop applications for a given operating system. With native application development, we don't have performance or compatibility issues in our apps. With cross-platform development frameworks, there will always be certain corner cases that cannot be resolved using cross-platform APIs alone. Regardless of whether you are a .NET MAUI, React Native, or Flutter developer, it is necessary to acquire a certain level of native programming knowledge to address these specific cases. For instance, I am currently waiting for the ZXing.Net.Maui project to be ready to support QR code functionality in my application.

However, we usually need to develop our application for multiple operating systems. Native application development incurs much higher costs than cross-platform frameworks. We must strike a balance between budget, time, and quality in a project. Again, we need to choose a solution based on the business requirements. This might mean we need to choose a cross-platform framework.

The most popular cross-platform frameworks on the market include Flutter, React Native, .NET MAUI/Xamarin, Ionic, and Apache Cordova.

 Gaining an understanding of various cross-platform technologies can greatly benefit .NET MAUI developers in making informed decisions when selecting their technology stack. It's important to note that, currently, there isn't a single cross-platform technology that can fulfill all requirements. As a result, we still come across new projects utilizing Ionic in business solutions.

In these frameworks, besides Flutter and .NET MAUI, React Native, Ionic, and Apache Cordova are JavaScript-based frameworks that originated from web development.

Apache Cordova

Apache Cordova is a hybrid framework that can be used to build mobile apps using web technologies such as HTML, CSS, and JavaScript. Cordova runs inside WebView, which provides a runtime environment to access device features. Cordova uses the same technologies as web apps, so Cordova can reuse the source code of web apps. Using a hybrid framework, the frontend team can work on both web and mobile applications.

The problem with hybrid frameworks is that the user interface for mobile is more similar to that of web apps than that of native apps, since the UI is created using web technology. Another concern is that the performance of hybrid apps is dependent on WebView's performance on the specific platform. Users may have different experiences on iOS and Android platforms.

Cordova is a hybrid framework that uses JavaScript, HTML, and CSS, but it doesn't provide a way to use modern JavaScript frameworks, such as React, Vue.js, and Angular.

Ionic

Ionic is a framework that was initially built on top of Apache Cordova. Another low-level framework called Capacitor can also be used in the more recent versions. Ionic can integrate with popular JavaScript frameworks such as React, Vue.js, and Angular, which means productivity can be improved significantly. Ionic also includes UI controls to support interactions, gestures, and animations.

Since Ionic is built using hybrid frameworks such as Cordova and Capacitor, the performance is similar to that of the underlying frameworks. However, Ionic includes optimizations for animations and transitions to deliver native-like performance for built-in libraries.

React Native

React Native is another framework that originated from a web development framework. Since React Native uses React and JavaScript to develop mobile apps, React developers can pick up React Native with very little effort. A cross-platform team can work on both web and mobile apps using React and React Native.

Unlike hybrid frameworks, React Native uses a bridge to translate JavaScript UIs into native ones. React Native apps have the same look and feel as native apps. Since React Native uses native components for rendering UIs on iOS and Android instead of WebView, it can achieve better performance than hybrid apps. A downside of React Native using native components is that we cannot share UI design and UI code between React and React Native. The paradigm is, "Learn once, write anywhere," instead of, "Write once, run anywhere."

Since React Native uses a bridge in its architecture, it may have slower performance than Flutter or .NET MAUI. In newer React Native releases, this may be improved by the new architecture.

Flutter

Flutter is an open-source UI toolkit developed by Google using the programming language Dart. Using Dart, Flutter supports **just-in-time (JIT)** and **ahead-of-time (AOT)** compilation and also has powerful performance optimization tools. Flutter apps can achieve near-native app performance.

Flutter employs a distinct rendering technology in comparison to hybrid apps and React Native. It uses an internal graphics engine called Skia (or Impeller, in the preview) to convert a hierarchy of widgets into the actual pixels on the screen. Flutter apps have the same look and feel on different devices without specific customization.

To simulate the look and feel of different platforms, Flutter has two different UI libraries for iOS and Android. Cupertino widgets are used for iOS and Material widgets for Android.

.NET MAUI

.NET MAUI is a successor of Xamarin.Forms, which is a part of the larger Xamarin platform. Xamarin itself provides native UI controls as part of the .NET runtime environment on iOS, macOS, and Android. You can develop native applications using C# and Xamarin. On Windows, since .NET is the original framework, .NET is supported by default.

From .NET 6 or above, you have a full .NET runtime available on these four platforms. .NET MAUI is only one of the .NET cross-platform frameworks that uses Xamarin. There are other .NET cross-platform frameworks that use Xamarin, and some of them can support more operating systems than .NET MAUI, such as Uno Platform, Avalonia UI, and Blazor Hybrid.

Flutter, React Native, and Cordova/Ionic represent three different types of cross-platform framework implementations. In the .NET world, we can find .NET cross-platform implementations that can match all these three categories.

Cordova, or Ionic, is a hybrid framework that uses web technology JavaScript, HTML, and CSS to develop mobile applications that run inside WebView. In .NET, Blazor is a web technology that uses C#, HTML, and CSS to develop web applications. The hybrid solution in .NET is Blazor Hybrid. BlazorWebView is used to host Blazor Hybrid applications on different platforms. Currently, BlazorWebView is available for .NET MAUI, WFP, and Windows Forms. We can use BlazorWebView to develop hybrid applications on these three frameworks. It is like Cordova and Ionic in that the look and feel of Blazor Hybrid applications is the same as that of web applications. It is possible to reuse code between Blazor Hybrid and Blazor applications.

Flutter uses a rendering technology based on Skia's 2D engine or Impeller. In .NET, Avalonia UI uses a similar approach that builds UI controls using Skia's 2D engine.

.NET MAUI uses native components as UI controls, such as React Native, so the .NET MAUI UI looks the same as native applications.

For a summary and comparison of the different frameworks, see *Table 1.1*.

Cross-Platform Frameworks (Languages)		UI Feature
.NET MAUI (XAML/C#)	React Native (HTML/CSS/JavaScript)	Native UI
Blazor Hybrid (HTML/CSS/C#)	Ionic/Cordova (HTML/CSS/JavaScript)	Web UI
Avalonia UI (XAML/C#)	Flutter (Dart)	Custom UI using 2D engine (Skia)

Table 1.1: Comparison of cross-platform frameworks

Besides Flutter, we can see that cross-platform frameworks use either JavaScript or .NET. It is possible to set up a cross-platform full stack team to work on the entire solution using either JavaScript or .NET technologies. Let's review the complexity level of cross-platform full stack solutions in the next section by comparing different combinations.

Analysis of cross-platform full stack solutions

Now that we have analyzed cross-platform and full stack frameworks, we can see that we are able to use just one programming language, either JavaScript or C#, to build the entire technical stack for a solution.

Table 1.2 is a summary of cross-platform full stack frameworks that use JavaScript or .NET.

Layers	Frameworks	
	JavaScript	C#/.NET
🌐 Web Application	React, Angular or Vue.js, etc.	Blazor
📱 Mobile Application	Cordova or Ionic	Blazor Hybrid
	React Native	.NET MAUI
⌨️ Backend Services	Node.js/Nest.js/Koa/Express.js	ASP.NET Core

Table 1.2: Comparison of JavaScript and .NET cross-platform full stack technical stacks

To build a solution using JavaScript, we can develop a web client using JavaScript frameworks, such as React, Angular, and Vue.js. If cost and time to market are major considerations, we will want to reuse code between web and mobile as much as possible. In that case, we can choose hybrid frameworks, such as Ionic and Cordova. If performance and user experience are more important to the business, React Native can be a good choice for mobile development. For backend services, there are plenty of JavaScript-based backend frameworks, such as Nest.js, Koa, and Express.js. We can choose pure JavaScript frameworks for all layers in the solution.

In .NET, we have very similar choices to those we have in JavaScript. If choosing a pure .NET technical stack for a solution, Blazor can be used for web client development. We also have the option to choose between hybrid and native frameworks. If considering cost and time to market, we can choose Blazor Hybrid so that web and mobile development can be treated as one development task. To have a native user experience and better performance, we can choose .NET MAUI for mobile development. In backend development, ASP.NET Core already has a large market share and is a popular framework.

Using frameworks with one programming language is the most economical choice, as we saw in *Table 1.1* and *Table 1.2*. However, in real projects, we may have to consider many factors. Our actual solution can be a combination of different languages and frameworks. Let's review the complexity level of different combinations in *Table 1.3*.

Cost Time to Market	Performance User Experience	Complexity Level	Technical Stacks in a Solution		
			Mobile	Web	Backend
		1	Blazor Hybrid	Blazor	ASP.NET
			Ionic/Cordova	JavaScript	Node.js
		2	.NET MAUI	Blazor	ASP.NET
			React Native	ReactJS	Node.js
		3	React Native	ReactJS	Java/ASP. NET/...
		4	Flutter	JavaScript	Java/ASP. NET/...
		5	Android/iOS/ma-cOS/Windows/...	JavaScript	Java/ASP. NET/...

Table 1.3: Complexity levels for cross-platform full stack solutions

In *Table 1.3*, I have summarized the different levels of complexity for different technology choices in each layer of a solution.

The complexity of your solution is determined by how many programming languages and frameworks are involved. The more languages and frameworks are involved, the greater the time to market and cost.

We have more choices with cross-platform and backend frameworks than we do with the frontend. In terms of programming languages, we can choose either JavaScript or C# to develop web clients. For this reason, the most economical choice to make for a backend framework is to select either a JavaScript- or C#-based backend framework. This is what we can see at complexity levels 1 and 2 in *Table 1.3*.

If we choose a hybrid framework, such as Ionic or Blazor Hybrid, to develop mobile apps, we can use one language and framework to cover all frontend and mobile development. In this case, if we also choose a backend framework in the same language, the time required and cost for this profile is minimal compared to all other profiles. As we can see in *Table 1.3*, we have JavaScript and .NET options at complexity level 1.

The most economical option may not be the best one for the product owner, since the product owner may have concerns about the user experience and performance of the solution. In terms of frontend and backend frameworks, .NET and JavaScript frameworks are mature and proven solutions. The real concern when thinking about solution performance, however, should be to do with hybrid frameworks. We can choose either .NET MAUI or React Native for mobile development. When using React Native, the most economical option is to use React as the frontend framework. In this way, we can still use one language and similar frameworks to cover both mobile and web development. There are many commercial solutions that go with this option. Since we won't be able to share UI code between .NET MAUI and Blazor or React and React Native, this category is a complexity level 2 option.

In backend development, there are too many options available in terms of languages and frameworks, and many of them are proven solutions. There is a very long list of languages that can be used in backend development, such as Java, C#, JavaScript, Python, Ruby, Go, and Rust. For whatever reason, we may not be able to choose the same backend programming language as the one we use for mobile and web development. This means a complexity level 3 solution. In this situation, the project team can reduce the complexity by choosing React and React Native together with a backend framework. In a real project, .NET MAUI and Blazor usually go with a .NET backend. We don't see many cases of .NET MAUI or Blazor being used with a non-.NET backend framework.

Flutter and React Native are the two most popular cross-platform frameworks in the market. .NET MAUI still needs more time to catch up with the market. If using Flutter, we go to complexity level 4. In this case, we have to involve three programming languages in the solution profile.

In some large projects, the user experience is a more important consideration than other factors. In such cases, we go with native application development. The number of languages and frameworks involved increases significantly, since every operating system added to the list adds one more programming language to the profile. This is the most complex case, at complexity level 5.

Comparison of .NET and JavaScript

There is no single best choice of cross-platform tool or framework. The final choice is usually decided according to the specific business requirements. However, from the above table, we can see that the .NET ecosystem provides a full spectrum of tools for your requirements. The development team of a large system usually requires people with experience in different programming languages and frameworks. With .NET, the complexity of programming languages and frameworks can be dramatically simplified.

We had an overview of tools and frameworks used in web app, native app, and backend service development. If we look at a higher level, that is, the .NET ecosystem level, the ecosystem of JavaScript almost matches what we have in a .NET solution. JavaScript and .NET solutions can provide tools or frameworks at nearly all layers. It would be interesting to do a comparison of JavaScript and .NET at a higher level.

JavaScript is a language created for web browsers, but its capability is extended due to the demands of web development. The limitation of JavaScript is that it is a scripting language, so it lacks the language features that can be found in C#. However, this limitation doesn't limit its usage and popularity. *Table 1.4* is a comparison of two technologies:

Area of Comparison	.NET	JavaScript
Programming languages	C#, F#, VB, C++	JavaScript, TypeScript, CoffeeScript, etc.
Runtime	CLR	V8/ SpiderMonkey/ JavaScriptCore
Supported IDE	Microsoft Visual Studio, Rider, MonoDevelop, Visual Studio Code	Visual Studio Code, Webstorm, Atom
Web	ASP.NET MVC/Blazor	React, Angular, Vue.js, etc.
Native apps	WinForms, WinUI, WPF, UWP	-
Desktop apps	.NET MAUI/Avalonia/Uno Platform/ Xamarin	Electron, NW.js
Mobile apps		React Native, Cordova, or Ionic
Backend	ASP.NET Core	Node.js

Table 1.4: Comparison of .NET and JavaScript

From *Table 1.4*, we can see that .NET has a good infrastructure for supporting multiple languages. With the **Common Type System (CTS)** and **Common Language Runtime (CLR)** as the core of .NET implementation, it supports multiple languages naturally, with the capability to share the **Base Class Library (BCL)** in all supported languages. JavaScript has its limitations as a scripting language, so languages such as TypeScript and CoffeeScript were invented to enhance it. TypeScript was developed by Microsoft to bring modern, object-oriented language features to JavaScript. TypeScript is compiled into JavaScript for execution, so it can work well with existing JavaScript libraries.

The cross-platform frameworks of .NET and JavaScript can cover not only mobile development but also desktop development. In a .NET environment, .NET MAUI, Uno Platform, and Avalonia can support both desktop and mobile cross-platform development. In the JavaScript ecosystem, React Native, Ionic, and Cordova are used for mobile development, and Electron or NW.js are used for desktop development.

Since .NET is a built-in component of Windows operating systems, it is used to develop native applications such as WinForms, UWP, and WPF. The Windows operating system itself is one of the major targets for support in cross-platform programming frameworks.

This comparison has helped us to choose between and evaluate technical stacks for cross-platform full stack development. As a .NET MAUI developer, this analysis can help you understand where .NET MAUI is located in the .NET ecosystem. To find out more about the .NET ecosystem, let's have a quick overview of the history of the .NET landscape in the next section.

Exploring the .NET landscape

Before we dive into the details of .NET MAUI, let's have an overview of the .NET landscape. This is a section for those who are new to .NET. If you are a .NET developer, you can skip this section.

Since Microsoft introduced the .NET platform, it has evolved from a proprietary software framework for Windows to a cross-platform and open-source platform.

There are many ways to look at the .NET technology stack. Basically, it contains the following components:

- Common infrastructure (compiler and tools suite)
- Base Class Library (BCL)
- Runtime (WinRT or Mono)

.NET Framework

The history of .NET started with .NET Framework. It is a proprietary software framework developed by Microsoft that runs primarily on Microsoft Windows. .NET Framework started as a future-oriented application framework to standardize the software stack in the Windows ecosystem. It is built around the **Common Language Infrastructure (CLI)** and C#. Even though the primary programming language is C#, it is designed to be a language-agnostic framework. Supported languages can share the same CTS and CLR. Most Windows desktop applications are developed using .NET Framework and it is shipped as a part of the Windows operating system.

Mono

The first attempt to make .NET an open-source framework was made by a company called Ximian. When the CLI and C# were ratified by ECMA in 2001 and ISO in 2003, it opened the door for independent implementations.

In 2001, the open-source project Mono was launched and aimed to implement .NET Framework on Linux.

Since .NET Framework was a proprietary technology at the time, .NET Framework and Mono had their own compiler, BCL, and runtime.

Over time, Microsoft moved toward open-source; .NET source code is available to the open-source community. The Mono project adopted some source code and tools from the .NET code base.

At the same time, the Mono project went through many changes as well. At one time, Mono was owned by Xamarin. Xamarin developed the Xamarin platform, based on Mono, to support the .NET platform on Android, iOS, UWP, and macOS. In 2016, Microsoft acquired Xamarin and Xamarin became a cross-platform solution in the .NET ecosystem.

.NET Core

Before the acquisition of Xamarin, Microsoft had already started work to make .NET a cross-platform framework. The first attempt was the release of .NET Core 1.0 in 2016. .NET Core is a free and open-source framework available for Windows, Linux, and macOS. It can be used to create modern web apps, microservices, libraries, and console applications. Since .NET Core applications can run on Linux, we can build microservices using containers and cloud infrastructure.

After .NET Core 3.x was released, Microsoft worked to integrate and unify .NET technology on various platforms. This unified version was to supersede both .NET Core and .NET Framework. To avoid confusion with .NET Framework 4.x, this unified framework was named .NET 5. Since .NET 5, a common BCL can be used on all platforms. In .NET 5, there are still two runtimes, which are the **Windows runtime (WinRT)**, which is used for Windows, and the Mono runtime, which is used for mobile and macOS.

Since .NET 5, .NET releases support two types of release, which are **Long Term Support (LTS)** and **Standard Term Support (STS)**. In this book, we use will .NET 8 releases, which are LTS releases.

.NET Standard and Portable Class Libraries

Before .NET 5, with .NET Framework, Mono, and .NET Core, we had different subsets of BCLs on different platforms. In order to share code between different runtimes or platforms, a technique called **Portable Class Libraries (PCLs)** was used. When you create a PCL, you have to choose a combination of platforms that you want to support. The level of compatibility is decided by the developer. If you want to reuse a PCL, you must carefully study the list of platforms that are supported.

Even though the PCL provides a way to share code, it cannot resolve compatibility issues well. To overcome compatibility issues, Microsoft introduced .NET Standard.

.NET Standard is not a separate .NET release but a specification of a set of .NET APIs that must be supported on most .NET implementations (.NET Framework, Mono, .NET Core, .NET 5 and 6, etc.).

Since .NET 5, a unified BCL is available, but .NET Standard will still be part of this unified BCL. If your applications only need to support .NET 5 or later, you don't really need to care too much about .NET Standard. However, if you want to be compatible with old .NET releases, .NET Standard is still the best choice for you. We will use .NET Standard 2.0 in this book to build our data model since this is a version that can support most existing .NET implementations and all future .NET releases.

There will be no new versions of .NET Standard from Microsoft, but .NET 5, .NET 6, and all future versions will continue to support .NET Standard 2.1 and earlier. *Table 1.5* shows the platforms and versions that .NET Standard 2.0 can support. This also happens to be a compatibility list for our data model in this book.

.NET Implementation	Version support
.NET and .NET Core	2.0, 2.1, 2.2, 3.0, 3.1, 5.0, 6.0
.NET Framework 1	4.6.1.2, 4.6.2, 4.7.1, 4.7.2, 4.8
Mono	5.4, 6.4
Xamarin.iOS	10.14, 12.16
Xamarin.Mac	3.8, 5.16
Xamarin.Android	8.0, 10.0
Universal Windows Platform	10.0.16299, TBD
Unity	2018.1

Table 1.5: .NET Standard 2.0-compatible implementations

Using Xamarin for cross-platform development

As we mentioned in the previous section, Xamarin was part of the Mono project and was an effort to support .NET on Android, iOS, and macOS. Xamarin exports the underlying operating system features to the .NET runtime. Xamarin.Forms is the cross-platform UI framework of Xamarin. .NET MAUI is an evolution of Xamarin.Forms. Before we discuss .NET MAUI and Xamarin.Forms, let us review the following diagram of Xamarin implementations on various platforms.

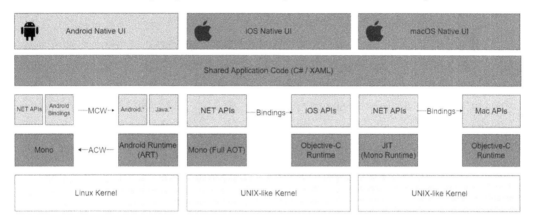

Figure 1.1: Xamarin implementations

Figure 1.1 shows the overall architecture of Xamarin. Xamarin allows developers to create native UIs on each platform and write business logic in C# that can be shared across platforms.

 The transition from Xamarin to .NET MAUI, or more specifically from Xamarin.Forms to .NET MAUI, is not a revolution. .NET MAUI essentially represents a new version of Xamarin.Forms rather than other components of Xamarin. Xamarin.Android has now become .NET Android, with the primary difference being the name change. The overall architecture, however, has not undergone significant modifications.

On supported platforms, Xamarin contains bindings for nearly the entire underlying platform SDK. Xamarin also provides facilities for directly invoking Objective-C, Java, C, and C++ libraries, giving you the power to use a wide array of third-party code. You can use existing Android, iOS, or macOS libraries written in Objective-C, Swift, Java, and C/C++.

The Mono runtime is used as the .NET runtime on these platforms. It has two modes of operation – JIT and AOT. JIT, or Just-in-Time, compilation generates code dynamically as it is executed. In AOT, or Ahead-of-Time, compilation mode, Mono precompiles everything so it can be used on operating systems where dynamic code generation is not possible.

As we can see in *Figure 1.1*, JIT can be used on Android and macOS, while AOT is used for iOS, where dynamic code generation is not allowed.

There are two ways to develop native applications using Xamarin.

We can develop native applications just like Android, iOS, and macOS developers using native APIs on each platform. The difference is that you use .NET libraries and C# instead of the platform-specific language and libraries directly. The advantage of this approach is that we can use one language and share a lot of components through the .NET BCL, even while working on different platforms. We can also leverage the power of underlying platforms, just as native application developers can.

If we want to reuse the code at the user interface layer, Xamarin.Forms can be used instead of the native UI.

Xamarin.Forms

Xamarin.Android, Xamarin.iOS, and Xamarin.Mac provide a .NET environment that exposes almost all the original SDK capabilities on their respective platforms. For example, as a developer, you nearly have the same capabilities with Xamarin.Android as you would with the original Android SDK. To improve code sharing, the open-source UI framework Xamarin.Forms was created. Xamarin.Forms includes a collection of cross-platform UI components. The user interface design can be implemented using XAML markup language, which is similar to Windows user interface design in WinUI or WPF.

Xamarin.Essentials

Since Xamarin exposes the capability of the underlying platform SDK, you can access device features using .NET APIs. However, the implementation is platform-specific. For example, when you use the location service on Android or iOS, the .NET API to use can be different. To further improve code sharing across platforms, Xamarin.Essentials can be used to access native device features. Xamarin.Essentials provides a unified .NET interface for native device features. If you use Xamarin.Essentials instead of native APIs, your code can be reused across platforms.

Some examples of functionality provided by Xamarin.Essentials include:

- Device info
- File system
- Accelerometer
- Phone dialer
- Text-to-speech
- Screen lock

Using Xamarin.Forms together with Xamarin.Essentials, most implementations, including of the business logic, user interface design, and some device-specific features, can be shared across platforms. In Chapter 7, *Using Platform-Specific Features,* we will learn how Xamarin.Essentials has been ported and thus made available for .NET MAUI.

Comparing user interface design on different platforms

Most modern application development on various platforms uses the **Model View Controller (MVC)** design pattern. To separate the business logic and user interface design, there are different approaches used on Android, iOS/macOS, and Windows. On all these platforms, even though the programming languages used are different, they use XML or HTML to design user interfaces.

On iOS/macOS, developers can use Interface Builder in Xcode to generate *.storyboard* or *.xib* files. Both are XML-based script files used to keep user interface information, and this script is interpreted at runtime together with Swift or Objective-C code to create the user interface. In 2019, Apple announced a new framework, SwiftUI. Using SwiftUI, developers can build user interfaces using the Swift language in a declarative way directly.

On the Android platform, developers can use Layout Editor in Android Studio to create user interfaces graphically and store the result in layout files. The layout files are in XML format and can be loaded at runtime to create the user interface.

On the Windows platform, XAML is used in user interface design. XAML, or Extensible Application Markup Language, is an XML-based language used for user interface design on the Windows platform. For WPF or UWP applications, XAML Designer can be used for user interface design. In .NET MAUI, a XAML-based UI is the default application UI. Another pattern, MVU, can also be used. In the MVU pattern, the user interface is implemented in C# directly without XAML. The coding style of MVU is similar to SwiftUI.

Compared to Xamarin.Forms, we can see in *Table 1.7* that there are many improvements in .NET MAUI.

.NET MAUI uses a single project structure to simplify project management. We can manage resources, dependency injection, and configuration in one location instead of managing them separately per platform. We will learn more about the single project structure in *Chapter 2, Building Our First .NET MAUI App.*

.NET MAUI is fully integrated as part of .NET, so we can create and build projects using the .NET SDK command line. In this case, we have more choice in terms of development environment.

Features	.NET MAUI	Xamarin.Forms
Project structure	Single project	Multiple projects
Resource management	One location for all platforms	Managed per platform

Fully integrated with .NET	Namespace in `Microsoft.Maui` and other IDEs can be chosen besides Visual Studio
	
	Command-line support. We can create, build, and run in console:
	
	`dotnet new maui`
	
	`dotnet build -t:Run -f net8.0-android`
	
	`dotnet build -t:Run -f net8.0-ios`
	
	`dotnet build -t:Run -f net8.0-maccatalyst`
		Namespace in `Xamarin.Forms` and Visual Studio as IDE

Design improvement	Configuration through .NET Generic Host Dependency injection support	Configuration scattered in different locations
Model View Update (MVU) pattern	A modern way of UI implementation	No
Blazor Hybrid	Support through `BlazorWebView`	No

Table 1.7: .NET MAUI improvements

.NET MAUI Blazor apps

In *Table 1.6*, where we compared user interface design options on different platforms, we mentioned that there is another way to design cross-platform user interfaces in .NET MAUI, which is Blazor.

Blazor, released in ASP.NET Core 3.0, is a framework for building interactive client-side web UIs with .NET. With .NET MAUI and Blazor, we can build cross-platform apps in the form of Blazor Hybrid apps. In this way, the boundary between native application and web application becomes blurred. .NET MAUI Blazor Hybrid apps enable Blazor components to be integrated with native platform features and UI controls. Blazor components have full access to the native capabilities of the device.

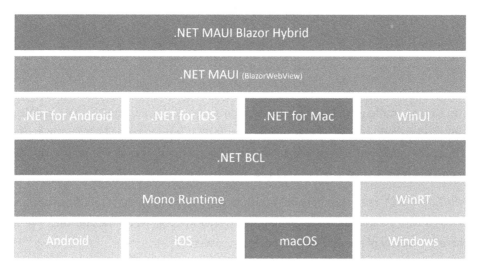

Figure 1.3: .NET MAUI Blazor Hybrid

As we can see in *Figure 1.3*, the way to use the Blazor web framework in .NET MAUI is through a BlazorWebView component. We can use .NET MAUI Blazor to mix native and web UIs in a single view. In .NET MAUI Blazor apps, applications can leverage the Blazor component model (Razor components), which uses HTML, CSS, and C# in Razor syntax. The Blazor part of an app can reuse components, layouts, and styles that are used in an existing regular web app. BlazorWebView components can be composed alongside native elements; additionally, these components leverage platform features and share state with their native counterparts.

Developing native apps using .NET

With .NET MAUI, Xamarin.Android, Xamarin.iOS, and Xamarin.Mac have been updated to .NET for Android, and .NET for iOS and .NET for Mac. We can develop native applications using .NET as we can see in *Figure 1.4*.

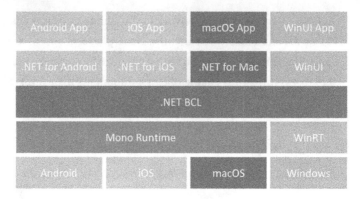

Figure 1.4: Native app development using .NET

Since we have a complete .NET implementation on Android, iOS, and macOS, we can develop native applications on these platforms using .NET tools. This is the same as for Xamarin-native projects. The open-source project keepass2android is a good example of developing native Android apps using Xamarin.Android: https://play.google.com/store/search?q=keepass2android.

With the latest .NET releases, there are multiple ways to develop cross-platform applications, such as .NET MAUI apps, native apps, and Blazor Hybrid apps, Avalonia, and Uno. We can see that there is a variety of possibilities in the .NET ecosystem.

What's new in .NET 8 for .NET MAUI?

.NET 8 introduced many new changes, and here we will review the aspects related to .NET MAUI.

Native AOT support for iOS-like platforms

.NET 8 introduces native AOT support for iOS-like platforms, allowing the building and running of .NET iOS and .NET MAUI applications on various platforms. Preliminary testing shows a 40% disk size decrease for .NET iOS apps and a 25% increase for .NET MAUI iOS apps using native AOT. However, as this is only the first step in support, performance conclusions should not be drawn yet. Native AOT support is an opt-in feature for app deployment, while Mono remains the default runtime for development and deployment.

.NET MAUI extension of Visual Studio Code

Although still in its preview stage, Visual Studio Code now offers a .NET MAUI extension, making it available for use in .NET MAUI development. The .NET MAUI extension is a new Visual Studio Code extension that lets you develop and debug your app on devices, emulators, and simulators from VS Code. It is built on top of the C# and C# Dev Kit extensions, which supercharge your .NET development with powerful IntelliSense, an intuitive Solution Explorer, package management, and more.

Development environment setup

In this section, we will introduce the development environment setup in Visual Studio and Visual Studio Code.

Using Visual Studio

Both Windows and macOS can be used for.NET MAUI development, but you won't be able to build all the targets with only one of them. You will need both Windows and Mac computers to build all the targets. In this book, the Windows environment is used to build and test Android and Windows targets, while iOS and macOS targets are built on a Mac computer.

.NET MAUI apps can target the following platforms:

- Android 5.0 (API 21) or higher
- iOS 11 or higher
- macOS 10.15 or higher, using Mac Catalyst
- Windows 11 and Windows 10 version 1809 or higher, using Windows UI Library (WinUI) 3

.NET MAUI Blazor apps use the platform-specific WebView control, so they have the following additional requirements:

- Android 7.0 (API 24) or higher
- iOS 14 or higher
- macOS 11 or higher, using Mac Catalyst

.NET MAUI build targets of Android, iOS, macOS, and Windows can be built using Visual Studio on a Windows computer. In this environment, a networked Mac is required to build iOS and macOS targets. Xcode must be installed on the paired Mac to debug and test an iOS MAUI app in a Windows environment.

.NET MAUI targets of Android, iOS, and macOS can be built and tested on macOS. Please refer to *Table 1.8* to find out about the build configurations on Windows and macOS.

Target platform	Windows	macOS
Windows	Yes	No
Android	Yes	Yes
iOS	Yes (pair to Mac)	Yes
macOS	Build only (pair to Mac)	Yes

Table 1.8: Development environment of .NET MAUI

Installing .NET MAUI on Windows

.NET MAUI can be installed as part of Visual Studio 2022. Visual Studio Community Edition is free, and we can download it from the Microsoft website at: `https://visualstudio.microsoft.com/vs/community/`.

After launching the Visual Studio Installer, we see what is shown in *Figure 1.5*. Please select **.NET Multi-platform App UI development** and **.NET desktop development** in the list of options. We also need to select **ASP.NET and web development** for the .NET MAUI Blazor app, which will be covered in part 2 of this book.

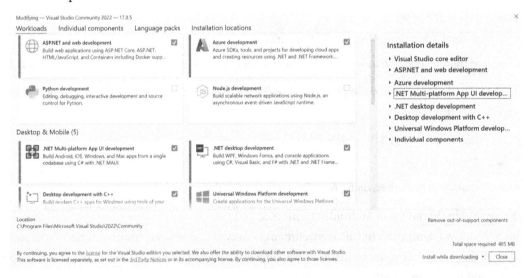

Figure 1.5: Visual Studio 2022 installation

After the installation is completed, we can check the installation from the command line using the dotnet command as follows.

```
C:\>dotnet workload list

Installed Workload Id      Manifest Version        Installation Source
--------------------------------------------------------------------------
maui-windows               8.0.0.8333/8.0.100      VS 17.7.33711.374
maui-maccatalyst           8.0.0.8333/8.0.100      VS 17.7.33711.374
maccatalyst                16.4.8377/8.0.100       VS 17.7.33711.374
maui-ios                   8.0.0.8333/8.0.100      VS 17.7.33711.374
ios                        16.4.8377/8.0.100       VS 17.7.33711.374
maui-android               8.0.0.8333/8.0.100      VS 17.7.33711.374
android                    34.0.0.273/8.0.100      VS 17.7.33711.374

Use `dotnet workload search` to find additional workloads to install.
```

Figure 1.6: Checking the dotnet workload list

We are now ready to create, build, and run a .NET MAUI app on Windows.

Installing .NET MAUI on macOS

Despite Microsoft's announcement of Visual Studio for Mac's retirement in August 2023, developers can still utilize it for .NET MAUI development on Mac. Visual Studio for Mac 17.6 will continue to be supported for another 12 months, until August 31st, 2024. Please refer to the following announcement: https://devblogs.microsoft.com/visualstudio/visual-studio-for-mac-retirement-announcement/.

The installation of Visual Studio Community Edition is similar to what we have done on Windows. The installation package can be downloaded from the same link.

After launching the Visual Studio Installer, we see what is shown in *Figure 1.7.*

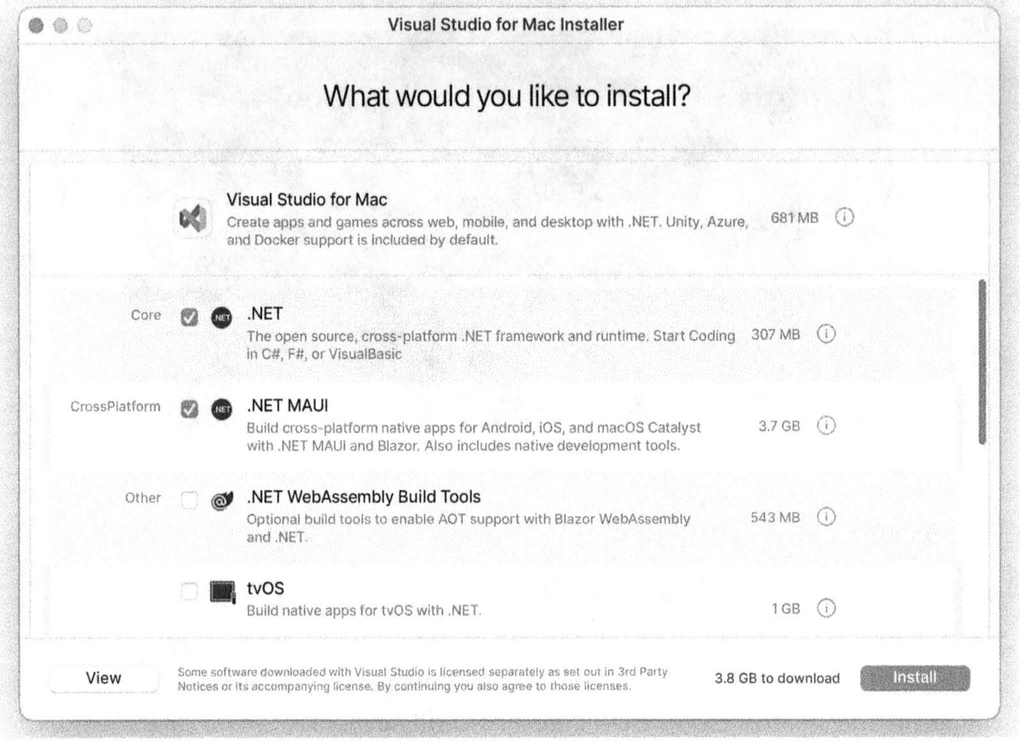

Figure 1.7: Visual Studio for Mac 2022 Installer

Please select **.NET** and **.NET MAUI** from the list of options in *Figure 1.7.*

After the installation is complete, we can check the installation from the command line using the dotnet command as well.

We are ready to create, build, and run a .NET MAUI app on macOS.

Visual Studio Code with the .NET MAUI extension

We can also set up a development environment using Visual Studio Code. It's straightforward to get started with the .NET MAUI extension by installing it in Visual Studio Code. You can search for the .NET MAUI extension and install it, as shown in *Figure 1.8*.

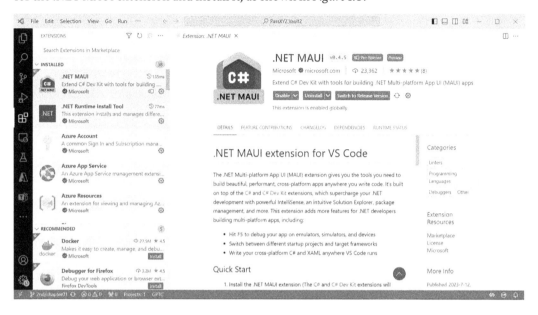

Figure 1.8: Visual Studio Code with .NET MAUI extension

When you install the **.NET MAUI extension**, the C# Dev Kit and C# extension will be installed automatically. Once the .NET MAUI extension is installed, you can load the project and explore the project in the solution explorer just as you can in Visual Studio.

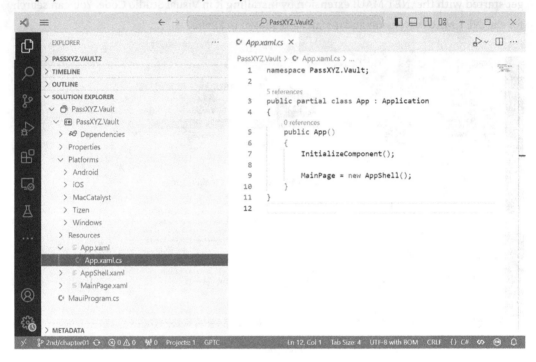

Figure 1.9: Solution explorer in Visual Studio Code

Since Visual Studio Code can support Windows, macOS, and Linux, we can develop .NET MAUI apps on these three platforms. Please refer to the following table to find out about the supported target platforms.

Operating System	Supported Target Platform
Windows	Windows, Android
macOS	Android, iOS, macOS
Linux	Android

Table 1.9: Supported target platforms

With Visual Studio Code, it is possible to develop .NET MAUI apps on Linux, but it can support Android as a target only.

Summary

In this chapter, we explored topics related to .NET MAUI and Xamarin, discussing various cross-platform technologies in comparison to .NET MAUI. This analysis provided insight into the advantages and disadvantages of different frameworks. Additionally, we compared the JavaScript and C# ecosystems, as most cross-platform frameworks utilize these languages. By introducing the .NET landscape and the available cross-platform frameworks, you now have a comprehensive understanding of the essentials before delving into the world of .NET MAUI.

In the next chapter, we will explore how to build a .NET MAUI application from scratch.

Further reading

- Avalonia UI and MAUI – Something for everyone: `https://avaloniaui.net/`
- **.NET MAUI** – You can find more information about .NET MAUI in the Microsoft official documentation: `https://docs.microsoft.com/en-us/dotnet/maui/`
- **KeePass** – The official website for KeePass can be found at: `https://keepass.info/`

Learn more on Discord

Join our community's Discord space for discussions with the author and other readers:

`https://packt.link/cross-platform-app`

2

Building Our First .NET MAUI App

In this chapter, we will create a new .NET MAUI project and customize it so that we can use it in the development of an app. The app that we will develop is a password management app. We will gradually introduce various features to it in the subsequent chapters. By the end of *Part 1*, we will possess a fully functional password management app.

Those who have prior experience with Xamarin.Forms will recall that the **Shell** serves as a convenient application container that simplifies app development by offering a unified structure for defining an application's key components. While there isn't a direct Visual Studio template for .NET MAUI Shell from Microsoft, we can effectively utilize the one from Xamarin.Forms. To incorporate Shell in our app, we'll reuse the project template found in Xamarin.Forms. As well as from providing us with a proficient project template, the process of migrating the Xamarin.Forms Shell template to .NET MAUI will provide valuable insights into the migration of a Xamarin.Forms project to .NET MAUI.

The following topics will be covered in this chapter:

- Setting up a new .NET MAUI project
- App startup and lifecycle management
- Configuring resources
- Creating a new Xamarin.Forms project with Shell support
- Migrating this Xamarin.Forms project to .NET MAUI

Technical requirements

To test and debug the source code in this chapter, you need Visual Studio 2022 installed on either Windows or macOS. Please refer to the *Development environment setup* section in *Chapter 1, Getting Started with .NET MAUI*, for details.

To check out the source code of this chapter, we can use the following Git command:

```
$ git clone https://github.com/PacktPublishing/.NET-MAUI-Cross-Platform-
Application-Development-Second-edition.git -b 2nd/chapter02
```

Managing the source code in this book

Since we will develop a password manager app incrementally in this book, the source code of each chapter is built on top of the previous chapters. To continuously improve our app, we will have separate branches for the source code of each chapter. If you want to clone the source code of all chapters in one command, you can clone it from the main branch. In the main branch, all the chapters are in separate folders. If you don't want to use Git, you can also download the source code as a compressed file from the release area, as shown in the following screenshot (*Figure 2.1*):

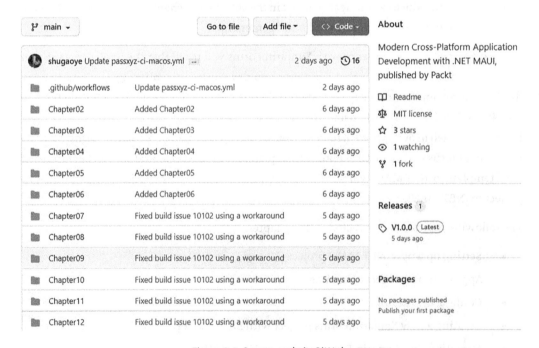

Figure 2.1: Source code in GitHub

Since new .NET MAUI releases may be available from time to time, the Git tags and versions in the release area will be updated according to the new .NET MAUI releases and bug fixes.

The source code of this book can be found in the following GitHub repository: `https://github.com/PacktPublishing/.NET-MAUI-Cross-Platform-Application-Development-Second-edition`.

There are three ways to download the source code from GitHub.

Download the source code in a compressed file

The source code can be downloaded in the release area, or use the following URL: `https://github.com/PacktPublishing/.NET-MAUI-Cross-Platform-Application-Development-Second-edition/releases/tag/V1.0.0`.

The release tag may be changed when a new release is available.

Clone the source code per chapter

To check out the source code for a chapter, you can use the following command, for example:

```
$ git clone https://github.com/PacktPublishing/.NET-MAUI-Cross-Platform-
Application-Development-Second-edition.git -b 2nd/chapter02
```

I use the following naming convention for branches: `[xxx]/chapter[yy]`, where x is the edition number and y is the chapter number, such as `2nd/chapter01`.

Clone the source code from the main branch

To check out the source code of all chapters from the main branch, you can use the following command:

```
$ git clone https://github.com/PacktPublishing/.NET-MAUI-Cross-Platform-
Application-Development-Second-edition.git
```

Setting up a new .NET MAUI project

In this chapter, we will create and configure a new .NET MAUI project, which will form the basis for further development of our password manager app. Given that the default .NET NAUI project template is a very simple one, we require a more robust project framework to establish the base project structure.

Xamarin.Forms project templates provide suitable options. In particular, there is a template that incorporates the Shell and **Model-View-View Model (MVVM)** pattern setup. We'll migrate this into our .NET MAUI project, which will also provide us with the opportunity to learn how to migrate a Xamarin.Forms project to .NET MAUI. Ultimately, we'll create our very own Visual Studio project template.

To create a new .NET MAUI project, we can use Visual Studio or the command line.

Creating a new project using Visual Studio

To create a new .NET MAUI project, follow these steps:

1. Launch Visual Studio 2022 and select **Create a new project** on the startup screen. This will open the **Create a new project** wizard.

2. At the top of the screen, there is a search box. We can type maui in the search box, and .NET MAUI-related project templates will be shown (see *Figure 2.2*):

Figure 2.2: New project setup – Create a new project

There are three templates for the .NET MAUI app or library:

- **.NET MAUI App** – This is for a XAML-based .NET MAUI app.

- **.NET MAUI Blazor Hybrid App** – This template can be used to create a .NET MAUI Blazor app.

- **.NET MAUI Class Library** – This is the option for building a .NET MAUI class library. We can build shared components as a .NET MAUI class library when we develop a .NET MAUI app.

3. Let's select **.NET MAUI App** and click the **Next** button; it goes to the next step to configure our new project, as shown in *Figure 2.3*:

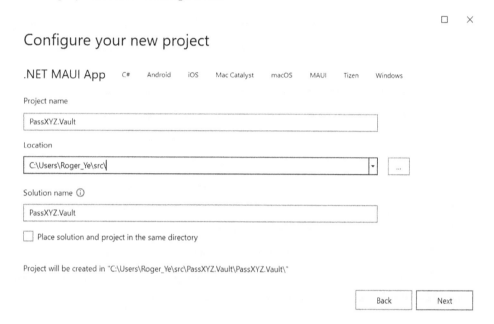

Figure 2.3: New project setup – Configure your new project

4. Enter the project name and solution name as PassXYZ.Vault and click the **Next** button. After the project is created, the project structure will look like *Figure 2.4* and will display the following:

- *Common files* – In a new project, three files are included in the template – App.xaml, MainPage.xaml, and MauiProgram.cs. This is the group of files that we will work on throughout the book. They are platform agnostic. Both business logic and UI can be developed here and shared on all platforms.

- *Platform-specific files* – There are five subfolders (Android, iOS, MacCatalyst, Windows, and Tizen) in the Platforms folder. Since we won't support Tizen, we can remove it from our project.

- *Resources* – A variety of resources ranging from images, fonts, splash screens, styles, and raw assets are in the Resources folder. These resources can be used in all supported platforms.

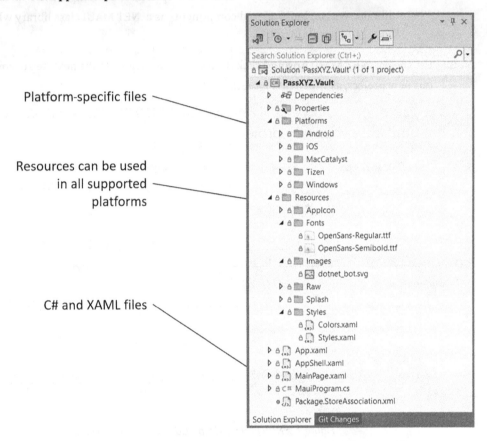

Platform-specific files

Resources can be used in all supported platforms

C# and XAML files

Figure 2.4: .NET MAUI project structure

In the .NET MAUI project, there is only one project structure. Later, we will see that the development of Xamarin.Forms involves multiple projects.

Creating a new project using the dotnet command

Although .NET MAUI was installed as part of the Visual Studio installation, it can also be installed independently using the command line. This flexibility allows the use of alternative development tools, such as Visual Studio Code, instead of Visual Studio. To create and build a .NET MAUI application from the command line, we can use the dotnet command.

To find out which project templates have been installed, we can refer to the following command:

```
C:\ > dotnet new --list
```

To create a new project using the command line, we can execute the following command:

```
C:\ > dotnet new maui -n "PassXYZ.Vault"
```

Once the new .NET MAUI project has been created, we can build and test it. Before we move on to that, let's spend some time looking at the .NET MAUI app startup code and lifecycle.

App startup and lifecycle

Lifecycle management in .NET MAUI is crucial for efficient resource management, ensuring smooth and consistent user experiences, secure application handling, and understanding and troubleshooting app behavior. It allows the application to conserve resources, appropriately saving and restoring the application's state when it's in the background or foreground. It provides opportunities to perform certain actions when an app goes to the background, such as saving data or pausing activities. Moreover, it provides enhanced security by managing sensitive data when apps switch to and from the active state. Hence, understanding the application lifecycle is crucial for crafting robust, efficient, and user-friendly .NET MAUI applications.

In .NET MAUI projects, app startup and lifecycle management are handled in the following two files:

- MauiProgram.cs
- App.xaml/App.xaml.cs

.NET Generic Host is used for app startup and configuration. When the application starts, a .NET Generic Host object is created to encapsulate an app's resources and lifetime functionality, such as the following:

- **Dependency injection (DI)**
- Logging
- Configuration
- Lifecycle management

This enables apps to be initialized in a single location and provides the ability to configure fonts, services, and third-party libraries. This chapter will explore everything except DI, which will be introduced in *Chapter 6, Software Design with Dependency Injection*.

.NET Generic Host

If you are a Xamarin developer, you may not be familiar with .NET Generic Host. Introduced in .NET Core, .NET Generic Host is a unified hosting model for building cross-platform .NET applications. It provides a consistent way to configure, run, and manage services and background tasks across various types of .NET applications, such as console apps, microservices, and web applications. In .NET MAUI, the same pattern is borrowed and used for startup and configuration management.

Let's examine the app start up code in *Listing 2.1*:

```
namespace PassXYZ.Vault;

public static class MauiProgram
{
  public static MauiApp CreateMauiApp()                    //(1)
  {
    var builder = MauiApp.CreateBuilder();                 //(2)
    builder
      .UseMauiApp<App>()                                   //(4)
      .ConfigureFonts(fonts =>
      {
        fonts.AddFont("OpenSans-Regular.ttf", "OpenSansRegular");
      });
    return builder.Build();                                //(3)
  }
}
```

Listing 2.1: MauiProgram.cs *(https://epa.ms/MauiProgram2-1)*

We can see the following in *Listing 2.1*:

(1) In each platform, the entry point is in platform-specific code. The entry point calls the CreateMauiApp function, which is a method of the MauiProgram static class.

(2) Inside CreateMauiApp, the code calls the CreateBuilder function, which is a method of the MauiApp static class, and returns a MauiAppBuilder instance, which provides a .NET Generic Host interface. We can use this instance of the .NET Generic Host interface to configure resources or services used in our app.

(3) The return value of `CreateMauiApp` is a `MauiApp` instance, which is the entry point of our app.

(4) The `App` class referenced in the `UseMauiApp` method is the root object of our application. Let's review the definition of the `App` class in *Listing 2.2*:

```
namespace PassXYZ.Vault;

public partial class App : Application            //(1)
{
  public App()
  {
    InitializeComponent();
    MainPage = new AppShell();                    //(2)
  }
}
```

Listing 2.2: `App.xaml.cs` *(https://epa.ms/App2-2)*

In *Listing 2.2*, we can see the following:

(1) The `App` class is derived from the `Application` class, and the `Application` class is defined in the `Microsoft.Maui.Controls` namespace.

(2) `AppShell` is an instance of Shell, and it defines the UI of the initial page of the app.

`Application` creates an instance of the `Window` class within which the application will run and views will be displayed. In the `App` class, we can overwrite the `CreateWindow` method to manage the lifecycle, which we will see soon.

Lifecycle management

.NET MAUI app generally operates in four execution states:

- Running
- Not running
- Deactivated
- Stopped

During the state transitions, the predefined lifecycle events will be triggered. Six cross-platform lifecycle events are defined, as we can see in *Table 2.1*:

Event	Description	State transition	Override method
Created	This event is raised after the native window has been created.	Not running -> Running	`OnCreated`
Activated	This event is raised when the window has been activated and is or will become the focused window.	Not running -> Running	`OnActivated`
Deactivated	This event is raised when the window is no longer the focused window. However, the window might still be visible.	Running -> Deactivated	`OnDeactivated`
Stopped	This event is raised when the window is no longer visible.	Deactivated -> Stopped	`OnStopped`
Resumed	This event is raised when an app resumes after being stopped.	Stopped -> Running	`OnResumed`
Destroying	This event is raised when the native window is destroyed and deallocated.	Stopped -> Not running	`OnDestroying`

Table 2.1: Lifecycle events and override methods

Please refer to the following Microsoft document to find out more about lifecycle events: `https://learn.microsoft.com/en-us/dotnet/maui/fundamentals/app-lifecycle`.

These lifecycle events are associated with the instance of the `Window` class created by `Application`. For each event, a corresponding override method is defined. We can either subscribe to the lifecycle events or create override functions to handle lifecycle management.

Subscribing to the Window lifecycle events

To subscribe to the lifecycle events, as we can see in *Listing 2.3*, at **(1)**, we can override the `CreateWindow` method in the `App` class to create a `Window` instance on which we can subscribe to events:

```
using System.Diagnostics;
namespace PassXYZ.Vault;

public partial class App : Application {
```

```
    public App() {
      InitializeComponent();
      MainPage = new MainPage();
    }


    protected override Window CreateWindow(IActivationState
      activationState)                                    //(1)
    {
      Window window = base.CreateWindow(activationState);
      window.Created += (s, e) => {
        Debug.WriteLine("PassXYZ.Vault.App: 1. Created event");
      };
      window.Activated += (s, e) => {
        Debug.WriteLine("PassXYZ.Vault.App: 2. Activated event");
      };
      window.Deactivated += (s, e) => {
        Debug.WriteLine("PassXYZ.Vault.App: 3. Deactivated event");
      };
      window.Stopped += (s, e) => {
        Debug.WriteLine("PassXYZ.Vault.App: 4. Stopped event");
      };
      window.Resumed += (s, e) => {
        Debug.WriteLine("PassXYZ.Vault.App: 5. Resumed event");
      };
      window.Destroying += (s, e) => {
        Debug.WriteLine("PassXYZ.Vault.App: 6. Destroying event");
      };
      return window;
    }
  }
```

Listing 2.3: App.xaml.cs *with lifecycle events (*https://epa.ms/App2-3*)*

In *Listing 2.3*, we revised the code of App.xaml.cs, and we subscribed to all six events so that we can run a test and observe the state in the Visual Studio output window. As we can see in the following debug output, we run and test our app in the Windows environment.

After we launch our app, we can see that Created and Activated events are fired. Then, we minimize our app and we can see that Deactivated and Stopped events are fired. When we resume our app again, Resumed and Activated events are fired. Finally, we close our app, and a Destroying event is fired:

```
PassXYZ.Vault.App: 1. Created event
PassXYZ.Vault.App: 2. Activated event
PassXYZ.Vault.App: 4. Stopped event
PassXYZ.Vault.App: 3. Deactivated event
PassXYZ.Vault.App: 5. Resumed event
PassXYZ.Vault.App: 2. Activated event
PassXYZ.Vault.App: 5. Resumed event
PassXYZ.Vault.App: 2. Activated event
The thread 0x6f94 has exited with code 0 (0x0).
PassXYZ.Vault.App: 6. Destroying event
The program '[30628] PassXYZ.Vault.exe' has exited with code 0 (0x0).
```

Consuming the lifecycle override methods

Alternatively, we can consume the lifecycle override methods. We can create our own derived class from the Window class:

1. In Visual Studio, right-click on the project node and select **Add** and then **New Item…**.

2. In the **Add New Item** window, select **C# Class** from the template and name it PxWindow. We created a new class, as shown next in *Listing 2.4*:

```csharp
using System.Diagnostics;
namespace PassXYZ.Vault;

public class PxWindow : Window
{
    public PxWindow() : base() {}
    public PxWindow(Page page) : base(page) {}

    protected override void OnCreated() {
        Debug.WriteLine("PassXYZ.Vault.App: 1. OnCreated");
    }
    protected override void OnActivated() {
```

```
            Debug.WriteLine("PassXYZ.Vault.App: 2. OnActivated");
        }
        protected override void OnDeactivated() {
            Debug.WriteLine("PassXYZ.Vault.App: 3. OnDeactivated");
        }
        protected override void OnStopped() {
            Debug.WriteLine("PassXYZ.Vault.App: 4. OnStopped");
        }
        protected override void OnResumed() {
            Debug.WriteLine("PassXYZ.Vault.App: 5. OnResumed");
        }
        protected override void OnDestroying() {
            Debug.WriteLine("PassXYZ.Vault.App: 6. OnDestroying");
        }
    }
}
```

Listing 2.4: PxWindow.cs *(*https://epa.ms/PxWindow2-4*)*

In *Listing 2.4*, we created a new class, PxWindow. In this class, we define our lifecycle override methods. We can use this new class in App.xaml.cs.

Next, let's look at the modified version of App.xaml.cs (*Listing 2.5*):

```
namespace PassXYZ.Vault;
public partial class App : Application
{
  public App()
  {
    InitializeComponent();
  }

  protected override Window CreateWindow(
    IActivationState activationState)                //(1)
  {
    return new PxWindow(new MainPage());
  }
}
```

*Listing 2.5: Modified App.xaml.cs with PxWindow (*https://epa.ms/App2-5*)*

When we repeat the previous test steps, we can see the following output in the Visual Studio output window. The output looks very similar to the previous one. Basically, both approaches have the same effect on lifecycle management:

```
PassXYZ.Vault.App: 1. OnCreated
PassXYZ.Vault.App: 2. OnActivated
PassXYZ.Vault.App: 4. OnStopped
PassXYZ.Vault.App: 3. OnDeactivated
PassXYZ.Vault.App: 5. OnResumed
PassXYZ.Vault.App: 2. OnActivated
PassXYZ.Vault.App: 5. OnResumed
PassXYZ.Vault.App: 2. OnActivated
PassXYZ.Vault.App: 6. OnDestroying
The program '[25996] PassXYZ.Vault.exe' has exited with code 0 (0x0).
```

We have learned about app lifecycle management in .NET MAUI through the `Window` class. We can either subscribe to lifecycle events or override the overridable methods to manage the app lifecycle. *Table 2.1* shows the comparison of these two approaches.

If you were a Xamarin.Forms developer, you might know that there were lifecycle methods defined in the `Application` class as well. In .NET MAUI, the following virtual methods are still available:

- `OnStart` – Called when the application starts
- `OnSleep` – Called each time the application goes to the background
- `OnResume` – Called when the application is resumed, after being sent to the background

To observe the behavior of these methods, we can override the following methods in our `App` class, as shown in *Listing 2.6*:

```
using System.Diagnostics;
namespace PassXYZ.Vault;

public partial class App : Application
{
  public App()
  {
    InitializeComponent();
    MainPage = new MainPage();
```

```
    }

    protected override void OnStart() {                    //(1)
      Debug.WriteLine("PassXYZ.Vault.App: OnStart");
    }
    protected override void OnSleep() {                    //(2)
      Debug.WriteLine("PassXYZ.Vault.App: OnSleep");
    }
    protected override void OnResume() {                   //(3)
      Debug.WriteLine("PassXYZ.Vault.App: OnResume");
    }
  }
```

Listing 2.6: `App.xaml.cs` `(https://epa.ms/App2-6)`

When we test the preceding code on Windows, we can see the following debug message in the Visual Studio Output window:

```
PassXYZ.Vault.App: OnStart
PassXYZ.Vault.App: OnSleep
The thread 0x6844 has exited with code 0 (0x0).
The thread 0x6828 has exited with code 0 (0x0).
The thread 0x683c has exited with code 0 (0x0).
PassXYZ.Vault.App: OnResume
```

As demonstrated in *Listing 2.6*, specific methods will be activated according to the varying statuses of the application.

(1) When the app starts, the `OnStart` method is invoked.

(2) When we minimize our app, the `OnSleep` method is invoked.

(3) When we resume the app from the taskbar, the `OnResume` method is invoked.

We've learned about the lifecycle states of a .NET MAUI app and also learned that we can either subscribe to lifecycle events or use override methods to manage the app's lifecycle. Let's now focus on the configuration of resources during the app's startup.

Configuring the resources

Resource management is one of the major differences between .NET MAUI and Xamarin.

Cross-platform development presents unique challenges as each platform has its own method for managing resources. This diversity can pose significant management tasks for development teams. For instance, we must incorporate multiple image sizes to accommodate various resolutions.

In Xamarin, most of the resources are managed separately in platform-specific projects. If we want to add an image, we must add the image files with different sizes to all platform projects separately.

.NET MAUI provides an elegant solution to manage resources effectively. The design goal of one single project for all supported platforms helps to manage resources in one place.

In .NET MAUI, resource files can be tagged into different categories using a build action based on the role they play in the project, as we can see in *Table 2.2*:

Resource Type	Build Action	Example
Images	`MauiImage`	`dotnet_bot.svg`
Icons	`MauiIcon`	`appicon.svg`
Splash screen image	`MauiSplashScreen`	`appiconfg.svg`
Fonts	`MauiFont`	`OpenSans-Regular.ttf`
Style definition using external CSS	`MauiCss`	N/A
Raw assets	`MauiAsset`	N/A
XAML UI definition	`MauiXaml`	N/A

Table 2.2: .NET MAUI resource types

The last three are not used frequently, so we will focus on examples using the more common resource types.

After adding a resource file, the build action can be set in the **Properties** window in Visual Studio. If we look at the project file, we can see the following `ItemGroup`:

```
<ItemGroup>
  <!-- App Icon -->
  <MauiIcon Include="Resources\AppIcon\appicon.svg"
    ForegroundFile="Resources\AppIcon\appiconfg.svg"
    Color="#512BD4" />

  <!- Splash Screen -->
  <MauiSplashScreen Include= "Resources\Splash\splash.svg"
    Color="#512BD4" BaseSize="128,128" />
```

```
    <!-- Images -->
    <MauiImage Include="Resources\Images\*" />

    <!-- Custom Fonts -->
    <MauiFont Include="Resources\Fonts\*" />
  </ItemGroup>
```

If we put resources according to the convention of default folder setup, the resources will be treated as the respective category and the build action will be set automatically.

App icon

In our app setup, as we can see in the `ItemGroup` above, we have an SVG image file, `appicon.svg`, in the `Resources\AppIcon` folder, with the build action set to `MauiIcon`. At build time, this file is used to generate icon images on the target platform for various purposes, such as on the device or in the app store.

It is possible to move this SVG file together with other images to the `Resources\Images` folder. In that case, we should use the following entry in the project file:

```
<MauiIcon Include="Resources\Images\appicon.png"
ForegroundFile="Resources\Images\appiconfg.svg" Color="#512BD4" />
```

The downside is that the build action treats the files in the same folder inconsistently – `appicon.svg` resides in the **Resources\AppIcon** folder instead of **Resources\Images** in our project.

Splash screen

The configuration of the splash screen is similar to configuration of the app icon. We have an SVG image file, `splash.svg`, in the `Resources/Splash` folder, with the build action set to `MauiSplashScreen`:

```
<MauiSplashScreen Include="Resources\Splash\splash.svg" Color="#512BD4" />
```

Resources like app icons, splash screens, and other images are simple and can be directly configured in the project file.

Some frequently used resources, such as custom fonts and services, may have to be configured in code, or in both code and project files. We will discuss the configuration of custom fonts in the next section and leave DI until *Chapter 6*, *Software Design with Dependency Injection*.

Setting custom font icons

Custom fonts can be managed as part of resources. Using custom font icons, we can dramatically reduce the number of image resources in our app. In a mobile app, the visual representation is generally delivered through images. We use images in all kinds of navigation activities. In Android and iOS development, we need to manage image resources for different screen resolutions.

There are many advantages of using custom fonts as icons instead of images. Font icons are vector icons instead of bitmap icons. Vector icons are scalable, meaning you don't need different images with different sizes and different resolutions based on the device. Icon font scaling can be handled through the FontSize property. The font file size is also much smaller than the images. A font file with hundreds of icons in it can be only a few KB in size.

The icon color can be changed with the TextColor property. With static images, we are not able to change the icon color.

Finally, font files can be managed in the shared project, so we don't have to manage fonts separately on different platforms.

In both Xamarin.Forms and .NET MAUI, we can use a custom font (icon font) instead of images for application icons.

In .NET MAUI, controls that display text typically have definable properties for configuring font settings. The properties that can be configured include:

- FontAttributes, which is an enumeration with three members: None, Bold, and Italic. The default value of this property is None.
- FontSize, which is the property of the font size, and the type is double.
- FontFamily, which is the property of the font family, and the type is string.

Custom font setup

The setup of custom fonts has two stages – adding font files and configuring them. Custom font files can be added to a shared project in both .NET MAUI and Xamarin.Forms. However, the configuration process differs between them. In Xamarin.Forms, the configuration is handled through AssemblyInfo.cs. In .NET MAUI, this is managed via .NET Generic Host.

In Xamarin.Forms, the process for accomplishing this is as follows:

1. Add the font file to the Xamarin.Forms shared project as an embedded resource (build action: EmbeddedResource).

2. Register the font file with the assembly in a file such as `AssemblyInfo.cs` using the `ExportFont` attribute. An optional alias can also be specified.

In .NET MAUI, the process is as follows:

1. Add the font files to the `Resources->Fonts` folder. The build action is set to **MauiFont**, as we can see in *Figure 2.5*:

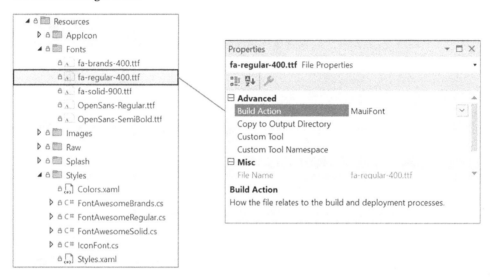

Figure 2.5: .NET MAUI Resources

2. Instead of registering the font file with the assembly, .NET MAUI initializes most of the resources through .NET Generic Host in the startup code, as shown in *Listing 2.7* at **(1)**. Font files are added using the `ConfigureFonts` method, which is an extension method of the `MauiAppBuilder` class.

In our project, we use the Font Awesome icon library from the following open-source project: `https://github.com/FortAwesome/Font-Awesome`.

The `fa-brands-400.ttf`, `fa-regular-400.ttf`, and `fa-solid-900.ttf` font files can be downloaded from the preceding website.

Let's review the source code in *Listing 2.7* and see how to add these fonts to the app configuration:

```
namespace PassXYZ.Vault;

public static class MauiProgram
{
```

```
public static MauiApp CreateMauiApp()
{
  var builder = MauiApp.CreateBuilder();
  builder
    .UseMauiApp<App>()
    .ConfigureFonts(fonts =>                                      //(1)
    {
      fonts.AddFont("fa-regular-400.ttf","FontAwesomeRegular");
      fonts.AddFont("fa-solid-900.ttf", "FontAwesomeSolid");
      fonts.AddFont("fa-brands-400.ttf","FontAwesomeBrands");
      fonts.AddFont("OpenSans-Regular.ttf","OpenSansRegular");
      fonts.AddFont("OpenSans-SemiBold.ttf","OpenSansSemiBold");
    });
  return builder.Build();
}
}
```

Listing 2.7: `MauiProgram.cs` *(*`https://epa.ms/MauiProgram2-7`*)*

In the above code, we can add fonts by calling the `ConfigureFonts` **(1)** method on the `MauiAppBuilder` object. To pass arguments to `ConfigureFonts`, we call the extension method `AddFont` of interface `IFontCollection` to add a font.

Displaying font icons

To display font icons in .NET MAUI applications, the font icon data can be defined in a `FontImageSource` object. This class, a derivative of the `ImageSource` class, comprises the properties shown in *Table 2.3*:

Property name	Type	Description
`Glyph`	`string`	Unicode character value, such as ""
`Size`	`double`	The size of the font in device-independent units
`FontFamily`	`string`	A string representing the font family, such as `FontAwesomeRegular`
`Color`	`Color`	Font icon color in `Microsoft.Maui.Graphics.Color`

Table 2.3: Properties of FontImageSource

The following XAML example has a single font icon being displayed in an Image view:

```
<Image BackgroundColor="#D1D1D1">
    <Image.Source>
        <FontImageSource Glyph="&#xf007;"
                         FontFamily="FontAwesomeRegular"
                         Size="32" />
    </Image.Source>
</Image>
```

If you are not familiar with the XAML syntax in the preceding example, don't worry. We will cover it in the following chapter. In the preceding code, a User icon is displayed in an Image control, which is from the FontAwesomeRegular font family that we just added in the configuration. The Glyph of the User icon in the hexadecimal format is \uf007, presented here in C# escaped format. When we use it in XML, the escaped format we have to use is .

The equivalent C# code is as follows:

```
Image image = new Image {
    BackgroundColor = Color.FromHex("#D1D1D1")
};
image.Source = new FontImageSource {
    Glyph = "\uf007",
    FontFamily = "FontAwesomeRegular",
    Size = 32
};
```

In the preceding example, we referred to a font icon using a string representation of a hex number for its Glyph. However, this is not the most practical for real-world usage. It's preferable to define font glyphs as C# string constants, allowing more meaningful references. Several approaches can be applied here. In our case, we make use of the open-source **IconFont2Code** tool to generate string constants. **IconFont2Code** can be found on GitHub using the following URL: https://github.com/andreinitescu/IconFont2Code.

In our project, we use Font Awesome. Through the **IconFont2Code** website, we can upload the font library from our project's Resources\Fonts folder. **IconFont2Code** then generates the corresponding code for us, as demonstrated in the following example:

```
namespace PassXYZ.Vault.Resources.Styles;

static class FontAwesomeRegular
{
    public const string Heart = "\uf004";
    public const string Star = "\uf005";
    public const string Scan = "\uf006";
    public const string User = "\uf007";
    public const string Qrcode = "\uf008";
    public const string Fingerprint = "\uf009";
    public const string Clock = "\uf017";
    public const string ListAlt = "\uf022";
    public const string Flag = "\uf024";
    public const string Bookmark = "\uf02e";


    ...


    public const string SmileBeam = "\uf5b8";
    public const string Surprise = "\uf5c2";
    public const string Tired = "\uf5c8";
}
```

We can save the generated C# files in the Resources\Styles folder. The preceding file can be found here: Resources\Styles\FontAwesomeRegular.cs.

With the preceding FontAwesomeRegular static class, a font icon can be used just like the normal text in a XAML file:

```
<Button
  Text="Click me"
  FontAttributes="Bold"
```

```
    Grid.Row="3"
    SemanticProperties.Hint="Counts the number of times …"
    Clicked="OnCounterClicked"
    HorizontalOptions="Center">
    <Button.ImageSource>
<FontImageSource
        FontFamily="FontAwesomeSolid"
        Glyph="{x:Static app:FontAwesomeSolid.PlusCircle}"
        Color="{DynamicResource SecondaryColor}"
        Size="16" />
    </Button.ImageSource>
</Button>
```

In the preceding code, we have added a circle plus icon to the `Button` control, which appears before the text `"Click me"`. In order to reference the icon name in the generated C# class, we introduce an app namespace, as defined here:

```
xmlns:app="clr-namespace:PassXYZ.Vault.Resources.Styles"
```

So far, we have created our project and configured the resources that we need. It's time to build and test our app.

Building and debugging

As we mentioned in *Chapter 1*, *Getting Started with .NET MAUI*, we cannot build and test every target using a single platform. Please refer to *Table 1.8* for the available build targets on Windows and macOS platforms. For the sake of simplicity, we will build and test targets Windows and Android on Windows. For iOS and macOS builds, we will do it on the macOS platform.

Once we've set things up, we can start building and debugging our application.

Let's begin with building and testing on the Windows platform. We can choose the framework that we want to run or debug, depending on our needs, as depicted in *Figure 2.6*:

```
File   Edit   View   Git   Project   Build   Debug   Test   Analyze   Tools   Extensions   Window   Help        🔎        Pass...ault

⊕ ▾  ▾  | 🗗 ▾ 🖆 🖫 🖺 | ↺ ▾ ↻ ▾ | Debug ▾ | Any CPU       ▾ | ▶ Windows Machine ▾  ▷ 🔧 ▾ | 🖳 🗐 ▾ 🎛 | " ...

                                                    ▷  Windows Machine                                              er
MauiProgram.cs  ⊕ ✕  What's New?
                                                       Framework (net8.0-windows10.0.19041.0)        ▸              🗐  🕐 ▾
[C#] PassXYZ.Vault (net8.0-android)      ▾  ⚙PassXYZ.Vault.MauiProgram      ▾  🔖                                   n Explorer
{🔖     1       using Microsoft.Extensions.Logging;     Android Emulators                           ▸              'PassXYZ.
        2                                               iOS Local Devices                            ▸
        3     ⊟namespace PassXYZ.Vault                  iOS Remote Devices                           ▸              XYZ.Vault
        4      {                                        iOS Simulators                               ▸              ependenci
        5     ⊟    public static class MauiProgram      🔧 PassXYZ.Vault Debug Properties                           operties
        6          {                                    ⚙ Configure Startup Projects...                             atforms
        7     ⊟        public static MauiApp CreateMauiApp()                                          ▷  🖿  Resources
        8              {                                                                              ▷  🗋  App.xaml
        9                  var builder = MauiApp.CreateBuilder();                                     ▷  🗋  AppShell.xa
       10                  builder                                                                    ▷  🗋  MainPage.x
       11                      .UseMauiApp<App>()                                                     ▷  C# MauiProgra
       12     ⊟                .ConfigureFonts(fonts =>
       13                      {
       14                          fonts.AddFont("OpenSans-Regular.ttf", "OpenSansRegula
       15                          fonts.AddFont("OpenSans-Semibold.ttf", "OpenSansSemib
       16                      });
       17
       18     #if DEBUG
       19              builder.Logging.AddDebug();
       20     #endif
```

Figure 2.6: Building and debugging

Windows

We can run or debug a Windows build on a local machine by choosing **net8.0-windows10.0.19041.0** as the framework. However, to accomplish this, we must first enable Developer Mode on Windows, if it's not yet been activated. Please refer to *Figure 2.7* for guidance on enabling Developer Mode on Windows 10 or 11:

1. Open the **Start** menu.

2. Search for **Developer settings** and select it.

3. Turn on **Developer Mode**.

4. If you receive a warning message about Developer Mode, read it, and select **Yes**.

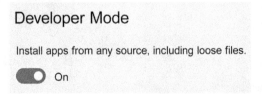

Figure 2.7: Developer Mode

Android

For Android builds, testing can be done using an Android emulator or device. However, prior to building or debugging, we need to connect a device or set up an instance of an emulator. For instructions on how to configure a device or create an emulator instance, please refer to the following Microsoft documentation: `https://learn.microsoft.com/en-us/dotnet/maui/`.

We can run or debug from Visual Studio (*Figure 2.6*) by selecting **net8.0-android** as the framework.

Alternatively, we can also build and run `net8.0-android` from the command line using the following command:

```
dotnet build -t:Run -f net8.0-android
```

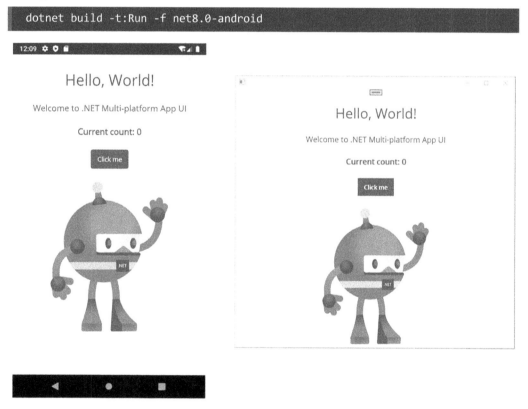

Figure 2.8: Running on Android and Windows

After we run the app on Android and Windows targets, we can see the preceding screen (*Figure 2.8*).

iOS and macOS

We're able to build and test iOS and macOS targets on a Mac computer. Given Microsoft's announcement regarding the retirement of Microsoft Visual Studio 2022 for Mac, we will proceed to demonstrate how to build and test iOS and macOS targets utilizing command-line operations.

Building and testing the iOS target

To build and test the iOS target, we can use the following command in the project folder:

```
dotnet build -t:Run -f net8.0-ios -p:_DeviceName=:v2:udid=02C556DA-64B8-
440B-8F06-F8C56BB7CC22
```

To select a target iOS emulator, we need to provide the device ID using the following parameter:

```
-p:_DeviceName=:v2:udid=
```

To find the device ID, we can launch Xcode on a Mac computer and go to **Windows -> Devices and Simulators**, as shown in *Figure 2.9*:

Figure 2.9: Devices and simulators in Xcode

As an addition to building on a Mac, it's worth noting that iOS targets can also be built and tested using Visual Studio 2022 on Windows, provided the configuration is set up accordingly. Refer to the following Microsoft documentation for instructions on how to deploy an iOS app using hot restart: `https://learn.microsoft.com/en-us/dotnet/maui/ios/hot-restart`.

Building and testing the macOS target

For the macOS target, we can use the following command to build and test:

```
dotnet build -t:Run -f net8.0-maccatalyst
```

In *Figure 2.10*, we can see a screenshot of our project in both iOS and macOS. The look and feel are similar to Android and Windows.

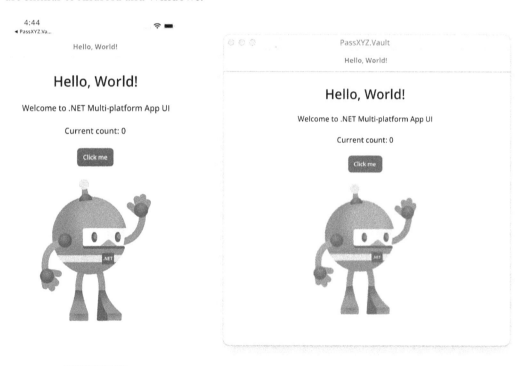

Figure 2.10: Running on iOS and macOS

The environment setup for Android, iOS, and macOS involves platform-specific details. Please refer to the Microsoft documentation for detailed instructions.

Our app works well now, but you can see that it is a very simple one with only one window. To lay a better foundation for our subsequent development, we will use Shell as the navigation framework. There is a good Shell-based template in Xamarin.Forms, and we can use it to create the initial code for our app.

Migrating from Xamarin

In this section, we will showcase the process of migrating a Xamarin.Forms project template to .NET MAUI. It should be noted that this serves only as an example, given that there are many types of Xamarin projects. Therefore, only an example of migrating a Xamarin.Forms project to .NET MAUI is discussed in this chapter. For additional information on migrating Xamarin-native projects and other related topics, please refer to the Microsoft documentation: `https://learn.microsoft.com/en-us/dotnet/maui/migration/`.

Though we are primarily porting the Xamarin.Forms Shell template as an example in this chapter, this new project template is crucial for our subsequent developments. To provide further context, I will briefly introduce the planned migration of PassXYZ.Vault from Xamarin.Forms to .NET MAUI. This will outline the challenges we'll need to tackle in this book, which should prepare you for the challenges you may encounter when migrating your own apps.

We can run the app that we have created successfully now. We are going to develop a password manager app named PassXYZ.Vault in the rest of this book. Version *1.x.x* of this app is implemented in Xamarin.Forms, and you can find it on GitHub: `https://github.com/passxyz/Vault`.

Version *1.0.0* is developed using Xamarin.Forms *5.0.0*. We plan to rebuild it using .NET MAUI and will discuss the process in this book. The .NET MAUI release will be labeled as *2.x.x*, and the source code will be available at the following location: `https://github.com/passxyz/Vault2`.

Both the *1.x.x* and *2.x.x* versions utilize Shell as the navigation framework, supported in .NET MAUI and Xamarin.Forms through `Microsoft.Maui.Controls.Shell` and `Xamarin.Forms.Shell`, respectively. Shell provides a consistent navigation user experience across all platforms. We will delve deeper into Shell and its navigation features in *Chapter 5, Navigation Using .NET MAUI Shell and NavigationPage*.

Project templates created from the Visual Studio for both .NET MAUI and Xamarin.Forms incorporate Shell. However, the default .NET MAUI project template contains only the simplest form of Shell, as seen in *Listing 2.8*:

```xml
<?xml version="1.0" encoding="UTF-8" ?>
<Shell
    x:Class="PassXYZ.Vault.AppShell"
    xmlns="http://schemas.microsoft.com/dotnet/2021/maui"
    xmlns:x="http://schemas.microsoft.com/winfx/2009/xaml"
    xmlns:local="clr-namespace:PassXYZ.Vault"
    Shell.FlyoutBehavior="Disabled">
    <ShellContent
        Title="Home"
        ContentTemplate="{DataTemplate local:MainPage}"
        Route="MainPage" />
</Shell>
```

Listing 2.8: `AppShell.xaml` *(https://epa.ms/AppShell2-8)*

`MainPage` is displayed in `ShellContent`, presenting a basic UI without much content. In our app, we will employ the **MVVM pattern** to build our user interface via Shell. In order to do so, boilerplate code is required that encompasses both the MVVM pattern and the Shell navigation structure.

 The MVVM pattern is a frequently used UI design pattern in .NET MAUI app development. We will encounter it several times as we progress through the topics in this book.

We have the option of creating this code from scratch. However, the Xamarin.Forms template includes the boilerplate code that I used in version *1.x.x* of `PassXYZ.Vault`. Thus, the same project template can be created for .NET MAUI. This process also gives us an insight into how to migrate or reuse existing Xamarin.Forms code.

Migrating and reusing the Shell template from Xamarin. Forms

Xamarin.Forms provides a more versatile Shell template that can be used to generate boilerplate code with either flyout or tabbed Shell navigation options. We can set up a new Xamarin.Forms project using this template. Then, we can implement this boilerplate code in the .NET MAUI application that we just created.

To create a new Xamarin.Forms project, follow these steps:

1. Launch Visual Studio 2022 and select **Create a new project**. This opens the **Create a new project** wizard. In the search box, we can type Xamarin, and all Xamarin-related project templates will be shown (see *Figure 2.11*):

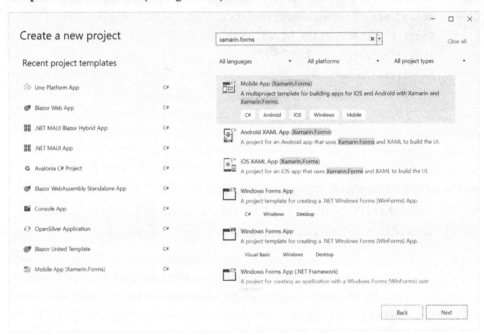

Figure 2.11: New Xamarin project

2.   Select **Mobile App (Xamarin.Forms)** from the list and click **Next**. On the next screen, as shown in *Figure 2.12*, we can choose a different location and use the same project name, PassXYZ.Vault, and then click the **Create** button:

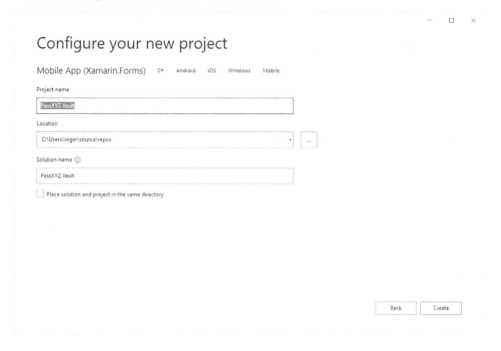

Figure 2.12: Configure the Xamarin project

3.   We have one more step, as shown in *Figure 2.13*. Let's select the **Flyout** template and click
     Create:

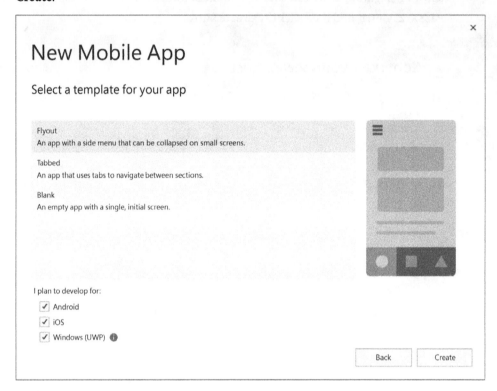

Figure 2.13: Configure the Xamarin project – Flyout

After the new solution has been created, we can see that there are four projects in the solution,
as shown in *Figure 2.14*:

- **PassXYZ.Vault** – This is a .NET Standard project that is shared by other projects, and all
  platform-independent code should be here.

- **PassXYZ.Vault.Android** – This is the Android platform-specific project.

- **PassXYZ.Vault.iOS** – This is the iOS platform-specific project.

- **PassXYZ.Vault.UWP** – This is the UWP-specific project.

We observe that the project structure of Xamarin.Forms is quite different from that of .NET MAUI. The solution consists of multiple projects, with resources managed separately in platform-specific projects. The bulk of the development work is carried out in the .NET Standard project, **PassXYZ. Vault**. We will focus on migrating and reusing the code present in this project.

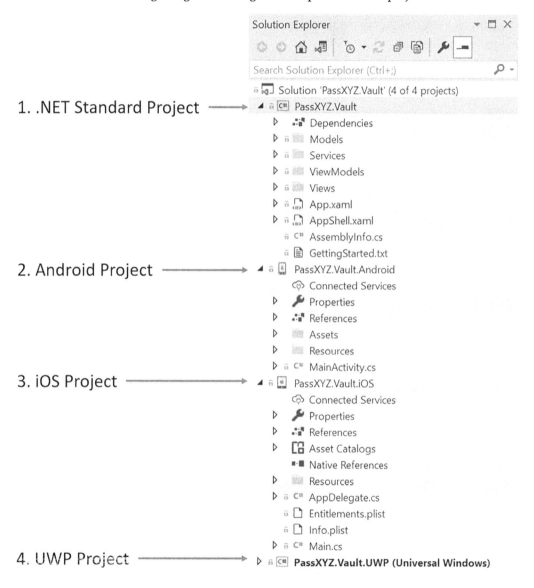

Figure 2.14: Xamarin.Forms project structure

The source code of this Xamarin.Forms project can be found here: `https://github.com/shugaoye/` `PassXYZ.Vault2/tree/xamarin`.

The migration process is relatively straightforward when it does not involve platform-specific code. We are tackling the simplest case here, but it's important to note that production code might be far more complex than this example. Therefore, any migration should only occur after meticulous analysis.

Let's concentrate on the .NET Standard project. Its content includes the boilerplate code required for the MVVM pattern and Shell UI – precisely what we need. We can copy the files highlighted in *Table 2.4* to the .NET MAUI project and adjust the namespaces in the source code accordingly.

Below are the steps of the migration process:

1. Please refer to *Table 2.4*, which shows a list of actions corresponding to the list of files and folders in the .NET Standard project:

Xamarin.Forms	Actions	.NET MAUI
`App.xaml`	No	Keep the .NET MAUI version. It defines the instance of the `Application` class.
`AppShell.xaml`	Replace	Overwrite the .NET MAUI version and change namespaces to .NET MAUI. This file defines the Shell navigation hierarchy.
`Views/`	Copy	New folder in .NET MAUI project. Need to change namespaces.
`ViewModels/`	Copy	New folder in .NET MAUI project. Need to change namespaces.
`Services/`	Copy	Interface to export models. New folder in .NET MAUI project. Need to change namespaces.
`Models/`	Copy	New folder in .NET MAUI project. Need to change namespaces.

Table 2.4: Actions in the .NET Standard project

2. In the .NET MAUI project, please refer to *Table 2.5* to replace the following namespaces:

Old namespace	New namespace
xmlns="http://xamarin.com/schemas/2014/forms"	xmlns="http://schemas.microsoft.com/dotnet/2021/maui"
using Xamarin.Forms	using Microsoft.Maui AND using Microsoft.Maui.Controls
using Xamarin.Forms.Xaml	using Microsoft.Maui.Controls.Xaml

Table 2.5: Namespaces in .NET MAUI and Xamarin.Forms

3. Test and fix any errors.

    In *Figure 2.15*, we can see the list of files changed in the process:

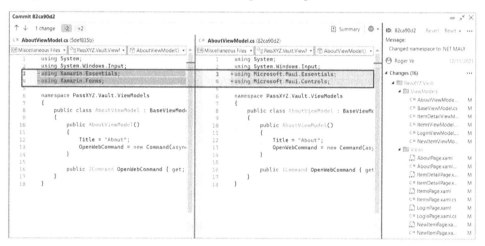

Figure 2.15: Changed files in migration (https://bit.ly/3NlfqvO)

For this straightforward case, all the necessary changes relate to the namespace. However, real-world situations may not always follow this pattern. Despite the simplicity of the process, it can still be somewhat daunting for newcomers to .NET MAUI. In fact, you are not required to carry out this process yourself. As an alternative, I've created a new .NET MAUI project template that you can use.

After building and testing this updated app, we'll be able to view the outcome in the screenshot provided in *Figure 2.16*:

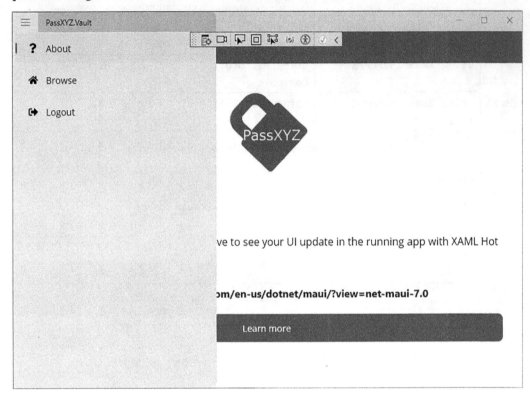

Figure 2.16: PassXYZ.Vault with .NET MAUI Shell

In *Figure 2.16*, we can see that there are three pages included in the default Shell menu:

- **About:** This is a page that informs users about the app's functionality.
- **Browse:** This is the entry point of a list of items.
- **Logout:** This is the link to the login page where you can log in or log out.

This boilerplate code will serve as the foundation for the further development of our project in this book. To encapsulate the work we've done in this section, I've created a corresponding Visual Studio project template. Utilizing this template allows us to generate the desired project structure with ease.

Note that this example merely illustrates the basic migration process. In a real-life project, numerous other factors would need to be taken into account, such as:

- Moving resources (font, images, and so on) out of platform folders
- Converting Customer Renderer to Handler
- Updating dependencies (NuGet packages)
- Changing `DependencyService` to DI

The above list is just an example. We can only find out all the considerations after a detailed analysis of a project.

Visual Studio project template

The project template can be downloaded as a Visual Studio extension package from the Visual Studio Marketplace at: `https://marketplace.visualstudio.com/items?itemName=shugaoye.maui`.

When you go to the above URL, you will see the page shown in *Figure 2.17*:

Figure 2.17: Project template in Visual Studio Marketplace

After the installation of this project template, we can create a new .NET MAUI project, as shown in *Figure 2.18*:

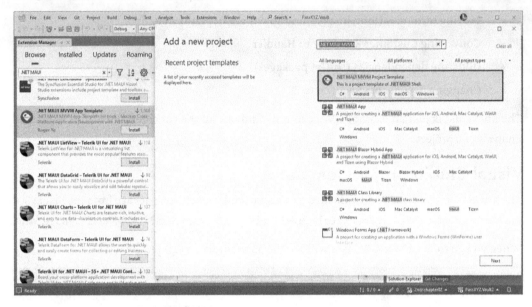

Figure 2.18: Creating a new .NET MAUI MVVM project

In the project created using this template, the project structure is the same as the one in this chapter. The source code of this project template can be found here: `https://github.com/passxyz/MauiTemplate`.

Summary

In this chapter, we created a new .NET MAUI project. We learned how to configure our .NET MAUI app using .NET Generic Host and adjusted the resources configuration to utilize a custom font (Font Awesome). We also learned about the .NET MAUI application lifecycle and tested the process of subscribing to lifecycle events by overriding the `CreateWindow` method and by creating a derived class of the `Window` class. To generate boilerplate code with MVVM pattern and Shell support, we created a new .NET MAUI project template. This walkthrough served to demonstrate how to migrate Xamarin.Forms code to .NET MAUI.

In our next chapter, we will learn how to create a user interface using XAML, which can be used to build user interfaces for WPF, UWP, Xamarin.Forms, and .NET MAUI. We will continue to create and enhance the user interfaces of our password manager app using XAML.

Learn more on Discord

Join our community's Discord space for discussions with the author and other readers:

`https://packt.link/cross-platform-app`

3

User Interface Design with XAML

In the previous chapter, we created a new .NET MAUI project named PassXYZ.Vault. As we progress through this book, we will enhance it with the skills and knowledge we acquire. In the last chapter, we got a glimpse of user interface implementation in XAML. In this chapter, we will delve deeper into creating user interfaces using XAML.

The **eXtensible Application Markup Language (XAML)** is an XML-based language that is used to define user interfaces for **Windows Presentation Foundation (WPF)**, **Universal Windows Platform (UWP)**, Xamarin.Forms, and .NET MAUI. The XAML dialects in these platforms share the same syntax but differ in their vocabularies.

XAML allows developers to define user interfaces in XML-based *markup language* rather than in any *programming language*. It is possible to write all our user interfaces in code, but user interface design with XAML will be more succinct and more visually coherent. Because XAML does not use a programming language, it cannot contain code. This is a disadvantage, but it is also an advantage as it forces the developer to separate the logic from the user interface design.

The following topics will be covered in this chapter:

- How to create a XAML page
- Basic XAML syntax
- XAML markup extension
- How to design user interfaces with the master-detail pattern
- Localization of .NET MAUI apps

Technical requirements

To test and debug the source code in this chapter, you need to have Visual Studio 2022 installed on your PC. Please refer to the *Development environment setup* section in *Chapter 1, Getting Started with .NET MAUI*, for the details.

The source code for this chapter is available in the following GitHub repository:

https://github.com/PacktPublishing/.NET-MAUI-Cross-Platform-Application-Development-Second-edition/tree/2nd/chapter03

To check out the source code of this chapter, we can use the following command:

```
$ git clone -b 2nd/chapter03 https://github.com/PacktPublishing/.NET-MAUI-
Cross-Platform-Application-Development-Second-edition.git PassXYZ.Vault2
```

To find out more about the source code in this book, please refer to the *Managing the source code in this book* section in *Chapter 2, Building Our First .NET MAUI App*.

Creating a XAML page

Before we delve into XAML syntax, let's first understand how to create a XAML page in Visual Studio and through the **dotnet** command line.

To create a XAML page using Visual Studio, right-click on the project node, then select **Add > New Item....** This will bring up the dialog box shown in *Figure 3.1*:

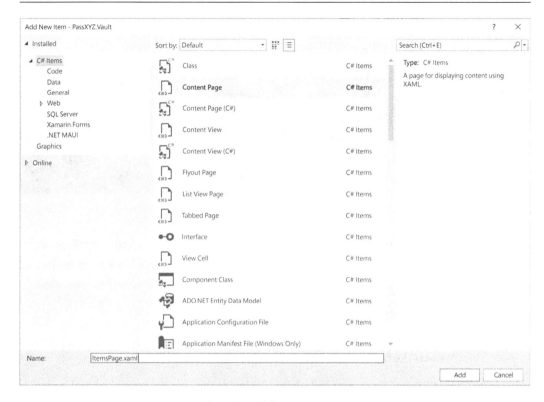

Figure 3.1: Adding a XAML page

On this screen, select **Content Page** from the templates and click **Add**. This action will generate a pair of files – a XAML file and a C# code-behind file.

The same can be achieved using a dotnet command. To locate all .NET MAUI templates, we can use the following dotnet command in the PowerShell console:

```
C:\>dotnet new --list | findstr -i maui
.NET MAUI App                    maui                [C#]    MAUI/Android/iOS/…
.NET MAUI Blazor App             maui-blazor         [C#]    MAUI/Android/iOS/…
.NET MAUI Class Library          mauilib             [C#]    MAUI/Android/iOS/…
.NET MAUI ContentPage (C#)       maui-page-csharp    [C#]    MAUI/Android/iOS/…
.NET MAUI ContentPage (XAML)     maui-page-xaml      [C#]    MAUI/Android/iOS/…
.NET MAUI ContentView (C#)       maui-view-csharp    [C#]    MAUI/Android/iOS/…
.NET MAUI ContentView (XAML)     maui-view-xaml      [C#]    MAUI/Android/iOS/…
.NET MAUI ResourceDictionary (XAML)  maui-dict-xaml  [C#]    MAUI/Android/iOS/…
```

Figure 3.2: dotnet command for listing templates

From the preceding output, we can observe that the short name of the XAML content page is
`maui-page-xaml`. We can create a XAML page using the following command:

```
C:\>dotnet new maui-page-xaml -n ItemsPage
The template ".NET MAUI ContentPage (XAML)" was created successfully.

Processing post-creation actions...
The post action 84c0da21-51c8-4541-9940-6ca19af04ee6 is not supported.
Description: Opens NewPage1.xaml in the editor.
```

Figure 3.3: Creating a XAML page

The preceding command will generate two files named `ItemsPage.xaml` and `ItemsPage.xaml.`
`cs`. You may notice a warning message about post-creation actions. This is a known issue, and
you can find more information about it at `https://github.com/dotnet/maui/issues/4994`.

However, this is not something we need to worry about.

What is the "code-behind"?

In .NET MAUI, the term **code-behind** refers to the code file associated with a **user
interface (UI)** definition file, typically a XAML file. The code-behind file contains
the logic for handling UI events, data binding, and other app functionality related
to the UI. The code-behind file is a C# (.cs) file with the same name as the related
XAML file. For example, if we have an `ItemsPage.xaml` file, the code-behind file will
be named `ItemsPage.xaml.cs`.

The code-behind file includes a class that inherits from a .NET MAUI base page type,
usually `ContentPage`, `NavigationPage`, or `TabbedPage`. The class declaration is
marked as a partial class that matches the class definition in the XAML file, allowing
for seamless integration between the XAML UI definition and its corresponding code.

XAML syntax

Since XAML is an XML-based language, to understand it better, we need to understand basic XML
syntax first. In an XML file, it starts with an XML declaration or prolog. The content of XML or
XAML files includes a hierarchy of elements. Each element may have attributes associated with it.

Let's review `App.xaml` in the project that we created in *Chapter 2, Building Our First .NET MAUI App*, as an example:

```xml
<?xml version = "1.0" encoding = "UTF-8" ?>
<Application
  xmlns="http://schemas.microsoft.com/dotnet/2021/maui"
  xmlns:x="http://schemas.microsoft.com/winfx/2009/xaml"
  xmlns:local="clr-namespace:PassXYZ.Vault"
  x:Class="PassXYZ.Vault.App">
    <Application.Resources>
      <ResourceDictionary.MergedDictionaries>
        <ResourceDictionary Source="…/Colors.xaml" />
        <ResourceDictionary Source="…/Styles.xaml" />
      </ResourceDictionary.MergedDictionaries>
    </Application.Resources>
</Application>
```

Listing 3.1: `App.xaml` *(https://epa.ms/App3-1)*

XML declaration

At the start of `App.xaml`, we can see the following XML declaration:

```xml
<?xml version = "1.0" encoding = "UTF-8" ?>
```

This declaration specifies the version of XML being used and the character encoding. In `App.xaml`, XML version 1.0 is used and the character encoding is set to UTF-8.

Element

In *Listing 3.1*, the content of `App.xaml` begins with the `Application` root element. Every XML document must contain a single root element that encompasses all other elements. Elements can have child elements, also known as nested elements, such as `ResourceDictionary`.

Elements are composed of a start tag, the content, and an end tag, as seen in the `Application` tag:

```xml
<Application>
…
</Application>
```

The start tag is enclosed in angle brackets (e.g., `<Application>`), and the end tag includes a forward slash before the element name (e.g., `</Application>`). The content can be any text or nested elements.

For an empty element, the end tag can be omitted by adding a forward slash at the end of the start tag, like so:

```
<Application />
```

When discussing an XML element, we may use the terms **element, node**, and **tag. Element** refers to the start and end tag of that element together. **Tag** refers to either the start or end tag of the element. **Node** refers to an element and all its inner content, including all child elements.

A XAML document consists of many nested elements, with only one top element, known as the root element. In .NET MAUI, the root element is usually `Application`, `ContentPage`, `Shell`, or `ResourceDictionary`.

For each XAML file, we typically have a corresponding C# code-behind file. Let's review the code-behind file in *Listing 3.2*:

```
using PassXYZ.Vault.Services;
using PassXYZ.Vault.Views;

namespace PassXYZ.Vault;

public partial class App : Application                                    //(1)
{
  public App()
  {
    InitializeComponent();                                               //(2)
    MainPage = new AppShell();
  }
}
```

Listing 3.2: `App.xaml.cs` *(https://epa.ms/App3-2)*

In XAML, elements usually represent actual C# classes that are instantiated to objects at runtime. Together, the XAML and code-behind files define a complete class. For example, `App.xaml` (*Listing 3.1*) and `App.xaml.cs` (*Listing 3.2*) define the App class, which is a sub-class of `Application`.

(1) The App class, whose full name is PassXYZ.Vault.App, is the same as the one defined in the XAML file using the x:Class attribute:

```
x:Class="PassXYZ.Vault.App"
```

(2) In the constructor of the App class, the InitializeComponent method is called to load the XAML and parse it. UI elements defined in the XAML file are created at this point. We can access these UI elements by the name defined with the x:Name attribute, as we'll see shortly.

Attribute

An element can have multiple unique attributes. An attribute provides additional information about XML elements. An XML attribute is a name-value pair attached to an element. In XAML, an element represents a C# class and the attributes represent the members of this class:

```
<Button x:Name="loginButton" VerticalOptions="Center"
IsEnabled="True" Text="Login"/>
```

As we can see in the above, four attributes – x:Name, VerticalOptions, IsEnabled, and Text – are defined for the Button element. To define an attribute, we need to specify the attribute's name and value with an equal sign. The attribute value should be enclosed in double or single quotes. For example, IsEnabled is the attribute name and "True" is the attribute value.

In this example, the x:Name attribute is a special one. It does not refer to a member of the Button class, but rather refers to the variable holding the instance of the Button class. Without the x:Name attribute, an anonymous instance of the Button class will be created. With the x:Name attribute declared, we can refer to the instance of the Button class using the loginButton variable in the code-behind file.

XML and XAML namespaces

In XML or XAML, we can declare namespaces just like we do in C#. Namespaces help to group elements and attributes to avoid name conflicts when the same name is used in a different scope. Namespaces can be defined using the xmlns attribute with the following syntax:

```
xmlns:prefix="identifier"
```

The XAML namespace definition has two components: a prefix and an identifier. Both the prefix and the identifier can be any string, as allowed by the W3C namespaces in the XML 1.0 specification. If the prefix is omitted, the namespace becomes the default namespace.

In *Listing 3.1*, the following namespace is the default one:

```
xmlns="http://schemas.microsoft.com/dotnet/2021/maui"
```

This default namespace allows us to refer to .NET MAUI classes without a prefix, such as ContentPage, Label, or Button.

For the namespace declaration, the x prefix is used, like so:

```
xmlns:x="http://schemas.microsoft.com/winfx/2009/xaml"
```

The xmlns:x namespace declaration specifies elements and attributes that are intrinsic to XAML. This namespace is one of the most important ones that we will use in the UI design with XAML. To comprehend its usage, we can create a content page with an identical structure using both C# and XAML in the subsequent sections.

Creating a new page using XAML

First, let's create a new page using XAML. To create a content page in XAML, we can use the dotnet command, as we have done previously:

```
dotnet new maui-page-xaml -n NewPage1
The template ".NET MAUI ContentPage (XAML)" was created successfully.
Processing post-creation actions...
The post action 84c0da21-51c8-4541-9940-6ca19af04ee6 is not supported.
Description: Opens NewPage1.xaml in the editor.
```

The preceding command generates a XAML file (NewPage1.xaml) and a C# code-behind file (NewPage1.xaml.cs). We can update the XAML file to the following. Since we aren't adding any logic, we can ignore the code-behind file (NewPage1.xaml.cs) in this example:

NewPage1.xaml

```
<ContentPage
   xmlns="http://schemas.microsoft.com/dotnet/2021/maui"
   xmlns:x="http://schemas.microsoft.com/winfx/2009/xaml"
   x:Class="MauiApp1.NewPage1"                                    //(1)
   Title="NewPage1">
   <StackLayout x:Name="layout">                                  //(2)
     <Label Text="Welcome to .NET MAUI!"
        VerticalOptions="Center"
        HorizontalOptions="Center" />
```

```
      <BoxView HeightRequest="150" WidthRequest="150"
        HorizontalOptions="Center">
        <BoxView.Color>
          <Color x:FactoryMethod="FromRgba">                  //(3)
            <x:Arguments>                                     //(4)
              <x:Int32>192</x:Int32>                          //(5)
              <x:Int32>75</x:Int32>
              <x:Int32>150</x:Int32>
              <x:Int32>128</x:Int32>
            </x:Arguments>
          </Color>
        </BoxView.Color>
      </BoxView>
    </StackLayout>
  </ContentPage>
```

NewPage1.xaml.cs

```
namespace MauiApp1;
public partial class NewPage1 : ContentPage {
  public NewPage1() {
    InitializeComponent();
  }
}
```

For comparison purposes with the XAML version we just created, let's create the same content page using C# only in the next section. Then we will have a look at the lines numbered in the preceding code.

Creating the same new page using C#

To create the same content page using only C# code, let's use the following command:

```
dotnet new maui-page-csharp -n NewPage1
The template ".NET MAUI ContentPage (C#)" was created successfully.
Processing post-creation actions...
The post action 84c0da21-51c8-4541-9940-6ca19af04ee6 is not supported.
Description: Opens NewPage1.cs in the editor.
```

The preceding command generates a content page in the NewPage1.cs C# file. We can implement the same logic in C# like so:

NewPage1.cs

```
namespace MauiApp1;
public class NewPage1 : ContentPage {                        //[1]
  public NewPage1() {
    var layout = new StackLayout                             //[2]
    {
      Children = {
        new Label { Text = "Welcome to .NET MAUI!" },
        new BoxView {
          HeightRequest = 150,
          WidthRequest = 150,
          HorizontalOptions = LayoutOptions.Center,
          Color = Color.FromRgba(192, 75, 150, 128)          //[3]
        }
      }
    };
    Content = layout;
  }
}
```

Here, we have created the same content page (NewPage1) twice in both XAML and C#. XAML cannot contain programming logic, but it can be used to declare user interface elements and put the logic in the C# code-behind file. Within both versions of NewPage1, we created a content page that contains Label and BoxView elements. In the XAML version, we used attributes defined in the xmlns:x namespace to specify the UI elements:

(1) A content page called NewPage1 is created in XAML. The x:Class attribute specifies the class name – that is, NewPage1. In the C# code-behind file, a partial class of NewPage1 is defined. In the constructor, the InitializeComponent method is invoked to load the UI defined in XAML.

[1] We can create the same content page, NewPage1, using C# directly as a derived class of ContentPage.

We defined a StackLayout in the content page and the variable name used to refer to it is **layout** in both the XAML and C# versions:

(2) In XAML, x:Name specifies the variable name of StackLayout.

[2] In C#, we can declare the variable as layout.

(3) x:FactoryMethod specifies a factory method that can be used to initialize an object.

[3] In C# code, we can call the Color.FromRgba function directly, but we have to use the x:FactoryMethod attribute in XAML to do the same.

(4) x:Arguments is used to specify arguments when we call Color.FromRgba in XAML.

(5) x:Int is used to specify integer arguments. For other data types, we can use x:Double, xChar, or x:Boolean.

For more information about the xmlns:x namespace, please refer to the Microsoft documentation at https://learn.microsoft.com/en-us/dotnet/maui/xaml/namespaces/.

Common Language Runtime (CLR) types can be referenced in XAML by declaring a XAML namespace with a prefix. As shown in *Listing 3.1*, we can refer to our C# namespace, PassXYZ.Vault, like so:

```
xmlns:local="clr-namespace:PassXYZ.Vault"
```

To declare a CLR namespace, we can use clr-namespace: or using:. If the CLR namespace is defined in a different assembly, assembly= is used to specify the assembly that contains the referenced CLR namespace. The value is the name of the assembly without the file extension. In our case, it has been omitted since the PassXYZ.Vault namespace is within the same assembly as our application code.

We will see more uses of namespaces later in this chapter.

XAML markup extensions

Even though we can initialize class instances using XAML elements and set class members using XAML attributes, we can only set them as predefined constants in a XAML document.

To enhance the power and flexibility of XAML by allowing element attributes to be set from a variety of sources, we can use XAML markup extensions. With XAML markup extensions, we can set an attribute to values defined somewhere else, or a result processed by code at runtime.

XAML markup extensions can be specified in curly braces, as shown here:

```
<Button Margin="0,10,0,0" Text="Learn more"
        Command="{Binding OpenWebCommand}"
        BackgroundColor="{DynamicResource PrimaryColor}"
        TextColor="White" />
```

In the preceding code, both the `BackgroundColor` and `Command` attributes have been set to markup extensions. `BackgroundColor` has been set to `DynamicResource` and `Command` has been set to the `OpenWebCommand` method defined in the view model.

Here, we've provided a brief introduction to markup extensions, so don't concern yourself with the usage of markup extensions for now. We will delve deeper into markup extensions when we use them later. In the next chapter, *Chapter 4, Exploring MVVM and Data Binding*, we will detail the usage of data binding.

Please refer to the following Microsoft documentation to find out more information about markup extensions: `https://learn.microsoft.com/en-us/dotnet/maui/xaml/markup-extensions/consume`.

Now that we've learned the basics about XAML, we can use it to work on our user interface design.

Building a user interface

Equipped with basic knowledge of XAML, let's take a bird's-eye view of the .NET MAUI user interface building blocks. We will explore them in greater depth as we encounter them in subsequent chapters.

A page is the top-level user interface element that typically occupies all the screens or windows. We introduced how to create pages using the Visual Studio template or `dotnet` command at the beginning of this chapter. Each page generally contains at least one layout element, which is used to organize the design of controls on a page. Examples of pages are `ContentPage`, `NavigationPage`, `TabbedPage`, `FlyoutPage`, and `Shell`.

Within a content page, we utilize views (or controls) as the building blocks of the user interface. To organize views into groups, we can use layout components as containers for the views.

Layouts

Layouts are container components that help organize and arrange UI elements (or views) within your app. They control the position, size, and alignment of the UI components based on specific rules.

Layouts allow you to create consistent and adaptive user interfaces that work on different screen sizes and device orientations. Examples include StackLayout, Grid, FlexLayout, RelativeLayout, and AbsoluteLayout.

StackLayout

StackLayout organizes elements in a one-dimensional stack, either horizontally or vertically. It is often used as a parent layout, which contains other child layouts. The default orientation is vertical. However, we should not use StackLayout to generate a layout similar to a table by using nested StackLayout horizontally and vertically. The following code shows an example of bad practice:

```
<StackLayout>
    <StackLayout Orientation="Horizontal">
        <Label Text="Name:" />
        <Entry Placeholder="Enter your name" />
    </StackLayout>
    <StackLayout Orientation="Horizontal">
        <Label Text="Age:" />
        <Entry Placeholder="Enter your age" />
    </StackLayout>
    <StackLayout Orientation="Horizontal">
        <Label Text="Address:" />
        <Entry Placeholder="Enter your address" />
    </StackLayout>
</StackLayout>
```

In the preceding code, we employed a StackLayout as the parent layout, where the default orientation is vertical. Then, we nested multiple StackLayout controls with a horizontal orientation to generate a form for data entry.

However, using nested StackLayouts to create a layout similar to a table is not optimized for such scenarios, and it might lead to performance and layout issues. In this situation, we should utilize the Grid control.

StackLayout is a frequently used layout control. There are two sub-types of StackLayout that help us directly design the layout horizontally or vertically.

HorizontalStackLayout

`HorizontalStackLayout` is a one-dimensional horizontal stack. For example, we can generate a row like so:

```
<HorizontalStackLayout>
    <Label Text="Name:" />
    <Entry Placeholder="Enter your name" />
</HorizontalStackLayout>
```

VerticalStackLayout

`VerticalStackLayout` is a one-dimensional vertical stack. For example, we can display an error message after a form is submitted with an error like so:

```
<VerticalStackLayout>
  <Label Text="The Form Is Invalid" />
  <Button Text="OK"/>
</VerticalStackLayout>
```

Grid

`Grid` organizes elements in rows and columns. We can specify rows and columns with the `RowDefinitions` and `ColumnDefinitions` properties. In the previous example, we created a form where the user can enter their name, age, and address using a nested `StackLayout`. We can do this in the `Grid` layout like so:

```
<Grid>
    <Grid.RowDefinitions>
        <RowDefinition Height="50" />
        <RowDefinition Height="50" />
        <RowDefinition Height="50" />
    </Grid.RowDefinitions>
    <Grid.ColumnDefinitions>
        <ColumnDefinition Width="Auto" />
        <ColumnDefinition />
    </Grid.ColumnDefinitions>
    <Label Text="Name:" />
    <Entry Grid.Column="1"
            Placeholder="Enter your name" />
    <Label Grid.Row="1" Text="Age:" />
```

```
    <Entry Grid.Row="1" Grid.Column="1"
           Placeholder="Enter your age" />
    <Label Grid.Row="2" Text="Address:" />
    <Entry Grid.Row="2"
           Grid.Column="1"
           Placeholder="Enter your address" />
  </Grid>
```

In the preceding example, we created a Grid layout with two columns and three rows.

FlexLayout

FlexLayout is similar to a StackLayout in that it displays child elements either horizontally or vertically in a stack. The difference is a FlexLayout can also wrap its children if there are too many to fit in a single row or column. As an example, we can create a FlexLayout with five labels in a row. If we specify the Direction property as Row, these labels will be displayed in one row. We can also specify the Wrap property, which can cause the items to wrap to the next row if there are too many items to fit in a row:

```
        <FlexLayout Direction="Row" Wrap="Wrap">
            <Label Text="Item 1" Padding="10"/>
            <Label Text="Item 2" Padding="10"/>
            <Label Text="Item 3" Padding="10"/>
            <Label Text="Item 4" Padding="10"/>
            <Label Text="Item 5" Padding="10"/>
        </FlexLayout>
```

AbsoluteLayout

AbsoluteLayout is a layout control that enables you to position and size child elements based on X and Y coordinates in addition to width and height. It is particularly useful in scenarios where you need fine-grained control over the exact position and size of your UI elements.

Here are some common use cases for AbsoluteLayout:

- **Overlap UI elements**: AbsoluteLayout allows you to position elements on top of others, which can create some effective visuals or display content over a background image.

- **Custom controls**: If you are developing custom controls that require precise control over the layout of their components, AbsoluteLayout should be your go-to choice.

- **Complex UI presentation:** You may need to create intricate UIs that don't fit within a standard grid or stack layout. In such scenarios, AbsoluteLayout gives you the control required to position items accurately.

- **Positioning based on the parent size:** AbsoluteLayout allows you to position children relative to the bounds of their parent. This makes it easier to place elements at specific positions or in response to certain events.

- **Animations:** If you need to animate elements, such as moving them around the screen or resizing them, AbsoluteLayout can simplify this process by providing direct access to the location, width, and height properties of child elements.

Generally speaking, there are three benefits of using AbsoluteLayout for building layouts:

- **Precise control:** AbsoluteLayout provides control over the position, size, and layering of child elements, which can be beneficial when working on custom or complex UI designs.

- **Performance:** Since AbsoluteLayout doesn't require complex calculations to arrange elements, it can offer better performance compared to other layout types, especially when dealing with a large number of child elements.

- **Responsive layouts:** With the support of proportional values, AbsoluteLayout can help create responsive designs that can scale with different screen sizes and orientations.

However, it's important to note that using AbsoluteLayout everywhere is not recommended. It is better suited for specific scenarios where other layouts cannot meet the required design or functionality requirements. The disadvantages of AbsoluteLayout include the difficulty of maintaining the responsive behavior of the UI and the potential for unexpected behavior when there are changes to the parent or child elements. Instead, you should use other layouts (e.g., Grid, StackLayout, or FlexLayout) whenever their features are adequate for your design needs.

In the following example, we are creating a BoxView control in the layout at (0, 0) with both width and height equal to 10:

```
<AbsoluteLayout Margin="20">
    <BoxView Color="Silver"
        AbsoluteLayout.LayoutBounds="0, 0, 10, 10" />
</AbsoluteLayout>
```

We have provided an overview of layout controls. For more detailed information, please refer to the following Microsoft documentation: https://learn.microsoft.com/en-us/dotnet/maui/user-interface/layouts/.

Views

Views (also known as controls) are the individual UI elements that users interact with or that display content on a screen. They are placed within layouts and, in turn, on pages. Views include basic UI controls like Label, Button, Entry, and Image, as well as more advanced UI controls, such as CollectionView, ListView, and WebView.

Please refer to the following Microsoft document about the controls in .NET MAUI: https:// learn.microsoft.com/en-us/dotnet/maui/user-interface/controls/.

In this section, we'll go through some controls that will be frequently used in this book.

Label

Label is used to display single-line or multi-line text. It can display text with a certain format, such as color, space, text decorations, and even HTML text. To create a Label, we can use the simplest format, like so:

```
<Label Text="Hello world" />
```

Image

In the user interface design, we usually use icons to decorate other controls or display images as backgrounds. The Image control can display an image from a local file, a URI, an embedded resource, or a stream. The following code shows an example of how to create an Image control in the simplest form:

```
<Image Source="dotnet_bot.png" />
```

Editor

In our app, the users need to enter or edit a single line of text or multiple lines of text. We have two controls to serve this purpose: Editor and Entry.

Editor can be used to enter or edit multiple lines of text. The following is an example of the Editor control:

```
<Editor Placeholder="Enter your description here" />
```

Entry

Entry can be used to enter or edit a single line of text. To design a login page, we can use Entry controls to enter a username and password. When users interact with an Entry, the behavior of the keyboard can be customized through the Keyboard property.

When users enter their passwords, the `IsPassword` property can be set to reflect the typical behavior on a login page. The following is an example of a password entry:

```
<Entry Placeholder="Enter your password" Keyboard="Text"
IsPassword="True" />
```

ListView

In user interface design, a common use case involves displaying a collection of data. In .NET MAUI, several controls can be utilized to display a collection of data, such as `CollectionView`, `ListView`, and `CarouselView`. In our app, we will employ `ListView` to display password entries, groups, and the contents of an entry. We will introduce the usage of `ListView` when introducing `ItemsPage` and `ItemDetailPage` in *Chapter 4, Exploring MVVM and Data Binding*.

With all these building blocks in place, we can construct a content page. Typically, an application consists of multiple pages implementing different functionalities. To create a functional app, we need to navigate between these pages.

Navigation refers to the process of moving between various pages or views within your app, enabling users to interact with multiple screens and access a range of features. Navigation is a crucial aspect of app design, as it determines the user's journey through the app and assists them in finding the information they require. In .NET MAUI, navigation management is handled using `NavigationPage`, `TabbedPage`, `Shell`, or custom navigation if necessary.

Master-detail UI design

There are various ways to implement navigation within an app. In our app's navigation design, we employ the master-detail pattern.

The master-detail pattern is a widely utilized user interface design approach. Many examples of it can be found in frequently used apps. For instance, in the Mail app on Windows, a list of emails is displayed in the master view along with the details of the selected email:

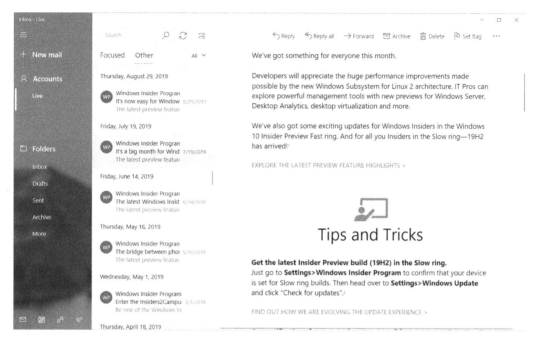

Figure 3.4: Mail in Windows

In *Figure 3.4*, three panels are present in the design. The left panel resembles a navigation drawer. When selecting a folder from the left panel, a list of emails is shown in the middle panel. The currently selected email is displayed in the right panel.

Note

Navigation drawers provide access to destinations and app functionality, such as the menu in the desktop environment. It typically slides in from the left and is triggered by tapping an icon in the top-left corner of the screen. It displays a list of choices to navigate to and is widely used in mobile and web user interface design. Xamarin. Forms and .NET MAUI Shell use navigation drawers as their top-level navigation methods.

The original KeePass UI design, shown in *Figure 3.5*, also uses three panels (left, right, and bottom) on the main page. The left panel is a classic tree view that acts like a navigation drawer. The right panel is used to display the list of password entries, while the bottom panel serves to exhibit the details of an entry:

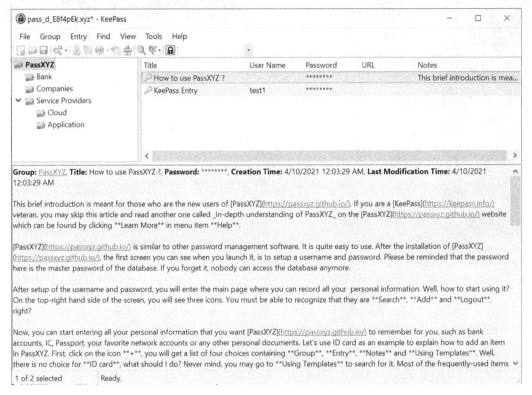

Figure 3.5: KeePass UI design

The master-detail pattern works well on a wide range of device types and display sizes.

Considering different display sizes, two popular modes can be used:

- Side-by-side
- Stacked

Side-by-side

When ample horizontal space is available on a large display, the side-by-side approach tends to be a sensible choice. The Mail app in *Figure 3.4* and the KeePass app in *Figure 3.5* serve as good examples. In this mode, both the master view and the detail view can be seen simultaneously.

Stacked

When using a mobile device, the screen size is typically smaller, with the vertical space being larger than the horizontal one. In such instances, the stacked approach is more suitable.

In the stacked mode, the master view occupies the entire screen space. Upon making a selection, the detail view then takes up the full screen space:

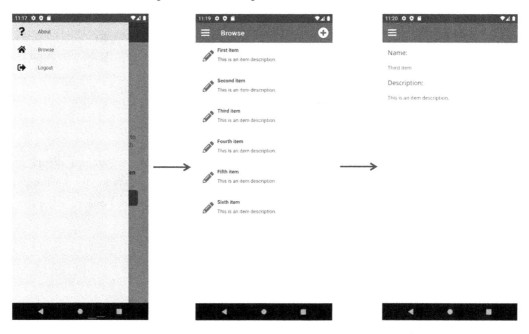

Figure 3.6: PassXYZ.Vault

In *Figure 3.6*, we can observe the app navigation from the user's perspective. We have a list of flyout items to choose from:

- **About**
- **Browse**
- **Logout**

Upon selecting **Browse**, we view the list of items on the master page (ItemsPage). From this page, if we choose an item, we will go to the item's detail page (ItemDetailPage). If we want to select another item, we must return to the master page and make another selection.

We will discuss flyout items in _Chapter 5, Navigation Using .NET MAUI Shell and NavigationPage_. In this section, we will examine the implementation of `ItemsPage` and `ItemDetailPage`. However, before delving into the specifics, let's explore layouts, which serve as containers for user interface elements.

Navigation in the master-detail UI design

As shown in _Figure 3.6_, we employ a stacked master-detail pattern in our navigation scheme. There is a flyout menu to display a list of pages. Within this list of pages, a page of the `ItemsPage` type is utilized to display a list of password entries. When users select an entry, details about the password entry are shown in `ItemDetailPage`.

Let's review the implementation of `ItemsPage` and `ItemDetailPage`.

ItemDetailPage

In our app, `ItemDetailPage` serves as the detail page of the master-detail pattern, displaying an item's content. In `ItemDetailPage`, we essentially present the `Item` data model. Although it appears quite simple for now, we will gradually enhance it throughout this book:

```
using System;
namespace PassXYZ.Vault.Models {
    public class Item {
        public string Id { get; set; }
        public string Text { get; set; }
        public string Description { get; set; }
    }
}
```

Listing 3.3: `Item.cs` (https://epa.ms/Item3-3)

As shown in _Listing 3.3_, the `Item` class includes three properties: `ID`, `Text`, and `Description`. The `Item` instance is loaded by the `LoadItemId` function in `ItemDetailViewModel`, as shown here:

```
public async void LoadItemId(string itemId)
{
  if (itemId == null) {
    throw new ArgumentNullException(nameof(itemId)); }

  var item = await dataStore.GetItemAsync(itemId);
  if (item == null) {
    logger.LogDebug("cannot find {itemId}", itemId);
```

```
        return; }
    Id = item.Id;
    Name = item.Name;
    Description = item.Description;
  }
```

In `LoadItemId`, the `GetItemAsync` method of the `IDataStore` interface is invoked to obtain the item by its ID.

After loading the item, we can present the data to the user in `ItemDetailPage.xaml`, as shown in *Listing 3.4*:

```
<?xml version="1.0" encoding="utf-8" ?>
<ContentPage
  xmlns="http://schemas.microsoft.com/dotnet/2021/maui"
  xmlns:x="http://schemas.microsoft.com/winfx/2009/xaml"
  x:Class="PassXYZ.Vault.Views.ItemDetailPage"
  Title="{Binding Title}">

  <StackLayout Spacing="20" Padding="15">
    <Label Text="Name:" FontSize="Medium" />
    <Label Text="{Binding Name}" FontSize="Small"/>
    <Label Text="Description:" FontSize="Medium" />
    <Label Text="{Binding Description}" FontSize="Small"/>
  </StackLayout>
</ContentPage>
```

Listing 3.4: `ItemDetailPage.xaml` *(https://epa.ms/ItemDetailPage3-4)*

Listing 3.4 represents the XAML file of `ItemDetailPage`. The item detail content page includes an instance of `StackLayout` and four instances of `Label`.

Within `StackLayout`, the default orientation is `Vertical`, causing the `Label` controls to be arranged vertically on the item detail page (refer to *Figure 3.4*). Both `Name` and `Description` are linked to the model data in the view model through data binding, which will be introduced in the next chapter.

ItemsPage

`ItemsPage` serves as the master page of the master-detail pattern in our app, presenting a list of items that users can browse.

Listing 3.5 showcases the implementation of `ItemsPage`. To display a list of items, a `ListView` control is employed. `ListView` is a control designed for displaying a scrollable vertical list of selectable data items:

```xml
<?xml version="1.0" encoding="utf-8" ?>
<ContentPage
  xmlns="http://schemas.microsoft.com/dotnet/2021/maui"
  xmlns:x="http://schemas.microsoft.com/winfx/2009/xaml"
  x:Class="PassXYZ.Vault.Views.ItemsPage"              //(1)
  Title="{Binding Title}"
  xmlns:local="clr-namespace:PassXYZ.Vault.ViewModels" //(5)
  xmlns:model="clr-namespace:PassXYZ. Vault.Models"    //(6)
  x:DataType="local:ItemsViewModel"                    //(2)
  x:Name="BrowseItemsPage">                            //(3)

  <ContentPage.ToolbarItems...>

  <StackLayout>
    <ListView x:Name="ItemsListView"                   //(4)
      ItemsSource="{Binding Items}"
      VerticalOptions="FillAndExpand"
      HasUnevenRows="False"
      RowHeight="84"
      RefreshCommand="{Binding LoadItemsCommand}"
      IsPullToRefreshEnabled="true"
      IsRefreshing="{Binding IsBusy, Mode=OneWay}"
      CachingStrategy="RetainElement"
      ItemSelected="OnItemSelected">
        <ListView.ItemTemplate>
          <DataTemplate...>
        </ListView.ItemTemplate>
    </ListView>
  </StackLayout>
</ContentPage>
```

Listing 3.5: `ItemsPage.xaml` (https://epa.ms/ItemsPage3-5)

Let's examine this code in greater detail:

(1) x:Class: This is utilized to define the class name of a partial class shared between the markup and code-behind file. PassXYZ.Vault.Views.ItemsPage is the class name defined here.

(3) x:Name: While x:Class defines the class name in XAML, x:Name defines the instance name. We can refer to the BrowseItemsPage instance name in the code-behind file.

(2) x:DataType: Setting x:DataType to the appropriate type defined in the view model enables compiled binding, which can significantly improve performance. The view model referred to here is ItemsViewModel.

In addition to the standard namespace, we have defined two more namespaces so that we can reference the objects in the view model **(5)** and model **(6)**. We will discuss the view model and model in the next chapter.

(4) We define a ListView control for displaying the list of items. The ListView control comprises numerous properties. The following properties must be defined when using the ListView control:

- ItemsSource, of the IEnumerable type, specifies the collection of items to display. It binds to Items, which is defined in the view model.

- ItemTemplate, of the DataTemplate type, specifies the template to apply to each item in the collection of items to be displayed.

In *Listing 3.5*, DataTemplate is collapsed. Upon expanding it, we will see the following code snippet. This default implementation comes from the Visual Studio template. The appearance of this data template is inadequate, and we will enhance it later:

```
<DataTemplate>
    <ViewCell>
        <StackLayout Padding="10" x:DataType="model:Item">
            <Label Text="{Binding Text}"
              LineBreakMode="NoWrap"
              Style="{DynamicResource ListItemTextStyle}"
              FontSize="16" />
            <Label Text="{Binding Description}"
              LineBreakMode="NoWrap"
              Style="{DynamicResource
                  ListItemDetailTextStyle}"
              FontSize="13" />
        </StackLayout>
```

```
    </ViewCell>
  </DataTemplate>
```

This `DataTemplate` implementation comprises a `ViewCell` consisting of a `StackLayout` with two `Label` controls, as seen in the preview in *Figure 3.6*.

The `DataTemplate` implementation must reference a `Cell` class to display items. There are built-in cells available, as follows:

- `TextCell`, which displays primary and secondary text on separate lines.
- `ImageCell`, which exhibits an image alongside primary and secondary text on separate lines.
- `SwitchCell`, which showcases text and a switch that can be switched on or off.
- `EntryCell`, which presents a label and text that's editable.
- `ViewCell`, which is a custom cell with an appearance defined by a `View`. This cell type should be utilized when fully customizing the appearance of each item in a `ListView`.

Typically, `SwitchCell` and `EntryCell` are only used in a `TableView` and can't be employed in a `ListView`.

The preview of `ViewCell` in the preceding code snippet doesn't look very good. Differentiating between `Name` and `Description` is not straightforward. In KeePass, an icon is usually attached to the password entry. By using a new data template, we can enhance its appearance, like so:

```
<DataTemplate>
  <ViewCell>
    <Grid Padding="10" x:DataType="model:Item" >          //(1)
      <Grid.RowDefinitions>                                //(2)
        <RowDefinition Height="32" />
        <RowDefinition Height="32" />
      </Grid.RowDefinitions>
      <Grid.ColumnDefinitions>
        <ColumnDefinition Width="Auto" />
        <ColumnDefinition Width="Auto" />
      </Grid.ColumnDefinitions>
      <Grid Grid.RowSpan="2" Padding="10">                 //(3)
        <Grid.ColumnDefinitions>
          <ColumnDefinition Width="32" />
        </Grid.ColumnDefinitions>
        <Image Grid.Column="0" Source="icon.png"
```

```
                HorizontalOptions="Fill" VerticalOptions="Fill" />
        </Grid>
        <Label Text="{Binding Text}" Grid.Column="1"
          LineBreakMode="NoWrap" MaxLines="1"
          Style="{DynamicResource ListItemTextStyle}"
          FontAttributes="Bold" FontSize="Small" />
        <Label Text="{Binding Description}"
          Grid.Row="1" Grid.Column="1"
          LineBreakMode="TailTruncation" MaxLines="1"
          Style="{DynamicResource ListItemDetailTextStyle}"
          FontSize="Small" />
      </Grid>
    </ViewCell>
  </DataTemplate>
```

Let's examine this code in more detail:

(1) To improve ViewCell's appearance, we replaced the StackLayout with Grid as the layout class. Grid is a layout that organizes its children into rows and columns.

(2) Since we want to display two rows with an icon on the left, we created a grid containing two columns and two rows, as shown here:

Figure 3.7: Layout of an entry or a group

We can use different font styles for Name and Description so that users can easily differentiate them visually.

(3) To center the icon within the first two columns, we merged the two rows into a Grid control. The attached Grid.RowSpan property can be used to merge rows.

A Grid can function as a parent layout containing other child layouts. To maintain a specific size for the icon and position it at the center of the merged cell, we can use another Grid as the parent of the Image control. This child Grid contains only one row and one column with a specific size.

In the Image control, we can use a default image (icon.png) from the resource. Customization can be applied once we introduce our model in the next chapter.

In the customized ViewCell, we can display a key-value pair of data with an associated icon.

Refer to *Figure 3.8* for the improved preview:

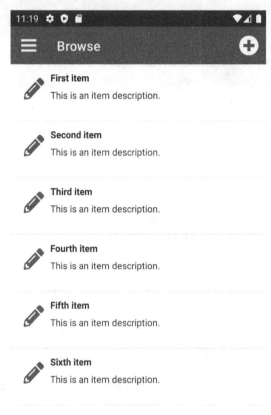

Figure 3.8: Improved ItemsPage

With this knowledge, we've covered the fundamentals of user interface design using XAML. A common challenge in user interface design is providing support for multiple languages. In the remainder of this chapter, we will learn how to support multiple languages when designing user interfaces in XAML.

Supporting multiple languages — localization

To accommodate multiple languages, we can utilize the .NET built-in mechanism for localizing applications. In .NET, resources files can be used to support localization by consolidating all text and other resources required for an application's user interface in one location. In a XAML file, we can use the x:Static markup extension to access the string defined in resources files.

Creating a .resx file

We can generate a resources file for each supported language. Resources files are XML files with a .resx extension, which are compiled into binary resources files during the build process. To add a resources file, right-click the project node and select **Add > New Item... > Resources File**, as shown in *Figure 3.9*:

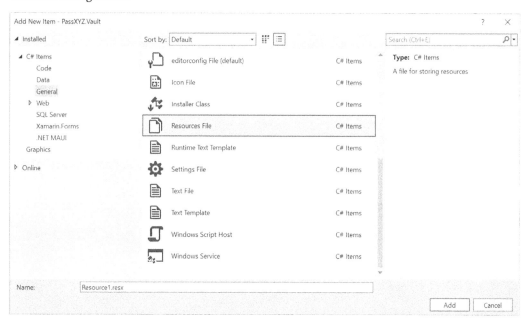

Figure 3.9: Creating a resources file

We can create the Resources.resx resources file in the Properties folder.

To support different cultures, we can add additional resources files with cultural information as part of the resources file's name:

- `Resources.resx`: The resources file for the default culture, which we will set to **en-US** (US English).

- `Resources.zh-Hans.resx`: The resources file for the **zh-Hans** culture, which is simplified Chinese.

- `Resources.zh-Hant.resx`: The resources file for the **zh-Hant** culture, which is traditional Chinese.

Upon creating the resources file, the following `ItemGroup` will be added to the project file:

```
<ItemGroup>
  <Compile Update="Properties\Resources.Designer.cs">
    <DesignTime>True</DesignTime>
      <AutoGen>True</AutoGen>
      <DependentUpon>Resources.resx</DependentUpon>
  </Compile>
</ItemGroup>
<ItemGroup>
  <EmbeddedResource Update="Properties\Resources.resx">
    <Generator>ResXFileCodeGenerator</Generator>
    <LastGenOutput>Resources.Designer.cs</LastGenOutput>
  </EmbeddedResource>
</ItemGroup>
```

To edit a resources file, click on the resources file and edit it in the resource editor, as shown in *Figure 3.10*:

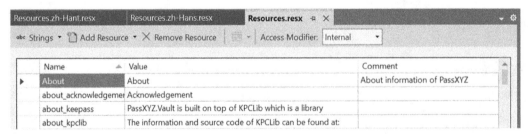

Figure 3.10: Resource editor

The resources file includes a list of key-value pairs for different languages:

- The Name field represents the string name that can be referenced in both XAML and C# files.
- The Value field contains the language-specific string that will be used according to the system language settings.
- The Comment field is employed as a remark for the key-value pair.

To specify the default language, we need to set the value of NeutralLanguage in <PropertyGroup> in the project file, as shown here:

```
<PropertyGroup>
...
<NeutralLanguage>en-US</NeutralLanguage>
...
</PropertyGroup>
```

In our project, we will use US English as the default culture, so NeutralLanguage is set to en-US.

Localizing text

Once the resources files have been configured, we can use localized content in our XAML file or C# files. Currently, our project contains five content pages. Let's modify AboutPage to support localization, as shown in *Listing 3.6*:

```
<?xml version="1.0" encoding="utf-8" ?>
<ContentPage
    xmlns="http://schemas.microsoft.com/dotnet/2021/maui"
    xmlns:x="http://schemas.microsoft.com/winfx/2009/xaml"
    x:Class="PassXYZ.Vault.Views.AboutPage"
    xmlns:res="clr-namespace:PassXYZ.Vault.Properties"          //(1)
    Title="{Binding Title}">

    <ContentPage.Resources...>

    <ScrollView>
      <StackLayout Margin="20">
        <Grid Padding="10"...>
        <StackLayout Padding="10" >
          <Label HorizontalOptions="Center"
```

```
            Text="{x:Static res:Resources.Appname}"              //(2)
            FontAttributes="Bold" FontSize="22" />
        <Label x:Name="AppVersion"
          HorizontalOptions="Center"
          FontSize="Small" />
        <Grid HorizontalOptions="Center"...>
        <StackLayout...>
      </StackLayout>
    </StackLayout>
  </ScrollView>
</ContentPage>
```

Listing 3.6: `AboutPage.xaml` (https://epa.ms/AboutPage3-6)

Text localization is done using the generated `Resources` class. This class is named based on the default resources file name. In *Listing 3.6* `AboutPage.xaml`, we added a new namespace **(1)** for the `Resources` class:

```
xmlns:res ="clr-namespace:PassXYZ.Vault.Properties "
```

In the `Label` control **(2)**, to display our application name, we can refer to the resource string using the `x:Static` XAML markup extension, as follows:

```
        <Label HorizontalOptions="Center"
          Text="{x:Static res:Resources.Appname}"
          FontAttributes="Bold" FontSize="22" />
```

In *Listing 3.6*, we collapsed most of the source code for conciseness. Please refer to the short URL of this book's GitHub repository to review the full source code.

Localized text can be used in both XAML and C#. To use a resource string in C#, we can examine the `Title` property in *Listing 3.6*. The `Title` property of `AboutPage` is connected to the `Title` property in the `AboutViewModel` class. Let's see how we can use a resource string in *Listing 3.7*:

```
using System;
using System.Windows.Input;
using CommunityToolkit.Mvvm.ComponentModel;
using CommunityToolkit.Mvvm.Input;
using Microsoft.Maui.Controls;

using PassXYZ.Vault.Properties;                                    //(1)

namespace PassXYZ.Vault.ViewModels
{
  public partial class AboutViewModel : ObservableObject
  {
    [ObservableProperty]
    private string? title = Properties.Resources.About;            //(2)

    [RelayCommand]
private async Task OpenWeb()...

public string GetStoreName()...
    public DateTime GetStoreModifiedTime()...
  }
}
```

Listing 3.7: AboutViewModel.cs *(https://epa.ms/AboutViewModel3-7)*

As shown in *Listing 3.7*, **(1)** we added the PassXYZ.Vault.Properties namespace first. **(2)** We refer to the resource string as Properties.Resources.About.

After we update `AboutPage` with localization support, we can test it in the supported languages, as shown in *Figure 3.11*:

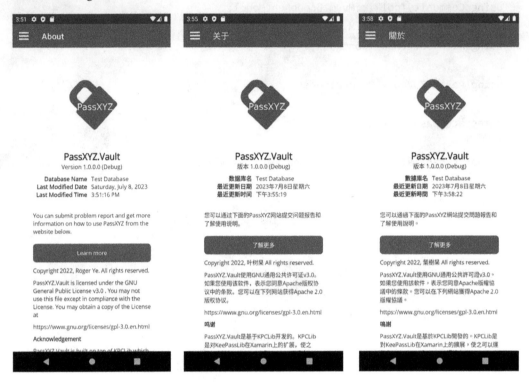

Figure 3.11: AboutPage in different languages

In `AboutPage`, many resource strings are used for localization. In *Listing 3.6* and *Listing 3.7*, we collapsed most of the code; you can refer to the short URL for this book's GitHub repository to review the source code online.

.NET MVVM Community Toolkit

The .NET MVVM Community Toolkit is a comprehensive collection of helpers and tools aimed at simplifying the development process of applications following the **Model-View-View-Model (MVVM)** pattern based on .NET libraries.

The toolkit provides a wide array of features aimed at reducing boilerplate code, including converters, helpers, behaviors, commands, and services aimed at facilitating communication between classes in the MVVM pattern.

More details about the .NET MVVM Community Toolkit will be introduced in the next chapter.

Summary

In this chapter, we explored XAML syntax and applied the knowledge we gained to enhance the appearance of ItemsPage. We will persist in refining the user interface of other pages throughout this book. To support multiple languages, we delved into .NET localization and created multiple resources files for the US-en, zh-Hans, and zh-Hant languages. Additionally, we discovered how to access strings in the resources files using the XAML markup extension. Lastly, we utilized AboutPage as an example to demonstrate the use of localized text in both XAML and C#.

In the next chapter, we will continue improving our app by introducing MVVM and data binding.

Further reading

- .NET Multi-platform App UI documentation: https://learn.microsoft.com/en-us/dotnet/maui/

- XAML - .NET MAUI: https://learn.microsoft.com/en-us/dotnet/maui/xaml/

- XAML markup extensions: https://learn.microsoft.com/en-us/dotnet/maui/xaml/fundamentals/markup-extensions

- KeePass – An open-source password manager: https://keepass.info/

Leave a review!

Enjoying this book? Help readers like you by leaving an Amazon review. Scan the QR code below for a 40% discount code.

*Limited Offer

4

Exploring MVVM and Data Binding

In the previous chapter, we explored how to construct **user interfaces** (**UIs**) using XAML. In this chapter, we will dive into the **Model-View-View-Model** (**MVVM**) pattern and data binding. The MVVM pattern, a widely adopted architectural pattern, is key in creating maintainable, scalable, and testable applications. In the context of .NET MAUI, MVVM separates the user interface logic, data, and the app's structure into three distinct components: Model, View, and ViewModel. This separation leads to a clean and organized codebase, making it easier to develop and maintain the application. Data binding is a technique that connects the view (UI) with the ViewModel in a way that the UI reflects the ViewModel's data and changes synchronously and automatically.

In this chapter, our initial focus will be on introducing **MVVM** and data binding. For a better design and cleaner code, we will employ the MVVM Toolkit, part of the .NET Community Toolkit. The use of the MVVM Toolkit results in more concise and clean ViewModel code.

In real-world applications, a majority of the logic is implemented in the model and service layers. Without a more complex model layer, we cannot delve into complicated topics about MVVM and data binding. Therefore, in the second half of this chapter, we present the actual model layer, which includes two .NET libraries, **KPCLib** and **PassXYZLib**.

With the real model layer in place, we introduce two advanced topics in data binding: binding to collections and using custom views.

The following topics will be covered in this chapter:

- Understanding **MVVM** and **MVC**
- Data binding
- .NET Community Toolkit
- Introducing the data model and service layer
- Binding to collections
- Using custom views

Technical requirements

To test and debug the source code in this chapter, you need to have Visual Studio 2022 installed on your PC or Mac. Please refer to the *Development environment setup* section in *Chapter 1, Getting Started with .NET MAUI*, for the details.

The source code for this chapter is available in the following GitHub repository: `https://github.com/PacktPublishing/.NET-MAUI-Cross-Platform-Application-Development-Second-edition/tree/2nd/chapter04`.

To check out the source code of this chapter, we can use the following command:

```
$ git clone -b 2nd/chapter04 https://github.com/PacktPublishing/.NET-MAUI-
Cross-Platform-Application-Development-Second-edition.git PassXYZ.Vault2
```

To find out more about the source code in this book, please refer to the *Managing the source code in this book* section in *Chapter 2, Building Our First .NET MAUI App*.

Understanding MVVM and MVC

In software design, we usually follow and reuse good practices and design patterns. The **Model-View-Controller** (**MVC**) pattern is an approach to decoupling the responsibilities of a system. It can help to separate the implementation of the UI and the business logic into different parts.

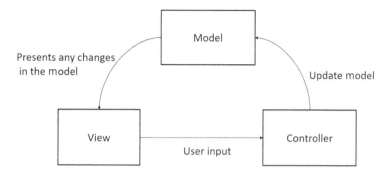

Figure 4.1: The MVC pattern

The MVC pattern, as shown in *Figure 4.1*, divides the responsibilities of the system into three distinct parts:

- **Model:** The model represents the data and the business logic of the application. It is responsible for storing the app's data, handling data validation, and performing any necessary data processing. Model classes typically interact with data sources, such as databases, web APIs, or file storage, to fetch and store data. Model classes usually can be implemented as **Plain Old CLR Objects (POCOs)** or **Data Transfer Objects (DTOs)**. POCO is a class that doesn't depend on any framework-specific classes, so POCO classes can be used with LINQ or Entity Framework well. DTO is a subset of a POCO class that only contains data without logic or behavior. DTO classes can be used to pass data between layers. The model has no dependency on the view or the controller so it can be implemented and tested separately.

- **View:** The view is responsible for the app's user interface and user interaction. The view should not contain any business logic or direct data processing. Instead, it displays data and interface elements to the user and captures their input.

- **Controller:** The controller updates the model and view in response to the user's action. Our understanding of the model and the view hasn't changed too much over time, but there have been different understandings and implementations of the controller since the MVC pattern was introduced.

The MVVM pattern was inspired by the MVC pattern, but it aimed to provide an improved approach specifically for UI development in XAML-based applications. With the rise of XAML-based UI frameworks, MVVM gained traction and became the de facto pattern for WPF, Silverlight, and later Xamarin.Forms applications.

With the evolution of Xamarin.Forms into .NET MAUI, MVVM continues to be a prominent pattern in multi-platform mobile and desktop application development.

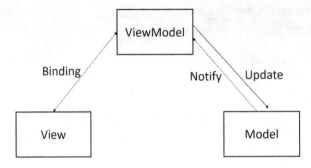

Figure 4.2: The MVVM pattern

As we can see in *Figure 4.2*, in MVVM, the ViewModel is used to replace the controller. The differences between MVVM and MVC are as follows:

- **Decoupling of view and model**: The ViewModel is used to handle the communication between the view and the model. The view accesses the data and logic in the model via the ViewModel.

- **Data binding between the view and ViewModel**: Using data binding, changes to the view or ViewModel can automatically be updated in the other one. This can help to reduce the complexity of implementation.

In both MVC and MVVM, the model can be tested separately. In MVVM, it is possible to design unit tests for the ViewModel as well.

When the view changes, the changes will be reflected in the ViewModel via data binding. The ViewModel will process the data changes in the model. Similarly, when the data changes in the model, the ViewModel is notified to update the view. The common solution for notifications is to install event handlers that prompt the notifications. With data binding, the implementation is simplified significantly.

MVVM in PassXYZ.Vault

In our app, PassXYZ.Vault, we use MVVM to handle the data exchange between the view and the ViewModel. As we can see in *Figure 4.3*, we have five XAML content pages and the same number of ViewModels defined. In our model, we have an Item class, which is our model class, and it can be accessed through the **IDataStore** interface.

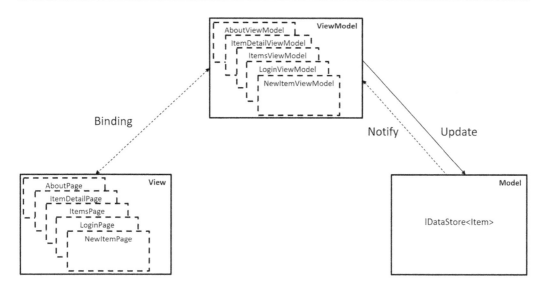

Figure 4.3: MVVM in PassXYZ.Vault

Data binding is used as the communication channel between views and ViewModels. The ViewModel will update the Item model via the **IDataStore** service interface. We will learn how to use data binding in the next section by analyzing the ItemDetailPage and ViewModel.

Data binding

Let's explore how MVVM and data binding works. We can use an item detail page implementation in our app to analyze **how data binding works**. The following list includes the view, ViewModel, and model that we are going to explore:

- **View**: ItemDetailPage, see *Listing 3.4* in the previous chapter
- **ViewModel**: ItemDetailViewModel, see *Listing 4.1*
- **Model**: Item (access through the **IDataStore** interface), see *Listing 3.3* in the previous chapter

ItemDetailPage is a view used to display the content of an instance of Item. The data is retrieved from the ViewModel. The UI elements presenting the content of Item are connected to the ViewModel instance through data binding.

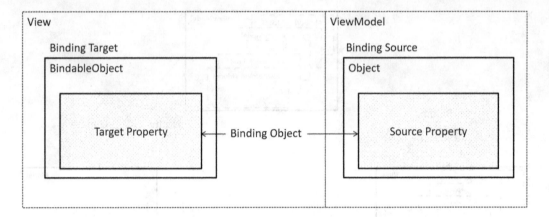

Figure 4.4: Data binding

As we can see in *Figure 4.4*, data binding is used to synchronize the properties of target and source objects. There are three objects involved in data binding and they are the `binding target`, `binding source`, and `binding object`.

Binding object

In *Figure 4.4*, the object of the `Binding` class (`Microsoft.Maui.Controls.Binding`) represents the connection between the target property (in the View) and the source property (in the ViewModel). It manages the synchronization of property values and handles the communication between the source and the target. The binding object is created when you define a binding expression in your XAML markup or create a binding in code.

Example of creating a binding object in XAML:

```
<Label Text="{Binding FirstName}" />
```

Example of creating a binding object in C#:

```
label.SetBinding(Label.TextProperty, new Binding("FirstName"));
```

Binding target

In *Figure 4.4*, the target refers to the UI element (control) in the view that is bound to the View-Model property. More specifically, the target is the property of the UI element involved in the binding. Examples of target properties include `Text` on a `Label` or `Entry`, `Source` on an `Image`, and `IsEnabled` on a `Button`. The target property must be a bindable property to participate in data binding.

Binding source

The source is the object containing the property that is bound to the target property in the view. Typically, the source object is the ViewModel, which should be set as the BindingContext of the view or one of its parents. The ViewModel exposes properties that define their data type, getter, and setter methods. The source property is identified through the Binding Path in the binding expression.

When you define a binding expression in XAML or create a binding object in code, a binding object is created and set for the specified target property. The XAML parser or the binding system creates the binding object and initializes it with the provided binding properties, such as Path, Source, Mode, Converter, and so on.

Here is a list of involved properties of target and source objects:

- **Target** – This is the UI element involved and this UI element has to be a child of BindableObject. The UI element used in ItemDetailPage is Label.
- **Target property** – This is the property of the target object. It is a BindableProperty. If the target is Label, as we mentioned here, the target property can be the Text property of Label.
- **Source** – This is the source object referenced by data binding. It is ItemDetailViewModel here.
- **Source object value path** – This is the path to the value in the source object. Here, the path is a ViewModel property, such as Name or Description.

Let's look at the following code in ItemDetailPage:

```
<StackLayout Spacing="20" Padding="15">
  <Label Text="Name:" FontSize="Medium" />
  <Label Text="{Binding Name}" FontSize="Small"/>          //(1)
  <Label Text="Description:" FontSize="Medium" />
  <Label Text="{Binding Description}" FontSize="Small"/>    //(2)
</StackLayout>
```

In the XAML here, there are two data binding source paths, which are Name, **(1)**, and Description, **(2)**. The binding target is Label and the target property is the Text property of Label. If we review the inheritance hierarchy of Label, it looks like so:

```
Object -> BindableObject -> Element -> NavigableElement -> VisualElement
-> View -> Label
```

We can see that `Element`, `VisualElement`, and `View` are the derivatives of `BindableObject`. The data binding target has to be a child of `BindableObject`.

The binding source is the `Name`, **(1)**, and `Description`, **(2)**, properties of the ViewModel as shown in *Listing 4.1* here:

```
using PassXYZ.Vault.Models;
namespace PassXYZ.Vault.ViewModels {
[QueryProperty(nameof(ItemId), nameof(ItemId))]
public class ItemDetailViewModel : BaseViewModel {
        private string itemId;
        private string name;
        private string description;
        public string Id { get; set; }
        public string Name {                                       //(1)
            get => name;
            set => SetProperty(ref name, value);
        }
        public string Description...                               //(2)
        public string ItemId...
        public async void LoadItemId(string itemId) {              //(3)
            try {
                var item = await DataStore.GetItemAsync
                    (itemId);
                Id = item.Id;
                Name = item.Name;
                Description = item.Description;
            }
            catch (Exception) {
                Debug.WriteLine("Failed to Load Item");
            }
        }
    }
}
```

Listing 4.1: `ItemDetailViewModel.cs` *(https://epa.ms/ItemDetailViewModel4-1)*

The values of `Name`, **(1)**, and `Description`, **(2)**, are loaded from the model in the `LoadItemId()` method, **(3)**. You may notice that the class is decorated by a `QueryPropertyAttribute` attribute. This is used to pass parameters during page navigation, and it will be introduced in the next chapter.

Let's use the following, *Table 4.1*, to summarize the data binding components in the code.

Data binding elements	Example
Target	`Label`
Target property	`Text`
Source object	`ItemDetailViewModel`
Source object value path	`Name` or `Description`

Table 4.1: Data binding settings

Properties of a Binding object

Having analyzed the preceding code, let us have a look at the syntax of the binding expression:

```
<object property="{Binding bindProp1=value1[, bindPropN=valueN]*}" ... />
```

Binding properties can be set as a series of name-value pairs in the form of `bindProp=value`. For example, see the following:

```
<Label Text="{Binding Path=Description}" FontSize="Small"/>
```

The `Path` property is the default property, and it can be omitted if it is the first one in the property list as shown here:

```
<Label Text="{Binding Description}" FontSize="Small"/>
```

The binding properties that we mentioned here are the properties of the `Binding` class, and you can find the details by referring to the Microsoft document about the `Binding` class here: `https://learn.microsoft.com/en-us/dotnet/api/microsoft.maui.controls.binding`.

As well as the `Path` property, let's review another two important binding properties, `Source` and `Mode`.

Source

The Source property represents the object containing the source property (which will be bound to the target property). By default, the source object is the BindingContext of the element, which is typically the ViewModel. However, you can use the Source property to bind to other objects if needed.

Example:

```
<Label Text="{Binding Source={x:Reference someLabel}, Path=Text}" />
```

When we set data binding to the target, we can use the following two members of the target class:

- The BindingContext property gives us the source object
- The SetBinding method specifies the target property and source property

In our case, we set the BindingContext property to an instance of ItemDetailViewModel, **(1)**, in the C# code-behind file of ItemDetailPage, as shown in *Listing 4.2* here. It is set at the page level, and it applies to all binding targets on this page:

```csharp
using PassXYZ.Vault.ViewModels;
using System.ComponentModel;
using Microsoft.Maui;
using Microsoft.Maui.Controls;

namespace PassXYZ.Vault.Views
{
  public partial class ItemDetailPage : ContentPage
  {
    public ItemDetailPage()
    {
      InitializeComponent();
      BindingContext = new ItemDetailViewModel();                //(1)
    }
  }
}
```

Listing 4.2: ItemDetailPage.xaml.cs *(https://epa.ms/ItemDetailPage4-2)*

Instead of using the `Binding` markup extension, we can also create the binding using the `SetBinding` method directly, as done here:

```
<StackLayout Spacing="20" Padding="15">
  <Label Text="Text:" FontSize="Medium" />
  <Label x:Name="labelText" FontSize="Small"/>                    //(2)
  <Label Text="Description:" FontSize="Medium" />
  <Label Text="{Binding Description}" FontSize="Small"/>
</StackLayout>
```

(2) In the XAML code, we removed the `Binding` markup extension and specified the instance name as `labelText`. In the C# code-behind file, we can call the `SetBinding` method, **(3)**, in the constructor of `ItemDetailPage` to create the data binding for the `Text` property:

```
public ItemDetailPage()
{
    InitializeComponent();
    BindingContext = new ItemDetailViewModel();
    labelText.SetBinding(Label.TextProperty, "Text");          //(3)
}
```

Binding mode

The `Mode` property specifies the direction of data flow in the binding, such as if data flows only from the ViewModel to the UI or if it flows in both directions.

In `ItemDetailPage`, all UI elements are `Label` objects, which are not editable for the user. This is one-way binding from the source to the target. The changes in the source object will cause updates in the target object.

There are four binding modes supported in .NET MAUI. Let's review them by referring to *Figure 4.5*.

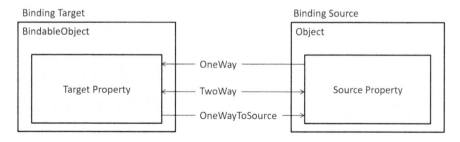

Figure 4.5: Binding mode

Let's look at the binding modes supported in `.NET MAUI`:

- OneWay binding is usually used in the case of presenting data to the user. In our app, we will retrieve a list of password entries and display this list on `ItemsPage`. When the user clicks an item in the list, the password details will show on `ItemDetailPage`. `OneWay` binding is used in both cases.

- TwoWay binding causes changes to either the source property or the target property to automatically update the other. In our app, when the user edits the fields of a password entry or when the user enters a username and password on `LoginPage`, the target UI `Entry` component and the source view model object are set with `TwoWay`.

- OneWayToSource is the reverse of the `OneWay` binding mode. When the target property is changed, the source property will be updated. When we add a new password entry on `NewItemPage`, we can use `OneWayToSource` instead of the `TwoWay` binding mode to improve performance.

- OneTime binding is a binding mode that is not shown in *Figure 4.4*. The target properties are initialized from the source properties, but any further changes to the source properties won't update the target properties. It is a simpler form of the `OneWay` binding mode with better performance.

If we don't specify the binding mode in data binding, the default binding mode is used. We can overwrite the default binding mode if it is needed.

In our `ItemsPage` code, we use the `ListView` control to display the list of password groups and entries, so we should set the `IsRefreshing` attribute to the `OneWay` binding mode:

```
IsRefreshing="{Binding IsBusy, Mode=OneWay}"
```

When we add a new item in `NewItemPage`, we use the `Entry` and `Editor` controls to edit the properties. We can use the `OneWayToSource` or `TwoWay` binding modes:

```
<Label Text="Text" FontSize="Medium" />
<Entry Text="{Binding Text, Mode=TwoWay}" FontSize="Medium"/>
<Label Text="Description" FontSize="Medium" />
<Editor Text="{Binding Description, Mode=OneWayToSource}"
  AutoSize="TextChanges" FontSize="Medium" Margin="0" />
```

Changing notifications in ViewModels

In *Figure 4.5*, we can see the data binding target is a derived class of BindableObject. Besides this requirement, in the data binding setup, the data source (ViewModel) needs to implement the INotifyPropertyChanged interface so that when the property changes, a PropertyChanged event is raised to notify the change.

In an MVVM pattern, the ViewModel is usually the data binding source so we need to implement the INotifyPropertyChanged interface in our ViewModels. If we do this for each ViewModel class, there will be a lot of duplicated code. In a Visual Studio template, a BaseViewModel class, as we can see in *Listing 4.3*, is included in the boilerplate code and we use it in our app. Other ViewModels inherit this class:

```
namespace PassXYZ.Vault.ViewModels;
public class BaseViewModel : INotifyPropertyChanged          //(1)
{
  public IDataStore<Item> DataStore =>
    DependencyService.Get<IDataStore<Item>>();
  bool isBusy = false;
  public bool IsBusy {
    get { return isBusy; }
    set { SetProperty(ref isBusy, value); }                  //(2)
  }
  string title = string.Empty;
  public string Title {
    get { return title; }
    set { SetProperty(ref title, value); }
  }
  protected bool SetProperty<T>(ref T backingStore,
      T value,
      [CallerMemberName] string propertyName = "",
      Action onChanged = null) {
    if (EqualityComparer<T>.Default.Equals
        (backingStore, value))
        return false;
    backingStore = value;
    onChanged?.Invoke();
```

```
    OnPropertyChanged(propertyName);
    return true;
  }
 #region INotifyPropertyChanged
  public event PropertyChangedEventHandler PropertyChanged;        //(4)
   protected void OnPropertyChanged([CallerMemberName]
     string propertyName = "") {                                   //(3)
     var changed = PropertyChanged;
     if (changed == null)
         return;
     changed.Invoke(this, new PropertyChangedEventArgs(propertyName));
   }
 #endregion
 }
```

Listing 4.3 `BaseViewModel.cs` *(*`https://epa.ms/BaseViewModel4-3`*)*

In the `BaseViewModel` class (*Listing 4.3*), we can see the following:

(1) `BaseViewModel` implements the `INotifyPropertyChanged` interface and this interface defines a single event, `PropertyChanged`, **(4)**.

(3) When a property is changed in the setter, the `OnPropertyChanged` method is called. In `OnPropertyChanged`, the `PropertyChanged` event is fired. A copy of the `PropertyChanged` event handler is stored in the **changed** local variable, so this implementation is safe in a multi-thread environment. When the `PropertyChanged` event is fired, it needs to pass the property name as a parameter to indicate which property is changed. The `CallerMemberName` attribute can be used to find the method name or property name of the caller, so we don't need to hardcode the property name.

(2) When we define a property in the ViewModel, the `OnPropertyChanged` method is called in the setter – but as you can see, in our code, we call `SetProperty<T>` instead of `OnPropertyChanged` directly. `SetProperty<T>` will do additional work before it calls `OnPropertyChanged`. It checks whether the value is changed. If there is no change, it will return and do nothing. If the value is changed, it will update the backing field and call `OnPropertyChanged` to fire the change event.

If we recall `ItemDetailViewModel` in *Listing 4.1*, it inherits from the `BaseViewModel` class. In the setter of the `Name` and `Description` properties, we call `SetProperty<T>` to set the values and fire the `PropertyChanged` event:

```
public string Name {
    get => name;
    set => SetProperty(ref name, value);
}
public string Description {
    get => description;
    set => SetProperty(ref description, value);
}
```

In this section, we learned about data binding and the `INotifyPropertyChanged` interface. We need to create boilerplate code to define a property with change notification support. To simplify the code and autogenerate boilerplate code behind the scenes, we can use the MVVM Toolkit.

.NET Community Toolkit

In this section, we will use the MVVM Toolkit to refactor our ViewModel code. The MVVM Toolkit is a module within the .NET Community Toolkit, specifically designed for building applications following the MVVM design pattern.

The .NET Community Toolkit (formerly Windows Community Toolkit) is a collection of helper functions, custom controls, and app services designed to simplify and accelerate .NET app development. The toolkit is open source and maintained by the community, offering a suite of tools for various .NET development platforms, such as .NET MAUI, Xamarin, UWP, WPF, and WinUI. The toolkit provides useful components that developers can use out of the box to easily build applications with a rich user interface, common app services, animations, and more.

The MVVM Toolkit supplies a set of base classes, utilities, and attributes that make implementing the MVVM pattern in your .NET applications more efficient and straightforward. The MVVM Toolkit provides the following key components:

- `ObservableObject`: A base class that simplifies the implementation of objects that raise PropertyChanged events, such as ViewModels. It implements the `INotifyPropertyChanged` interface and provides the `SetProperty` method to handle property change notifications.

- RelayCommand and AsyncRelayCommand: Classes implementing the ICommand interface, designed to handle executing methods and checking if a command can execute. They make it easy to create commands for your ViewModel that react to UI actions.

- **Dependency Injection support**: The MVVM Toolkit offers built-in support for dependency injection, making it simple to integrate services into your ViewModels using popular dependency injection libraries like Microsoft.Extensions.DependencyInjection.

- **Messenger (Event Aggregator)**: The MVVM Toolkit provides a lightweight messenger service that enables decoupled, message-based communication between components, like different ViewModels. This promotes a separation of concerns and makes each component more testable.

Please find more information about the MVVM Toolkit in the *Further reading* section.

How to use the MVVM Toolkit

To use the MVVM Toolkit in .NET MAUI, follow these steps:

1. Add the .NET CommunityToolkit.Mvvm NuGet package to our project file as follows:

```
<ItemGroup>
  <PackageReference Include="CommunityToolkit.Mvvm"
    Version="8.2.1" />
</ItemGroup>
```

2. Refactor ViewModel using MVVM Toolkit Source Generators. Source Generators is a C# compiler feature that allows executing custom code at compile time to modify the compilation output. The MVVM Toolkit supports using Source Generators to automatically generate ViewModel and ICommand boilerplate code based on attributes, which can simplify ViewModel creation.

The MVVM Toolkit can help us to simplify ViewModel by using Source Generators. If we want to add a property in ViewModel as a data binding source, we need to implement the INotifyPropertyChanged interface. For example, in ItemDetailViewModel, we implement the Description property as follows:

```
private string description;
public string Description {
  get => description;
  set => SetProperty(ref description, value);
}
```

In the Setter, the `SetProperty` method is called, and it will update the backing field and call `OnPropertyChanged` to fire the change event. Both `SetProperty` and `OnPropertyChanged` are defined in the `BaseViewModel` class, as we can see in *Listing 4.3*.

Using the MVVM Toolkit, we can inherit from `ObservableObject` instead of `BaseViewModel`. `ObservableObject` implements the `INotifyPropertyChanged` interface similar to what we have done in `BaseViewModel`. With `ObservableObject`, we can simplify the above implementation as follows:

```
[ObservableProperty]
private string description;
```

As we can see, using the `ObservableProperty` attribute, we can define the backing field only in the code. Source Generators will help us to generate boilerplate code. We can use the `Description` property in XAML as follows:

```
<Label Text="{Binding Description}"
    FontSize="Small"
    TextType ="Html"
    Style="{DynamicResource ListItemDetailTextStyle}" />
```

In the MVVM pattern, we can define a ViewModel property as an observable property to support TwoWay binding. We can also define a ViewModel property as an `ICommand` interface to handle UI events using data binding.

In our app, we display a list of items in `ItemsPage`. In `ItemsPage`, we need to load a list of items from the data source, and we also need to support adding a new item. We need to define two `ICommand` interfaces as follows:

```
public class ItemsViewModel : BaseViewModel
{
  ...
  public Command LoadItemsCommand { get; }            //(1)
  public Command AddItemCommand { get; }              //(2)

  public ItemsViewModel()
  {
    ...
    LoadItemsCommand = new Command(
        async () => await LoadItems());               //(3)
```

```
      AddItemCommand = new Command(AddItem);                    //(4)
      ...
    }

    private async Task LoadItems()                              //(5)
    {
      ...
    }

    private async void AddItem(object obj)                      //(6)
    {
      await Shell.Current.GoToAsync(nameof(NewItemPage));
    }
    ...
}
```

In the above implementation, we define two properties, LoadItemsCommand(**1**) and AddItemCommand(**2**), as the type Microsoft.Maui.Controls.Command. In the constructor of View-Model, we initialize them(**3**)(**4**) with the private methods LoadItems(**5**) and AddItem(**6**).

Using the MVVM Toolkit, we can simplify the implementation as follows:

```
public partial class ItemsViewModel : BaseViewModel
{
  ...
  [RelayCommand]
  private async void AddItem(object obj)                        //(1)
  {
    await Shell.Current.GoToAsync(nameof(NewItemPage));
  }


  ...


  [RelayCommand]
  private async Task LoadItems()                                //(2)
  {
    ...
  }
}
```

We can see that we just need to add `RelayCommandAttribute` in front of `AddItem` **(1)** and `LoadItems` **(2)** to implement `ICommand` properties. Source Generators will help us generate the rest of the code.

Having introduced the basic knowledge of XAML UI design, the MVVM pattern, and data binding, we can improve our app using the knowledge we just learned.

Improving the data model and service

After introducing the MVVM pattern, data binding, and the MVVM Toolkit, we have the fundamental knowledge of how to use data binding. In the rest of this chapter, we will explore advanced topics about data binding. We will discuss how to bind to collections first and then we will introduce custom views. Using custom views, we can make XAML code cleaner and more concise.

To examine these topics, a more intricate model layer is required. Instead of creating a hypothetical model layer, we'll work with the actual model layer in our app, which includes two .NET libraries: **KPCLib** and **PassXYZLib**.

To introduce the model layer of our app, let us review the use cases again. We are developing a cross-platform password manager app that is compatible with the popular **KeePass** database format. We have the following use cases:

- **Use case 1**: `LoginPage` – As a password manager user, I want to log in to the password manager app so that I can access my password data.

- **Use case 2**: `AboutPage` – As a password manager user, I want to have an overview of my database and the app that I am using.

- **Use case 3**: `ItemsPage` – As a password manager user, I want to see a list of groups and entries so that I can explore and examine my password data.

- **Use case 4**: `ItemDetailPage` – As a password manager user, I want to see the details of a password entry after I select it in the list of password entries.

- **Use case 5**: `NewItemPage` – As a password manager user, I want to add a password entry or create a new group in my database.

These five use cases are inherited from the Visual Studio template, and they are sufficient for the user stories of our password manager app for the moment. We will improve our app using these user stories in this chapter.

We implemented our app using the MVVM pattern, but the `Item` model below is too simple and is not sufficient to be used in a password manager app:

```
public class Item
{
  public string Id { get; set; }
  public string Name { get; set; }
  public string Description { get; set; }
}
```

The major functionalities of our password manager app are encapsulated in the model layer. We will build our model using two .NET packages, KPCLib and PassXYZLib. These two packages include all the password management features we need.

KPCLib

The model that we will use is a library from **KeePass** called `KeePassLib`. Both KeePass and `KeePassLib` are built for .NET Framework, so they can only be used on Windows. I ported `KeePassLib` and rebuilt it as a .NET Standard 2.0 library packaged as KPCLib. KPCLib can be found on NuGet and GitHub here:

- NuGet: `https://www.nuget.org/packages/KPCLib/`
- GitHub: `https://github.com/passxyz/KPCLib`

KPCLib is used both as a package name and a namespace. The package of KPCLib includes two namespaces, `KeePassLib` and `KPCLib`. The `KeePassLib` namespace is the original one from KeePass with the following changes:

- Updated and built for .NET Standard 2.0
- Updated `PwEntry` and `PwGroup` to be classes derived from the `Item` abstract class

In the KPCLib namespace, an `Item` abstract class is defined. The reason I created a new class and made it the parent class of `PwEntry` and `PwGroup` is due to the navigation design difference between `KeePass` and `PassXYZ.Vault`.

If we look at the UI of KeePass in *Figure 4.5*, we can see that it is a classic Windows desktop UI. The navigation is designed around a tree view like Windows Explorer.

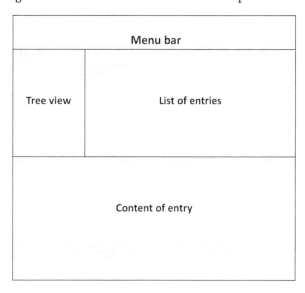

Figure 4.6: KeePass UI

Two classes, PwGroup and PwEntry, behave like directories and files. A PwGroup instance is just like a directory, and it includes a list of children – PwGroup and PwEntry. All PwGroup instances are displayed in a tree view on the right-hand panel. When a PwGroup instance is selected, the list of PwEntry in this group is shown on the right-hand panel. PwEntry includes the content of a password entry, such as a username and password. The content of PwEntry is displayed on the bottom panel.

In the PassXYZ.Vault UI design, we use a .NET MAUI Shell template. It is an implementation of the stacked Master-Detail pattern. In the stacked Master-Detail pattern, a single list is used to display items. In this case, the instances of both PwGroup and PwEntry can be displayed in the same list. After an item is selected, we will take an action according to the type of the item.

Abstraction of PwGroup and PwEntry

To work with the PassXYZ.Vault UI design better, we can abstract PwGroup and PwEntry as the Item abstract class, as shown in *Figure 4.7*.

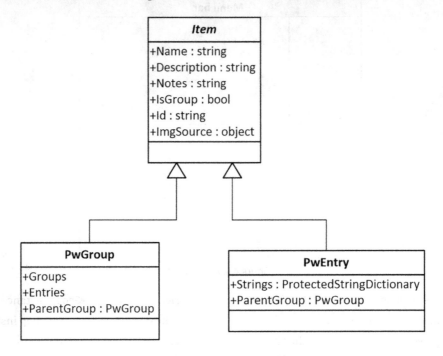

Figure 4.7: Class diagram of Item

Referring to the UML class diagram in *Figure 4.7* and the source code of Item.cs in *Listing 4.4*, we can see the following properties are defined in the Item abstract class. These properties are implemented in both PwEntry and PwGroup:

(1) Name: the Item name

(2) Description: the Item description

(3) Notes: Item comments defined by the user

(4) IsGroup: true if the instance is PwGroup or false if it is PwEntry

(5) Id: ID of the instance (a unique value that is like the primary key in a database)

(6) `ImgSource`: image source of the icon (both `PwGroup` and `PwEntry` can have an associated icon)

(7) `LastModificationTime`: the last modification time of the item

(8) `Item`: implements the `INotifyPropertyChanged` interface, and it can work well in the MVVM model for data binding:

```
using System.Text;
namespace KPCLib
{
  public abstract class Item : INotifyPropertyChanged          //(8)
  {
    public abstract DateTime LastModificationTime {get;
        set;};}                                                //(7)
    public abstract string Name { get; set; }                  //(1)
    public abstract string Description { get;}                 //(2)
    public abstract string Notes { get; set; }                 //(3)
    public abstract bool IsGroup { get; }                      //(4)
    public abstract string Id { get; }                         //(5)
    virtual public Object ImgSource { get; set; }              //(6)
#region INotifyPropertyChanged ...
  }
}
```

Listing 4.4: `Item.cs` `(https://epa.ms/Item4-4)`

PassXYZLib

To use KeePassLib in `PassXYZ.Vault`, we need to use some .NET MAUI APIs to extend the functionalities required of our app. To separate the business logic from the UI and extend the functionalities of `KeePassLib` for .NET MAUI, a .NET MAUI class library, PassXYZLib, is created to encapsulate the extended model in a separate library. PassXYZLib is both a package name and a namespace.

To add PassXYZLib to our project, we can add it to a `PassXYZ.Vault.csproj` project file, as seen here:

```
<ItemGroup>
  <PackageReference Include="PassXYZLib" Version="2.1.2" />
</ItemGroup>
```

We can also add a PassXYZLib package from the command line here. From the command line, go to the project folder and execute this command to add the package:

```
dotnet add package PassXYZLib
```

Updating the model

After we add a PassXYZLib package to the project, we can access the KPCLib, KeePassLib, and PassXYZLib namespaces. To replace the current model, we need to remove the Models/Item.cs file from the project.

After that, we need to replace the PassXYZ.Vault.Models namespace with KPCLib. In *Figure 4.8a*, we can see that the Item in namespace PassXYZ.Vault.Models is used.

```
1   using PassXYZ.Vault.Models;
2   using System;
3   using System.Collections.Generic;
4   using System.Linq;
5   using System.Threading.Tasks;
6
7   namespace PassXYZ.Vault.Services
8   {
9       public class MockDataStore : IDataStore<Item>
10      {
11          readonly List<Item> items;
12
13          public MockDataStore()
14          {
15              items = new List<Item>()
16              {
17                  new Item { Id = Guid.NewGuid().ToString(), Name = "First item", Description="This is an item description." },
18                  new Item { Id = Guid.NewGuid().ToString(), Name = "Second item", Description="This is an item description." },
19                  new Item { Id = Guid.NewGuid().ToString(), Name = "Third item", Description="This is an item description." },
20                  new Item { Id = Guid.NewGuid().ToString(), Name = "Fourth item", Description="This is an item description." },
21                  new Item { Id = Guid.NewGuid().ToString(), Name = "Fifth item", Description="This is an item description." },
22                  new Item { Id = Guid.NewGuid().ToString(), Name = "Sixth item", Description="This is an item description." }
23              };
24          }
25
26          public async Task<bool> AddItemAsync(Item item)
27          {
28              if (item == null) { throw new ArgumentNullException(nameof(item)); }
29              items.Add(item);
30              return await Task.FromResult(true);
31          }
32
```

Figure 4.8a: PassXYZ.Vault.Models before update to KPCLib

After the PassXYZ.Vault.Models namespace is replaced, in *Figure 4.8b*, the Item from the KBCLib namespace is utilized. Comparing the implementation before and after the transition, we can observe that the rest of the code remains largely unchanged. By adopting the MVVM pattern, most of the business logic is encapsulated within the model layer.

```
1    using KPCLib;
2    using PassXYZLib;
3
4    namespace PassXYZ.Vault.Services;
5
6    public class MockDataStore : IDataStore<Item>
7    {
8        static string[] jsonData = {
9            "pxtem://{'IsPxEntry':true,'Strings':{'000UserName':{'Value':'PassXYZ Tester','IsProtected':false},'00:
10           "pxtem://{'IsPxEntry':true,'Strings':{'000UserName':{'Value':'PassXYZ Tester','IsProtected':false},'00:
11           "pxtem://{'IsPxEntry':false,'Strings':{'Password':{'Value':'','IsProtected':true},'Mobile':{'Value':''
12           "pxtem://{'IsPxEntry':false,'Strings':{'Password':{'Value':'12345','IsProtected':true},'Mobile':{'Valu
13           "pxtem://{'IsPxEntry':true,'Strings':{'000UserName':{'Value':'PassXYZ Tester','IsProtected':false},'00:
14       };
15
16       readonly List<Item> items;
17
18       public MockDataStore()
19       {
20           items = new List<Item>()
21           {
22               new PxEntry(jsonData[0]),
23               new PxEntry(jsonData[1]),
24               new PxEntry(jsonData[2]),
25               new PxEntry(jsonData[3]),
26               new PxEntry(jsonData[4])
27           };
28       }
29
30       public async Task<bool> AddItemAsync(Item item)
31       {
32           if (item == null) { throw new ArgumentNullException(nameof(item)); }
33           items.Add(item);
34           return await Task.FromResult(true);
35       }
```

Figure 4.8b: Updated to KPCLib

For the remaining changes in view models and views, all modifications pertain to namespace changes, so further explanations aren't necessary.

Updating the service

The major changes can be found in MockDataStore.cs. In the MockDataStore class, we changed the namespace and the mock data initialization.

To decouple the model from the rest of the system, we use an IDataStore interface to encapsulate the actual implementation. At this stage, we use mock data to implement the service for testing, so the MockDataStore class is used. We will replace it with the actual implementation in *Chapter 6, Software Design with Dependency Injection,* using dependency injection.

Dependency inversion and dependency injection

We will learn about the **Dependency Inversion Principle (DIP)**, which is one of the SOLID design principles, in *Chapter 6, Software Design with Dependency Injection*. We will learn how to use dependency injection to manage the mapping of the `IDataStore` interface to the actual implementation.

In the original code, we created new instances of `PassXYZ.Vault.Models.Item` to initialize mock data. After we replace the model, we cannot create `KPCLib.Item` directly, since it is an abstract class. Instead, we can create new instances of `PxEntry` using JSON data and assign `PxEntry` instances to the `Item` list:

```
Static string[] jsonData =…;
readonly List<Item> items;
public MockDataStore() {
    items = new List<Item>() {
        new PxEntry(jsonData[0]),
        new PxEntry(jsonData[1]),
        new PxEntry(jsonData[2]),
        new PxEntry(jsonData[3]),
        new PxEntry(jsonData[4])
    };
}
```

To create the instances of an abstract class, the factory pattern can be used. To make the testing code simple, we did not use it here. The factory pattern is used in the actual implementation later in this book.

We have replaced the model in the sample code with our own model now. With this change, we can improve `ItemsPage` and `ItemDetailPage` to reflect the updated model.

We will update the view and ViewModel using data binding to collections in the next section.

Binding to collections

In the previous section, we replaced the model using PassXYZLib. When we introduced data binding, we used `ItemDetailPage` and `ItemDetailViewModel` to explain how to bind the source property to the target property.

For the item detail page, we created data binding from one source to one target. However, there are many cases in which we need to bind a data collection to the UI, such as ListView or CollectionView, to display a group of data.

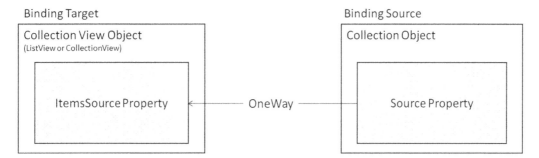

Figure 4.9: Binding to collections

As we can see in *Figure 4.9*, when we create a data binding from a collection object to a collection view, the ItemsSource property is the one to use. In .NET MAUI, collection views such as ListView and CollectionView can be used, and both have an ItemsSource property.

For the collection object, we can use any collection that implements the IEnumerable interface. However, the changes to the collection object may not be able to update the UI automatically. In order to update the UI automatically, the source object needs to implement the INotifyCollectionChanged interface.

We can implement our collection object with the INotifyCollectionChanged interface, but the simplest approach is to use the ObservableCollection<T> class. If any item in the observable collection is changed, the bound UI view is notified automatically.

With this in mind, let's review the class diagram of our **models**, **ViewModels**, and **views** as shown in *Figure 4.9*:

- **Model**: Item, PwEntry, PwGroup, Field
- **View Model**: ItemsViewModel, ItemDetailViewModel
- **View**: ItemsPage, ItemDetailPage

When we display a list of items to the user, the user may act on the selected item. If the item is a group, we will show the groups and entries in an instance of ItemsPage. If the item is an entry, we will show the content of the entry on a content page, which is an instance of ItemDetailPage. On ItemDetailPage, we display a list of fields to the user. Each field is a key value pair and is implemented as an instance of the Field class.

In summary, we display two kinds of lists to the user – a list of items or a list of fields. The list of items is shown in `ItemsPage` and the list of fields is shown in `ItemDetailPage`.

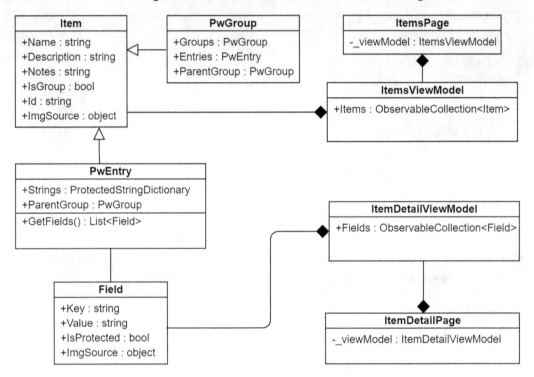

Figure 4.10: Class diagram of the model, view, and ViewModel

In this class diagram, we can see both `PwEntry` and `PwGroup` are derived from `Item`. There is a list of items in `ItemsViewModel` and there is a list of fields in `ItemDetailViewModel`. In the views, `ItemsPage` contains a reference to `ItemsViewModel`, and `ItemDetailPage` contains a reference to `ItemDetailViewModel`.

After we refine our design, we can look at the implementation. We will review the implementation of `ItemDetailViewModel` and `ItemDetailPage` to verify the design change:

```
[QueryProperty(nameof(ItemId), nameof(ItemId))]
public partial class ItemDetailViewModel : BaseViewModel
{
    readonly IDataStore<Item> dataStore;
    ILogger<ItemDetailViewModel> logger;
    public ObservableCollection<Field> Fields { get; set; }         //(1)
```

```
public ItemDetailViewModel(IDataStore<Item> dataStore,
  ILogger<ItemDetailViewModel> logger)
{
  this.dataStore = dataStore;
  this.logger = logger;
  Fields = new ObservableCollection<Field>();                //(2)
}

[ObservableProperty]
private string? title;

[ObservableProperty]
private string? id;

[ObservableProperty]
private string? description;

[ObservableProperty]
private bool isBusy;

private string? itemId;
public string ItemId {
  get {
    if(itemId == null)
    { throw new NullReferenceException(nameof(itemId)); }
    return itemId;
  }

  set {
    itemId = value;
    LoadItemId(value);
  }
}

public override void OnItemSelecteion(object sender)
{
  logger.LogDebug("OnItemSelecteion is invoked.");
```

```
    }

    public async void LoadItemId(string itemId)
    {
      if (itemId == null)
      { throw new ArgumentNullException(nameof(itemId)); }
      var item = await dataStore.GetItemAsync(itemId);
      if (item == null)
      { throw new NullReferenceException(itemId); }
      Id = item.Id;
      Title = item.Name;
      Description = item.Description;

      if (!item.IsGroup) {
        PwEntry dataEntry = (PwEntry)item;                        //(3)
        Fields.Clear();
        List<Field> fields =
          dataEntry.GetFields(GetImage: FieldIcons.GetImage);     //(4)
        foreach (Field field in fields) {
          Fields.Add(field);
        }
        logger.LogDebug($"ItemDetailViewModel:
          Name={dataEntry.Name}.");
      }
    }
  }
```

As shown in the code here, we can see the difference in `ItemDetailViewModel` compared to *Listing 4.1* at the beginning of this chapter:

(1) A `Fields` property is defined as the `ObservableCollection<Field>` type to hold the `Field` list.

(2) The `Fields` variable is initialized in the constructor of `ItemDetailViewModel`.

(3) We can cast `item` to a `PwEntry` instance.

(4) We can get the list of fields by calling an extension method, `GetFields`, which is defined in the PassXYZLib library.

Having reviewed the changes in `ItemDetailViewModel`, let's review the changes in `ItemDetailPage` in *Listing 4.5*:

```xml
<?xml version="1.0" encoding="utf-8" ?>
<ContentPage
  xmlns="http://schemas.microsoft.com/dotnet/2021/maui"
  xmlns:x="http://schemas.microsoft.com/winfx/2009/xaml"
  x:Class="PassXYZ.Vault.Views.ItemDetailPage"
  xmlns:local="clr-namespace:PassXYZ.Vault.ViewModels"
  xmlns:model="clr-namespace:KPCLib;assembly=KPCLib"        //(1)
  x:DataType="local:ItemDetailViewModel"
  Title="{Binding Title}">

  <StackLayout>
    <ListView
      x:Name="FieldsListView"
      ItemsSource="{Binding Fields}"                          //(2)
      VerticalOptions="FillAndExpand"
      HasUnevenRows="False"
      RowHeight="84"
      IsPullToRefreshEnabled="true"
      IsRefreshing="{Binding IsBusy, Mode=OneWay}"
      CachingStrategy="RetainElement"
      ItemSelected="OnFieldSelected">

      <ListView.ItemTemplate>
        <DataTemplate>                                        //(3)
          ...
        </DataTemplate>
      </ListView.ItemTemplate>
      <ListView.Footer>
        <StackLayout Padding="5" Orientation="Horizontal">
          <Label
            Text="{Binding Description}"
            FontSize="Small"
            Style="{DynamicResource ListItemDetailTextStyle}"
            TextType ="Html"/>
        </StackLayout>
      </ListView.Footer>
```

```
      </ListView>
    </StackLayout>
  </ContentPage>
```

Listing 4.5: `ItemDetailPage.xaml` *(https://epa.ms/ItemDetailPage4-5)*

In `ItemDetailPage`, we can see there are many changes compared to *Listing 3.4* in *Chapter 3, User Interface Design with XAML*. `ListView` is used to display the fields in an entry:

(1) To use `Field` in `DataTemplate`, an `xmlns:model` namespace is added. Since the `Field` class is in a different assembly, we need to specify the assembly's name as follows:

```
xmlns:model="clr-namespace:KPCLib;assembly=KPCLib"
```

(2) We bind the `Fields` property to the `ItemsSource` property of `ListView`.

(3) `DataTemplate` is used to define the appearance of each item in `ListView`. It is collapsed in *Listing 4.5*.

Let's expand it and review the implementation of `DataTemplate` in this code block:

```
<DataTemplate>
  <ViewCell>
    <Grid Padding="10" x:DataType="model:Field" >            //(1)
      <Grid.RowDefinitions...>
      <Grid.ColumnDefinitions...>
      <Grid Grid.RowSpan="2" Padding="10">
        <Grid.ColumnDefinitions...>
        <Image Grid.Column="0" Source="{Binding ImgSource}"  //(2)
        HorizontalOptions="Fill"
        VerticalOptions="Fill" />
      </Grid>
      <Label Text="{Binding Key}"  Grid.Column="1".../>       //(3)
      <Label Text="{Binding Value}" Grid.Row="1"              //(4)
        Grid.Column="1".../>
    </Grid>
  </ViewCell>
</DataTemplate>
```

In `DataTemplate`, the layout of each field is defined in a `ViewCell` element. In the `ViewCell` element, we defined a 2x2 `Grid` layout. The first column is used to display the field icon. The key and value in the field are displayed in the second column with two rows:

(1) The x:DataType attribute in the Grid layout is set to Field and the following data binding in Grid will refer to the property of Field. The Field class is defined in our model, which is in the KPCLib package.

(2) To display the field icon, the Source property of the Image control is set to the ImgSource property of Field.

The Key property and the Value property of Field are assigned to the Text property of the Label control.

With this analysis, we learned how to create data binding for a collection. The data binding used in ItemsPage and ItemsViewModel is similar to this implementation. The difference is we use a collection of Field here and a collection of Item classes is used in ItemsPage. Having completed the changes, we can see the improvement of the UI in *Figure 4.11*.

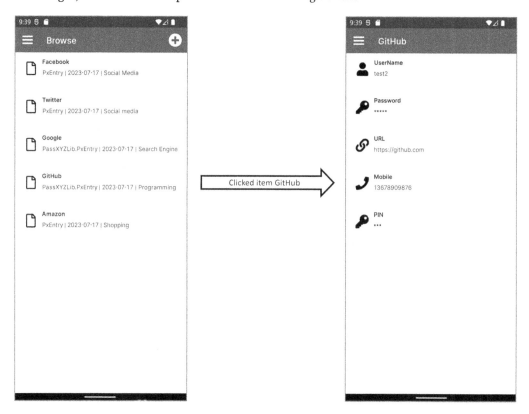

Figure 4.11: Improved ItemsPage and ItemDetailPage

In the improved UI, we display a list of items on `ItemsPage` (on the left). The items in the list can be entries (such as on Facebook, Twitter, or Amazon), or groups, which we will see in the next chapter.

When the user clicks on an item, such as **GitHub**, details about **GitHub** are displayed on `ItemDetailPage` (on the right). On the item detail page, the information about this account (**GitHub**) is shown.

Using custom views

We implement an instance of `ViewCell` in `DataTemplate` in *Listing 4.5*. This `ViewCell` is used to display a key-value pair with an icon. The same implementation is employed in both `ItemsPage` and `ItemDetailPage`, with the sole distinction being the data binding. We have duplicated code here. To refactor the implementation, we can create a custom view (or custom control).

A custom view in .NET MAUI is a user interface component created by developers to meet custom requirements, provide reusable UI logic, or extend the functionality of existing UI components. Custom views can be built by combining existing controls, deriving from base classes like `View`, `ViewCell`, or `ContentView`, and overriding specific methods to customize rendering or behavior.

To create a custom view that can be reused in both `ItemsPage` and `ItemDetailPage`, we should first create a new folder called `Templates` within the `Views` directory. In Visual Studio, we can right-click on the *Templates* folder to add a new item based on the **.NET MAUI ContentView (XAML)** template, naming it `KeyValueView`:

```xml
<?xml version="1.0" encoding="utf-8" ?>
<ViewCell ...
  xmlns:vm="clr-namespace:PassXYZ.Vault.ViewModels"
  x:Class="PassXYZ.Vault.Views.Templates.KeyValueView">        //(1)

  <Grid Padding="10" VerticalOptions="FillAndExpand">          //(2)
    <Grid.RowDefinitions>
      <RowDefinition Height="Auto" />
      <RowDefinition Height="Auto" />
    </Grid.RowDefinitions>
    <Grid.ColumnDefinitions>
      <ColumnDefinition Width="Auto" />
      <ColumnDefinition Width="Auto" />
    </Grid.ColumnDefinitions>
    <Grid Grid.RowSpan="2" Padding="10">
```

```xml
      <Grid.ColumnDefinitions>
        <ColumnDefinition Width="32" />
      </Grid.ColumnDefinitions>
      <Image x:Name="imageField" Grid.Column="0"             //(5)
        HorizontalOptions="Fill" VerticalOptions="Fill">
        <Image.Source>

        ...

        </Image.Source>
      </Image>
    </Grid>
    <Label x:Name="keyField" ... />                           //(3)
    <Label x:Name="valueField" ... />                         //(4)
    <Grid.GestureRecognizers>
      <TapGestureRecognizer
        NumberOfTapsRequired="1"
        Command="{Binding Source=
        {RelativeSource AncestorType=
        {x:Type vm:BaseViewModel}},
        Path=ItemSelectionChangedCommand}"
        CommandParameter="{Binding .}">
      </TapGestureRecognizer>
    </Grid.GestureRecognizers>
  </Grid>
</ViewCell>
```

Listing 4.6: `KeyValueView.xaml` (https://epa.ms/KeyValueView4-6)

We can see in *Listing 4.6* that the class name is `KeyValueView` **(1)** and we have created a 2x2 grid **(2)**. In this grid, there are two rows used to display key **(3)** and value **(4)** with an icon **(5)**.

When we use `KeyValueView`, we can establish data binding for the key, value, and icon. To support data binding, we need to define the key, value, and icon as bindable properties. Let's review the implementation shown in *Listing 4.7*.

```csharp
public partial class KeyValueView : ViewCell {
  public KeyValueView() {
    InitializeComponent();
  }
```

```
public static readonly BindableProperty KeyProperty =
  BindableProperty.Create(nameof(Key), typeof(string),
  typeof(KeyValueView), string.Empty,
  propertyChanging: (bindable, oldValue, newValue) =>
  {
    var control = bindable as KeyValueView;
    var changingFrom = oldValue as string;
    var changingTo = newValue as string;
    if(control == null) {
      throw new NullReferenceException(nameof(control)); }
    if(changingTo == null) {
      throw new NullReferenceException(nameof(changingTo));
    }
    control.Key = changingTo;
  });

public string Key {                                        //(1)
  get { return (string)GetValue(KeyProperty); }
  set {
      keyField.Text = value;
      SetValue(KeyProperty, value);
  }
}

public static readonly BindableProperty ValueProperty =
  BindableProperty.Create(nameof(Value), typeof(string),
  typeof(KeyValueView), string.Empty,
  propertyChanging: (bindable, oldValue, newValue) =>
  {
    var control = bindable as KeyValueView;
    var changingFrom = oldValue as string;
    var changingTo = newValue as string;
    if (control == null)
      { throw new NullReferenceException(nameof(control)); }
    if (changingTo == null) {
      throw new NullReferenceException(nameof(changingTo));
    }
```

```
          control.Value = changingTo;
      });

  public string Value {                                       //(2)
      get { return (string)GetValue(ValueProperty); }
      set {
          valueField.Text = value;
          SetValue(ValueProperty, value);
      }
  }


  public static readonly BindableProperty SourceProperty =
    BindableProperty.Create(nameof(Source),
    typeof(ImageSource), typeof(KeyValueView), default!,
    propertyChanging: (bindable, oldValue, newValue) =>
    {
      var control = bindable as KeyValueView;
      var changingFrom = oldValue as ImageSource;
      var changingTo = newValue as ImageSource;
      if (control == null)
        { throw new NullReferenceException(nameof(control)); }
      if (changingTo == null) {
        throw new NullReferenceException(nameof(changingTo));
      }
      control.Source = changingTo;
    });

  public ImageSource Source {                                 //(3)
    get { return (ImageSource)GetValue(SourceProperty); }
    set {
      imageField.Source = value;
      SetValue(SourceProperty, value);
    }
  }
}
```

Listing 4.7: KeyValueView.xaml.cs *(https://epa.ms/KeyValueView4-7)*

To implement the bindable properties key **(1)**, Value **(2)**, and Source **(3)** within our custom control class, we must define the BindableProperty using the static BindableProperty.Create method. This method should include the property name, property type, declaring type, and a default value as parameters:

```
public static readonly BindableProperty KeyProperty =
  BindableProperty.Create(nameof(Key), typeof(string),
  typeof(KeyValueView), string.Empty,
  propertyChanging: (bindable, oldValue, newValue) =>
  {
    var control = bindable as KeyValueView;
    var changingFrom = oldValue as string;
    var changingTo = newValue as string;
    if(control == null) {
      throw new NullReferenceException(nameof(control)); }
    if(changingTo == null) {
      throw new NullReferenceException(nameof(changingTo));
    }
    control.Key = changingTo;
  });
```

After that, we need to implement the corresponding property with a getter and setter. They will interact with the BindableProperty through the GetValue and SetValue methods:

```
public string Key {
  get { return (string)GetValue(KeyProperty); }
  set {
    keyField.Text = value;
    SetValue(KeyProperty, value);
  }
}
```

We have now created the custom view KeyValueView, and are able to refactor the previous DataTemplate implementation accordingly. The revised implementation is as follows:

```
<DataTemplate x:DataType="model:Field">
  <template:KeyValueView
    Key="{Binding Key}"
    Value="{Binding Value}"
```

```
        Source="{Binding ImgSource}"/>
    </DataTemplate>
```

After introducing the new data model, the design has not experienced significant changes. We have enhanced the UI to make it more meaningful, but the majority of the complexity remains concealed within our model libraries – KPCLib and PassXYZLib. This is the advantage we observe by employing the MVVM pattern, which allows us to separate the model (business logic) from the UI design.

Summary

In this chapter, we learned about the MVVM pattern and applied it to our app development. One key feature of the MVVM pattern is data binding between the view and ViewModel. We delved into data binding and utilized it in the implementation of our app.

To delve deeper into the complexities of data binding, we examined binding to collections and the utilization of data binding in custom views. By employing data binding and custom views, we're able to refactor XAML code, resulting in a cleaner and more concise codebase.

To demonstrate advanced data binding usage, we need a more intricate model layer. We enhanced the model in this chapter by introducing two packages – KPCLib and PassXYZLib. We replaced the model in the sample code with the models found in these two packages. Subsequently, we updated the UIs of `ItemsPage` and `ItemDetailPage` to reflect the changes made to the model.

In the next chapter, we will refine our user stories and continue improving the UI, drawing upon our knowledge of Shell and navigation.

Further reading

- *Introduction to the MVVM Toolkit*: `https://learn.microsoft.com/en-us/dotnet/communitytoolkit/mvvm/`

- KeePass is a free open source password manager: `https://keepass.info/`

Learn more on Discord

Join our community's Discord space for discussions with the author and other readers:

https://packt.link/cross-platform-app

5

Navigation Using .NET MAUI Shell and NavigationPage

In the preceding chapters, we've tackled **user interface** (**UI**) design, the MVVM pattern, and data binding. These elements allow us to devise UIs at the page level. For real-world applications, the ability to navigate between pages is crucial. Consequently, most application frameworks include their own distinct navigation mechanisms, .NET MAUI being no exception. In this chapter, we'll introduce the navigation mechanisms in .NET MAUI. We'll start by demonstrating how to accomplish the most basic navigation using NavigationPage, then we'll delve into a more structured navigation mechanism – Shell.

Subsequently, we'll enhance the navigation capabilities of our application with Shell. In *Chapter 2, Building Our First .NET MAUI App*, we created our app using a Shell template. Despite this, our app has not yet reached the complexity required for multi-level navigation. With the integration of Shell, we'll execute multi-level navigation. In order to facilitate this, it's necessary to refine our model to support the navigation implementation. By the end of this chapter, our application will be able to support login, the selection of a page from the flyout menu, and switching to the item details or navigation to a child group. After delving deeper into the navigation design, we'll gain an understanding of how navigation functions within .NET MAUI.

The following topics will be covered in this chapter:

- Implementing navigation
- Using Shell
- Improving design and navigation

Technical requirements

To test and debug the source code in this chapter, you need to have Visual Studio 2022 installed on your PC or Mac. Please refer to the *Development environment setup* section in *Chapter 1, Getting Started with .NET MAUI*, for the details.

The source code for this chapter is available in the following branch on GitHub: `https://github.com/PacktPublishing/.NET-MAUI-Cross-Platform-Application-Development-Second-edition/tree/main/2nd/chapter05`.

To check out the source code of this chapter, we can use the following command:

```
$ git clone -b 2nd/chapter05 https://github.com/PacktPublishing/.NET-MAUI-
Cross-Platform-Application-Development-Second-edition.git PassXYZ.Vault2
```

To find out more about the source code in this book, please refer to the *Managing the source code in this book* section in *Chapter 2, Building Our First .NET MAUI App*.

Implementing navigation

In this chapter, we are going to implement the navigation logic of our password manager app. This will include the following functionalities:

- Logging in and connecting to the database
- Exploring data in the password database

Navigation design has a significant impact on user experience. In .NET MAUI, there is a built-in mechanism to help developers implement navigation efficiently. As we saw in the previous chapters, we can use `Shell` in our app. In this chapter, we will learn about `Shell` and enhance our app with features provided by `Shell`. Before we dive into `Shell`, we will explore the basic navigation mechanism in .NET MAUI.

The most common ways to implement navigation are hierarchial and modal:

- **Hierarchical navigation** provides a navigation experience where the user can navigate through pages, both forward and backward. This pattern typically uses a toolbar or navigation bar at the top of the screen to display an Up or Back button in the top-left corner. It usually maintains a LIFO stack of pages to handle the navigation. **LIFO** stands for **last in, first out**, which means the last page to enter is the first one to pop out.

- **Modal navigation** is different from hierarchical navigation in terms of how users can respond to it. If a modal page is displayed on the screen, the users must complete or cancel the required task on the page before they can take other actions. The users cannot navigate away from modal pages before the required task is completed or canceled.

INavigation interface and NavigationPage

In .NET MAUI, both hierarchical navigation and model navigation are supported through the INavigation interface. The INavigation interface is supported by a special page called NavigationPage. NavigationPage is used to manage the navigation of a stack of other pages. The inheritance hierarchy of NavigationPage looks like this:

- **Object** | **BindableObject** | **Element** | **NavigableElement** | **VisualElement** | **Page** | **NavigationPage**

NavigableElement defines a property called Navigation that implements the INavigation interface. This inherited property can be called from any VisualElement or Page for navigation purposes, as shown here:

```
public Microsoft.Maui.Controls.INavigation Navigation { get; }
```

To use NavigationPage, we must add the first page to a navigation stack as the root page of the application. We can see an example of this in the following code snippet:

```
public partial class App : Application
{
  ...
  public App ()
  {
    InitializeComponent();
    MainPage = new NavigationPage (new TheFirstPage());
  }
  ...
}
```

We build the navigation stack in the constructor of the App class, which is a derived class of Application. TheFirstPage, which is a derived class of ContentPage, is pushed onto the navigation stack.

Using the navigation stack

There are two ways to navigate to or from a page. When we want to browse a new page, we can add the new page to the navigation stack. This action is called a **push**. If we want to go back to the previous page, we can **pop** the previous page from the stack:

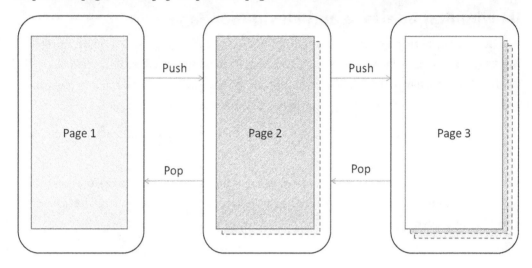

Figure 5.1: Push and pop

As shown in *Figure 5.1*, we can use the PushAsync() or PopAsync() method in the INavigation interface to change to a new page or go back to the previous page, respectively.

If we are on **Page1**, we can change to **Page2** with the GotoPage2() event handler. In this function, we are pushing the new page, **Page2**, to the stack:

```
async void GotoPage2 (object sender, EventArgs e) {
        await Navigation.PushAsync(new Page2());
}
```

Once we are on **Page2**, we can go back with the BackToPage1() event handler. In this function, we are popping the previous page from the stack:

```
async void BackToPage1 (object sender, EventArgs e) {
        await Navigation.PopAsync();
}
```

In the preceding example, we navigated to a new page using the hierarchical navigation method. To display a modal page, we can use the modal stack. For example, in our app, if we want to create a new item in `ItemsPage`, we can call `PushModalAsync()` in `ItemsViewModel`:

```
await Shell.Current.Navigation.PushModalAsync(NewItemPage(type));
```

After the new item has been created, we can call `PopModalAsync()` in `NewItemViewModel` to dismiss the modal page:

```
_ = await Shell.Current.Navigation.PopModalAsync();
```

On the `NewItemPage` model page, we cannot navigate to other pages before we complete or cancel the task. Both `PopAsync()` and `PopModalAsync()` return an awaitable task of the `Task<Page>` type.

To find more information about NavigationPage, please refer to the following Microsoft document:

`https://learn.microsoft.com/en-us/dotnet/maui/user-interface/pages/navigationpage`

Manipulating the navigation stack

In hierarchical navigation, we can not only push or pop pages from the stack, but we can also manipulate the navigation stack.

Inserting a page

We can insert a page into the stack using the `InsertPageBefore` method:

```
public void InsertPageBefore (Page page, Page before);
```

The `InsertPageBefore` method requires two parameters:

- page: This is the page to be added.
- before: This is the page before which the page is inserted.

In *Figure 5.1*, when we are at **Page2**, we can insert another page, **Page1**, before it:

```
Navigation.InsertPageBefore(new Page1(), this);
```

Removing a page

We can also remove a specific page from the stack using the `RemovePage()` method:

```
public void RemovePage (Page page);
```

In *Figure 5.1*, given we have a reference of **Page2** when we are at **Page3**, we can remove **Page2** from the stack. After PopAsync() is called, we will be back at **Page1**:

```
// the reference page2 is an instance of Page2
Navigation.RemovePage(page2);
await Navigation.PopAsync();
```

In conclusion, we have learned how to build a navigation stack using NavigationPage. Upon creating a navigation stack, we can utilize the INavigation interface to execute navigation actions. For a simple application, this method may suffice. However, for more complex applications, this approach can involve a significant amount of work. Fortunately, .NET MAUI offers a structured alternative called Shell. Shell is designed to improve the navigation structure of your applications by providing a unified, declarative syntax for defining the flyout menu, tab bars, and other navigational UIs. Utilizing Shell allows us to deliver an enhanced navigation experience to users with significantly less effort.

Using Shell

The INavigation interface and NavigationPage offer basic navigation functionality. Relying solely on them would require us to create complex navigation mechanisms by ourselves. Fortunately, .NET MAUI provides built-in page templates to choose from, which can deliver various navigation experiences.

As shown in the class diagram in *Figure 5.2*, there are built-in pages available for different use cases. All these pages – TabbedPage, ContentPage, FlyoutPage, NavigationPage, and Shell – are derived classes of Page:

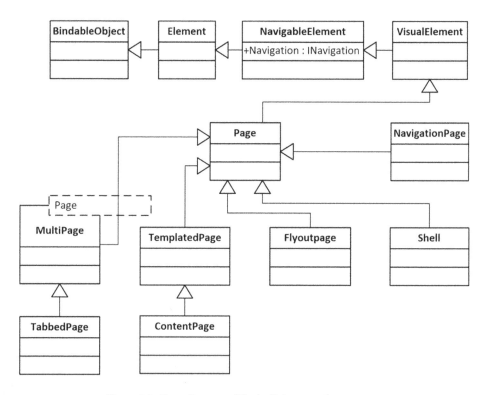

Figure 5.2: Class diagram of the built-in pages in .NET MAUI

ContentPage, TabbedPage, and FlyoutPage can be used to create various UIs per your requirements:

- ContentPage is the most commonly used page type and can include any layout and view
  elements. It is suitable for single-page designs.

- TabbedPage can be used to host multiple pages. Each child page can be selected by a series
  of tabs, located at either the top or bottom of the page.

- FlyoutPage can display a list of items, similar to menu items in a desktop application.
  Users can navigate to individual pages through the items in the menu.

Although Shell is also a derived class of Page, it includes a common navigation user experience that simplifies developers' tasks. Shell assists developers by reducing the complexity of application development and consolidating highly customizable, rich features in one location.

Shell provides the following features:

- A single place to describe the visual hierarchy of an app
- A highly customizable common navigation user experience
- A URI-based navigation scheme that is very similar to what we have in a web browser
- An integrated search handler

The top-level building blocks of Shell are flyouts and tabs. We can use flyouts and tabs to create the navigation structure of our app.

Flyout

A flyout can be used as the top-level menu of a Shell app. In our app, we must use both flyouts and tabs to create the top-level navigation design. In this section, we will explore flyouts; in the next section, we will discuss using tabs in our app.

In *Figure 5.3*, we can see what the flyout looks like in our app. From the flyout menu, we can switch to the AboutPage, ItemsPage, or LoginPage. To access the flyout menu, we can either swipe from the left edge of the screen or click the flyout icon, which is the hamburger icon **(1)**. When we click the **Root Group (2)** in the flyout menu, we will see a list of password entries or groups.

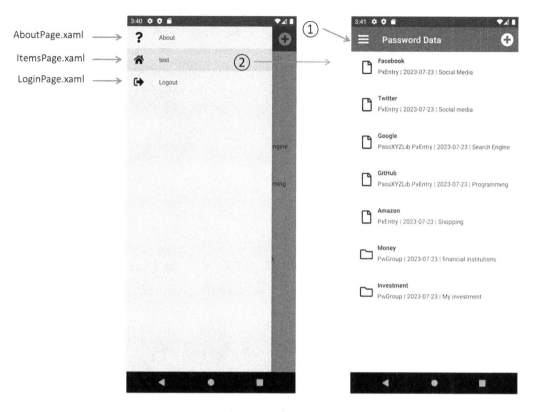

Figure 5.3: Flyout

The flyout menu consists of flyout items or menu items. In *Figure 5.3*, **About** and **Root Group** are flyout items, while **Logout** is a menu item.

Flyout items

Each flyout item is a `FlyoutItem` object that contains a `ShellContent` object. We can define flyout items like so in the `AppShell.xaml` file. We assign a `string` resource to the `Title` attribute **(1)** and an `ImageSource` to the `Icon` attribute **(2)**. These correspond to the properties of the `FlyoutItem` class:

```
<FlyoutItem
  Title="{x:Static resources:Resources.About}"          //(1)
  Icon="tab_info.png" >                                  //(2)
  <Tab>
    <ShellContent Route="AboutPage" ContentTemplate=
      "{DataTemplate local:AboutPage}" />
  </Tab>
</FlyoutItem>
<FlyoutItem x:Name="RootItem" Title="Browse"
    Icon="tab_home.png">
  <Tab>
    <ShellContent Route="RootPage" ContentTemplate=
      "{DataTemplate local:ItemsPage}" />
  </Tab>
</FlyoutItem>
```

`Shell` has implicit conversion operators that can be used to remove the `FlyoutItem` and `Tab` objects so that the preceding XAML code can also be simplified, like so:

```
<ShellContent Title="{x:Static resources:Resources.About}"
  Icon="tab_info.png" Route="AboutPage"
  ContentTemplate="{DataTemplate local:AboutPage}" />
<ShellContent x:Name="RootItem" Title="Browse"
  Icon="tab_home.png" Route="RootPage"
  ContentTemplate="{DataTemplate local:ItemsPage}" />
```

Menu items

In some instances, using flyout items for navigation to a content page might not be necessary; instead, we may desire to perform an action. In such cases, menu items can be utilized. For our scenario, we have designated `Logout` as a menu item to execute an action rather than navigating to another content page:

```
<MenuItem Text="Logout" IconImageSource="tab_login.png"
    Clicked="OnMenuItemClicked">
</MenuItem>
```

As we can see from the preceding XAML code, each menu item is a MenuItem object. The MenuItem class has a Clicked event and a Command property. When MenuItem is tapped, we can execute an action. In the preceding menu item, we assigned OnMenuItemClicked as the event handler.

Let's take a closer look at AppShell.xaml, as shown in *Listing 5.1*. In this file, we have defined two flyout items and one menu item. The flyout items allow us to select the AboutPage **(1)** and ItemsPage **(2)**, while the menu item enables us to log out **(3)**.

```
<Shell
  xmlns="http://schemas.microsoft.com/dotnet/2021/maui"
  ...
  Title="PassXYZ.Vault"
  x:Class="PassXYZ.Vault.AppShell"
  FlyoutIcon="{FontImage FontFamily=FontAwesomeSolid,
  Color=White,
  Glyph={x:Static style:FontAwesomeSolid.Bars}}"
  FlyoutBackgroundColor="{StaticResource Secondary}">

  <TabBar>                                                      //(4)
    <ShellContent Title="Login" Route="LoginPage"
      Icon="{FontImage FontFamily=FontAwesomeSolid,
      Color=Black,
      Glyph={x:Static style:FontAwesomeSolid.UserAlt}}"
      ContentTemplate="{DataTemplate local:LoginPage}" />
    <ShellContent Title="SignUp" Route="SignUpPage"
      Icon="{FontImage FontFamily=FontAwesomeSolid,
      Color=Black,
      Glyph={x:Static style:FontAwesomeSolid.Users}}"
      ContentTemplate="{DataTemplate local:SignUpPage}" />
  </TabBar>

  <FlyoutItem Title="About"                                     //(1)
```

```
    Icon="{FontImage FontFamily=FontAwesomeSolid, Color=Black,
    Glyph={x:Static style:FontAwesomeSolid.Question}}">
    <ShellContent Route="AboutPage"
      ContentTemplate="{DataTemplate local:AboutPage}">
    </ShellContent>
  </FlyoutItem>

  <FlyoutItem x:Name="RootItem" Title="Browse"                   //(2)
    Icon="{FontImage FontFamily=FontAwesomeSolid, Color=Black,
    Glyph={x:Static style:FontAwesomeSolid.Home}}">
    <ShellContent Route="RootPage"
      ContentTemplate="{DataTemplate local:ItemsPage}">
    </ShellContent>
  </FlyoutItem>

  <MenuItem Text="Logout" Clicked="OnMenuItemClicked"            //(3)
    IconImageSource="{FontImage FontFamily=FontAwesomeSolid,
    Color=Black,
    Glyph={x:Static style:FontAwesomeSolid.SignOutAlt}}">
  </MenuItem>

</Shell>
```

Listing 5.1: AppShell.xaml *in PassXYZ.Vault (*https://epa.ms/AppShell5-1*)*

There is also a TabBar **(4)** defined for LoginPage and SignUpPage. Let's review tabs now.

Tabs

Utilizing tabs in Shell enables the creation of a navigation experience akin to that of TabbedPage. As depicted in *Figure 5.4*, both Android and iOS platforms feature two tabs on the bottom tab bar. However, the appearance of the tabs differs when implemented on the Windows platform.

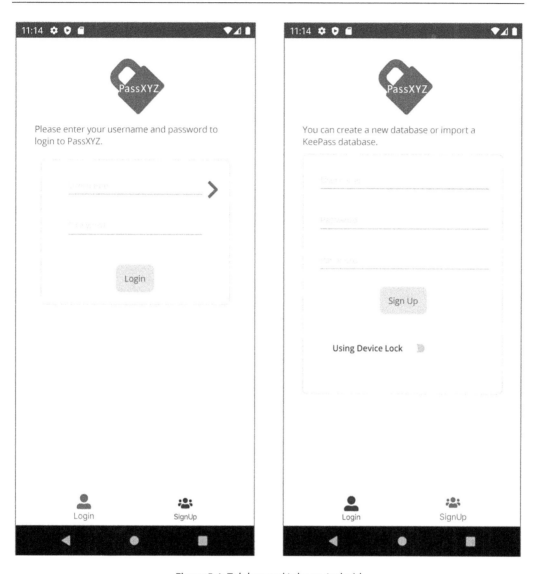

Figure 5.4: Tab bar and tabs on Android

As we can see in *Figure 5.5*, on Windows, the tab bar is at the top:

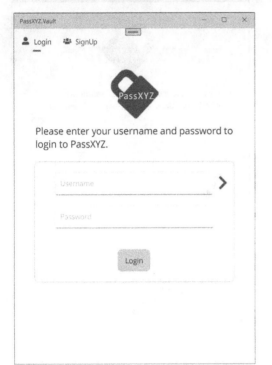 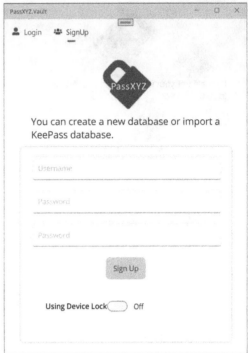

Figure 5.5: Tab bar and tabs on Windows

In order to incorporate tabs into our app, we need to create a TabBar object. This TabBar object can comprise one or more Tab objects, with each Tab object representing an individual tab on the tab bar. Additionally, each Tab object can encompass one or more ShellContent objects. The subsequent XAML code demonstrates its similarity to the code used when defining a flyout:

```
<TabBar>
  <Tab Title="{x:Static resources:Resources.action_id_login}"
    Icon="tab_login.png">
    <ShellContent Route="LoginPage"
    ContentTemplate="{DataTemplate local:LoginPage}" />
  </Tab>
  <Tab Title="{x:Static resources:Resources.menu_id_users}"
    Icon="tab_users.png">
    <ShellContent Route="SignUpPage"
    ContentTemplate="{DataTemplate local:SignUpPage}" />
  </Tab>
</TabBar>
```

Similar to the approach we took in the flyout XAML code, we can simplify the previous code by eliminating the Tab tags. By utilizing the implicit conversion operators of Shell, we can remove the Tab objects. As demonstrated, it is possible to omit the Tab tags and directly define the Title and Icon attributes within the ShellContent tags:

```
<TabBar>
  <ShellContent Title="{x:Static resources:Resources.action_id_login}"
                Icon="tab_login.png"
                Route="LoginPage"
                ContentTemplate="{DataTemplate local:LoginPage}" />
  <ShellContent Title="{x:Static resources:Resources.menu_id_users}"
                Icon="tab_users.png"
                Route="SignUpPage"
                ContentTemplate="{DataTemplate local:SignUpPage}" />
</TabBar>
```

In a situation where we define both TabBar objects and FlyoutItem objects in AppShell.xaml, the TabBar objects will disable the flyout items. This is why, upon launching our app, we are presented with a tabbed screen displaying either the login or signup pages. Once the user successfully logs in, we can navigate them to the RootPage, which is the registered route illustrated in *Listing 5.1*. In the following section, we will delve into the process of registering routes and navigating using these registered routes.

Shell navigation

In Shell, navigating to pages is achieved through registered routes. Similar to a web browser, .NET MAUI uses URI-based navigation. The URI might look something like the following:

```
//RootPage/ItemDetailPage?ID="your entry ID"
```

Or, it might look like the following:

```
Group1/ItemDetailPage1
```

As you can see, the URI format allows us to specify the path within the application interface and potentially, include additional parameters. Beginning the URI with a double slash "//" signifies the root of navigation. Just like in file system navigation, we can also utilize ".." to execute backward navigation. This way, programmers can navigate the navigation stack in a way that's both intuitive and efficient.

There are two methods for registering routes. The first method involves registering routes within Shell's visual hierarchy. The second method requires explicitly registering them by utilizing the `RegisterRoute` static method found in the `Routing` class.

Registering absolute routes

We have the option to register routes in Shell's visual hierarchy, as demonstrated in *Listing 5.1*. Routes can be specified through the `Route` property of `FlyoutItem`, `TabBar`, `Tab`, or `ShellContent`.

In the `AppShell.xaml` file, we registered the following routes.

Route	Page	Description
LoginPage	LoginPage	This route displays a page for user login
SignUpPage	SignUpPage	This route displays a page for user signup
AboutPage	AboutPage	This route displays a page about our app
RootPage	ItemsPage	This route displays a page for navigating the password database

Table 5.1: Registered routes in the visual hierarchy

To navigate to a route in Shell's visual hierarchy, we can use an absolute route URI. The absolute URI starts with a double slash "//", such as `//LoginPage`.

Registering relative routes

It is also possible to navigate to a page without predefining it in the visual hierarchy. For instance, the password entry detail page, `ItemDetailPage`, can be navigated to at any hierarchy level of the password groups. In our app, we can explicitly register the following routes using `RegisterRoute` in the code-behind file, `AppShell.xaml.cs`:

```
public static AppShell? CurrentAppShell
{ get; private set; } = default!;


public AppShell()
{
  InitializeComponent();

  Routing.RegisterRoute(nameof(ItemDetailPage),
    typeof(ItemDetailPage));
  Routing.RegisterRoute(nameof(NewItemPage),
    typeof(NewItemPage));
```

```
Routing.RegisterRoute(nameof(ItemsPage),
    typeof(ItemsPage));
CurrentAppShell = this;
}
```

In the preceding code, we defined the following routes.

Route	Page	Description
ItemDetailPage	ItemDetailPage	This is the route to display details about a password entry
NewItemPage	NewItemPage	This is the route to add a new item (entry or group)
ItemsPage	ItemsPage	This is the route to display a page for navigating the password database

Table 5.2: Registered detail page routes

In order to illustrate the usage of relative routes, we will proceed by adding a new item. When the need arises to add a new item, we can navigate to the NewItemPage utilizing a relative route, as shown here:

```
await Shell.Current.GoToAsync(nameof(NewItemPage));
```

In this scenario, the NewItemPage route is searched, and if the route is identified, the page will be displayed and added to the navigation stack. This navigation stack is the same as the one we discussed while explaining basic navigation using the INavigation interface. When defining a relative route and navigating to it, we pass a string as the route's name. To prevent errors, we can use the class name as the route name by employing the **nameof** expression.

Once we have entered the details for the new item in the NewItemPage, we can click either the **Save** or **Cancel** button. Within the event handler for the **Save** or **Cancel** button, we can navigate back to the previous page using the code provided:

```
await Shell.Current.Navigation.PopModalAsync();
```

Alternatively, we can also navigate back using the following code:

```
await Shell.Current.GoToAsync("..");
```

Just like in file system navigation, here, the ".." represents the parent page in the navigation stack.

As evident from the code mentioned earlier, there are two methods to navigate back. The first option involves using the `PopModalAsync` method of the `INavigation` interface. Due to `Shell` being a derived class of `Page`, it implements the `INavigation` interface through the inherited `Navigation` property. We can call the `PopModalAsync` modal navigation method to go back, with `NewItemPage` functioning as a modal page.

The second method involves utilizing the `GoToAsync` function to navigate back. As the `NewItemPage` serves as a modal page, you might be curious about how to distinguish between a modal page and a non-modal page when invoking `GoToAsync`. In `Shell` navigation, this distinction is determined by the page presentation mode. The content page of `NewItemPage` is defined as follows:

```xml
<?xml version="1.0" encoding="UTF-8"?>
<ContentPage
    xmlns="http://schemas.microsoft.com/dotnet/2021/maui"
    xmlns:x="http://schemas.microsoft.com/winfx/2009/xaml"
    x:Class="PassXYZ.Vault.Views.NewItemPage"
    Shell.PresentationMode="ModalAnimated"                        //(1)
    Title="New Item">

    <ContentPage.Content...>
</ContentPage >
```

As observed, the `Shell.PresentationMode` **(1)** property is defined within the content page. Based on our preference for implementing animation, we can assign different values to this property. For a standard content page, we can set it to either `NotAnimated` or `Animated`. In the case of a modal page, the options are `Modal`, `ModalAnimated`, or `ModalNotAnimated`. If left unchanged, the default value is set to `Animated`.

To navigate back, the `GoToAsync` method is utilized along with the route assigned to "..". This approach is reminiscent of file system navigation or browser URL navigation. The relative route, "..", signifies navigating back to the parent route. It can also be combined with a route to access a page at the parent level, as demonstrated here:

```
await Shell.Current.GoToAsync("../AboutPage");
```

In *Table 5.1* and *Table 5.2*, you will notice that `ItemsPage` is registered as both the absolute route `RootPage` and the relative route `ItemsPage`. It is important to note that `ItemsPage` may encompass password groups at various levels. When positioned at the top level, it serves as an absolute route, whereas at all subsequent navigation hierarchy levels, it functions as a relative route.

Passing data to pages

In order to elaborate on the reasoning behind registering ItemsPage with both absolute and relative routes, let's examine the navigation hierarchy of our app, as depicted in *Figure 5.6*.

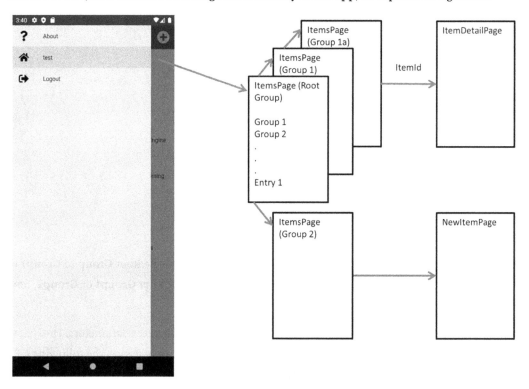

Figure 5.6: Navigation hierarchy

In our app, once the user successfully logs in, the main page showcases a list of entries and groups situated at the top tier of the password database, referred to as Root Group. This resembles the navigation structure of a file system that displays the top-level files and folders at its root.

The first instance of ItemsPage employs the RootPage route, which can be accessed via the flyout item. Assume there are sub-groups named **Group1** and **Group2** within the Root Group, as depicted in *Figure 5.6*. We can navigate to these sub-groups, which also represent instances of ItemsPage. Since these instances utilize relative routes and rely on navigation stacks that are pushed on demand, they cannot be pre-defined. These navigation stacks can extend as deep as the actual data present in the password database.

The two distinct routes of ItemsPage are defined in AppShell.xaml and AppShell.xaml.cs as follows:

The RootPage route (absolute route):

```
<FlyoutItem x:Name="RootItem" Title="Browse"
  Icon="{FontImage FontFamily=FontAwesomeSolid,
  Color=Black,
  Glyph={x:Static style:FontAwesomeSolid.Home}}">
  <ShellContent Route="RootPage"
    ContentTemplate="{DataTemplate local:ItemsPage}">
  </ShellContent>
</FlyoutItem>
```

The ItemsPage route (relative route):

```
Routing.RegisterRoute(nameof(ItemsPage),
    typeof(ItemsPage));
```

In this section, you might be curious about how to navigate from the Root Group to **Group1** or **Group2**. If the ItemsPage is capable of displaying the content of either **Group1** or **Group2**, how can we inform ItemsPage which group needs to be displayed?

In Shell navigation, data can be transmitted to a content page using query parameters. The syntax is akin to the parameters passed in a URL within a web browser. For instance, the following URL can be used to search for **.net** on Google: https://www.google.com.hk/search?q=.net.

The desired outcome is achieved by appending a question mark (?) after a route, along with a pair of query parameter IDs and their respective values. In the preceding example, the key is q and the value is .net.

Upon selecting an item in the list of Root Groups, it can be either an entry or a group. The click event activates the OnItemSelection method in ItemsViewModel, demonstrated in *Listing 5.2*:

```
using System.Collections.ObjectModel;
using CommunityToolkit.Mvvm.ComponentModel;
using CommunityToolkit.Mvvm.Input;
using Microsoft.Extensions.Logging;
using KPCLib;

using PassXYZ.Vault.Services;
using PassXYZ.Vault.Views;
```

```
namespace PassXYZ.Vault.ViewModels {
  [QueryProperty(nameof(ItemId), nameof(ItemId))]                  //(1)
  public partial class ItemsViewModel : BaseViewModel {
    readonly IDataStore<Item> dataStore;
    ILogger<ItemsViewModel> logger;

    public ObservableCollection<Item> Items { get; }

    public ItemsViewModel(IDataStore<Item> dataStore,
      ILogger<ItemsViewModel> logger) {
      this.dataStore = dataStore;
      this.logger = logger;
      Title = "Browse";
      Items = new ObservableCollection<Item>();
      IsBusy = false;
    }

    [ObservableProperty]
    private Item? selectedItem = default;

    [ObservableProperty]
    private string? title;

    [ObservableProperty]
    private bool isBusy;

    [RelayCommand]
    private async Task AddItem(object obj) {
      await Shell.Current.GoToAsync(nameof(NewItemPage));
    }

    public override async void OnItemSelecteion(object sender) {
      Item? item = sender as Item;
      if (item == null)
      {
        logger.LogWarning("item is null.");
```

```
      return;
    }
    logger.LogDebug($"Selected item is {item.Name}");
    if (item.IsGroup)
    {
      await Shell.Current.GoToAsync(                          //(3)
        $"{nameof(ItemsPage)}?
        {nameof(ItemsViewModel.ItemId)}={item.Id}");
    }
    else
    {
      await Shell.Current.GoToAsync(                          //(4)
        $"{nameof(ItemDetailPage)}?
        {nameof(ItemDetailViewModel.ItemId)}={item.Id}");
    }
}


[RelayCommand]
private async Task LoadItems() {
  try {
    Items.Clear();
    var items = await dataStore.GetItemsAsync(true);
    foreach (var item in items) {
        Items.Add(item);
    }
    logger.LogDebug($"IsBusy={IsBusy},
      added {Items.Count()} items");
  }
  catch (Exception ex) {
    logger.LogError("{ex}", ex);
  }
  finally {
    IsBusy = false;
    logger.LogDebug("Set IsBusy to false");
  }
}


public string ItemId {                                       //(2)
```

```
        get {
            return SelectedItem == null ?
              string.Empty : SelectedItem.Id;
        }
        set {
          if (string.IsNullOrEmpty(value))
          {
            SelectedItem = null;
          }
          else {
            var item = dataStore.GetItem(value);
            if (item != null) {
                SelectedItem = item;
            }
            else {
              throw new ArgumentNullException(nameof(ItemId),
                "cannot find the selected item");
            }
          }
        }
      }

      public void OnAppearing() {
        if (SelectedItem == null) {
          Title = dataStore.SetCurrentGroup();
        }
        else {
          Title = dataStore.SetCurrentGroup(SelectedItem);
        }
        // Load items
        logger.LogDebug($"Loading group {Title}");
        IsBusy = true;
      }
    }
  }
```

Listing 5.2: `ItemsViewModel.cs` *(*`https://epa.ms/ItemsViewModel5-2`*)*

Based on the item type, we might navigate to either the `ItemsPage` **(3)** or the `ItemDetailPage` **(4)**. In both instances, we transfer the `Id` of the item to the `ItemId` query parameter, which is defined in both the `ItemsViewModel` and the `ItemDetailViewModel`.

In the context of *Listing 5.2*, **(1)** `ItemId` is established as the `QueryPropertyAttribute` within the `ItemsViewModel`. The first argument of `QueryPropertyAttribute` corresponds to the name of the property designated to receive the data, which in this instance is `ItemId` **(2)**.

The second argument corresponds to the `id` parameter. Upon selecting a group from the list, the view model's `OnItemSelected` method **(3)** is triggered and the item `Id` of the chosen group is passed as the value for the `ItemId` query parameter.

When the `ItemsPage` is loaded along with the `ItemId` query parameter, the `ItemId` property **(2)** gets set. In the setter of the `ItemId` property, we examine whether the query parameter value is empty. If it is empty, it might be our initial navigation to the `RootPage` route without any query parameter. In this case, we just set `SelectedItem` to `null`.

If it is not empty, we will find the item and set it to `SelectedItem`.

(4) If we select an entry from the list, we can navigate to `ItemDetailPage` with the item `Id` as the value of the query parameter. To accommodate this query parameter, we can modify the `ItemId` property of the `ItemDetailViewModel` as follows:

```
[QueryProperty(nameof(ItemId), nameof(ItemId))]
public partial class ItemDetailViewModel : BaseViewModel
{
    readonly IDataStore<Item> dataStore;
    ILogger<ItemDetailViewModel> logger;
    public ObservableCollection<Field> Fields { get; set; }

    public ItemDetailViewModel(IDataStore<Item> dataStore,
        ILogger<ItemDetailViewModel> logger) {
            this.dataStore = dataStore;
            this.logger = logger;
            Fields = new ObservableCollection<Field>();
    }

    [ObservableProperty]
    private string? title;
```

```
    [ObservableProperty]
    private string? id;

    [ObservableProperty]
    private string? description;

    [ObservableProperty]
    private bool isBusy;

    private string? itemId;
    public string ItemId {                                              //(1)
      get {
        if(itemId == null) {
          throw new NullReferenceException(nameof(itemId));
        }
        return itemId;
      }

      set {
        itemId = value;
        LoadItemId(value);                                              //(2)
      }
    }

    public override void OnItemSelecteion(object sender) {
        logger.LogDebug("OnItemSelecteion is invoked.");
    }

    public void LoadItemId(string itemId) {
      if (itemId == null) {
        throw new ArgumentNullException(nameof(itemId)); }
      var item = dataStore.GetItem(itemId);                             //(3)
  if (item == null) {
    throw new NullReferenceException(itemId); }
      Id = item.Id;
      Title = item.Name;
      Description = item.Description;
```

```
    if (!item.IsGroup)
    {
      PwEntry dataEntry = (PwEntry)item;                        //(4)
      Fields.Clear();
      List<Field> fields = dataEntry.GetFields(
        GetImage: FieldIcons.GetImage);                         //(5)
      foreach (Field field in fields) {
          Fields.Add(field);
      }
      logger.LogDebug($"ItemDetailViewModel:
        Name={dataEntry.Name}.");
    }
  }
}
```

In the `ItemDetailViewModel` class, we implement the following logic:

- `ItemId` **(1)** serves as the property that accepts the query parameter.
- When setting the `ItemId`, the `LoadItemId` method **(2)** is called to load the item.
- Within `LoadItemId`, the data service method `GetItem` **(3)** is called to obtain the item using its corresponding `Id`.
- In this case, the item is an instance of `PwEntry` **(4)**, which can be cast accordingly.
- The PassXYZLib extension method, `GetFields` **(5)**, is utilized to update the list of fields.

In the previous two sections, we acquired knowledge of basic navigation and `Shell` navigation and enhanced our navigation design using `Shell`. At this point, it is essential to revisit the MVVM pattern and further refine our data model to improve the quality of our password manager app.

Improving our app

In *Chapter 4, Exploring MVVM and Data Binding*, we analyzed various use cases and developed a few. In this section, utilizing the knowledge we have acquired, we will augment the existing use cases and introduce new ones.

We will be working on the following use cases:

- **Use case 1**: As a password manager user, I want to log in to the password manager app so that I can access my password data.

In this use case, we have not yet fully implemented user login; we plan to complete this in the subsequent chapter. For now, we will implement a pseudo-logic that encompasses all aspects except the data layer.

Previously, in *Chapter 4, Exploring MVVM and Data Binding*, we covered a use case that supports one level of navigation.

- **Use case 3**: As a password manager user, I want to see a list of groups and entries so that I can explore my password data.

To accommodate multiple levels of navigation, we will implement the following use cases in this section:

- **Use case 6**: As a password manager user, when I click on a group in the current list, I want to see the groups and entries belonging to that group.
- **Use case 7**: As a password manager user, when navigating through my password data, I want to be able to go back to the previous group or parent group.

In the previous implementation (use case 1), after login, we implemented the navigation to the root page using an absolute route. However, the implementation of the `LoginService` is not done yet. We need to implement it in this chapter.

After loading the root page (use case 3), at present, we can only browse the root-level entries and groups. We are not yet able to enter a child group from the root level. To address this limitation, we are introducing use cases 6 and 7 in this chapter. In use cases 6 and 7, we aim to navigate forward and backward using relative routes.

With the MVVM pattern, we access our model through services, which are typically abstracted as interfaces, separate from the actual implementation. The `IDataStore` interface is an example of this. In order to support use case 6 and enhance use case 1, we need to develop a new interface called `IUserService` for user login support.

Understanding the improved design

To understand the services and the enhanced model, let's review the enhanced design in *Figure 5.7*:

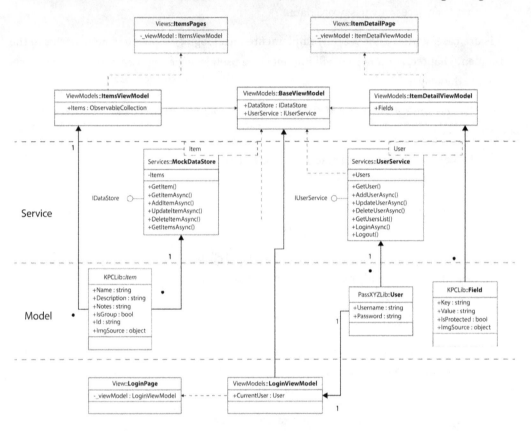

Figure 5.7: Model and service in MVVM

Figure 5.7 presents a class diagram that illustrates the majority of our design. To comprehend the design of our app, we can examine this class diagram in conjunction with the table provided. For the sake of simplicity, I have excluded some elements. For instance, you can add the `NewItemPage` or `SignUpPage` to *Figure 5.7* and *Table 5.3* by yourself.

Model		View	View Model
Data Model	**Service**		
`User`	`IUserService`	`LoginPage`	`LoginViewModel`
`Item`	`IDataStore`	`ItemsPage`	`ItemsViewModel`
`Field`		`ItemDetailPage`	`ItemDetailViewModel`

Table 5.3: Classes and interfaces in the MVVM pattern

Registering absolute routes and relative routes

In this section, when introducing pages and routes, you may notice that the names of pages and routes could be the same. To distinguish between them, I'll use bold font to identify a page and italic font to identify a route.

In our application, both absolute and relative routes are registered within the AppShell class. The absolute routes, *LoginPage*, *SignUpPage*, *RootPage*, and *AboutPage*, are created as parts of the Shell. Conversely, the relative routes – *ItemsPage*, *ItemDetailPage*, and *NewItemPage* – are defined within the constructor of the AppShell.

To facilitate multi-level navigation, the page **ItemsPage** is registered as both the absolute route *RootPage* and the relative route *ItemsPage*.

Upon application loading, the route *LoginPage* is utilized. Post-login, the app navigates to *RootPage*. If a user selects a child group, the relative route *ItemsPage* is loaded, thereby permitting navigation deeper into multi-levels. When a user selects an entry, the relative route *ItemsDetailPage* is loaded.

Model and services

To save application data, we typically store it in a database, which could be either a relational database or a NoSQL database. In our case, our password database is not a relational database. Nevertheless, while working on our design, we can employ the analogous logic of relational databases when formulating our business logic. Our model is represented by three distinct classes – User, Item, and Field.

In the context of our design, Item and Field represent a password entry and the content within that entry, respectively. An entry can be visualized as a row in a table, with a field acting as a cell. To model a password entry, we employ the PwEntry from KeePassLib. In this instance, a group refers to a collection of entries, and PwGroup is utilized to model this group. A group can be compared to a table within a database, and fields that share the same key values across a group are akin to a column. In order to develop the interface for our data services, we can adopt a similar approach for processing data within our database.

How can we manage data within a database? You might be familiar with the term CRUD operations. In our situation, we can employ the augmented create, read, update, delete, and list (**CRUDL**) operations for defining the interface of our service.

To process password entries and groups, we can use the following `IDataStore` interface:

```
public interface IDataStore<T>
{
    T? GetItem(string id, bool SearchRecursive = false);
    Task<T?> GetItemAsync(string id, bool SearchRecursive =
        false);
    Task AddItemAsync(T item);
    Task UpdateItemAsync(T item);
    Task<bool> DeleteItemAsync(string id);
    Task<IEnumerable<T>> GetItemsAsync(bool forceRefresh =
        false);
}
```

In the `IDataStore` interface, we define the following CRUDL operations:

- **Create**: We use `AddItemAsync` to add an entry or a group
- **Read**: We use `GetItem` or `GetItemAsync` to read an entry or a group
- **Update**: We use `UpdateItemAsync` to update an entry or a group
- **Delete**: We use `DeleteItemAsync` to delete an entry or a group
- **List**: We use `GetItemsAsync` to get a list of entries and groups in the current group

To manage users, we can utilize the following `IUserService` interface:

```
public interface IUserService<T>
{
    T GetUser(string username);
    Task AddUserAsync(T user);
    Task DeleteUserAsync(T user);
    List<string> GetUsersList();
    Task<bool> LoginAsync(T user);
    void Logout();
}
```

We can define a set of CRUDL operations to handle users as well:

- **Create**: We can create a new user using `AddUserAsync`
- **Read**: We can get the user information using `GetUser`
- **Delete**: We can delete a user using `DeleteUserAsync`

- **List**: We can get a list of users using `GetUsersList`
- **LoginAsync** and **Logout**: We can log in or log out using an instance of `User`

To remove the dependencies between the model and service, we can employ generic types in the interface definition, rather than utilizing concrete types. To decouple the dependency between services and view models, we can introduce instances of these services into our view models via dependency injection, a concept that will be elaborated upon in the subsequent chapter. The following code snippet demonstrates how to inject `IDataStore` into `ItemsViewModel` using constructor injection as an example:

```
readonly IDataStore<Item> dataStore;
ILogger<ItemsViewModel> logger;

public ObservableCollection<Item> Items { get; }

public ItemsViewModel(IDataStore<Item> dataStore, ILogger<ItemsViewModel>
logger)
{
  this.dataStore = dataStore;
  this.logger = logger;
  Title = "Browse";
  Items = new ObservableCollection<Item>();
  IsBusy = false;
}
```

In the constructor of `ItemsViewModel` class, we initialize the `IDataStore` and `ILogger` services through a dependency injection.

Implementation of IUserService

In our application, the `UserService` class serves as the implementation of the `IUserService` interface. The code for this can be found in *Listing 5.3*. For the sake of simplifying the testing process, we have not implemented all features in this chapter, as we continue to utilize a mock data store:

```
using KPCLib;
using Microsoft.Extensions.Logging;
using System.Collections.ObjectModel;
using User = PassXYZLib.User;

namespace PassXYZ.Vault.Services;
```

```csharp
public class UserService : IUserService<User>
{
  readonly IDataStore<Item> dataStore;
  ILogger<UserService> logger;
  private User? _user = default;

  public UserService(IDataStore<Item> dataStore,            //(1)
    ILogger<UserService> logger) {
    this.dataStore = dataStore;
    this.logger = logger;
  }

  public User GetUser(string username) {
    User user = new User();
    user.Username = username;
    logger.LogDebug($"Path={user.Path}");
    return user;
  }

  public async Task DeleteUserAsync(User user) {
    await Task.Run(() => {
      logger.LogDebug($"Remove Path={user.Path}");
    });
  }

  public List<string> GetUsersList() {
    return User.GetUsersList();
  }

  public async Task AddUserAsync(User user) {
    if (user == null) {
        throw new ArgumentNullException(nameof(user), "User cannot be
          null"); }
    _user = user;

    await dataStore.SignUpAsync(user);
```

```
        }

    public async Task<bool> LoginAsync(User user) {
        if (user == null) {
            throw new ArgumentNullException(nameof(user), "User cannot be
                null"); }
        _user = user;

        return await dataStore.ConnectAsync(user);
    }

    public void Logout() {
        dataStore.Close();
        logger.LogDebug("Logout");
    }
    }
```

Listing 5.3: `UserService.cs` *(https://epa.ms/UserService5-3)*

In the `UserService` constructor **(1)**, an `IDataStore` instance is initialized via dependency injection. The available functions can be classified into two types. Functions such as `GetUser`, `DeleteUserAsync`, and `GetUserList` can be implemented using methods from the `User` class. Meanwhile, methods like `AddUserAsync`, `LoginAsync`, and `Logout` are implemented using the `IDataStore` instance.

Improving the login process

In the process of user management, we may need to add new users or remove outdated users from the system. For our app, it only allows one user to log in at a time. To support this feature, we can implement a class using the singleton pattern. Alternatively, we can implement a class and utilize dependency injection to have a similar effect on the singleton pattern. For instance, we can create a `LoginService` class that inherits from the `User` class, as demonstrated in *Listing 5.4*:

```
using System.Diagnostics;

using PassXYZLib;

namespace PassXYZ.Vault.Services;
```

```csharp
public class LoginService : PxUser {                              //(1)
  private IUserService<User> _userService;
  private const string PrivacyNotice = "Privacy Notice";

  public static bool IsPrivacyNoticeAccepted {
    get => Preferences.Get(PrivacyNotice, false);
    set => Preferences.Set(PrivacyNotice, value);
  }

  public LoginService(IUserService<User> userService) {
    _userService = userService;                                   //(2)
  }

  public async Task<bool> LoginAsync() {
    return await _userService.LoginAsync(this);                   //(3)
  }

  public async Task SignUpAsync() {
    await _userService.AddUserAsync(this);                        //(4)
  }

  public override void Logout() {
    _userService.Logout();
  }

  public async Task<string> GetSecurityAsync() {
    if (string.IsNullOrWhiteSpace(Username)) {
      return string.Empty; }

    string data = await SecureStorage.GetAsync(Username);
    return data;
  }

  public async Task SetSecurityAsync(string password) {
    if (string.IsNullOrWhiteSpace(Username) ||
      string.IsNullOrWhiteSpace(password)) { return; }
```

```
      await SecureStorage.SetAsync(Username, password);
   }

   public async Task<bool> DisableSecurityAsync() {
      ...
   }
}
```

Listing 5.4: `LoginService.cs` (`https://epa.ms/LoginService5-4`)

(1) The LoginService class is derived from the PxUser subclass, which in turn inherits from the User class.

(2) Within LoginService, we initialize the IUserService interface through dependency injection.

(3) To execute user login, we can invoke the IUserService method by passing a LoginService instance as the argument. **(4)** The same process is applicable in the case of user signup.

Login view model

After introducing the model and service layer, we can now focus on the view model and view for the login and signup functionality. Let's start by examining the implementation of the view model, as presented in *Listing 5.5*:

```
using CommunityToolkit.Mvvm.ComponentModel;
using CommunityToolkit.Mvvm.Input;
using Microsoft.Extensions.Logging;

using PassXYZLib;
using PassXYZ.Vault.Views;
using PassXYZ.Vault.Services;
using System.Diagnostics;

namespace PassXYZ.Vault.ViewModels
{
   public partial class LoginViewModel : ObservableObject
   {
      private LoginService _currentUser;
      ILogger<LoginViewModel> _logger;

      public LoginViewModel(LoginService user,                    //(1)
```

```
   ILogger<LoginViewModel> logger)
{
  _currentUser = user;
  _logger = logger;
}


[RelayCommand(CanExecute = nameof(ValidateLogin))]
private async Task Login(object obj)
{
  ...
  bool status = await _currentUser.LoginAsync();              //(2)
  ...
}


private bool ValidateLogin()
{
  var canExecute = !String.IsNullOrWhiteSpace(Username)
      && !String.IsNullOrWhiteSpace(Password);
  return canExecute;
}


[RelayCommand(CanExecute = nameof(ValidateSignUp))]
private async Task SignUp()
{
  ...
  await _currentUser.SignUpAsync();                          //(3)
  ...
}


private bool ValidateSignUp()
{
  var canExecute = !String.IsNullOrWhiteSpace(Username)
      && !String.IsNullOrWhiteSpace(Password)
      && !String.IsNullOrWhiteSpace(Password2);

  if (canExecute) {
      return Password!.Equals(Password2);
```

```
    }

    return canExecute;
  }

  [ObservableProperty]
  private bool isBusy = false;

  [ObservableProperty]
  [NotifyCanExecuteChangedFor(nameof(LoginCommand))]              //(4)
  [NotifyCanExecuteChangedFor(nameof(SignUpCommand))]
  private string? username = default;

  [ObservableProperty]
  [NotifyCanExecuteChangedFor(nameof(LoginCommand))]
  [NotifyCanExecuteChangedFor(nameof(SignUpCommand))]
  private string? password = default;

  [ObservableProperty]
  [NotifyCanExecuteChangedFor(nameof(SignUpCommand))]
  private string? password2 = default;

  public bool IsDeviceLockEnabled
  {
    ...
  }

  public List<string> GetUsersList() {
      return User.GetUsersList();
  }

  public void Logout() {
    _currentUser.Logout();
  }
  }
}
```

Listing 5.5: LoginViewModel.cs *(https://epa.ms/LoginViewModel5-5)*

(1) In the `LoginViewModel`, we inject an instance of `LoginService` through dependency injection and save it in the private member variable `_currentUser`. This variable is utilized to track all login and signup activities.

Subsequently, we created the `LoginCommand` **(2)** and `SignUpCommand` **(3)** using the `RelayCommand` attribute from the .NET Community Toolkit. Within these functions, we call the `LoginAsync` and `SignUpAsync` methods from the `LoginService`.

To validate both commands, we created the `ValidateLogin` and `ValidateSignUp` methods to perform the necessary checks. In `ValidateLogin`, we ensure that both the username and password are not empty before allowing the login process to proceed. In `ValidateSignUp`, we not only verify the username and password but also confirm that the password and confirmation password fields match. **(4)** To trigger the validation methods, the `NotifyCanExecuteChangedFor` attribute is added to decorate the properties. This is part of the MVVM toolkit implementation, which we discussed in *Chapter 4, Exploring MVVM and Data Binding*.

Now, we have upgraded our model and services to optimize the login process. Reviewing the class diagram in *Figure 5.7*, we have modified the source code at the view, view model, and service layers to improve our application. The actual model is contained within two libraries, `KPCLib` and `PassXYZLib`. We have exposed the capabilities of these libraries through the `IDataStore` and `IUserService` interfaces. By creating the implementing classes for these two interfaces, we have further enhanced our model. In the following section, we will focus on the view layer and examine the upgraded UI.

Login UI

We can now enhance the login and signup UI. Currently, the login page only contains a single button. Let's add a username field and a password field to `LoginPage.xaml`, as illustrated in *Figure 5.8*.

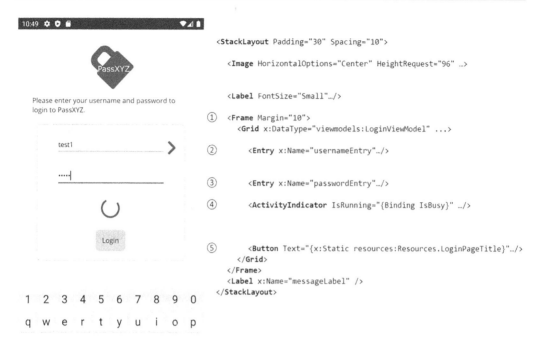

Figure 5.8: LoginPage

In this new UI design, we made the following changes:

- We created a 4x3 grid layout within a frame. **(1)**

- In the first two rows, we added two Entry controls to hold the username **(2)** and password **(3)**. We established a data binding between the Text fields of the Entry controls and the properties of the LoginViewModel.

- In the third row, we incorporated an ActivityIndicator control **(4)** to display the login status, which is bound to the IsBusy property of the view model.

- In the final row, we defined a Button control **(5)** for the login action. The Button control has a Command property that implements the ICommand interface. We used data binding to link this Command property to the method in the view model responsible for performing the login action.

Summary

In this chapter, we focused on fundamental navigation principles and the `Shell` framework. We chose `Shell` as the navigation foundation for our app design, examined its capabilities, and discussed how to integrate it into our app's UI.

After we completed most of the UI design, we enhanced our model by making changes to two service interfaces: `IDataStore` and `IUserService`. We improved the login process after making changes in the view, view model, and service layers. In the service layer, we are still using the `MockDataStore` class. However, we haven't finalized the implementation in the `IDataStore` service to perform the actual login activities yet. We will leave this to the next chapter.

Upon completing the majority of the UI design, we proceeded to refine our model by modifying two service interfaces: `IDataStore` and `IUserService`. By making alterations in the view, view model, and service layers, we enhanced the login process. In the service layer, we continued to utilize the `MockDataStore` class. However, the implementation of the `IDataStore` service for performing actual login activities has yet to be finalized, and we will address this in the subsequent chapter.

In the next chapter, we will delve into dependency injection in .NET MAUI, which is done quite differently compared to Xamarin.Forms. We will instruct you on how to register our services using dependency injection and how to initialize our service via constructor injection or property injection. Furthermore, we will develop the actual service to supersede the `MockDataStore`.

Learn more on Discord

Join our community's Discord space for discussions with the author and other readers:

```
https://packt.link/cross-platform-app
```

6

Software Design with Dependency Injection

Having introduced navigation and the Shell in .NET MAUI, we've laid the groundwork for building a comprehensive application. However, we are currently utilizing a mock data service, which we intend to modify in this chapter. Before diving into this, let's first review the best practices in software design, starting with an overview of design principles. Later, we will explore how to leverage dependency injection in our application.

Software design principles and patterns typically form the backbone of best practices in software design. These principles offer rules and guidelines that software designers adhere to in crafting an efficient and clean design structure. They play a key role in shaping the software design process as they dictate the most effective practices. Design patterns are effectively best practices that experienced developers in object-oriented software employ. They function as templates designed to address repetitive design problems in specific contexts, offering reusable solutions that can be applied to prevalent issues in software design.

Dependency Injection (DI) is a software design pattern and technique that ensures a class is not dependent on its dependencies. It achieves this through decoupling an object's utilization from its creation. The goal here is to create a system that is more adaptable, modular, and simpler to debug and maintain. DI is embodied in the **Dependency Inversion Principle (DIP)**, one of the five SOLID principles in object-oriented programming and design.

In this chapter, we will explore the following topics:

- A brief overview of design principles
- Implementing DI
- Replacing the mock data store

DI is a method for implementing the design principle of dependency inversion, also known as the DIP. The DIP is one of the SOLID design principles, and we will learn how to incorporate SOLID principles into our design process. An overview of the SOLID design principles will be provided at the beginning of this chapter, before delving into the discussion on DI.

Technical requirements

To test and debug the source code in this chapter, you need to have Visual Studio 2022 installed on your PC or Mac. Please refer to the *Development environment setup* section in *Chapter 1, Getting Started with .NET MAUI*, for the details.

The source code for this chapter is available in the following branch on GitHub: `https://github.com/PacktPublishing/.NET-MAUI-Cross-Platform-Application-Development-Second-edition/tree/main/2nd/chapter06`.

To check out the source code of this chapter, we can use the below command:

```
$ git clone -b 2nd/chapter06 https://github.com/PacktPublishing/.NET-MAUI-
Cross-Platform-Application-Development-Second-edition.git PassXYZ.Vault2
```

To find out more about the source code in this book, please refer to the *Managing the source code in this book* section in *Chapter 2, Building Our First .NET MAUI App*.

A brief overview of design principles

Design principles are high-level guidelines that offer valuable advice on design considerations. These principles can provide essential guidance to help you make better design decisions. Some general design principles are applicable not only to software design but also to other design disciplines.

Let's review some general design principles before we explore the commonly used design principles (SOLID) in software development.

Exploring types of design principles

Design principles encompass a vast subject area. Thus, rather than delving into intricate details, I will provide insights from my experiences in implementing design principles during development, offering a concise overview of the principles discussed in this book. We will begin with high-level principles such as **DRY**, **KISS**, and **YAGNI**, and then progress to those more commonly used in software development. In the realm of **object-oriented programming** (**OOP**), the most widely used design principles are the SOLID principles.

Don't Repeat Yourself (DRY)

As people often say, don't reinvent the wheel; we should strive to reuse existing components instead of redeveloping what has already been created.

Keep It Simple, Stupid (KISS)

We should choose a simple and straightforward approach rather than involve unnecessary complexity in a design.

You Aren't Gonna Need It (YAGNI)

We should implement functionality when it is required. In software development, there is a tendency to futureproof a design. This may create something that is actually not needed and increase the complexity of the solution.

SOLID design principles

SOLID design principles are widely employed in software development and serve as high-level guidelines for numerous design patterns. SOLID is an acronym that encapsulates the following five principles:

- **Single Responsibility Principle (SRP)**: A class should have a single responsibility. Adhering to this design principle, a developer should have only one reason to modify a class. By considering this principle during implementation, the resulting code becomes easier to comprehend and more effectively adapts to evolving requirements.

- **Open/Closed Principle (OCP)**: Classes should be open for extension but closed for modification. The central concept behind this principle is to prevent disruptions to existing code when introducing new features.

- **Liskov Substitution Principle (LSP)**: If the object of the parent type can be used in a context, an object with a child type should also be able to function in the same manner without causing any errors or disruptions.

- **Interface Segregation Principle (ISP):** A design should not implement an interface that it doesn't use, and a class should not be forced to depend on methods it doesn't intend to implement. We should design concise and simple interfaces rather than large and complex ones.

- **Dependency Inversion Principle (DIP):** This principle emphasizes the decoupling of software modules. High-level modules should not depend on low-level modules directly. Both should depend on abstractions. Abstractions should not depend on details. Details should depend on abstractions.

Design principles are guidelines to help us to make better design decisions. However, the responsibility ultimately lies with us to determine the most suitable course of action during the actual implementation, rather than solely relying on these principles.

Since we will focus on the usage of DI in this chapter, please refer to the *Further reading* section to find more information about design principles (SOLID) and design patterns.

Using design principles

Having discussed various design principles, allow me to share insights and lessons learned from implementing them in practice.

In our app's model, I utilized the **KeePassLib** from Dominik Reichl. While porting it to .NET Standard, I modified the inheritance hierarchy, as depicted in *Figure 6.1*:

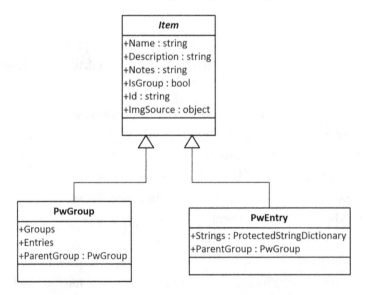

Figure 6.1: Class diagram of Item, PwEntry, and PwGroup

In the process of porting KeePassLib to .NET Standard, I developed an abstract parent class, `Item`, for the group (`PwGroup`) and entry (`PwEntry`). This modification appears to violate OCP within the SOLID principles. The rationale behind this approach is rooted in a lesson I learned from the past implementation.

In earlier versions, prior to 1.2.3, I had not implemented **KPCLib** in the manner described. Instead, I directly used `PwGroup` and `PwEntry`, which required handling groups and entries separately. This resulted in increased complexity in `ItemsPage` and `ItemsViewModel`. This approach's most significant consequence was the inability to distinctly separate the model and the view model. Consequently, I had to manage numerous details using **KeePassLib** directly within the view model. However, upon introducing the `Item` abstract parent class, I successfully concealed most of the intricate implementation within services (`IDataStore` and `IUserService`) and `PassXYZLib`. This led to the elimination of any code reliant on KeePassLib within the view and view model.

The inspiration behind this change came from the KISS principle rather than merely adhering to OCP. When considering other SOLID principles, such as LSP and SRP, this modification significantly improved the overall architecture. It's essential to recognize that, in practical work, conflicts can arise among various design principles. It is ultimately our responsibility to make informed decisions instead of adhering dogmatically to design principles. The most effective design decisions typically arise from the insights gained from prior failures.

Returning to our main focus, we will now discuss enhancing the design by employing one of the SOLID principles—dependency inversion. As part of the SOLID design principles, dependency inversion emphasizes the separation of software modules, and it also provides guidelines on how to achieve this. The fundamental concept behind it is the preference of relying on abstractions whenever possible. In practice, DI is a technique routinely used to implement the idea of dependency inversion.

Implementing DI

DI is a technique that can be utilized in .NET MAUI. Although not a novel concept, it has been extensively employed in backend frameworks like ASP.NET Core and the Java Spring Framework. DI facilitates dependency inversion (DIP) by decoupling an object's usage from its creation, eliminating the need for direct reliance on the object. In our app, once we have separated the `IDataStore` interface implementation, we can commence with a mock implementation and subsequently replace it with the actual implementation.

In .NET MAUI, the `Microsoft.Extensions.DependencyInjection` service, which we will refer to as MS.DI throughout this chapter, is readily available for us to utilize as a built-in feature.

In the realm of .NET, numerous DI containers are available besides MS.DI. Some of these alternatives, such as the Autofac DI container and the Simple Injector DI container, offer enhanced power and flexibility compared to MS.DI. At this point, one may wonder why we are choosing MS.DI over the other potent and adaptable DI containers. It is essential to revisit the KISS and YAGNI principles in this context. We should not opt for a more powerful solution with the assumption that we may utilize certain features in the future. Instead, the most straightforward and efficient approach is to leverage what we already possess without any additional effort.

With MS.DI, we can avoid introducing extra dependencies. Regardless of our intention to use it, it is already incorporated in the .NET MAUI configuration. By simply adding a few lines of code, we can enhance our design. Alternative DI containers may offer more sophisticated features, but we would need to include additional dependencies and perform the necessary configuration in our code before utilizing them. If you are working on a complex system design, it's recommended to evaluate the available DI containers and select the most suitable one for your system. In our scenario, **PassXYZ.Vault** is a relatively straightforward app, and we will not directly benefit from the advanced DI features offered by Autofac or Simple Injector. The functionalities provided by MS.DI are adequate for our implementation.

In our app, the module we aim to decouple is the model layer, which derives from a third-party library provided by KeePass. As depicted in the package diagram in *Figure 6.2*, our system comprises three distinct assemblies: **KPCLib**, **PassXYZLib**, and **PassXYZ.Vault**.

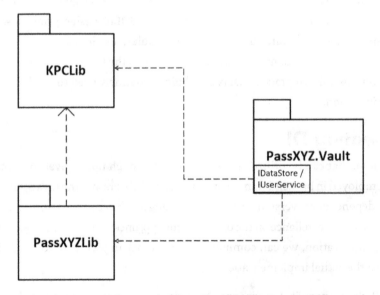

Figure 6.2: Package diagram

The **KPCLib** package encompasses two namespaces, **KeePassLib** and **KPCLib. PassXYZLib** serves as an extension package to augment the **KPCLib** package's functionality using .NET MAUI-specific implementation. **PassXYZ.Vault**, our app, relies directly on the **PassXYZLib** package and indirectly on the **KPCLib** package. In accordance with the DI principle, we aim to establish dependencies on abstractions rather than concrete implementations. To achieve this, we have designed two interfaces, IDataStore and IUserService, which enable us to decouple from the actual implementations.

The actual implementations that require access to KPCLib and PassXYZLib are encapsulated in the classes that implement these two interfaces: IDataStore and IUserService. The remainder of the code needed to access the functionalities in **KPCLib** and **PassXYZLib** can utilize these two interfaces. The key point is that we always have the flexibility to replace the implementations of IDataStore and IUserService if necessary. The remaining code will not be affected by these changes.

In order to utilize MS.DI as a DI service, two primary steps are involved: registration and resolution.

Initially, we must register our interfaces (such as IDataStore) and their corresponding implementations (such as MockDataStore) during the program's startup. Following that, we can utilize these registered interfaces throughout our program without manually creating them. We can then resolve these registered dependencies using the DI container.

The ServiceCollection class serves as the means for registration, while the ServiceProvider class facilitates resolution, as depicted in *Figure 6.3*:

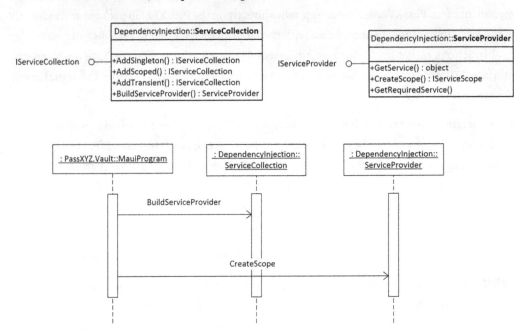

Figure 6.3: Usage of MS.DI

Figure 6.3 presents a simplified class diagram of ServiceCollection and ServiceProvider at the top. ServiceCollection serves as the default implementation of the IServiceCollection interface, while ServiceProvider acts as the default implementation of the IServiceProvider interface.

These interfaces, IServiceCollection and IServiceProvider, allow us to register and resolve dependencies. At the bottom of *Figure 6.3*, there's a sequence diagram illustrating how to use both interfaces to achieve this. For a clearer understanding, we'll use the IDataStore service as an example to explain the utilization of IServiceCollection and IServiceProvider.

To utilize DI for implementing the IDataStore service, we can follow the steps outlined in the subsequent code block:

```
// Registration
var services = new ServiceCollection();                          //(1)
services.AddSingleton <IDataStore<Item>, MockDataStore>();       //(2)
// Resolution
```

```
ServiceProvider provider =
    services.BuildServiceProvider(validateScopes: true);        //(3)
IDataStore<Item> dataStore =
    provider.GetRequiredService<IDataStore<Item>>();            //(4)
```

(1) To begin, we must first create an instance of the `ServiceCollection` class that implements the `IServiceCollection` interface.

(2) The `IServiceCollection` interface does not inherently specify any methods. Instead, a collection of extension methods is defined in the MS.DI namespace. Among these, the `AddSingleton` extension method can be utilized to register the concrete `MockDataStore` class that implements the `IDataStore` interface. The method `AddSingleton` is explained in the following section. This method employs a generic type to specify both the interface and its implementation. Additionally, there are several overloaded variations of the `AddSingleton` extension method at your disposal.

(3) In order to access objects, we can obtain an instance of `ServiceProvider` by invoking the `BuildServiceProvider` extension method associated with `IServiceCollection`. The `ServiceProvider` class complies with the `IServiceProvider` interface. Notably, the `IServiceProvider` interface is located within the `System` namespace and exclusively defines the `GetService` method. Additional methods are designated as extension methods and can be found in the `Microsoft.Extensions.DependencyInjection` namespace, as illustrated in *Figure 6.3*.

(4) Once we have an instance of `ServiceProvider`, we can resolve the `IDataStore` interface using the `GetRequiredService` extension method.

To manage the scope of a service, we can resolve it within the scope as follows:

```
IServiceScope scope = provider.CreateScope();
IDataStore<Item> dataStore = scope.ServiceProvider
    .GetRequiredService<IDataStore<Item>>();
```

We will discuss the scope in the next section.

Though MS.DI is a lightweight DI service, it offers a sufficient range of features for .NET MAUI applications, as outlined below:

- Lifetime management of instances
- Constructor, method, and property injections

In the upcoming sections, we will delve deeper into these features.

Lifetime management

When using DI, you should consider how long instances of a registered service should be reused or retained before they are disposed of or new instances are created. Lifetime management is crucial in defining the scope within which a service instance is generated and shared.

Here are a few aspects to consider for lifecycle management:

- **Resource management**: Resources, such as database connections utilized by a service, should not be left open indefinitely. For example, if a singleton service keeps a database connection open, it holds that resource for the application's lifespan.

- **Performance**: It might not always be the most efficient approach to create a new instance of a service each time it's needed, particularly if constructing the service is resource-intensive.

- **Isolation**: If your service requires isolation (for instance, if it maintains some state), it's essential to configure its lifecycle in accordance with the scope that satisfies such isolation requirements.

- **Threading issues**: Singleton services need to be thread-safe as they're shared among different requests, usually processed in parallel on separate threads.

Using MS.DI, we can manage the lifespan of these instances by configuring the `ServiceCollection`.

There are commonly three types of lifetimes in dependency injection, and we can configure them using extension methods:

- **Singleton**: A single instance of the service is created when requested for the first time and then reused for all subsequent requests throughout the application's lifetime. All callers receive the same instance, meaning a singleton service behaves like a shared global resource. Singleton services can retain state and are useful for providing centralized management of resources, such as logging, caching, or configuration. The extension method `AddSingleton` can be used to create a single instance throughout the life of the application.

- **Scoped**: A scoped service creates a new instance per scope, typically per request in a web application. Each scope has its instance of the service, which is shared among all components within that specific scope. Scoped services are useful for maintaining state specific to a single request or user interaction, such as user information, request details, or database connections in a per-request context. The extension method `AddScoped` can be used to create one instance and reuses the same instance within the defined scope.

- **Transient:** Transient services create a new instance each time the service is requested, en-suring that each caller gets a unique instance without sharing state or resources. Transient services are useful for services without an internal state or a need for resource management. They are often lightweight and don't require sharing across different components. The extension method `AddTransient` can be used to create an instance for each call.

In order to illustrate the lifetime management of MS.DI, let's examine the following code snippet in conjunction with *Figure 6.4*:

```
var services = new ServiceCollection();
services.AddSingleton< IUserService<User>, UserService>();        //(1)
services.AddScoped<IDataStore<Item>, DataStore>();                //(1)
services.AddTransient<ItemsViewModel>();                          //(1)
ServiceProvider rootContainer =
    services.BuildServiceProvider(validateScopes: true);         //(2)
var userService =
    rootContainer.GetRequiredService<IUserService<User>>();
IServiceScope scope1 = rootContainer.CreateScope();              //(3)
IDataStore<Item> dataStore1 =
  scope1.ServiceProvider.GetRequiredService<IDataStore<Item>>();
IServiceScope scope2 = rootContainer.CreateScope();              //(3)
IDataStore<Item> dataStore2 = Scope2.ServiceProvider.
GetRequiredService<IDataStore<Item>>();
```

In the aforementioned code, in the lines marked by **(1)**, we registered `IUserService` as a `Singleton` object, `IDataStore` as a `Scoped` object, and `ItemsViewModel` as a `Transient` object.

Following the registration, in the line marked by **(2)**, we instantiated a `ServiceProvider` and stored it in a `rootContainer` variable. In the lines marked by **(3)**, utilizing the `rootContainer`, we generated two scopes, named **scope1** and **scope2**.

The lifetime management of these created objects can be examined in *Figure 6.4*:

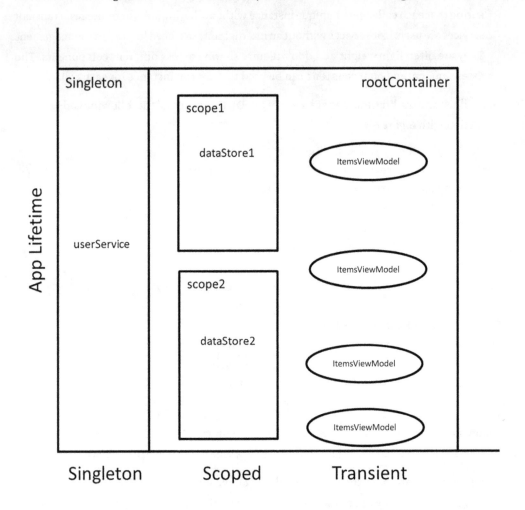

Figure 6.4: Lifetime management in MS.DI

The variable `userService` is created as a `Singleton` object, ensuring that only one instance exists, and its lifetime is equal to that of the application. The two scopes—namely, **scope1** and **scope2**—possess distinct lifetimes determined by our design. The `Scoped` objects—**dataStore1** and **dataStore2**—have the same lifetime as the scope to which they belong. Meanwhile, the instances of `ItemViewModel` are `Transient` objects.

In the case of the three methods—`AddSingleton`, `AddScoped`, and `AddTransient`—numerous overloaded variations have been defined to cater to an array of requirements pertaining to `ServiceCollection` configuration.

In our application, we have two versions of the IDataStore interface implementation:

- DataStore: This version represents the actual implementation.
- MockDataStore: This version is employed for testing purposes.

With MS.DI, we have the ability to utilize MockDataStore in the Debug build and employ DataStore in the Release build. This configuration can be executed as demonstrated in the subsequent code snippet:

```
bool isDebug = false;
var services = new ServiceCollection();
services.AddSingleton<DataStore, DataStore>();
services.AddSingleton<MockDataStore, MockDataStore>();
services.AddSingleton<IDataStore<Item>>(c => {
    if (isDebug)
    {
        return c.GetRequiredService<MockDataStore>();
    }
    else
    {
        return c.GetRequiredService<DataStore>();
    }
});
```

In the code snippet mentioned earlier, we are able to set up concrete classes, DataStore and MockDataStore, and the interface IDataStore for distinct build configurations. When configuring IDataStore, a delegate can be employed to resolve the object. The isDebug variable may be adjusted using build configurations, enabling it to be set as true or false, depending on whether the build is for debugging or release purposes.

Configuring DI in .NET MAUI

MS.DI is incorporated into the .NET release, making it accessible for all types of applications in .NET 5 or subsequent versions. As we discussed in the previous section, we can implement DI using ServiceCollection and ServiceProvider. However, there is a more straightforward approach to utilizing MS.DI in .NET MAUI. With DI integrated as part of the .NET Generic Host configuration, there is no need for us to create an instance of ServiceCollection manually. This allows us to employ the preconfigured DI service directly, without any additional effort.

To gain a deeper understanding of the preconfigured DI service in .NET MAUI, let's revisit the .NET MAUI application startup process as depicted in *Figure 6.5*. This figure encompasses both a class diagram and a sequence diagram, illustrating the classes involved in the process.

Please be aware that the number in *Figure 6.5* represents the type of object (**(1)** = MauiProgram, **(2)** = MauiApp, and **(3)** = MauiAppBuilder):

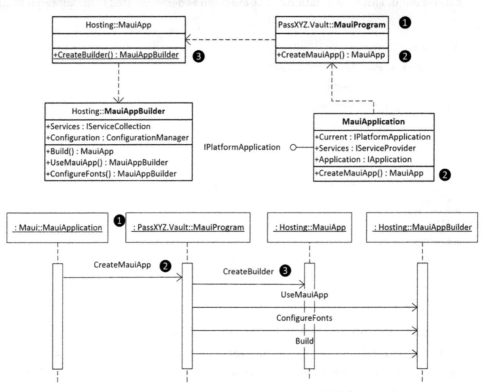

Figure 6.5: .NET MAUI DI configuration

In *Figure 6.5*, at the top, we observe that the initiation of the .NET MAUI application involves four different classes:

- **Platform entry point:** The initiation of the .NET MAUI application occurs in platform-specific code. For the .NET MAUI project, this can be found in the **Platforms** folder. Distinct classes have been defined for each platform, as illustrated in *Table 6.1*. In *Figure 6.5*, we use the MauiApplication Android version as a representative example.

Platform	Entry point class	Implement Interface
Android	`MauiApplication`	
iOS/macOS	`MauiUIApplicationDelegate`	`IPlatformApplication`
Windows	`MauiWinUIApplication`	

Table 6.1: Entry points in different platforms

All entry-point classes implement the `IPlatformApplication` interface, as we can see in the following code snippet:

```
public interface IPlatformApplication
{
    static IPlatformApplication? Current { get; set; }
    IServiceProvider Services { get; }
    IApplication Application { get; }
}
```

The `IPlatformApplication` interface defines a property called `Services`, which is of the type `IServiceProvider`. Once the application is initialized, this property can be utilized directly to resolve DI objects.

All platform entry-point classes also implement an override method, `CreateMauiApp`, which calls the static method `CreateMauiApp` defined in the `MauiProgram` class. Please refer to the following code, *Table 6.1*, and *Figure 6.5*.

- `MauiProgram` (**1**): In the subsequent `MauiProgram` implementation code, it becomes apparent that every .NET MAUI application must define a static `MauiProgram` class and include a `CreateMauiApp` method. The `CreateMauiApp` method gets called by an override function, which is present in all platform entry points. This override function ultimately returns a `MauiApp` instance:

```
protected override MauiApp
    CreateMauiApp() => MauiProgram.CreateMauiApp();
```

- `MauiApp` (**2**): Inside `CreateMauiApp`, it creates a `MauiAppBuilder` instance by calling the function `MauiApp.CreateBuilder`.
- `MauiAppBuilder` (**3**): `MauiAppBuilder` incorporates an attribute called `Services`, which is of the `IServiceCollection` interface type. This attribute allows us to configure DI for the .NET MAUI application.

Based on the above analysis of the .NET MAUI app startup process, it is apparent that both
`IServiceCollection` and `IServiceProvider` are initialized during this procedure. As a result,
we can conveniently utilize them without the need for additional configuration.

The `MauiProgram` implementation can be observed in the code provided below. Here, we have
registered interfaces—`IDataStore` and `IUserService`—as well as multiple classes including
`LoginService`, view models, and pages. It is important to note that all of these components are
singleton objects, except for `ItemsViewModel` and `ItemsPage`:

```
public static class MauiProgram {                                    //(1)
  public static MauiApp CreateMauiApp() {                            //(2)
    var builder = MauiApp.CreateBuilder();                           //(3)
    builder
      .UseMauiApp<App>()
      .ConfigureFonts(fonts => {
        fonts.AddFont("fa-regular-400.ttf",
            "FontAwesomeRegular");
        fonts.AddFont("fa-solid-900.ttf",
            "FontAwesomeSolid");
        fonts.AddFont("fa-brands-400.ttf",
            "FontAwesomeBrands");
        fonts.AddFont("OpenSans-Regular.ttf",
            "OpenSansRegular");
        fonts.AddFont("OpenSans-SemiBold.ttf",
            "OpenSansSemiBold");
      });
#if DEBUG
    builder.Logging.AddDebug();
    builder.Logging.SetMinimumLevel(LogLevel.Debug);
#endif
    builder.Services.AddSingleton<IDataStore<Item>, DataStore>();
    builder.Services.AddSingleton<IUserService<User>, UserService>();
    builder.Services.AddSingleton<LoginService>();
    builder.Services.AddSingleton<LoginViewModel>();
    builder.Services.AddSingleton<LoginPage>();
    builder.Services.AddSingleton<SignUpPage>();
    builder.Services.AddSingleton<ItemDetailViewModel>();
    builder.Services.AddSingleton<ItemDetailPage>();
```

```
builder.Services.AddSingleton<NewItemViewModel>();
builder.Services.AddSingleton<NewItemPage>();
builder.Services.AddSingleton<AboutViewModel>();
builder.Services.AddSingleton<AboutPage>();
builder.Services.AddTransient<ItemsViewModel>();
builder.Services.AddTransient<ItemsPage>();

return builder.Build();   }
}
```

After configuring DI for interfaces and classes, we can utilize them in our implementation. The IServiceProvider interface enables us to resolve objects effectively. When implementing DI, there are three primary methods for injecting dependencies: constructor injection, method injection, and property injection. In the subsequent sections, we will explore how to apply these methods to our programming.

Constructor injection

With constructor injection, the necessary dependencies for a class are supplied as arguments to the constructor, allowing us to resolve dependencies using the constructor itself. In the code-behind of ItemsPage, ItemsPage relies on its view model, ItemsViewModel. We can establish the constructor of ItemsPage as follows:

```
public partial class ItemsPage : ContentPage {
  ItemsViewModel viewModel;

  public ItemsPage(ItemsViewModel viewModel) {
    InitializeComponent();
    BindingContext = this.viewModel = viewModel;
  }

  protected override void OnAppearing() {
    base.OnAppearing();
    viewModel.OnAppearing();
  }
}
```

In the ItemsPage constructor, we inject the dependency through the argument viewModel. In this instance, MS.DI resolves viewModel according to the configuration defined in MauiProgram.

Constructor injection is the most common and most advised form of DI because the object always gets created with the required dependencies. The biggest advantage is that it makes dependencies explicit, and the object never exists in an incomplete state.

Often, it may not be feasible to inject dependencies through the constructor, such as when a class comprises optional dependencies or when there's a need to alter dependencies dynamically. In these circumstances, utilizing method injection or property injection would be the recommended approach.

Method injection

Instead of using constructor injection to provide required dependencies when the object is instantiated, method injection passes the dependencies directly to the methods that use them. Method injection is a technique in DI where dependencies are provided to an object through method parameters.

In our code, we can set up dependencies through a method instead of a constructor, as illustrated in the following code:

```
namespace PassXYZ.Vault.ViewModels {
  [QueryProperty(nameof(ItemId), nameof(ItemId))]
  public partial class ItemsViewModel : BaseViewModel {
    readonly IDataStore<Item> dataStore;
    ILogger<ItemsViewModel> logger;

    public ObservableCollection<Item> Items { get; }

    public ItemsViewModel(ILogger<ItemsViewModel> logger) {
        this.logger = logger;
        Items = new ObservableCollection<Item>();
    }

    public SetDataStore(IDataStore<Item> store) {
      this.dataStore = store;
    }

    ...

    public async Task AddItem(Item item) {
```

```
        if (item == null) {
          logger.LogDebug("Item cannot be null");
          return;
        }

        await dataStore.AddItemAsync(item);
      }


      ...

    }
  }
```

In this example, IDataStore is set using the method SetDataStore instead of being injected through the constructor. However, it has a disadvantage where the dependent object might forget to set the dependency. As a result, the object can exist in an incomplete state.

In the code example provided, using method injection enables us to utilize both the actual and mock DataStore implementations within the same code. Method injection also allows for more fine-grained control over when dependencies are created, passed, and disposed of compared to constructor injection. However, it can also make the method's call more complex since the caller is responsible for providing the dependencies as parameters.

In general, constructor injection is often preferred for simplicity and better encapsulation, but method injection can be valuable for specific use cases.

Property injection

In property injection, dependencies are set through properties. Generally, method and property injection can be used to replace each other. It is similar to method injection—in numerous situations, we might be unable to utilize constructor injection, so we have to use method or property injection. The issue with method or property injection is that the dependent object might forget to set the dependency, so the object can exist in an incomplete state.

This problem can be partially mitigated through the use of attributes or annotations in object-oriented languages, an approach we will explore later.

In .NET MAUI, we can resolve the dependencies through IServiceProvider. Within a .NET MAUI application, the hosting environment generates an IServiceProvider interface for us, as demonstrated in *Figure 6.5*.

To obtain the ISeviceProvider interface, we can employ the IPlatformApplication interface defined in the platform-specific entry points, as depicted in *Listing 6.1*:

```
namespace PassXYZ.Vault.Services;
public static class ServiceHelper
{
    public static TService GetService<TService>()
        => Current.GetService<TService>();                          //(2)
    public static IServiceProvider Current =>                       //(1)
#if WINDOWS10_0_17763_0_OR_GREATER
        MauiWinUIApplication.Current.Services;
#elif ANDROID
        MauiApplication.Current.Services;
#elif IOS || MACCATALYST
        MauiUIApplicationDelegate.Current.Services;
#else
        null;
#endif
}
```

Listing 6.1: ServiceHelper.cs *(https://epa.ms/ServiceHelper6-1)*

(1) In the ServiceHelper class, we define a static variable called Current, which maintains a reference to the IServiceProvider. We can obtain the IServiceProvider through the Services property of the IPlatformApplication interface.

(2) A GetService static method is defined, which, in turn, invokes the GetService method of the IServiceProvider interface.

ServiceHelper

For the **ServiceHelper** implementation, I referred to the **MauiApp-DI** GitHub project. Thanks to James Montemagno for the sample code on GitHub!

(https://github.com/jamesmontemagno/MauiApp-DI)

By utilizing the ServiceHelper class, we can obtain an instance of IDataStore, as demonstrated below:

```
public static IDataStore<Item> DataStore =>
        ServiceHelper.GetService<IDataStore<Item>>();
```

You might notice that the property injection code provided earlier appears less elegant when compared to constructor injection. We have to set the dependencies manually. In the worst case, the object can exist in an incomplete state.

As of now, I have not discovered a more efficient method for implementing this in .NET MAUI. Nonetheless, in the subsequent sections of this book, when we introduce the Blazor Hybrid app, we will be able to utilize C# attributes to address property injection more effectively. To resolve the IDataStore interface in Blazor, a more straightforward approach can be employed, which is demonstrated in the following example:

```
[Inject]
public IDataStore<Item> DataStore { get; set; } = default!;
```

We can use the Inject C# attribute to implicitly resolve dependencies without explicitly invoking the GetService method from the ServiceHelper.

By employing DI, we can seamlessly substitute the mock implementation of the IDataStore interface with the actual one. This implementation can facilitate the CRUD operations of the password database. In the upcoming section, we will examine this new class in greater detail.

Replacing the mock data store

As explored in previous sections, we can register the implementation of data store services in MauiProgram.cs as follows:

```
builder.Services.AddSingleton<IDataStore<Item>, MockDataStore>();
builder.Services.AddSingleton<IUserService<User>, UserService>();
```

In the above code snippet, we receive an instance of MockDataStore for the IDataStore interface. This is a mock implementation to simplify the initial development. Now, it's time to substitute this with the actual implementation. We will replace the above code with the following:

```
builder.Services.AddSingleton<IDataStore<Item>, DataStore>();
builder.Services.AddSingleton<IUserService<User>, UserService>();
```

Here, DataStore is the actual implementation of the IDataStore service, which we will fully implement in the remainder of this chapter.

The password database is a local database in the KeePass 2.x format. Within this database, password information is organized into groups and entries. The KeePassLib namespace contains a PwDatabase class, which is designed to manage database operations.

To comprehend the relationship between PwDatabase, PwGroup, and PwEntry, we can refer to the class diagram in *Figure 6.6*:

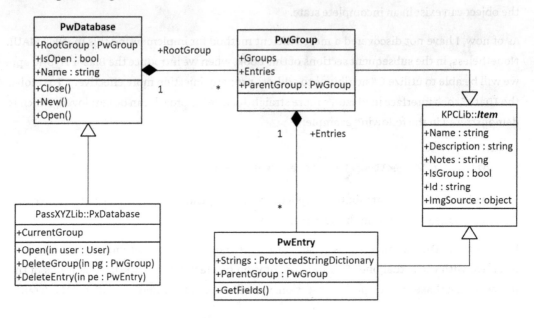

Figure 6.6: Class diagram of KeePass database

In **PwDatabase**, the **RootGroup** property of type **PwGroup** is defined, which contains all groups and entries stored in the database. The data structure of the KeePass database can be navigated from **RootGroup** to a specific entry. **PwEntry** defines a set of standard fields, as illustrated in *Figure 6.7*:

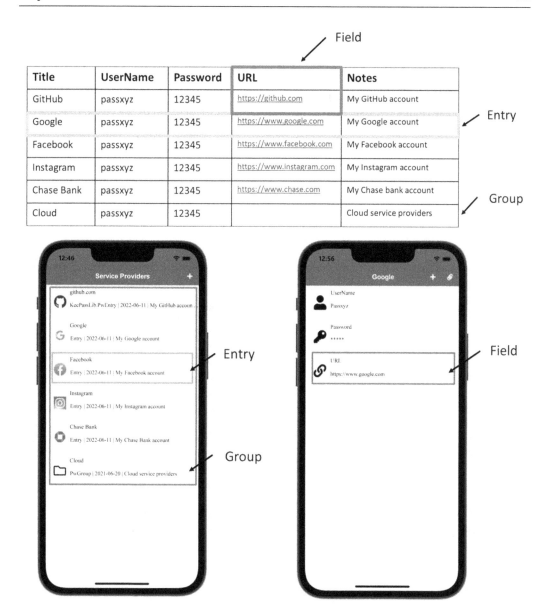

Title	UserName	Password	URL	Notes
GitHub	passxyz	12345	https://github.com	My GitHub account
Google	passxyz	12345	https://www.google.com	My Google account
Facebook	passxyz	12345	https://www.facebook.com	My Facebook account
Instagram	passxyz	12345	https://www.instagram.com	My Instagram account
Chase Bank	passxyz	12345	https://www.chase.com	My Chase bank account
Cloud	passxyz	12345		Cloud service providers

Figure 6.7: Group, entry, and field

If we possess a list of entries containing only standard fields, it will resemble a table. In *Figure 6.7*, the current group consists of five entries (**GitHub**, **Google**, **Facebook**, **Instagram**, and **Chase Bank**) along with a sub-group (**Cloud**). On the left, a screenshot of the `ItemsPage` displays the items within the current group. If the **Google** item is selected, it will appear as an entry in the screenshot on the right side. Users have the option to add extra fields to the entry, making the KeePass database dissimilar to a relational database; it is more akin to a key-value database. Each field consists of a key-value pair, such as a URL field.

In order to utilize `PwDatabase` in our application, we have defined a derived class called `PxDatabase`. This class introduces additional properties and methods, such as `CurrentGroup`, `DeleteGroup`, `DeleteEntry`, and more.

To access a database, one can open the database file and perform CRUD operations on it. However, when building a cross-platform app, handling the database file directly may not be convenient for the end users. In **PassXYZ.Vault**, the concept of users is employed rather than using a data file. Within **PassXYZLib**, a `User` class has been defined to encapsulate the underlying file operations.

In order to access the database, we have defined database initialization and CRUD operations within the `IDataStore` and `IUserService` interfaces. The `DataStore` and `UserService` concrete classes serve to implement these two interfaces.

Initializing the database

The database initialization is incorporated within the login process, so the subsequent login method is defined in the `IUserService` interface:

```
Task<bool> LoginAsync(T user);
```

The `UserService` class serves as an implementation of the `IUserService` interface. Within the `UserService` class, the `LoginAsync` method is defined as an asynchronous method, as illustrated here:

```
public async Task<bool> LoginAsync(User user)
{
  if (user == null) {
    throw new ArgumentNullException(
      nameof(user), "User cannot be null"); }

  _user = user;

  return await dataStore.ConnectAsync(user);
}
```

In `LoginAsync`, the `IDataStore` method `ConnectAsync` is invoked to perform the actual task. Let's examine the `ConnectAsync` implementation below:

```
public async Task<bool> ConnectAsync(User user)
{
  return await Task.Run(() =>                                    //(1)
  {
    if (string.IsNullOrEmpty(user.Username) ||
      string.IsNullOrEmpty(user.Password)) {
        throw new ArgumentNullException(nameof(user),
        "Username or password cannot be null");
    }

    _db.Open(user);                                             //(2)
    if (_db.IsOpen)
    {
        _db.CurrentGroup = _db.RootGroup;
    }
    return _db.IsOpen;
  });
}
```

In the `ConnectAsync` function, **(1)**, a distinct task is employed to manage the opening process of the database. The `Open` method of `PxDatabase` is invoked, **(2)**, and an instance of the `User` class is provided as an argument to the `Open` method.

After successfully establishing a connection and initializing the database, we need to implement the methods required for database operations. These can include tasks such as data retrieval, data insertion, data update, and data deletion, among others. These represent the fundamental operations to interact, manage, and maintain data within the database system.

Performing CRUD operations

The data manipulation in the KeePass database closely resembles the CRUD operations found in a relational database. These operations are outlined in the `IDataStore` interface, as demonstrated in the subsequent code snippet. Upon logging in and connecting to a database, we can access our stored password data. Initially, we must retrieve a list of items. Upon login, the root group provides the first list. We use the `SetCurrentGroup` method **(1)** to establish the current navigation location.

When the user navigates to another group, SetCurrentGroup is invoked with an argument to set the new location in the navigation:

```
public interface IDataStore<T>
{
  Task<bool> AddItemAsync(T item);
  Task<bool> UpdateItemAsync(T item);
  Task<bool> DeleteItemAsync(string id);
  T? GetItem(string id);
  Task<IEnumerable<T>> GetItemsAsync(
    bool forceRefresh = false);
  string SetCurrentGroup(T? group = default);                    //(1)
  Task<bool> ConnectAsync(User user);
  Task SignUpAsync(User user);
  void Close();
  T? CreateNewItem(ItemSubType type);
}
```

Listing 6.2: IDataStore.cs *(https://epa.ms/IDataStore6-2)*

Adding an item

The initial operation in CRUD involves creating or adding an item. This item could be an entry or a group that is added to the current group. The user interface for performing this add operation can be found as a toolbar item in ItemsPage, as illustrated below:

```
<ContentPage.ToolbarItems>
  <ToolbarItem Text="Add" Command="{Binding AddItemCommand}"
    IconImageSource="{FontImage FontFamily=FontAwesomeSolid,
    Color=White,
    Glyph={x:Static style:FontAwesomeSolid.PlusCircle}}"/>
</ContentPage.ToolbarItems>
```

We can see a toolbar item icon is shown in the top-right corner of ItemsPage in *Figure 6.8*:

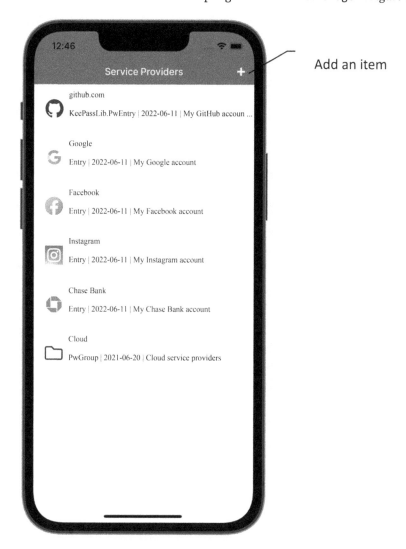

Figure 6.8: Adding an item

When the + button is clicked, the AddItemCommand command in the ItemsViewModel is invoked through data binding.

The AddItemCommand command invokes the following AddItem method in the view model:

```
[RelayCommand]
private async Task AddItem(object obj)
{
  string[] templates = {
      Properties.Resources.item_subtype_group,
      Properties.Resources.item_subtype_entry,
      Properties.Resources.item_subtype_notes,
      Properties.Resources.item_subtype_pxentry
  };

  var template = await Shell.Current.DisplayActionSheet(
    Properties.Resources.pt_id_choosetemplate,
    Properties.Resources.action_id_cancel, null, templates);        //(1)

  ItemSubType type;

  if (template ==
    Properties.Resources.item_subtype_entry) {
    type = ItemSubType.Entry;
  }
  else if (template ==
    Properties.Resources.item_subtype_pxentry) {
    type = ItemSubType.PxEntry;
  }
  else if (template ==
    Properties.Resources.item_subtype_group) {
    type = ItemSubType.Group;
  }
  else if (template ==
    Properties.Resources.item_subtype_notes) {
    type = ItemSubType.Notes;
  }
  else if (template ==
    Properties.Resources.action_id_cancel) {
    type = ItemSubType.None;
  }
```

```
    else {
      type = ItemSubType.None;
    }

    if (type != ItemSubType.None) {
      var itemType = new Dictionary<string, object> {          //(2)
          { "Type", type }
      };
      await Shell.Current.GoToAsync(                           //(3)
        nameof(NewItemPage), itemType);
    }
  }
}
```

Listing 6.3: ItemsViewModel.cs *(https://epa.ms/ItemsViewModel6-3)*

(1) In the AddItem function, an ActionSheet is displayed, allowing the user to select an item type. The item type can either be a group or an entry.

(2) Upon obtaining the item type, we can construct a dictionary that includes the item type and the query parameter's name. Then, we store this dictionary object in a variable called itemType.

(3) This itemType variable can be passed to NewItemPage as a query parameter. In *Chapter 5, Navigation Using .NET MAUI Shell and NavigationPage*, we learned how to pass a string value as a query parameter to a page in Shell navigation. Here, we can pass an object as a query parameter to a page after we wrap it in a dictionary.

To add a new item, the user interface is defined in NewItemPage, while the logic is managed within the NewItemViewModel. Let's examine the NewItemViewModel implementation as shown in *Listing 6.4*:

```
using CommunityToolkit.Mvvm.ComponentModel;
using CommunityToolkit.Mvvm.Input;
using Microsoft.Extensions.Logging;
using KPCLib;
using PassXYZLib;
using PassXYZ.Vault.Services;
using static System.Net.Mime.MediaTypeNames;

namespace PassXYZ.Vault.ViewModels;
```

```
[QueryProperty(nameof(Type), nameof(Type))]                        //(1)
public partial class NewItemViewModel : ObservableObject
{
  readonly IDataStore<Item>? _dataStore;
  ILogger<NewItemViewModel> _logger;
  private ItemSubType _type = ItemSubType.Group;

  public NewItemViewModel(IDataStore<Item> dataStore,
    ILogger<NewItemViewModel> logger) {
    this._dataStore = dataStore ??
      throw new ArgumentNullException(nameof(dataStore));
    this._logger = logger;
  }

  private void SetPlaceholder(ItemSubType type) {
    if (type == ItemSubType.Group) {
      Placeholder = Properties.Resources.action_id_add +
        " " + Properties.Resources.item_subtype_group;
    }
    else
    {
      Placeholder = Properties.Resources.action_id_add +
        " " + Properties.Resources.item_subtype_entry;
    }
  }

  public ItemSubType Type {                                        //(2)
    get => _type;
    set {
      _ = SetProperty(ref _type, value);
      SetPlaceholder(_type);
    }
  }

  [ObservableProperty]
  [NotifyCanExecuteChangedFor(nameof(SaveCommand))]
  private string? name;
```

```
    [ObservableProperty]
    [NotifyCanExecuteChangedFor(nameof(SaveCommand))]
    private string? description;

    [ObservableProperty]
    private string? placeholder;

    [RelayCommand]
    private async Task Cancel() {
        await Shell.Current.GoToAsync("..");
    }

    [RelayCommand(CanExecute = nameof(ValidateSave))]
    private async Task Save() {
      if(_dataStore == null) {
        throw new ArgumentNullException(
        "dataStore cannot be null"); }

      Item? newItem = _dataStore.CreateNewItem(_type);            //(3)

      if (newItem != null) {
        newItem.Name = Name;
        newItem.Notes = Description;
        await _dataStore.AddItemAsync(newItem);                   //(4)
      }
      await Shell.Current.GoToAsync("..");
    }

  private bool ValidateSave() {
    var canExecute = !String.IsNullOrWhiteSpace(Name)
        && !String.IsNullOrWhiteSpace(Description);
    _logger.LogDebug("ValidateSave: {canExecute}", canExecute);
    return canExecute;
  }
 }
}
```

Listing 6.4: NewItemViewModel.cs *(https://epa.ms/NewItemViewModel6-4)*

The design of the NewItemPage is quite straightforward, featuring two controls: **Entry** and **Editor**, which serve to edit the name and notes of an item, respectively. The **Entry** control is employed for entering or editing a single line of text, whereas the **Editor** control is utilized for modifying multiple lines of text. Within the NewItemViewModel view model, we can observe the process of adding a new item as demonstrated below:

(1) The query parameter is defined using the QueryPropertyAttribute. **(2)** The Type property, declared as ItemSubType, is utilized to obtain the query parameter. The acquired item type is subsequently stored in the _type backing variable. Within the NewItemPage, two toolbar items are established, and their actions are associated with the **Save** and **Cancel** methods found in the view model.

Upon entering a name and notes in the user interface and clicking the **Save** button, **(3)**, a new item instance is created using the CreateNewItem factory method, which is defined in the IDataStore interface. **(4)** Once the new item instance is populated with the user input, it can be added to the database by calling the AddItemAsync method.

We have now implemented the addition operation. In the following section, let's proceed to implement the remaining data operations.

Editing or deleting an item

In CRUD operations, a create operation does not require an existing item. However, to perform update and delete operations, an instance of the existing item is necessary.

In a read operation, when an item is a group, we implement it by transmitting an ItemId query parameter to the ItemsPage and, subsequently, identifying the group within the setter of ItemId in the ItemsViewModel view model. Conversely, if the item is an entry, we transmit an ItemId query parameter to ItemDetailPage and locate the entry within the setter of ItemId in the ItemDetailViewModel.

For updating, editing, and deleting operations, we can utilize context actions. These actions allow us to manipulate items within a ListView effectively. It is important to note that context actions have a distinct appearance on various platforms, such as iOS, Android, and Windows, as depicted in *Figure 6.9*:

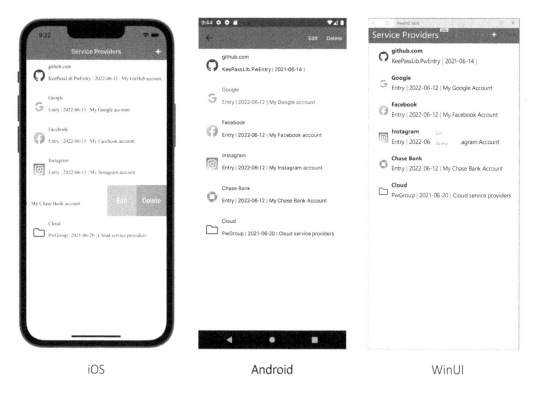

| iOS | Android | WinUI |

Figure 6.9: Context actions

On the iOS platform, you can perform an action on an item by swiping it to the left. In an Android system, you can access the contextual actions menu by long-pressing an item, which will then appear in the top-right corner of the screen. On Windows, you might be familiar with right-clicking your mouse to display the contextual actions menu.

In our application, we introduce a context actions menu within the `ItemsPage`. We configure the context actions in the `ItemViewCell` inside `ItemsPage`, as demonstrated below:

```
<ListView.ItemTemplate>
  <DataTemplate x:DataType="model:Item">
    <template:ItemViewCell Key="{Binding Name}"
      Value="{Binding Description}" Source="{Binding ImgSource}"
      ParentPage="{x:Reference itemsPage}"/>
  </DataTemplate>
</ListView.ItemTemplate>
```

The `ItemViewCell` is a custom view that inherits from `KeyValueView`, which was introduced in *Chapter 4*, *Exploring MVVM and Data Binding*. Let's examine the `ItemViewCell` code in *Listing 6.5*:

```
using System.Diagnostics;

using KPCLib;
using PassXYZ.Vault.ViewModels;

namespace PassXYZ.Vault.Views.Templates;

public class ItemViewCell : KeyValueView {
  public ItemViewCell() {
    SetContextAction(GetEditMenu(), OnEditAction);
    SetContextAction(GetDeleteMenu(), OnDeleteAction);
  }

  private void OnEditAction(object? sender,                         //(1)
    System.EventArgs e) {
    if(sender is MenuItem menuItem)
    {
      if(menuItem.CommandParameter is Item item &&
          ParentPage.BindingContext is ItemsViewModel vm)
      {
        vm.Update(item);
      }
    }
  }

  private async void OnDeleteAction(object? sender,                 //(2)
    System.EventArgs e) {
    if (sender is MenuItem menuItem) {
      if (menuItem.CommandParameter is Item item &&
          ParentPage.BindingContext is ItemsViewModel vm)
      {
        await vm.Delete(item);
      }
    }
```

```
    }
  }
```

Listing 6.5: ItemViewCell.cs *(https://epa.ms/ItemViewCell6-5)*

In the ItemViewCell, we define two menu items for editing and deleting context actions. We assign two event handlers (**(1)** OnEditAction and **(2)** OnDeleteAction) to their corresponding context actions. Within the event handlers, we invoke the view model methods, Update and Delete, to execute the required operations.

Let us examine the source code for the Update and Delete functions in the ItemsViewModel, as shown below:

```
public async void Update(Item item) {
  if (item == null) {
    return;
  }

  await Shell.Current.Navigation.PushAsync(
    new FieldEditPage(async (string k, string v,          //(1)
                    bool isProtected) => {
    item.Name = k;
    item.Notes = v;
    await dataStore.UpdateItemAsync(item);                //(2)
  }, item.Name, item.Notes, true));
}

public async Task Delete(Item item) {
  if (item == null) {
    return;
  }

  if (Items.Remove(item)) {
    _ = await dataStore.DeleteItemAsync(item.Id);          //(3)
  }
  else {
    throw new NullReferenceException("Delete item error");
  }
}
```

In the `ItemsViewModel`, to edit or update an item, **(1)**, we utilize a content page called `FieldEditPage` to carry out the editing process. Upon invoking the constructor of `FieldEditPage`, an anonymous function is passed as a parameter. This function is invoked when the user finishes editing within `FieldEditPage`. Within this function, **(2)**, the `UpdateItemAsync` method of the `IDataStore` interface is called to update the item.

The delete operation is fairly straightforward. We can simply invoke the `DeleteItemAsync` method, **(3)**, from the `IDataStore` interface to eliminate the item.

Once the CRUD operations are implemented, our application will possess the essential features required for a password manager app. We can establish a new database by registering a new user. Upon creating a new database, we can then log in to access our data. Additionally, after generating entries and groups, we have the ability to modify or remove them as needed.

Summary

In this chapter, we began by introducing design principles. Following this, we delved into the SOLID design principles, and I shared insights gleaned from the development of our app. Among the most crucial SOLID principles is the **DIP**. **DI** is a technique that applies the DIP in practical implementation. In our app, we utilize the built-in DI service of .NET MAUI to decouple dependencies, enabling us to separate the implementation of the service from the interface.

We accumulated extensive knowledge about .NET MAUI and successfully completed our app implementation by replacing `MockDataStore` with the actual implementation. We established CRUD operations on top of this new `IDataStore` service, resulting in a fully functional password manager app.

Although we have incorporated essential features in our app, users often expect additional desirable features in a password manager application, such as fingerprint scanning and one-time passwords. Some of these features are platform-specific, which requires knowledge of platform integration. In the next chapter, we will delve into various platform integration topics to further improve our app.

Further reading

- *Beginning SOLID Principles and Design Patterns for ASP.NET Developers*, by Bipin Joshi
- **Autofac** is an **inversion of control** (**IoC**) container for .NET Core, ASP.NET Core, .NET 4.5.1+, and more: `https://autofac.org/`
- **Simple Injector** is a DI container that can support .NET 4.5 and .NET Standard: `https://simpleinjector.org/`

Learn more on Discord

Join our community's Discord space for discussions with the author and other readers:

https://packt.link/cross-platform-app

7

Using Platform-Specific Features

In the last six chapters, we developed a fundamental password manager app. So far, all platform-specific features have been managed by .NET MAUI, making the developed features appear platform-agnostic. However, addressing platform-specific features is not always avoidable. In this chapter, we will delve into the implementation of such features.

We will explore how to utilize device features on supported platforms. By applying the knowledge gained in this chapter, we will incorporate fingerprint support and a customized Markdown view into our app.

While this chapter does touch on platform-specific features, its primary focus isn't platform-specific programming. Delving deeper into platform-specific implementations would require specific programming knowledge for Android, iOS, WinUI, and so on. Given this would require a considerable amount of knowledge, instead of teaching you to write your own plugins or specific UI controls for each platform, we will consider some of the high-level concepts involved in creating these elements. To help you become familiar with these concepts, our focus will be on how to extend these features and incorporate them into our app.

To use .NET for native application development, you would need to write a specialized book for each platform. You can refer to the *Further reading* section for more information about Android and iOS native application development using Xamarin.

The following topics will be covered in this chapter:

- Implementing platform-specific code
- .NET MAUI plugins
- Customizing controls

Technical requirements

To test and debug the source code in this chapter, you need to have Visual Studio 2022 installed on your PC or Mac. Please refer to the *Development environment setup* section in *Chapter 1, Getting Started with .NET MAUI*, for the details.

The source code for this chapter is available in the following GitHub repository: `https://github.com/PacktPublishing/.NET-MAUI-Cross-Platform-Application-Development-Second-edition/tree/main/2nd/chapter07`.

To check out the source code of this chapter, we can use the below command:

```
$ git clone -b 2nd/chapter07 https://github.com/PacktPublishing/.NET-MAUI-
Cross-Platform-Application-Development-Second-edition.git PassXYZ.Vault2
```

To find out more about the source code in this book, please refer to the section *Managing the source code in this book* in *Chapter 2, Building Our First .NET MAUI App*.

Implementing platform-specific code

In the realm of .NET MAUI application development, there are numerous instances where we might need to write platform-specific code. In this section, we will examine the guidelines for implementing such code. Following that, we will explore the two most common scenarios that necessitate writing platform-specific code in this chapter. The first scenario involves accessing platform features that are not readily available in .NET MAUI APIs. The second scenario may require creating custom controls or customizing existing controls.

Before delving into how to access platform APIs, it's important to distinguish between the terms .NET MAUI API and platform API. In *Chapter 1, Getting Started with .NET MAUI*, we have the following architecture diagram of a .NET MAUI application (*Figure 7.1*).

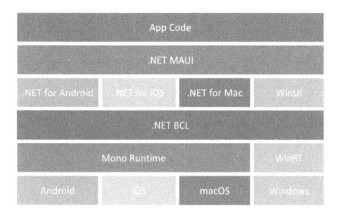

Figure 7.1: .NET MAUI architecture

Since most of the components in the architectural diagram are open-source, I've numbered the components for the discussion. You can reference these numbers in the *Further reading* section to locate the corresponding source code on GitHub:

- **.NET MAUI APIs (6)** are the cross-platform APIs offered by the .NET MAUI framework. These APIs maintain consistency and unification across various platforms.
- **Platform APIs (7)(8)(9)(10)**, on the other hand, pertain to the platform-specific APIs provided by the underlying target platforms (Android, iOS/macOS, and Windows). These APIs enable you to access native features, devices, and functionalities unique to each platform.

Generally, to incorporate platform code in .NET MAUI, we can utilize techniques such as conditional compilation and interfaces, as well as partial classes and methods.

Conditional compilation

In .NET MAUI, it is possible to employ conditional compilation to invoke platform-specific code by defining compiler directives tailored to each platform. These directives enable you to incorporate or omit particular code segments, depending on the target platform throughout the compilation process.

In the subsequent code snippet, the Markdown encoding varies on Android. By utilizing conditional compilation, we can manage the Android code independently:

```
public void DisplayMarkdown(string markdown)
{
#if !ANDROID
  string markDownTxt = HttpUtility.JavaScriptStringEncode(markdown);
#else
  string markDownTxt = markdown;
#endif
  MainThread.BeginInvokeOnMainThread(async () =>
  {
    await InvokeJsMethodAsync("MarkdownToHtml", markDownTxt);
  });
}
```

This modular approach enables the effective use of platform-specific APIs while preserving a shared codebase, facilitating a more seamless cross-platform development process. The conditional compilation method described is typically used for simple implementations. However, if platform-specific implementations involve more complex logic, it's best to utilize interfaces and partial classes. These provide a more structured approach, allowing for better organization and maintainability of the code, especially when dealing with complex, platform-specific logic.

Interfaces, partial class, and methods

Using interfaces, partial classes, and methods to implement platform-specific features provides several benefits to developers when building cross-platform applications, ensuring clean code organization, maintainability, and flexibility. Here are the advantages of using these techniques:

- Abstraction and modularity:
  - **Interfaces**: Interfaces provide a way to define contracts that must be implemented by the platform-specific classes, encapsulating platform-specific code while ensuring consistency across different platform implementations. This promotes a clear separation of concerns and allows for modular code that is easier to manage and maintain.
  - **Partial classes**: Partial classes enable you to split the implementation of a single class across multiple files, which is particularly useful when working with platform-specific features. Each platform's implementation can be separated into different files, resulting in cleaner and more organized code.

- Code reusability and maintainability:

  Using interfaces allows you to create reusable components that can be easily plugged into different platform-specific implementations without modifying the shared code. This improves maintainability, as changes in platform-specific code do not affect the rest of the application, reducing the potential for errors and simplifying updates.

  Partial methods serve as optional method implementations within partial classes. They enable you to define a method signature in the shared code without providing an implementation. The platform-specific code can then provide the implementation if needed, which can be left empty otherwise. This approach keeps the codebase cleaner by avoiding unnecessary empty method implementations and helps to maintain a more consistent structure across platforms.

- Flexibility and testability:

  Interfaces offer flexibility when implementing platform-specific features, as different implementations can be easily swapped for testing purposes or to support future platforms. It allows for dependency injection, making it easier to write unit tests and mock platform-specific components during development and testing.

  In order to utilize platform features that are not directly supported by .NET MAUI, we typically create components known as plugins. In the upcoming section, we will use the fingerprint plugin as a case study to gain insight into the implementation of .NET MAUI plugins through interfaces, partial classes, or abstract classes.

.NET MAUI/Xamarin plugins

To utilize platform features in a cross-platform manner, we typically create components known as plugins. In .NET MAUI plugins (or Xamarin plugins), we establish cross-platform APIs to access native platform features or services. These plugins empower you to write platform-independent code in your shared project while concurrently harnessing native functionality on each platform (Android, iOS, macOS, and Windows).

Plugins abstract platform-specific code, enabling you to use a standardized API in your shared project for accessing native features. This streamlines development and helps you maintain a neater and more readable codebase that adheres to the **Model-View-ViewModel** (**MVVM**) pattern.

Although I have used the term ".NET MAUI plugins," it's important to note that it's not limited purely to .NET MAUI. In fact, it's possible to develop a plugin that can be used by both .NET MAUI and Xamarin.Forms simultaneously. Typically, a plugin is a multi-target .NET project where the developer can decide the number of platforms to support. The content in this chapter regarding plugins is also applicable to .NET MAUI Blazor Hybrid apps. We will delve into .NET MAUI Blazor Hybrid app development in the next chapter.

As plugin development can be fairly flexible and potent, the compatibility of plugin libraries is determined by individual developers. To standardize a variety of plugins from the community, let's evaluate the evolutionary path of .NET MAUI or Xamarin plugins in the upcoming section.

The evolution of .NET MAUI/Xamarin plugins

Previously, in order to utilize a device feature without a built-in cross-platform interface, we could often find Xamarin plugins developed by the community. Xamarin plugins, created by Xamarin developers, are packaged in a cross-platform format. However, these plugins lack standardization, which may result in the existence of multiple plugins catering to the same device features.

As the Xamarin ecosystem evolved and matured, Xamarin.Essentials was introduced as an all-embracing, harmonized alternative. By consolidating popular plugins into a single cross-platform library, it simplified the utilization of native APIs across Android, iOS, and Windows devices.

Xamarin.Essentials serves as both a library and a namespace. Within this namespace, we can access hardware interfaces, such as a battery, flashlight, vibration, geolocation sensor, etc.

With the advent of .NET MAUI, Xamarin.Essentials has undergone further development, resulting in a collection of individual namespaces housed under the `Microsoft.Maui` namespace, as depicted in *Figure 7.2*.

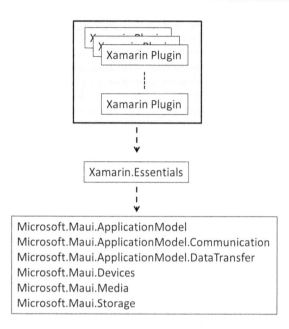

Figure 7.2: Evolution of Xamarin.Essentials

In Xamarin.Essentials, all features are consolidated under a single namespace, resulting in a sizable and flat library. In contrast, .NET MAUI adopts a more refined design by dividing the features into multiple namespaces, as illustrated in *Table 7.1*.

Namespace	Description
Microsoft.Maui. ApplicationModel	Within this namespace, it encompasses APIs that enable access to platform-specific application-level information and activities. Examples of these include app actions, app information, the browser, the launcher, the main thread, maps, permissions, and version tracking.
Microsoft.Maui. ApplicationModel. Communication	Within this namespace, we have access to various communication services, including contacts, email, networking, the phone dialer, sms, and web authenticator functionality.
Microsoft.Maui. ApplicationModel. DataTransfer	Clipboard and sharing APIs can be found in this namespace.

`Microsoft.Maui.Devices`	In this namespace, we have the capability to access various hardware sensors and accelerators, including the battery, the device display, device information, device sensors, the flashlight, geocoding, geolocation, haptic feedback, and vibration.
`Microsoft.Maui.Media`	We can access video and photos in this namespace, such as the media picker, screenshot, text-to-speech, or unit converters.
`Microsoft.Maui.Storage`	To access various local storage in preferences or secure storage, we can use this namespace. We can find a cross-platform file picker and filesystem helpers here.

Table 7.1: Device features in Microsoft.Maui

While the cross-platform APIs listed in *Table 7.1* allow us to access various device features, there are still some platform features unavailable. In such instances, we must either implement our own solutions or utilize plugins developed by the community. For instance, there are no cross-platform APIs available for fingerprint functionality. To incorporate fingerprint features in our app, we need to rely on community-developed plugins.

As .NET MAUI APIs currently do not support fingerprint functionality, we will employ an open-source plugin called `Plugin.Fingerprint`, which was previously used in the Xamarin version of `PassXYZ.Vault`. In this chapter, we will utilize the same plugin to facilitate fingerprint support in the .NET MAUI version of PassXYZ.Vault. `Plugin.Fingerprint` is an example of a library that can support both .NET MAUI and Xamarin.Forms.

The introduction of Plugin.Fingerprint

In this session, we will utilize `Plugin.Fingerprint` as a case study to demonstrate the implementation of .NET MAUI plugins. You can find the fingerprint plugin we will be using at the following GitHub URL: `https://github.com/smstuebe/xamarin-fingerprint`.

To use `Plugin.Fingerprint` in our project, we can add the package to our project by using the below command:

```
dotnet add package Plugin.Fingerprint
```

In order to implement a plugin, it is common practice to begin by defining an interface. This interface serves as a means to access the features provided by the plugin.

The concrete implementation is divided into two components, the cross-platform aspect and the platform-specific aspect, which are achieved using either a partial class or an abstract class.

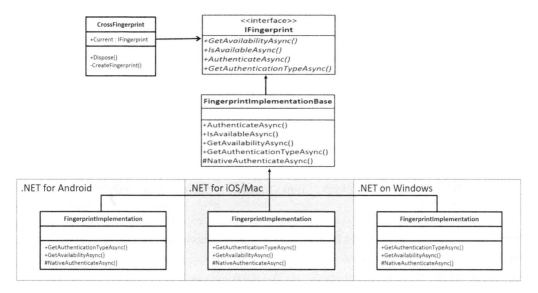

Figure 7.3: Plugin.Fingerprint

Figure 7.3 presents the class diagram of `Plugin.Fingerprint`. It is evident that `Plugin.Fingerprint` establishes an interface called `IFingerprint`. An abstract class, `FingerprintImplementationBase`, carries out the implementation of this interface. This abstract class is responsible for cross-platform functionality and outlines abstract methods designated for platform-specific implementation. `FingerprintImplementation`, a separate class on each platform, defines the platform-specific implementation. In the following block, we will examine the code of `IFingerprint`:

```
using System.Threading;
using System.Threading.Tasks;

namespace Plugin.Fingerprint.Abstractions
{
  public interface IFingerprint
  {
Task<FingerprintAvailability> GetAvailabilityAsync(
  bool allowAlternativeAuthentication = false);
    Task<bool> IsAvailableAsync(bool allowAlternativeAuthentication =
  false);
```

```
    Task<FingerprintAuthenticationResult> AuthenticateAsync(
AuthenticationRequestConfiguration authRequestConfig,
        CancellationToken cancellationToken = default);
    Task<AuthenticationType> GetAuthenticationTypeAsync();
  }
}
```

The IFingerprint interface defines four methods:

- GetAvailabilityAsync checks the availability of fingerprint authentication.

- IsAvailableAsync serves as a wrapper for GetAvailabilityAsync, offering easier access.

- AuthenticateAsync handles the actual authentication, using fingerprint data.

- GetAuthenticationTypeAsync allows users to retrieve the currently available authentication type.

Now, let's examine FingerprintImplementationBase, which implements the IFingerprint interface:

```
public abstract class FingerprintImplementationBase : IFingerprint
{
  public async Task<FingerprintAuthenticationResult>
    AuthenticateAsync(
    AuthenticationRequestConfiguration authRequestConfig,
    CancellationToken cancellationToken = default) {
    if (authRequestConfig is null)
        throw new ArgumentNullException(nameof(authRequestConfig));

    var availability = await GetAvailabilityAsync(
        authRequestConfig.AllowAlternativeAuthentication);
    if (availability != FingerprintAvailability.Available) {
      var status = availability == FingerprintAvailability.Denied ?
        FingerprintAuthenticationResultStatus.Denied :
        FingerprintAuthenticationResultStatus.NotAvailable;

        return new FingerprintAuthenticationResult {
          Status = status,
          ErrorMessage = availability.ToString() };
    }
```

```
  return await NativeAuthenticateAsync(
    authRequestConfig, cancellationToken);
    }


  public async Task<bool> IsAvailableAsync(
    bool allowAlternativeAuthentication = false) {
      return await GetAvailabilityAsync
        (allowAlternativeAuthentication)
        == FingerprintAvailability.Available;
  }


  public abstract Task<FingerprintAvailability>
    GetAvailabilityAsync(
      bool allowAlternativeAuthentication = false);


  public abstract Task<AuthenticationType>
    GetAuthenticationTypeAsync();


  protected abstract Task<FingerprintAuthenticationResult>
  NativeAuthenticateAsync(
    AuthenticationRequestConfiguration authRequestConfig,
    CancellationToken cancellationToken);
  }
```

In the `FingerprintImplementationBase` class, the `AuthenticateAsync` method is implemented by invoking the `NativeAuthenticateAsync` method. The latter is defined as an abstract method that is implemented in the platform layer.

It also defines `GetAvailabilityAsync` and `GetAuthenticationTypeAsync` as abstract methods, which are subsequently implemented in the platform layer.

The `IsAvailableAsync` method simply invokes `GetAvailabilityAsync` and then compares the return value.

In order to instantiate the `IFingerprint` interface, `Plugin.Fingerprint` employs a class named `CrossFingerprint`. This class utilizes a creational design pattern, along with lazy initialization, to generate `IFingerprint` interface instances during runtime, as we can see in the following code:

```
  public partial class CrossFingerprint {
    private static Lazy<IFingerprint> _implementation =            //(1)
```

```
new Lazy<IFingerprint>(CreateFingerprint,
  LazyThreadSafetyMode.PublicationOnly);

public static IFingerprint Current {                          //(2)
  get => _implementation.Value;
  set {
    _implementation = new Lazy<IFingerprint>(() => value);
  }
}
static IFingerprint CreateFingerprint() {                     //(3)
#if NETSTANDARD2_0
    throw NotImplementedInReferenceAssembly();
#else
    return new FingerprintImplementation();
#endif
}
public static void Dispose() {
  if (_implementation != null && _implementation.IsValueCreated)
  {
    _implementation = new Lazy<IFingerprint>(CreateFingerprint,
      LazyThreadSafetyMode.PublicationOnly);
  }
}
private static Exception NotImplementedInReferenceAssembly() {
    return new NotImplementedException("This functionality is not
implemented in the portable version of this assembly. You should reference
the NuGet package from your main application project in order to reference
the platform-specific implementation.");
}
}
```

In CrossFingerprint, a static property called Current **(2)** is defined, which can be utilized to obtain the instance of IFingerprint. The property Current returns the value of a Lazy<IFingerprint> object, specified in the variable _implementation **(1)**, which implements lazy initialization. Within Lazy<IFingerprint>, the IFingerprint instance is created using the factory method CreateFingerprint **(3)**.

Now that we have introduced `Plugin.Fingerprint`, let's explore how to incorporate fingerprint support in our app using this plugin.

Supporting fingerprint functionality using Plugin.Fingerprint

To incorporate fingerprint functionality using `Plugin.Fingerprint`, we must first configure it within our project before making any code modifications. This step involves adding the NuGet package `Plugin.Fingerprint` to our project file, as detailed below:

```
<ItemGroup>
<PackageReference Include="CommunityToolkit.Mvvm" Version="8.2.1" />
<PackageReference Include="EJL.MauiHybridWebView" Version="1.0.0-preview3"
/>
<PackageReference Include="Microsoft.Extensions.Logging.Debug"
Version="7.0.0" />
<PackageReference Include="Plugin.Fingerprint" Version="3.0.0-beta.1" />
<PackageReference Include="PassXYZLib" Version="2.1.2" />
</ItemGroup>
```

For now, please disregard the NuGet package `EJL.MauiHybridWebView`. We will delve into a discussion about it later in this chapter.

As users must access device-specific features within each platform, it is essential to configure the required permissions for our application in their respective configuration files.

For the Android platform, it is necessary to request specific permissions within the `AndroidManifest.xml` file:

```
<uses-permission android:name="android.permission.USE_BIOMETRIC" />
<!-- only if you target android below level 28 -->
<uses-permission android:name="android.permission.USE_FINGERPRINT" />
```

For the iOS platform, we need to do the same in `Info.plist`, as below:

```
<key>NSFaceIDUsageDescription</key>
<string>Need your face to unlock secrets!</string>
```

Incorporating fingerprint functionality is an objective we aim to achieve in our application. By employing the MVVM pattern, we can initially integrate this fingerprint feature within our view model. Subsequently, we can utilize this functionality in our XAML pages.

Our users will utilize fingerprint authentication to log in, so we can incorporate the fingerprint plugin into the `LoginViewModel`. The users will engage with `LoginPage` to carry out the login process. However, before they can employ fingerprint authentication within `LoginPage`, they must first enable the fingerprint feature in our app's settings. The implementation of these settings is found in the `SettingsPage`. The relationship between `IFingerprint`, `LoginViewModel`, `LoginPage`, and `SettingsPage` is illustrated in *Figure 7.4*:

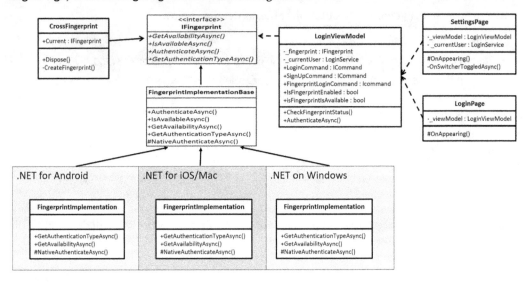

Figure 7.4: Plugin.Fingerprint integration

As we are utilizing dependency injection to manage dependencies, it is necessary to initially include the `IFingerprint` interface in the configuration found in `MauiProgram.cs`, as demonstrated below:

```
builder.Services.AddSingleton(typeof(IFingerprint), CrossFingerprint.
Current);
```

Having completed the aforementioned setup and configuration, let us now examine the code of the `LoginViewModel` provided below:

```
public partial class LoginViewModel : ObservableObject {
  private LoginService _currentUser;
  ILogger<LoginViewModel> _logger;
  private readonly IFingerprint _fingerprint;
  public LoginViewModel(LoginService user,
    ILogger<LoginViewModel> logger, IFingerprint fingerprint) {    //(1)
    _currentUser = user;
```

```
    _logger = logger;
    _fingerprint = fingerprint;
  }
  ...
  [RelayCommand(CanExecute = nameof(ValidateFingerprintLogin))]
  private async Task FingerprintLogin() {                          //(2)
    var cancel = new CancellationTokenSource();
var dialogConfig = new AuthenticationRequestConfiguration(
  Username,
      Properties.Resources.fingerprint_login_message) {
      CancelTitle = "Cancel fingerprint login",
      FallbackTitle = "Use Password",
      AllowAlternativeAuthentication = true,
    };
var result = await _fingerprint.AuthenticateAsync(
  dialogConfig, cancel.Token);
    if (result.Authenticated) {
      Password = await _currentUser.GetSecurityAsync();
      if (!string.IsNullOrWhiteSpace(Password)) {
          await Login();
      }
      else {
          _logger.LogWarning("GetSecurityAsync() error.");
      }
    }
    else {
        _logger.LogWarning("Failed to login with fingerprint.");
    }
  }
  ...
  public async void CheckFingerprintStatus() {                     //(3)
    _currentUser.Username = Username;
    var password = await _currentUser.GetSecurityAsync();
IsFingerprintIsAvailable =
  await _fingerprint.IsAvailableAsync();
IsFingerprintEnabled = IsFingerprintIsAvailable &&
  !string.IsNullOrWhiteSpace(password);
```

```
    }
    [ObservableProperty]
    private bool isFingerprintEnabled = false;                      //(4)

    [ObservableProperty]
    private bool isFingerprintAvailable = false;                    //(5)
    ...
    public async Task<bool> AuthenticateAsync(string reason,        //(6)
string? cancel = null, string? fallback = null,
string? tooFast = null) {
        CancellationTokenSource cancelToken;
        cancelToken = new CancellationTokenSource();
var dialogConfig = new AuthenticationRequestConfiguration(
    "Verify your fingerprint", reason) {
        CancelTitle = cancel,
        FallbackTitle = fallback,
        AllowAlternativeAuthentication = false
    };
    dialogConfig.HelpTexts.MovedTooFast = tooFast;
var result = await _fingerprint.AuthenticateAsync(
    dialogConfig, cancelToken.Token);

    return result.Authenticated;
    }
}
```

Listing 7.1: `LoginViewModel.cs` (https://epa.ms/LoginViewModel7-1)

In the `LoginViewModel`, we obtain an instance of the `IFingerprint` interface **(1)** via constructor dependency injection and save it in the member variable `_fingerprint`. This `IFingerprint` instance is then utilized to implement fingerprint status validation and authentication functions.

The function `CheckFingerprintStatus` **(3)** has been implemented to evaluate the device's capability and status, specifically determining if the device supports fingerprint recognition and if it is enabled for the current user. The properties `IsFingerprintEnabled` **(4)** and `IsFingerprintAvailable` **(5)** will be updated by this function.

To enable fingerprint authentication, `FingerprintLogin` **(2)** is incorporated to execute login via fingerprint recognition. The function `AuthenticateAsync` **(6)** is utilized for fingerprint verification; however, it does not carry out the login process.

After implementing the view model, we can focus on developing the user interface. To incorporate fingerprint functionality, it is necessary for the user to activate it initially. We employ a settings page for this purpose. When the fingerprint feature is enabled, the user can access the system using their fingerprint. This login function is incorporated into the LoginPage.

Fingerprint settings

Please refer to *Figure 7.5* for the fingerprint configuration. The user interface design is notably minimalistic, utilizing only a switch control to activate or deactivate the fingerprint function.

Figure 7.5: SettingsPage

The user interface for the SettingsPage is relatively straightforward, which allows us to bypass discussing its XAML. Instead, we will focus on examining the code-behind file of the SettingsPage in *Listing 7.2*:

```
public partial class SettingsPage : ContentPage {
  private LoginService _currentUser;
  ILogger<LoginViewModel> _logger;
  private readonly LoginViewModel _viewModel;
  public SettingsPage(LoginViewModel viewModel,                        //(1)
    LoginService user, ILogger<LoginViewModel> logger) {
    InitializeComponent();
    BindingContext = _viewModel = viewModel;
    _currentUser = user;
    _logger = logger;
    Title = Properties.Resources.menu_id_settings;
  }
  private void SetFingerprintSwitcher() {
    FingerprintSwitcher.IsEnabled =
      _viewModel.IsFingerprintAvailable;
    FingerprintSwitcher.On = _viewModel.IsFingerprintEnabled;
    if (_viewModel.IsFingerprintAvailable) {
      FingerprintSwitcher.Text =
        Properties.Resources.settings_fingerprint_remark;
    }
    else {
      FingerprintSwitcher.Text =
        Properties.Resources.settings_fingerprint_disabled;
    }
  }
  protected override void OnAppearing() {                               //(2)
    base.OnAppearing();
    ...
    try {
      _viewModel.CheckFingerprintStatus();                             //(3)
    }
```

```
      catch (Exception ex) {_logger.LogError($"{ex}");}
      SetFingerprintSwitcher();                                    //(4)
  }
  private async void OnTimerTappedAsync(object sender,
    System.EventArgs e) ...

  private async void SetResultAsync(bool result) {
    if (result) {
      try {
        await _currentUser.SetSecurityAsync(_currentUser.Password);
        _viewModel.IsFingerprintEnabled = true;
      }
      catch (Exception ex) {
        _logger.LogError(
          "SettingsPage: in SetResultAsync, {ex}", ex);
      }
    }
    else {
      FingerprintSwitcher.Text = "Turn on fingerprint error.";
    }
    SetFingerprintSwitcher();
  }
  private async void OnSwitcherToggledAsync(object sender,       //(5)
    ToggledEventArgs e) {
    if (!_viewModel.IsFingerprintAvailable) { return; }

    if (e.Value) {
      try {
        string data = await _currentUser.GetSecurityAsync();
        if (data == null) {
          var status = await _viewModel.AuthenticateAsync(       //(6)
            Properties.Resources.fingerprint_login_message);
          SetResultAsync(status);
        }
      }
```

```
        catch (Exception ex) {_logger.LogError("{ex}", ex); }
    }
    else {
        _ = await _currentUser.DisableSecurityAsync();
    }
    }
}
```

Listing 7.2: `SettingsPage.xaml.cs` *(*`https://epa.ms/SettingsPage7-2`*)*

In the `SettingsPage`, we incorporate `LoginViewModel` **(1)** and `LoginService` through dependency injection. We override the lifecycle method `OnAppearing` **(2)** to evaluate fingerprint support by invoking `CheckFingerprintStatus` **(3)**.

Following this, we execute the function `SetFingerprintSwitcher` **(4)** to update the UI. When users toggle the switch on or off, the event handler `OnSwitcherToggleAsync` **(5)** is activated. Within this event handler, we authenticate the fingerprint by calling `AuthenticateAsync` **(6)** and subsequently save the master password in secure storage. If fingerprint authentication is not used, we remove the master password from secure storage to disable this feature.

Login using a fingerprint

Upon activating the fingerprint feature in the `SettingsPage`, users can utilize fingerprint login, as illustrated in *Figure 7.6*. With the fingerprint function enabled, a fingerprint icon appears next to the password field. By clicking on this icon, users can access the fingerprint login user interface.

Figure 7.6: LoginPage

We can examine the implementation of this fingerprint icon by reviewing the XAML code provided below:

```
<ImageButton x:Name="fpButton" Grid.Row="1" Grid.Column="2"
    VerticalOptions="End" IsVisible="{Binding IsFingerprintEnabled}"
    Command="{Binding FingerprintLoginCommand}"
    BackgroundColor="White" BorderColor="White"
    HeightRequest="32"  WidthRequest="32" BorderWidth="0">
  <ImageButton.Source>
    <FontImageSource FontFamily="FontAwesomeSolid"
          Glyph="{x:Static styles:FontAwesomeSolid.Fingerprint}"
          Color="{DynamicResource Primary}" />
  </ImageButton.Source>
</ImageButton>
```

The fingerprint icon is designed as an `ImageButton`, which will only be visible when `IsFingerprintEnabled` is set to true through data binding. Upon clicking the icon, the `FingerprintLoginCommand` will be triggered. By leveraging the MVVM pattern, we simply need to add this `ImageButton` to the XAML page, while the remaining logic is implemented within the view model.

We have now completed the introduction of .NET MAUI/Xamarin plugins. Our app's fingerprint support was made possible through the use of `Plugin.Fingerprint`. In the upcoming section, we will explore another case – creating custom controls or customizing existing ones.

Customizing controls

.NET MAUI controls are built on the foundation of native controls. There may be instances where we would like these native controls to exhibit customized behavior to cater to our specific needs. Additionally, there might be situations when we need to create our own controls, particularly when the desired native controls are not readily available in .NET MAUI.

In this section, we will discuss the .NET MAUI implementations of cross-platform controls and use an example to illustrate how to enhance a cross-platform control with new capabilities.

In our application, we might want to present a password entry as a secure note, rather than as a standard password entry on the details page. To improve the user experience, we aim to support Markdown text instead of plain text. As .NET MAUI currently does not provide a Markdown view control, we must create our own. We will use this scenario as an example to demonstrate how to expand the functionality of existing controls to develop a new one.

Overview of handlers

In .NET MAUI, handlers play a crucial role in the rendering process by transforming cross-platform view elements (controls) into their corresponding platform-specific native UI components. The implementation of handlers bears a resemblance to the approach taken in the `Plugin.Fingerprint` implementation, where a control-specific interface is employed to distinguish between the cross-platform view and the native view. As we plan to implement our `MarkdownView` using the `WebView` control, we will use the `WebView` control as an example to explain handlers.

A `WebView` displays web content and HTML within a .NET MAUI application. In .NET MAUI, each supported platform (iOS, Android, macOS, and Windows) has corresponding handlers for the `WebView` control, mapping it to native controls. Such examples include `WKWebView` for iOS and macOS, `WebView` for Android, and `WebView2` for Windows.

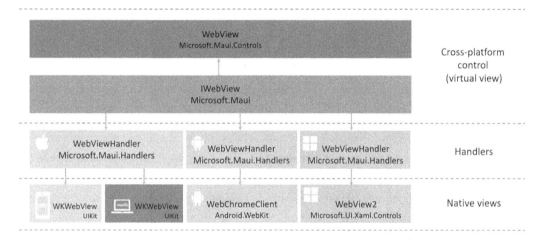

Figure 7.7: .NET MAUI handlers

As depicted in *Figure 7.7*, the architecture consists of three layers: a virtual view, handlers, and native views. Cross-platform controls interact with native views via a control-specific interface implemented by the handlers. In the case of `WebView`, it communicates with `WebViewHandler` through the `IWebView` interface.

The `IWebView` interface is implemented by `WebViewHandler`, which utilizes partial classes to segregate the platform-specific implementation, such as:

- `WebViewHandler.iOS.cs`
- `WebViewHandler.Android.cs`

- `WebViewHandler.WinUI.cs`
- `WebViewHandler.MacCatalyst.cs`

Within the handler, the `VirtualView` property is defined as a reference to the cross-platform control, while the `PlatformView` property refers to the native view. A property mapper is utilized to establish a connection between the cross-platform control's API and the native view's API.

The implementation of .NET MAUI handlers illustrates the architectural differences between .NET MAUI and Xamarin.Forms. For more information on .NET MAUI handlers, you can refer to the Microsoft article titled "*Create a custom control using handlers*" in the *Further reading* section. This article provides extensive insights into the creation and application of custom controls using handlers.

Using HybridWebView

As we introduce handlers, we will investigate the implementation of a Markdown view using `WebView`. A common approach to displaying Markdown text involves converting it into HTML and then presenting the HTML content within a `WebView`. Our challenge lies in transforming the Markdown text into HTML. There are .NET libraries available to accomplish this, such as Markdig, which can be found at `https://github.com/xoofx/markdig`.

Opting for this approach requires us to convert Markdown text into HTML at runtime and subsequently assemble an HTML page. Since `WebView` will be employed, a more straightforward method involves directly passing the Markdown text to `WebView` and allowing `WebView` to interpret the text, using a JavaScript library. However, the default `WebView` lacks sufficient JavaScript interoperability to facilitate this process. As a solution, we will implement our Markdown view using the open-source project `HybridWebView`, developed by Eilon Lipton, which can be found at `https://github.com/Eilon/MauiHybridWebView`.

`HybridWebView` improves `WebView` by supporting more sophisticated JavaScript interoperability. This enhancement allows for the following functionalities:

- We can configure a JavaScript library and resources by utilizing .NET MAUI raw resources, packaging them similarly to a static website. At runtime, we can load it in `WebView`, which resembles a **Single Page Application (SPA)**. There is a sample app that demonstrates how to convert an existing React application into a .NET MAUI application running in `WebView`.
- `HybridWebView` also augments event handling and enables JavaScript functions to invoke .NET functions, and vice versa.

With the assistance of `HybridWebView`, let's explore how to incorporate `MarkdownView` into our app.

Implementing MarkdownView

The concept behind MarkdownView is to directly pass the Markdown text that we wish to display to HybridWebView. This employs a JavaScript library to render the text. To achieve this, we require a JavaScript-based Markdown interpreter. Given that Markdown is widely utilized in numerous web applications, several JavaScript libraries are available for this purpose. We will use a compact, yet efficient library called Marked, which can be found at https://github.com/markedjs/marked.

Utilizing the Marked library is quite simple. You can simply invoke it as follows:

```html
<!doctype html>
<html>
<head>
  <meta charset="utf-8"/>
  <title>Marked in the browser</title>
</head>
<body>
  <div id="content"></div>
  <script src="https://cdn.jsdelivr.net/npm/marked/marked.min.js">
  </script>
  <script>
    document.getElementById('content').innerHTML =
      marked.parse('This is rendered by **marked**.');
  </script>
</body>
</html>
```

We can observe that displaying a Markdown string is achieved by passing it to the marked.parse function.

However, before we proceed, we must determine the appropriate moment to pass this Markdown string to WebView. If we simply call a JavaScript function from the .NET side, the JavaScript function in the HTML file may not be fully prepared. Hence, it is essential to wait for the HTML file to load completely in WebView.

By employing the jQuery library, we can obtain an event that notifies .NET when the HTML page is ready, as illustrated in *Figure 7.8*.

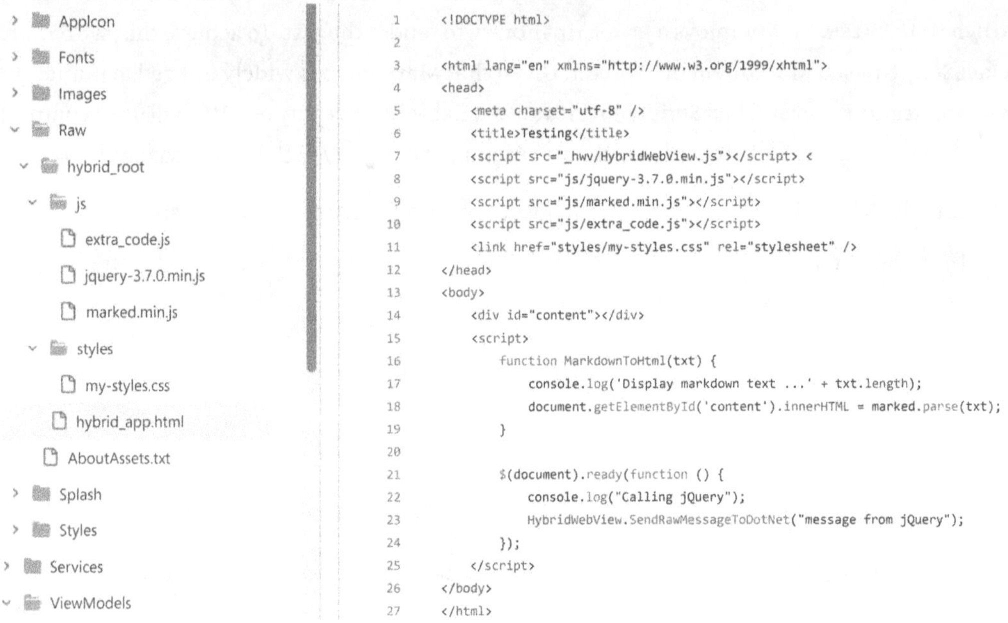

```
1    <!DOCTYPE html>
2
3    <html lang="en" xmlns="http://www.w3.org/1999/xhtml">
4        <head>
5            <meta charset="utf-8" />
6            <title>Testing</title>
7            <script src="_hwv/HybridWebView.js"></script> <
8            <script src="js/jquery-3.7.0.min.js"></script>
9            <script src="js/marked.min.js"></script>
10           <script src="js/extra_code.js"></script>
11           <link href="styles/my-styles.css" rel="stylesheet" />
12       </head>
13       <body>
14           <div id="content"></div>
15           <script>
16               function MarkdownToHtml(txt) {
17                   console.log('Display markdown text ...' + txt.length);
18                   document.getElementById('content').innerHTML = marked.parse(txt);
19               }
20
21               $(document).ready(function () {
22                   console.log("Calling jQuery");
23                   HybridWebView.SendRawMessageToDotNet("message from jQuery");
24               });
25           </script>
26       </body>
27   </html>
```

Folder tree (left side of figure):
- AppIcon
- Fonts
- Images
- Raw
  - hybrid_root
    - js
      - extra_code.js
      - jquery-3.7.0.min.js
      - marked.min.js
    - styles
      - my-styles.css
    - hybrid_app.html
    - AboutAssets.txt
- Splash
- Styles
- Services
- ViewModels

Figure 7.8: HTML and JavaScript resources

As depicted in *Figure 7.8*, we create a folder named `hybrid_root` within the `Raw` directory under the `Resources` folder. Within the `hybrid_root` folder, we store JavaScript files in the `js` folder and CSS files in the `styles` folder.

The `js` folder houses local copies of both Marked and jQuery, eliminating the need for network requests when displaying a Markdown string. The left side of *Figure 7.8* displays the contents of `hybrid_app.html`. Inside this file, we utilize the jQuery function `$(document).ready()` to send an event to the .NET side when the page has loaded. Once the .NET side receives this event, it can invoke the `MarkdownToHtml` function by passing a Markdown string to it. In this manner, we can display any Markdown string using `MarkdownView`.

Having explained the necessary preparations for HTML and JavaScript, let's examine what we need to implement on the .NET side. We can begin by looking at the implementation of `MarkdownView` in *Listing 7.3*:

```
public class MarkdownView : HybridWebView.HybridWebView
{
    public MarkdownView() {
```

```
        HybridAssetRoot = "hybrid_root";                          //(1)
        MainFile = "hybrid_app.html";                             //(2)
    }


    public void DisplayMarkdown(string markdown) {
#if !ANDROID
        string markDownTxt =
           HttpUtility.JavaScriptStringEncode(markdown);          //(3)
#else
        string markDownTxt = markdown;
#endif
        MainThread.BeginInvokeOnMainThread(async () => {          //(4)
           await InvokeJsMethodAsync("MarkdownToHtml", markDownTxt);
        });
    }
}
```

Listing 7.3: `MarkdownView.cs` *(https://epa.ms/MarkdownView7-3)*

In the `MarkdownView`, we must establish the web asset's root as `hybrid_root` **(1)**, and `hybrid_app.`
`html` **(2)** is the HTML file that needs to be loaded.

A function called `DisplayMarkdown` is created to showcase Markdown text, and it will invoke
the JavaScript function `MarkdownToHtml` **(4)** to display the text. Since the encoding of Markdown text varies between Android, Windows, and iOS/macOS, the string encoding function
`JavaScriptStringEncode` **(3)** has to be called for Windows and iOS/macOS platforms. After
implementing `MarkdownView`, we can develop the user interface to render Markdown text, as
demonstrated in *Listing 7.4*:

```
<?xml version="1.0" encoding="utf-8" ?>
<ContentPage
    xmlns="http://schemas.microsoft.com/dotnet/2021/maui"
    xmlns:x="http://schemas.microsoft.com/winfx/2009/xaml"
    xmlns:vw="clr-namespace:PassXYZ.Vault.Views"
    x:Class="PassXYZ.Vault.Views.NotesPage"
    Title="{Binding Title}">
    <vw:MarkdownView x:Name="markdownview"
      RawMessageReceived="OnHybridWebViewRawMessageReceived"
      VerticalOptions="FillAndExpand"/>
</ContentPage>
```

Listing 7.4: `NotesPage.xaml` *(https://epa.ms/NotesPage7-4)*

In *Listing 7.4*, a MarkdownView called markdownview is defined. An event handler, OnHybridWebVi
ewRawMessageReceived, is registered, and its implementation can be found in the code-behind
file in *Listing 7.5*:

```
using PassXYZ.Vault.ViewModels;
namespace PassXYZ.Vault.Views;

public partial class NotesPage : ContentPage {
  ItemDetailViewModel _viewModel;

  public NotesPage(ItemDetailViewModel viewModel) {
    InitializeComponent();
    BindingContext = _viewModel = viewModel;
#if DEBUG
    markdownview.EnableWebDevTools = true;
#endif
  }
  protected override void OnAppearing() {                          //(1)
    base.OnAppearing();
    markdownview.Reload();
  }

  private void OnHybridWebViewRawMessageReceived(object sender,
    HybridWebView.HybridWebViewRawMessageReceivedEventArgs e) {
    markdownview.DisplayMarkdown(_viewModel.MarkdownText);         //(2)
  }
}
```

Listing 7.5: NotesPage.xaml.cs *(*https://epa.ms/NotesPage7-5*)*

In the NotesPage.xaml.cs file, we override the OnAppearing function **(1)**. This function ensures
that MarkdownView is reloaded every time the page is loaded.

The OnHybridWebViewRawMessageReceived event handler is where we invoke DisplayMarkdown
(2) to showcase the Markdown text. *Figure 7.9* displays the completed user interface.

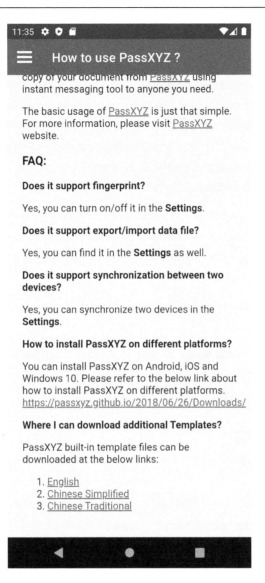

Figure 7.9: MarkdownView

With the introduction of MarkdownView, we have gained knowledge on expanding an existing control to accommodate the necessary new features.

Summary

In this chapter, we presented guidelines on implementing platform-specific code within a .NET MAUI project. There are numerous instances where platform-specific code implementation may be required. Regardless of whether we aim to create a plugin or a custom control, it is crucial to begin with an interface definition. A pre-defined interface facilitates the seamless separation of cross-platform and native implementations. To implement the interface, we have the option to employ either an abstract class or a partial class, allowing us to distribute the implementation for each platform across individual files.

The introduction of `HybridWebView` opens the door to integrating or reusing JavaScript libraries. By crafting hybrid solutions, we can harness the advantages of both .NET and the JavaScript ecosystem. `HybridWebView` enables the development of .NET solutions that incorporate various JavaScript frameworks.

Having completed the current version of the password manager app, we have now reached the end of *Part 1* of this book.

In *Part 2*, we will delve into the Blazor Hybrid app within .NET MAUI, which is a novel feature that is not present in Xamarin.Forms. By employing Blazor, we can introduce some cutting-edge frontend development methods to .NET MAUI development.

Further reading

- Biometric / fingerprint plugin for Xamarin: `https://github.com/smstuebe/xamarin-fingerprint`
- .NET MAUI HybridWebView: `https://github.com/Eilon/MauiHybridWebView`
- Marked – Markdown parser: `https://marked.js.org`
- Xamarin Mobile Application Development for Android: `https://www.oreilly.com/library/view/xamarin-mobile-application/9781785280375/`
- Beginning Xamarin Development for the Mac: Create iOS, watchOS, and Apple tvOS apps with Xamarin.iOS and Visual Studio for Mac: `https://www.oreilly.com/library/view/beginning-xamarin-development/9781484231326/`
- .NET MAUI source code: `https://github.com/dotnet/maui`
- .NET for Android source code – both .NET for Android and Xamarin.Android are built from this repository with different build configurations: `https://github.com/xamarin/xamarin-android`

- .NET for iOS source code – both .NET for iOS and Xamarin.iOS are built from this repository with different build configurations: `https://github.com/xamarin/xamarin-macios`

- .NET for Mac source code – .NET for iOS and .NET for Mac share the same codebase with different build configurations: `https://github.com/xamarin/xamarin-macios`

- WinUI: `https://github.com/microsoft/microsoft-ui-xaml`

- Create a custom control using handlers: `https://learn.microsoft.com/en-us/dotnet/maui/user-interface/handlers/create?view=net-maui-8.0`

- Introducing Shared Class Library – multi-target Xamarin.Forms and .NET MAUI from a single project: `https://egvijayanand.in/2022/05/25/introducing-shared-class-library-multi-target-xamarin-forms-and-dotnet-maui-from-a-single-project/`

Leave a review!

Enjoying this book? Help readers like you by leaving an Amazon review. Scan the QR code below for a 40% discount code.

*Limited Offer

Part 2

Implementing .NET MAUI Blazor

In the second part of this book, we will explore the process of building a .NET MAUI Blazor Hybrid application. Blazor is a modern web framework developed by Microsoft, allowing developers to create interactive web applications using C# and Razor syntax rather than JavaScript. You might be familiar with JavaScript frameworks like React, Angular, and Vue, among others. Unlike most frontend frameworks, which rely on JavaScript, Blazor utilizes C# as an alternative.

Moreover, Blazor can be employed for developing Blazor Hybrid applications. In a Blazor Hybrid app, Razor components function natively on the device through an embedded Web View control, which enables the app to access device features, just like a native app would.

In *Part 2*, we will redesign our app as a Blazor Hybrid app. We will cover Blazor Bindings, a new topic that allows you to leverage the power of Blazor within the .NET MAUI framework, expanding your options for application development.

Part 2 includes the following chapters:

- *Chapter 8, Introducing Blazor Hybrid App Development*
- *Chapter 9, Understanding Blazor Routing and Layout*
- *Chapter 10, Implementing Razor Components*

8

Introducing Blazor Hybrid App Development

In .NET MAUI, an alternative approach to constructing the **user interface** (UI) is by using Blazor. Blazor, a modern web framework developed by Microsoft, allows developers to create interactive web applications utilizing C# and Razor syntax instead of JavaScript. Additionally, Blazor can be employed in the development of .NET MAUI applications as part of a Blazor Hybrid app. The fundamental building blocks of Blazor are Razor components, which can be reused between native and web applications when utilizing Blazor and Blazor Hybrid. In comparison to XAML UIs, a Blazor UI offers increased reusability, encompassing both native and web applications. In this chapter, we will provide an introduction to Blazor and discuss its implementation in various scenarios. Additionally, we will introduce Razor components and explain how to develop a Blazor Hybrid app using these components.

We will cover the following topics in this chapter:

- What is Blazor?
- How to create a .NET MAUI Blazor project
- How to create a new Razor component

Technical requirements

To test and debug the source code in this chapter, you need to have Visual Studio 2022 installed on your PC or Mac. Please refer to the *Development environment setup* section in *Chapter 1, Getting Started with .NET MAUI*, for the details.

The source code for this chapter is available in the following GitHub repository: `https://github.com/PacktPublishing/.NET-MAUI-Cross-Platform-Application-Development-Second-edition/tree/main/2nd/chapter08`.

To check out the source code of this chapter, we can use the following command:

```
$ git clone -b 2nd/chapter08 https://github.com/PacktPublishing/.NET-MAUI-
Cross-Platform-Application-Development-Second-edition.git PassXYZ.Vault2
```

To find out more about the source code in this book, please refer to the *Managing the source code in this book* section in *Chapter 2, Building Our First .NET MAUI App*.

What is Blazor?

Blazor is a framework designed to build web applications utilizing HTML, CSS, and C#. When developing web applications with Blazor in ASP.NET Core, you have two options to consider: Blazor Server and Blazor **WebAssembly** (**Wasm**). Furthermore, .NET MAUI enables the use of Blazor to create native applications, introducing a third variant – the Blazor Hybrid app.

In web application development, tasks typically involve creating a frontend UI and a backend service. Backend services can be accessed through RESTful APIs or **remote procedure calls** (**RPCs**). UI components, comprised of HTML, CSS, and JavaScript, are loaded in a browser and displayed as web pages. In the ASP.NET Core architecture, components related to user interaction can be rendered on the server. This hosting model is known as Blazor Server. Alternatively, we can execute most of the UI components within the browser, which is referred to as the Blazor Wasm hosting model.

In some instances, applications may require access to device-specific features, such as sensors or cameras; to accommodate these requirements, developers usually create native applications. However, Blazor offers an additional solution – the Blazor Hybrid app. Now, let's discuss Blazor hosting models in more detail.

Hosting models

Blazor is a web framework designed for building web UI components, commonly referred to as Razor components, which can be hosted through various methods. These components can operate on the server side within ASP.NET Core (Blazor Server) or client side inside a web browser (Blazor Wasm).

Furthermore, Razor components can be implemented in native mobile and desktop applications by rendering them within an embedded Web View control (Blazor Hybrid). Despite the differences in hosting models, the process of building Razor components remains consistent. Consequently, the same Razor components can be utilized across all hosting models without any modification.

Blazor Server

In traditional web application development, the logic for user interactions is executed on the server side. Within the MVC design pattern, handling user interaction is an integral part of the application architecture. When a user interaction occurs in the browser, it is sent back to the server for processing. As a result, the entire page may be reloaded in response to the user's request.

To enhance performance, Blazor Server employs a design that resembles a **single-page application (SPA)** framework. When responding to a user request, Blazor Server processes it and only sends the **Document Object Model (DOM)** changes pertaining to the user action to the browser. As depicted in *Figure 8.1*, the processing logic in Blazor Server is similar to that of a SPA, with the key distinction being that Razor components are rendered on the server, rather than the browser. In order to facilitate real-time communication between the web client and the server, SignalR, an open source library, is utilized as the connection between the server and browser.

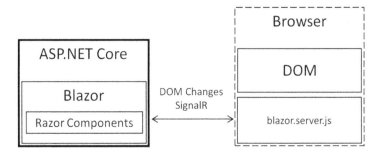

Figure 8.1: Blazor Server

Razor components versus Blazor components

People may get confused between Blazor and Razor. Razor was introduced as a template engine of ASP.NET in 2010. Razor syntax is a markup syntax in which developers can embed C# code into an HTML page. Blazor is a web framework that uses Razor syntax as the programming language. It was introduced around 2018. Blazor is a component-based framework, and a Blazor app consists of Razor components. In other words, Blazor is a hosting model for Razor components. Blazor components and Razor components are widely used interchangeably, but the correct terminology is Razor component.

A Razor component resides in a file with the `.razor` extension, and it is compiled as a .NET class at runtime. This `.razor` file can also be split into two files with `.razor` and `.razor.cs` extensions. The idea is quite similar to XAML and code-behind, which we learned about in *Part 1* of this book.

In Blazor Server, the app's state is maintained on the server, and the client does not need a .NET runtime. This model can result in a faster initial load time as the browser only downloads a small initial payload. However, it requires a constant connection with the server, which may affect the scalability and introduce latency in UI updates.

Blazor Wasm

Blazor Wasm is a hosting model that renders Razor components within a web browser. As illustrated in *Figure 8.2*, the Razor components are loaded into the browser and compiled into Wasm using the .NET runtime:

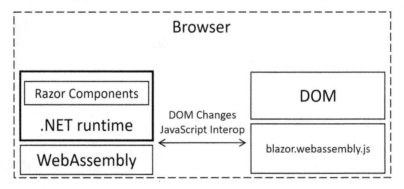

Figure 8.2: Blazor Wasm

In the browser, the startup page loads the .NET environment and Razor components. These Razor components are compiled to Wasm through a .NET **Intermediate Language** (IL) interpreter at runtime, which manages DOM changes. This process is commonly known as **just-in-time** (JIT) compilation. With JIT, the compilation takes place at runtime, which results in slower performance compared to **ahead-of-time** (AOT) compilation. Blazor Wasm apps can be compiled AOT to Wasm to improve runtime performance but at the expense of a much larger download size.

With the introduction of .NET 8, a new runtime feature called jiterpreter was introduced in .NET 8 that enables partial JIT support in the .NET IL interpreter to achieve improved runtime performance.

Blazor Wasm apps can be deployed as static files and hosted on various web server platforms or static site hosting providers. Optionally, Blazor Wasm can also communicate with a server through API calls to retrieve data or offload complex operations.

Wasm

Wasm is a binary instruction format for a stack-based virtual machine. Wasm is supported by most modern web browsers. With Wasm, we can use many programming languages to develop client-side components.

As a SPA framework, Blazor can be compared to other JavaScript-based SPA frameworks, such as React, Angular, and Vue. Numerous JavaScript SPA frameworks exist, and *Table 8.1* contains a comparison between Blazor and React. Although other JavaScript frameworks could also be used for comparison, the decision to choose React was based on the fact that React Native can be utilized to develop Hybrid apps. This shares some similarities with .NET MAUI Blazor, which will be discussed in the following section:

Feature	React	Blazor Wasm	Blazor Server
Language	JavaScript/JSX/Type-Script	C#	C#
Runtime	JavaScript engine	Wasm	ASP.NET Core
Progressive Web App (PWA) Support	Yes	Yes	No
Hosting	Flexible to choose	Flexible to choose	ASP.NET Core

Static Site Hosting	Yes	Yes	No
Offloads Processing to Clients	Yes	Yes	No
Performance	Lightweight with great performance	There is a heavier first-time load due to the extra download time of .NET runtimes	Similar performance to the JavaScript framework

Table 8.1: Comparison of Blazor and React

Both JavaScript and Wasm are integral features of modern browsers. SPA frameworks that utilize either JavaScript or Wasm require no additional dependencies to run in a browser. Blazor Wasm supports JavaScript Interop, enabling the use of JavaScript components with Blazor.

Both Blazor and React support PWA development, which allows SPAs to function in offline mode.

Blazor Wasm and React both operate on the client side, utilizing **client-side rendering (CSR)**. As a result, relying solely on these libraries for a web application could negatively affect **search engine optimization (SEO)** and the initial loading performance. This is because a considerable amount of time is necessary for the proper rendering of the content on the screen. In fact, in order to display the complete web app, the browser must download the entire application bundle, parse its content, execute it, and then render the result. This process could take several seconds for larger applications.

On the other hand, Blazor Server employs **server-side rendering (SSR)** to enhance the performance and user experience of web pages, particularly for users with slow internet connections or devices. SSR can decrease the initial loading time and bandwidth consumption of web pages by only sending the necessary HTML and CSS for the first render, while CSR necessitates downloading and executing a significant amount of JavaScript code before anything is rendered. Moreover, SSR facilitates faster interactions and transitions between pages, as the server can pre-render the upcoming page and transmit it to the browser as soon as the user clicks a link.

Another advantage of SSR is that it can improve the SEO and social media sharing of web pages, as the server can provide the full HTML content and metadata of each page to crawlers and bots. CSR can make it harder for crawlers and bots to access and index the content of web pages, as they may not be able to execute JavaScript or wait for asynchronous data fetching.

SSR can also ensure that the content and layout of web pages are consistent across different browsers and devices, as the server can handle browser compatibility and responsiveness issues.

In recent developments, both Blazor and JavaScript frameworks have transitioned to mixed rendering modes to harness the benefits of both CSR and SSR. With the introduction of .NET 8, Auto render mode is now available. This mode employs Wasm-based rendering when the .NET Wasm runtime can be loaded swiftly (within 100ms). This generally occurs when the runtime has already been downloaded and cached, or when a high-speed network connection is being used. If these conditions are not satisfied, the Auto render mode defaults to Server render mode while simultaneously downloading the .NET Wasm runtime in the background.

Blazor Hybrid

We can also utilize Blazor as the UI layer for desktop or mobile native frameworks, which are referred to as Blazor Hybrid applications. In such an app, Razor components are natively rendered on the device using an integrated WebView control. Wasm is not involved, so the application possesses the same capabilities as a native app.

In *Figure 8.3*, we observe that a Hybrid app allows us to utilize the **BlazorWebView** control for constructing and executing Razor components within an embedded WebView. The **BlazorWebView** control can be accessed in .NET MAUI and Windows desktop environments. By utilizing .NET MAUI and Blazor together, it is possible to use one set of web UI components across mobile, desktop, and web platforms.

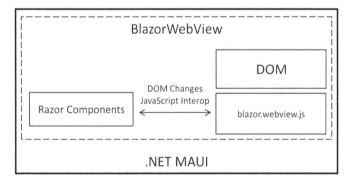

Figure 8.3: BlazorWebView

Blazor Hybrid applications can be developed using .NET MAUI, WPF, or Windows Forms. This means that it is possible to create a Blazor Hybrid application as a WPF, Windows Forms, or .NET MAUI application. In *Part 2*, we will focus solely on building a .NET MAUI Blazor Hybrid application.

We have presented three Blazor hosting models. Among these models, both Blazor Server and Blazor Hybrid applications offer full support for the .NET API. However, Blazor Wasm applications are limited to using a subset of the .NET APIs.

Blazor Bindings

Other than the hosting models that we previously introduced. There is a special type of Blazor app called Blazor Bindings available. Blazor Bindings or Mobile Blazor Bindings is an experimental project from Microsoft aimed at expanding the capabilities of Blazor, making it a cross-platform technology not only for creating web applications but also, eventually, for mobile development.

Blazor is a framework that allows you to build interactive web interfaces using C# instead of JavaScript, for both client and server code. It relies on Wasm to run the C# code directly in the browser.

With Mobile Blazor Bindings, the developer can write Blazor syntax and components but have them rendered as native controls on iOS, macOS, Windows, and Android – similar to how .NET MAUI XAML applications operate.

The key components of Mobile Blazor Bindings are:

- **.NET Runtime**: Since .NET 5, we have a common BCL on all support platforms.
- **Blazor**: Blazor allows running .NET Standard compatible code in the browser using Wasm. It also provides a way to define UI components using Razor files (`.razor`).
- **.NET MAUI**: .NET MAUI is a framework for building native UIs for iOS, macOS, Android, and Windows from a single, shared code base.
- **BlazorBindings.Maui:** This is the NuGet package published by Oleksandr Liakhevych. This package provides the basic Blazor Bindings functionality.

Mobile Blazor Bindings allow developers to use existing Blazor development skills for mobile application development, where developers can use Razor syntax with C# to build UI components for either Web UI or native UIs.

It's important to note that, as of January 2024, Mobile Blazor Bindings are still in the experimental phase and are not recommended for production applications. Microsoft's original source code repository can be found here: `https://github.com/dotnet/MobileBlazorBindings/`.

Currently, the project is in the preview stage and is not under active maintenance. However, some updates have been merged from the GitHub repository of Oleksandr Liakhevych. Oleksandr Liakhevych is actively developing and maintaining his own repository: `https://github.com/Dreamescaper/BlazorBindings.Maui`.

I have applied the Blazor Bindings from Oleksandr Liakhevych in implementing the source code for the first and second chapters of the book. The implemented code can be found in the designated branches: `BlazorBindings/chapter01` and `BlazorBindings/chapter02`: https://github.com/PacktPublishing/.NET-MAUI-Cross-Platform-Application-Development-Second-edition.

To gain an understanding of Blazor Bindings, let's compare the code and screenshot from the 2nd/chapter01 and `BlazorBindings/chapter01` branches, as exemplified in the following code and *Figure 8.4*. The branch 2nd/chapter01 code was created from the .NET MAUI project template, whereas the code in the branch `BlazorBindings/chapter01` is the equivalent implementation using Blazor.

`MainPage.xaml (2nd/chapter01)` — https://epa.ms/MainPage-CH01

```
<?xml version="1.0" encoding="utf-8" ?>
<ContentPage xmlns="http://schemas.microsoft.com/dotnet/2021/maui"
             xmlns:x="http://schemas.microsoft.com/winfx/2009/xaml"
             x:Class="PassXYZ.Vault.MainPage">

  <ScrollView>
    <VerticalStackLayout
      Padding="30,0"
      Spacing="25">
      <Image Source="dotnet_bot.png" HeightRequest="185"
        Aspect="AspectFit"
        SemanticProperties.Description=
          "dot net bot in a race car number eight" />

      <Label Text="Hello, World!"
        Style="{StaticResource Headline}"
        SemanticProperties.HeadingLevel="Level1" />

      <Label Text="Welcome to &#10;.NET Multi-platform App UI"
        Style="{StaticResource SubHeadline}"
        SemanticProperties.HeadingLevel="Level2"
        SemanticProperties.Description=
          "Welcome to dot net Multi platform App U I" />

      <Button x:Name="CounterBtn" Text="Click me"
```

```
            SemanticProperties.Hint=
              "Counts the number of times you click"
            Clicked="OnCounterClicked"
            HorizontalOptions="Fill" />
      </VerticalStackLayout>
    </ScrollView>

  </ContentPage>
```

Within `MainPage.xaml`, a `ScrollView` is included. This `ScrollView` contains an `Image`, two `Label` instances, and a `Button`, all of which are housed within the `VerticalStackLayout` control.

MainPage.Razor (BlazorBindings/chapter01) – https://epa.ms/MainPage-BlazorBindings

```
@page "/main"

<ContentPage>
  <ScrollView>
    <VerticalStackLayout Spacing="25"
      Padding="new(30,0)"
      VerticalOptions="LayoutOptions.Center">

      <Image Source="dotNetBotSource" HeightRequest="200"
          HorizontalOptions="LayoutOptions.Center" />

      <Label Text="Hello, World!" FontSize="32"
        HorizontalOptions="LayoutOptions.Center" />

      <Label Text=
        "Welcome to .NET Multi-platform Blazor Bindings App UI"
        FontSize="18"
        HorizontalOptions="LayoutOptions.Center" />
```

```
        <Button Text="@ButtonText"
          HorizontalOptions="LayoutOptions.Fill"
          OnClick="OnCounterClicked" />
      </VerticalStackLayout>
    </ScrollView>
  </ContentPage>

@code {
  ImageSource dotNetBotSource =
    ImageSource.FromFile("dotnet_bot.png");

  int count = 0;

  string ButtonText => count switch
  {
    0 => "Click me",
    1 => $"Clicked 1 time",
    _ => $"Clicked {count} times"
  };

  void OnCounterClicked()
  {
    count++;
  }
}
```

Within `MainPage.razor`, we've replicated the same UI but used Razor syntax. We'll delve deeper into the particulars of Razor syntax later in this chapter. Meanwhile, we can compare the UIs in *Figure 8.4*. They appear to be identical:

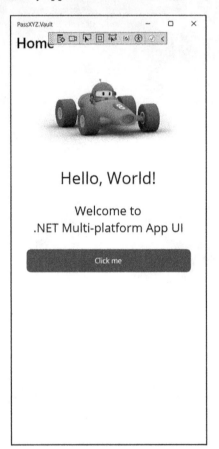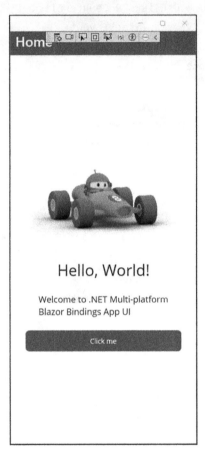

Figure 8.4: Recreating the main page UI using Razor syntax

What's new in .NET 8 Blazor hosting models

In our previous discussion of Blazor hosting models, we touched upon the topic of Blazor render modes. Prior to .NET 8, ASP.NET Core supported two render modes: SSR and CSR. These render modes were tied to a project type at compile time.

However, .NET 8 introduced a new feature to harness the benefits of both SSR and CSR – the Interactive Auto rendering. This new rendering mode initially uses a server-side ASP.NET Core for content rendering and interactivity.

It then switches to the .NET Wasm runtime on the client side for subsequent rendering and interactivity, after the Blazor bundle is downloaded and the Wasm runtime activated. Interactive Auto rendering frequently offers the quickest app startup experience.

This constitutes a significant departure from previous ASP.NET Core versions. With .NET 8, developers can designate the render modes of individual components at both compile time and runtime. Moreover, these render modes can be defined at both the component and page levels.

To illustrate this, in the following example, we apply SSR to the `Dialog` component:

```
<Dialog @rendermode="InteractiveServer" />
```

To designate the render modes at the page level, consult the following code snippet:

```
@page "..."
@rendermode InteractiveServer
```

In this code, the entire page will be rendered server side.

With support for specifying render modes at runtime, the boundary between SSR and CSR has become blurry. Developers now have the flexibility to switch render modes within a single application.

Before .NET 8, developers could create either a Blazor Server app or a Blazor Wasm app using Visual Studio templates. But .NET 8 introduced a new project template – the Blazor Web app. We'll examine these project templates further in the next segment.

Project templates of .NET MAUI and Blazor apps

Blazor Server, Blazor Wasm, and Blazor Hybrid run in different hosting models at runtime, so they have different capabilities. Blazor Web app is the new project template introduced in .NET 8. With this template, we can mix render modes at runtime. In this book, our focus is on Blazor Hybrid applications.

We can create different project types using either the command line or Visual Studio.

To conserve space, we will examine the project templates using the command line only. To list the installed project templates, we can run the following command:

```
dotnet new --list
These templates matched your input:
Template Name          Short Name           Language
----------------       ------------------   ----------
```

```
.NET MAUI App        maui              [C#]
.NET MAUI Blazo...   maui-blazor       [C#]
.NET MAUI Class...   mauilib           [C#]
Blazor Server App    blazorserver      [C#]
Blazor Web App       blazor            [C#]
Blazor WebAssem...   blazorwasm        [C#]
Razor Class Lib...   razorclasslib     [C#]
Class Library        classlib          [C#],F#,VB
```

In the preceding list, we filtered out irrelevant project types. To understand the different project types better, we can review the summary depicted in *Table 8.2*:

Template Name/Short Name	SDK	Target Framework
Blazor Wasm app (blazorwasm)	Microsoft.NET.Sdk.BlazorWebAssembly	net8.0
Blazor Server app (blazorserver)	Microsoft.NET.Sdk.Web	net8.0
Blazor Web app (blazor)	Microsoft.NET.Sdk.Web Microsoft.NET.Sdk.BlazorWebAssembly	net8.0
.NET MAUI app (maui)	Microsoft.NET.Sdk	net8.0-android net8.0-ios net8.0-maccatalyst net8.0-windows10.0.19041.0
.NET MAUI Blazor app (maui-blazor)	Microsoft.NET.Sdk.Razor	net8.0-android net8.0-ios net8.0-maccatalyst net8.0-windows10.0.19041.0
.NET MAUI Class Library (mauilib)	Microsoft.NET.Sdk	net8.0-android net8.0-ios net8.0-maccatalyst net8.0-windows10.0.19041.0
Razor Class Library (razorclasslib)	Microsoft.NET.Sdk.Razor	net8.0
Class Library (classlib)	Microsoft.NET.Sdk	net8.0

Table 8.2: .NET MAUI and Blazor-related project types

The project types illustrated in *Table 8.2* can be categorized into two groups – Blazor apps and .NET MAUI apps. Let's examine these groups in more detail.

Blazor apps

In both Blazor Server and Blazor Wasm templates, the target framework is net8.0, but they utilize different SDKs. The Blazor Server application can fully leverage the server's capabilities using `Microsoft.NET.Sdk.Web`, while Blazor Wasm has access to only a limited set of .NET APIs via `Microsoft.NET.Sdk.BlazorWebAssembly`. In the template of Blazor Web app, it mixes both Blazor Server and Blazor Wasm.

To share Razor components between Blazor Server and Blazor Wasm, a Razor Class Library may be employed. This library employs `Microsoft.NET.Sdk.Razor`. Additionally, the standard .NET class library, which can be shared across all .NET 8.0 applications, utilizes `Microsoft.NET.Sdk`.

.NET MAUI apps

In a .NET MAUI application, one can create XAML-based .NET MAUI apps utilizing the `Microsoft.NET.Sdk`, while for .NET MAUI Blazor apps, the `Microsoft.NET.Sdk.Razor` is employed. Both project types cater to the same collection of target frameworks.

In order to share components, the standard .NET class library can be utilized. If it is necessary to incorporate .NET MAUI features within the shared components, the .NET MAUI class library may be employed. For instance, `PassXYZLib` is a .NET MAUI class library. Although both the .NET class library and the .NET MAUI class library utilize the same `Microsoft.NET.Sdk`, they target distinct frameworks.

Creating a new .NET MAUI Blazor project

To learn how to develop a Blazor Hybrid app, we need to upgrade our `PassXYZ.Vault` project to accommodate a Blazor-based UI. Fortunately, we don't need to start from scratch – we can simply modify our existing project to support the Blazor UI. By doing this, we can efficiently build both an XAML-based app and a Hybrid app within the same project. Before incorporating the Blazor UI into our app, let's first establish a new .NET MAUI Blazor project with an identical app name. This will allow us to reference the new project when converting our current project into a .NET MAUI Blazor project.

We have the option to create this new .NET MAUI Blazor project either through the command line or via Visual Studio. We will demonstrate both methods in this section.

Generating a .NET MAUI Blazor project with the dotnet command line

Let us begin by creating a new project using the .NET command line. This can be accomplished on both Windows and macOS platforms. To create a new project, we will utilize the short name maui-blazor, as mentioned in *Table 8.2*:

```
dotnet new maui-blazor -o PassXYZ.Vault
The template ".NET MAUI Blazor Hybrid App" was created successfully.
```

In the previous command, we selected the project template by specifying the short name, maui-blazor, and designated PassXYZ.Vault as the project name. After creating the project, it can be built and executed:

```
C:\ > dotnet build -t:Run -f net8.0-android
MSBuild version 17.8.0-preview-23367-03+0ff2a83e9 for .NET
  Determining projects to restore...
  All projects are up-to-date for restore.
  PassXYZ.Vault -> C:\PassXYZ.Vault\bin\Debug\net8.0-android\PassXYZ.
Vault.dll

Build succeeded.
    0 Warning(s)
    0 Error(s)
Time Elapsed 00:01:43.79
```

In the build command, we designate net8.0-android as the target framework for testing our new app. We can replace the target framework with other supported frameworks such as net8.0-ios, net8.0-maccatalyst, or net8.0-windows10.0.19041.0.

Refer to *Figure 8.6* to view a screenshot of this new app and its project structure. With this, we have successfully created a new project using the command line. Now, let's explore how to accomplish the same task using Visual Studio on Windows.

Creating a .NET MAUI Blazor Hybrid App using Visual Studio on Windows

To create a .NET MAUI Blazor Hybrid App project using Visual Studio, begin by launching Visual Studio and selecting Create a new project, and then in the search box, type MAUI to filter the available options. As shown in *Figure 8.5*, choose .NET MAUI Blazor Hybrid App from the list of project templates:

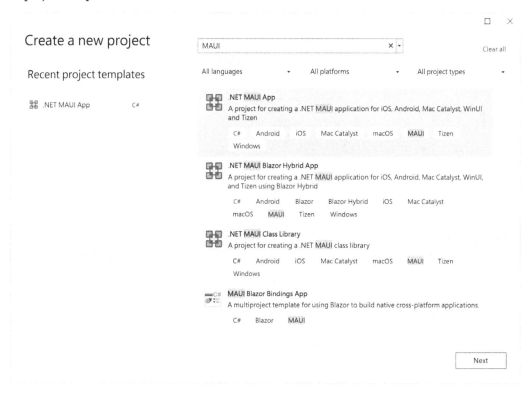

Figure 8.5: Creating a new .NET MAUI Blazor Hybrid App project

After completing the project creation using the wizard, we can choose net8.0-android as the target framework for building and running the project. To conserve space, the Android platform will be used as our primary example in this section; however, you are welcome to explore and test other target frameworks if desired.

Running the new project

To execute the project, press *F5* or *Ctrl + F5* in Visual Studio, or use the dotnet command from the command line. Refer to *Figure 8.6* for screenshots illustrating this process and the project structure.

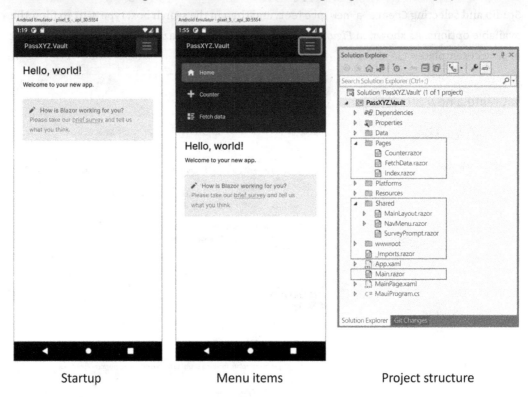

| Startup | Menu items | Project structure |

Figure 8.6: Screenshots and project structure

The UI of the app, created using the template, resembles a SPA with a navigation menu at the top for Android devices. When executed on Windows with a larger screen, the navigation menu displays on the left side of the screen in a side-by-side manner. The project structure closely mirrors that of a standard .NET MAUI app but with the following notable differences:

- wwwroot/: This folder is the root of static files for web pages.
- Pages/: This folder contains Razor pages in the app.
- Shared/: This folder contains Razor components that can be shared.
- Main.razor: This is the main page of the Blazor app.
- _Imports.razor: This is a helper to import Razor components at the folder or project level.

To understand the difference between the .NET MAUI app and the .NET MAUI Blazor app, it is helpful to analyze their respective startup code.

The startup code of the .NET MAUI Blazor Hybrid App

All .NET MAUI apps contain a file named MauiProgram.cs, which handles their startup and configuration. Let's examine the startup code of the .NET MAUI Blazor Hybrid App:

```
namespace PassXYZ.Vault;
public static class MauiProgram {
  public static MauiApp CreateMauiApp() {
    var builder = MauiApp.CreateBuilder();
    builder.UseMauiApp<App>()
      .ConfigureFonts(fonts => {
        fonts.AddFont("OpenSans-Regular.ttf",
            "OpenSansRegular");
      });
    builder.Services.AddMauiBlazorWebView();                    //(1)
#if DEBUG
    builder.Services.AddBlazorWebViewDeveloperTools();          //(2)
#endif
    builder.Services.AddSingleton<WeatherForecastService>();
    return builder.Build();
  }
}
```

In the .NET MAUI Blazor Hybrid App, we can see that the following Blazor configurations have been added:

(1) BlazorWebView is added by calling AddMauiBlazorWebView().

(2) Developer tools are added by calling AddBlazorWebViewDeveloperTools() for debugging.

The rest of the startup process is the same as that for an XAML-based .NET MAUI app. In the App.xaml.cs file, the MainPage property, which is inherited from the App class, is assigned to an instance of MainPage.xaml as we can see in the following:

```
namespace PassXYZ.Vault;
public partial class App : Application {
  public App() {
    InitializeComponent();
```

```
        MainPage = new MainPage();
    }
}
```

The primary distinction between XAML-based applications and Blazor Hybrid applications lies in the UI controls used within `MainPage.xaml`. Let's examine the code of `MainPage.xaml` closely to better understand this difference:

```
<?xml version="1.0" encoding="utf-8" ?>
<ContentPage
    xmlns="http://schemas.microsoft.com/dotnet/2021/maui"
    xmlns:x="http://schemas.microsoft.com/winfx/2009/xaml"
    xmlns:local="clr-namespace:PassXYZ.Vault"
    x:Class="PassXYZ.Vault.MainPage"
    BackgroundColor="{DynamicResource PageBackgroundColor}">

    <BlazorWebView HostPage="wwwroot/index.html">             //(1)
        <BlazorWebView.RootComponents>                        //(2)
            <RootComponent Selector="#app"                    //(3)
                ComponentType="{x:Type local:Main}" />        //(4)
        </BlazorWebView.RootComponents>
    </BlazorWebView>
</ContentPage>
```

In the `MainPage.xaml`, only one UI element named `BlazorWebView` is defined. With the `HostPage` property and the nested node `RootComponent`, it is possible to customize the `BlazorWebView` efficiently.

We can consider `BlazorWebView` to be similar to a browser. In a browser, the UI is typically loaded from an HTML file. The `HostPage` property **(1)** serves to indicate the static HTML page that should load within the web view control. In our specific case, this refers to `wwwroot/index.html`, which we will examine in *Listing 8.1*.

In this static HTML file, we must designate the location for the Razor component and determine the root component. Both can be specified using the attributes of the nested node `RootComponent` **(2)**.

In the previous chapter, we discovered that an XAML tag ultimately maps to a C# class. In this context, both `BlazorWebView` and `RootComponent` are also C# classes.

In the RootComponent, we utilize the Selector attribute **(3)** to define a CSS selector that determines the placement of the root Razor component within our application. In our specific instance, we use the #app CSS selector defined in the index.html file. The ComponentType attribute **(4)** establishes the type of the root component, which in our case is Main.

Finally, let's revisit the HTML file (index.html) that was mentioned earlier.

```
<!DOCTYPE html>
<html lang="en">
<head>
  <meta charset="utf-8" />
  <meta name="viewport" content="width=device-width,
      initial-scale=1.0, maximum-scale=1.0,
      user-scalable=no, viewport-fit=cover" />
  <title>PassXYZ.Vault</title>
  <base href="/" />
  <link rel="stylesheet"
      href="css/bootstrap/bootstrap.min.css" />          //(1)
  <link href="css/app.css" rel="stylesheet" />
  <link href="PassXYZ.Vault.styles.css" rel="stylesheet" />
</head>
<body>
  <div class="status-bar-safe-area"></div>
  <div id="app">Loading...</div>                          //(2)
  <div id="blazor-error-ui">
    An unhandled error has occurred.
    <a href="" class="reload">Reload</a>
    <a class="dismiss">X</a>
  </div>
  <script src="_framework/blazor.webview.js"
      autostart="false">                                  //(3)
  </script>
</body>
</html>
```

Listing 8.1: index.html *(https://epa.ms/index8-1)*

We can see that `index.html` is a simple HTML file:

(1) It uses the CSS stylesheet from the Bootstrap framework.

(2) The `id` selector is specified as `app`, which is then passed to the `Selector` attribute of the `RootComponent` within the `MainPage.xaml` file.

(3) A JavaScript file called `blazor.webview.js` is loaded at the end of `index.html`. This is responsible for initializing the runtime environment for `BlazorWebView`.

With that, we have provided an overview of the .NET MAUI Blazor Hybrid app. In the following section, we will substitute the XAML-based UI with one that utilizes Blazor.

Migrating to a .NET MAUI Blazor Hybrid App

In the previous section, we created a new Hybrid app, which will serve as a reference for migrating our existing application. Instead of starting from scratch, we can take advantage of both the XAML and Blazor UIs within our current app by adjusting the project configuration. For now, we will implement a combination of XAML and Blazor UIs in a single application and, later on, transition entirely to Blazor in the following chapter.

To convert our app into a .NET MAUI Blazor Hybrid app, it is necessary to implement the following modifications.

Change the SDK in the project file by replacing `Microsoft.NET.Sdk` with `Microsoft.NET.Sdk.Razor`, as the .NET MAUI Blazor Hybrid app relies on a different SDK.

1. In the `PassXYZ.Vault.csproj` project file, the following line is present:

    ```
    <Project Sdk="Microsoft.NET.Sdk">
    ```

2. This line needs to be replaced with the following:

    ```
    <Project Sdk="Microsoft.NET.Sdk.Razor">
    ```

3. Transfer the subsequent folders from the newly established project into our application:

    *   `wwwroot`
    *   `Shared`

4. Transfer the subsequent files from the new project to our app:

    *   `_Imports.razor`
    *   `MainPage.xaml`

- MainPage.xaml.cs

- Main.razor

5. Revise MauiProgram.cs by adding the following code:

```
    Builder.Services.AddMauiBlazorWebView();
#if DEBUG
    builder.Services.AddBlazorWebViewDeveloperTools();
#endif
```

To review the commit history of these changes, go to https://epa.ms/Blazor7-1.

With these adjustments, we have implemented all the necessary modifications to the configuration and can now proceed to the subsequent step. Nonetheless, before we delve into working on these changes, let us first acquaint ourselves with the fundamental Razor syntax.

Understanding Razor syntax

Blazor applications are composed of Razor components. As discussed in *Chapter 3, User Interface Design with XAML*, XAML is a language that has its roots in XML. UI elements based on XAML consist of XAML pages and their corresponding C# code-behind files. Razor components closely resemble this pattern, with the primary difference being that Razor employs HTML as its markup language and C# code can be directly embedded within the HTML. Alternatively, we can opt to separate the C# code into a code-behind file, thus maintaining a clear distinction between the UI and its underlying logic.

Code blocks in Razor

To create the simplest Razor component, it would appear as follows:

```
<h3>Hello World!</h3>
@code {
  // Put your C# code here
}
```

In the previous example, we can design our page similarly to an HTML page while incorporating programming logic within a code block. Razor pages or Razor components are generated as C# classes, with the filename serving as the class name. The newly created Razor components can be utilized as HTML tags in another Razor page.

Implicit Razor expressions

In Razor syntax, we can transition from HTML to C# using the @ symbol. These are referred to as implicit Razor expressions. For instance, we can use the following implicit expression to set the text of the `label` tag with the C# variable `currentUser.Username`:

```
<label>@currentUser.Username</label>
```

There should be no spaces between implicit expressions. Using C# generics in implicit expressions is not possible, as the characters within the angle brackets (<>) are interpreted as an HTML tag.

Explicit Razor expressions

In order to address the challenges posed by implicit expressions (e.g., white space or utilizing generics), we can employ explicit Razor expressions. These explicit expressions are composed of an @ symbol followed by parentheses. A generic method can be invoked as demonstrated in the following:

```
<p>@(GenericMethod<int>())</p>
```

When we intend to concatenate text with an expression, it is necessary to employ explicit expressions, as demonstrated in the following:

```
<p>@(currentUser.FirstName)_@(currentUser.LastName)</p>
```

In more complex scenarios, we can utilize explicit Razor expressions, like passing a lambda expression to an event handler. Let's examine another instance of employing an explicit Razor expression when embedding HTML within C# code.

Expression encoding

Occasionally, we might need to incorporate HTML as a string within our C# code; however, the outcome could be different from what we anticipated.

Let's say we write the following C# expression:

```
@("<span>Hello World!</span>")
```

The result will look like this after rendering:

```
&lt;span&gt;Hello World&lt;/span&gt;
```

To preserve the HTML string, it is necessary to utilize the `MarkupString` keyword, as demonstrated in the following:

```
@((MarkupString)"<span>Hello World</span>")
```

The result of the preceding C# expression is as follows:

```
<span>Hello World!</span>
```

This is the desired output. We will delve deeper into explicit Razor expressions as we progress with the creation of Razor components.

Directives

In addition to HTML code and C# code blocks, there are reserved keywords designed for use as Razor directives. These Razor directives are denoted by implicit expressions that follow the @ symbol and contain specific reserved keywords. In the previous section, we encountered the code block represented as @code. In this instance, @code serves as a directive, containing the reserved keyword code. Throughout this book, we will be using the following directives:

- @attribute: This is used to add the given attribute to the class.
- @code: This is used to define a code block.
- @implements: This is used to implement an interface for the generated class.
- @inherits: This is used to specify the parent class for the generated class.
- @inject: This is used to inject a service using dependency injection.
- @layout: This is used to specify a layout for routable Razor components.
- @namespace: This is used to define the namespace for the generated class.
- @page: This is used to define a route for the page.
- @using: This is similar to the using keyword in C#, which imports a namespace.

Directive attributes

In a Razor page, HTML tags can act as classes, and attributes can serve as members of the class. Let's examine the following example:

```
<input type="text" @bind="currentUser.Username">
```

Here, input is an HTML tag, which is a class. The attribute type serves as a property of the input tag and its value is text, which indicates the type of this input tag. You might have noticed another attribute, @bind, which appears somewhat different from regular attributes.

It looks like a Razor implicit expression. In fact, it is an implicit expression, with bind being a reserved keyword. This attribute functions as a directive attribute. The distinction between a Razor directive and a Razor directive attribute lies in the fact that the latter acts as an attribute for an HTML tag. Throughout this book, we will be using the following directive attributes:

- @bind: This is used in data binding.
- @on{EVENT}: This is used in event handling.
- @on{EVENT}:preventDefault: This is used to prevent the default action for the event.
- @on{EVENT}:stopPropagation: This is used to stop event propagation.
- @ref: This is used to provide a way to reference a component instance.
- @typeparam: This is used to declare a generic type parameter.

Having familiarized ourselves with the fundamental syntax of the Razor markup language, it is time to put it into practice by developing a Razor component within our application.

Creating a Razor component

In developing a .NET MAUI Blazor Hybrid application, we have the option to either construct the entire UI utilizing Blazor or combine Razor components with XAML components. We will initially explore the second option, as we have already completed a password manager application in the first part of this book.

Redesigning the login page using a Razor component

The first UI we aim to replace is the login page. We can accomplish this by utilizing a Razor page instead of the XAML page, thereby maintaining the same functionality.

In a Blazor Hybrid application, the BlazorWebView serves as the control that hosts Razor components. We can modify LoginPage.xaml to the following:

```
<?xml version="1.0" encoding="utf-8" ?>
<ContentPage
  xmlns="http://schemas.microsoft.com/dotnet/2021/maui"
  xmlns:x="http://schemas.microsoft.com/winfx/2009/xaml"
  xmlns:b="clr-namespace:Microsoft.AspNetCore.Components.
    WebView.Maui;
    assembly=Microsoft.AspNetCore.Components.WebView.Maui"
  xmlns:local="clr-namespace:PassXYZ.Vault.Pages"
  x:Class="PassXYZ.Vault.Views.LoginPage"
```

```
      Shell.NavBarIsVisible="False">

    <b:BlazorWebView HostPage="wwwroot/login.html">          //(1)
      <b:BlazorWebView.RootComponents>
        <b:RootComponent Selector="#login-app"               //(3)
          ComponentType="{x:Type local:Login}" />            //(2)
      </b:BlazorWebView.RootComponents>
    </b:BlazorWebView>
  </ContentPage>
```

On the previous page, there is only a `BlazorWebView` control. We should focus on the following aspects:

(1) The `HostPage` attribute is utilized to indicate the HTML page that should be loaded in `BlazorWebView`. In this instance, `login.html` (as shown in *Listing 8.2*) is the specified page.

The attributes of `RootComponent` specify the Razor component and CSS selector to be used:

(2) The `ComponentType` attribute indicates the Razor `Login` component, which we will be discussing in detail shortly.

(3) The `Selector` attribute indicates the CSS selector where our web UI will be loaded. We have defined the CSS `#login-app` ID in `login.html`. This `login.html` HTML page is created and saved in the `wwwroot` folder. Let's take a look at it in *Listing 8.2*:

```html
<!DOCTYPE html>
<html lang="en">
<head>
  <meta charset="utf-8" />
  <meta name="viewport" content="width=device-width,
    initial-scale=1.0, maximum-scale=1.0, user-scalable=no,
      viewport-fit=cover" />
  <title>PassXYZ.Vault Login</title>
  <base href="/" />
  <link rel="stylesheet"
    href="css/bootstrap/bootstrap.min.css" />
  <link href="css/app.css" rel="stylesheet" />
  <link href="PassXYZ.Vault.styles.css" rel="stylesheet" />
</head>
```

```
<body class="text-center">
  <div id="login-app">Loading...</div>                                        //(1)
  <div id="blazor-error-ui">
    An unhandled error has occurred.
    <a href="" class="reload">Reload</a>
    <a class="dismiss">X</a>
  </div>
  <script src="_framework/blazor.webview.js"
      autostart="false">
  </script>
</body>
</html>
```

Listing 8.2: `login.html` *(https://epa.ms/Login8-2)*

In *Listing 8.2*, we observe that it closely resembles `index.html`, which we have examined earlier. The CSS ID `"login-app"` **(1)** is defined here, serving the purpose of loading our Razor component:

```
<div id="login-app">Loading...</div>
```

In the .NET MAUI Blazor Hybrid app template, the default CSS framework is Bootstrap (`bootstrap.min.css`). At the time of writing, the embedded Bootstrap version was 5.1. However, you might find a newer version in your project.

Bootstrap is a renowned framework for web development, which provides numerous examples of its usage. For instance, there is a sign-in example available on the Bootstrap website for creating a login page, as illustrated in *Figure 8.7*. We will utilize this example to construct our Login component:

Figure 8.7: Bootstrap sign-in example

You can find this sign-in example at https://getbootstrap.com/docs/5.1/examples/sign-in/.

This sign-in example includes two files:

index.html (*Listing 8.3*) is the UI of the sign-in page. It defines the following:

- Two <input> tags for the username **(1)** and password **(2)**
- An <input> tag **(3)** for a checkbox to remember the username
- A <button> tag **(4)** to process the login activity

It uses Bootstrap CSS styles and its own styles defined in signin.css.

signin.css (*Listing 8.4*) defines the CSS styles specific to the sign-in page:

```
<!doctype html>
<html lang="en">
  <head> ... </head>
  <body class="text-center">
<main class="form-signin">
  <form>
<img class="mb-4" src=".../bootstrap-logo.svg"
  alt="" width="72" height="57">
    <h1 class="h3 mb-3 fw-normal">Please sign in</h1>
    <div class="form-floating">
      <input type="email" class="form-control"
        id="floatingInput" placeholder="name@example.com">        //(1)
      <label for="floatingInput">Email address</label>
    </div>
    <div class="form-floating">
      <input type="password" class="form-control"
        id="floatingPassword" placeholder="Password">             //(2)
      <label for="floatingPassword">Password</label>
    </div>
    <div class="checkbox mb-3">
      <label>
        <input type="checkbox" value="remember-me">               //(3)
        Remember me
      </label>
    </div>
<button class="w-100 btn btn-lg btn-primary"
  type="submit">Sign in</button>                                  //(4)
    <p class="mt-5 mb-3 text-muted">&copy; 2017–2021</p>
  </form>
</main>
  </body>
</html>
```

Listing 8.3: index.html *(Bootstrap sign-in example)*

In signin.css (*Listing 8.4*), we modify the form-signin CSS class, which is used in the sign-in
section of index.html:

```css
html,
body {
  height: 100%;
}
body {
  display: flex;
  align-items: center;
  padding-top: 40px;
  padding-bottom: 40px;
  background-color: #f5f5f5;
}
.form-signin {
  width: 100%;
  max-width: 330px;
  padding: 15px;
  margin: auto;
}
.form-signin .checkbox {
  font-weight: 400;
}
.form-signin .form-floating:focus-within {
  z-index: 2;
}
.form-signin input[type="email"] {
  margin-bottom: -1px;
  border-bottom-right-radius: 0;
  border-bottom-left-radius: 0;
}
.form-signin input[type="password"] {
  margin-bottom: 10px;
  border-top-left-radius: 0;
  border-top-right-radius: 0;
}
```

Listing 8.4: signin.css *(Bootstrap sign-in example)*

To create a new Razor component, first, a folder named Pages needs to be created within the project. Next, right-click on the newly created Pages folder in Visual Studio and select **Add | Razor Component....** Name this component Login.razor and proceed to create the file. Once created, copy the part between the <main> tag from *Listing 8.3* and paste it into the Razor page within a <div> tag, as demonstrated in *Listing 8.5*:

```
@using System.Diagnostics
@using PassXYZ.Vault.Services
@using PassXYZ.Vault.ViewModels
@inject LoginViewModel viewModel                                     //(1)
@inject LoginService currentUser                                     //(2)
<div>
  <main class="form-signin">
    <form>
      <img class="mb-4"...>
      <h1 class="h3 mb-3 fw-normal">Please sign in</h1>
      <div class="form-floating">
        <label for="floatingInput">Username</label>
        <input type="text" @bind="@currentUser.Username"             //(3)
          class="form-control" id="floatingInput"
          placeholder="Username">
      </div>
      <div class="form-floating">
        <label for="floatingPassword">Password</label>
        <input type="password"
          @bind="@currentUser.Password" class="form-control"
          id="floatingPassword" placeholder="Password">              //(4)
      </div>
      <div class="checkbox mb-3">
        <label>
          <input type="checkbox" value="remember-me">
            Remember me
        </label>
      </div>
      <button class="w-100 btn btn-lg btn-primary"
          type="submit" @onclick="OnLogin">Sign in</button>
      <p class="mt-5 mb-3 text-muted">&copy; 2017–2021</p>
    </form>
```

```
    </main>
  </div>
  @code {
    protected override void OnInitialized() {
    }
    private void OnLogin(MouseEventArgs e) {
viewModel.Username = currentUser.Username;
viewModel.Password = currentUser.Password;
      viewModel.LoginCommand.Execute(null);
    }
  }
```

Listing 8.5: `Login.razor`

We employ the directive inject to instantiate `LoginViewModel` as the `viewModel` variable **(1)**, and `LoginService` as the `currentUser` variable **(2)**. This enables us to reference the `Username` **(3)** and `Password` **(4)** properties of `currentUser` in the HTML via the @ symbol. Similarly, we can define the `OnLogin` event handler and associate it with the `onclick` event.

Upon entering their username and password, the `currentUser` properties are populated accordingly. When the login button is clicked, the `OnLogin` function is triggered. Consequently, the view model's `LoginCommand` is executed to initiate the login process.

The Model-View-ViewModel (MVVM) pattern in Blazor

One of the benefits of utilizing Blazor for UI design is that it allows us to create most of the UI using HTML initially. After ensuring the UI design meets our expectations, we can then implement the programming logic. By employing the MVVM pattern, which we explored in *Chapter 3, User Interface Design with XAML*, we can effectively separate responsibilities within the Razor component development. For a Razor component, we can consider the HTML markup as the view and the code block as the ViewModel. Should the logic in the code block become overly complex, we have the option to separate it into a C# code-behind file.

On the login page, we may proceed with utilizing the `LoginViewModel` from the XAML domain. This is made possible by the transition from Blazor to the XAML UI occurring within `LoginViewModel`. The primary objective is to demonstrate the seamless integration of Blazor and XAML UIs within a single application. In the subsequent chapter, we will completely replace the XAML UI with the Blazor UI.

In a Razor component, it is possible to incorporate both HTML and C# within a single file or divide them between a Razor file and a C# code-behind file, similar to XAML.

Let's apply this concept to `Login.razor`. By splitting it into two files, the component will be divided into two partial classes found in `Login.razor` and `Login.razor.cs`, as demonstrated in *Listing 8.6* and *Listing 8.7*:

```
@namespace PassXYZ.Vault.Pages
<div>
  <main class="form-signin">
    <form>
      <img class="mb-4"...>
      <h1 class="h3 mb-3 fw-normal">Please sign in</h1>
      <div class="form-floating">
        <label for="floatingInput">Username</label>
        <input type="text" @bind="@currentUser.Username"
            class="form-control" id="floatingInput"
                placeholder="Username">
      </div>
      <div class="form-floating">
        <label for="floatingPassword">Password</label>
        <input type="password" @bind="@currentUser.
            Password" class="form-control"
                id="floatingPassword" placeholder="Password">
      </div>
      <div class="checkbox mb-3">
        <label>
          <input type="checkbox" value="remember-me"> Remember me
        </label>
      </div>
      <button class="w-100 btn btn-lg btn-primary"
          type="submit" @onclick="OnLogin">Sign in</button>
      <p class="mt-5 mb-3 text-muted">&copy; 2021-2022</p>
    </form>
  </main>
</div>
```

Listing 8.6: `Login.razor` (https://epa.ms/Login8-6)

In *Listing 8.6*, the HTML markup is solely present in Login.razor, which effectively separates the UI from the underlying logic, resulting in a cleaner design. Now, let's examine the corresponding C# code in *Listing 8.7*:

```
using Microsoft.AspNetCore.Components;
using System.Diagnostics;
using PassXYZ.Vault.Services;
using PassXYZ.Vault.ViewModels;
using Microsoft.AspNetCore.Components.Web;
namespace PassXYZ.Vault.Pages;
public partial class Login : ComponentBase {
  [Inject]
  LoginViewModel viewModel { get; set; } = default!;
  [Inject]
  LoginService currentUser { get; set; } = default!;

  protected override void OnInitialized()
  {
  }

  private void OnLogin(MouseEventArgs e)
  {
      viewModel.Username = currentUser.Username;
      viewModel.Password = currentUser.Password;
      viewModel.LoginCommand.Execute(null);
  }
}
```

Listing 8.7: Login.razor.cs *(https://epa.ms/Login8-7)*

In *Listing 8.7*, we have transferred all the code from the @code block to the C# file within the Login class, which inherits from the ComponentBase class. All Razor components inherit from ComponentBase.

You might have observed the usage of the Inject attribute in the declaration of the viewModel and currentUser properties. These properties are initialized using dependency injection.

Dependency injection in Blazor

In *Chapter 6, Software Design with Dependency Injection*, we introduced how to use dependency injection in .NET MAUI development. All the concepts presented in that chapter are equally applicable here; however, Blazor offers additional features. With Blazor, we can utilize dependency injection in both HTML and C# code.

As demonstrated in *Listing 8.5*, the following declaration is defined at the beginning of the `Login. razor` file:

```
@inject LoginViewModel viewModel
```

In the preceding code, we initialize the `viewModel` property through dependency injection. This approach employs property injection using the Razor directive, which has become more straightforward to use in Blazor than in previous versions.

When we move it to the C# code-behind file, we can use the `Inject` attribute to do the same:

```
[Inject]
LoginViewModel viewModel { get; set; } = default!;
```

In web development, we frequently utilize HTML and CSS in conjunction to design UIs for websites. In the Bootstrap example, a `signin.css` file is present. Now, where should we store our CSS styles? We will explore this topic in the subsequent section.

CSS isolation

In the earlier discussion of the Bootstrap sign-in example, we mentioned the presence of an HTML file and a CSS file. Now, the question arises – where should the CSS file be placed in order to effectively reuse the sign-in CSS styles on our login page?

In HTML design, using a CSS framework like Bootstrap may require customization of styles at the page level. To facilitate this in Blazor, a technique called CSS isolation for Razor components is employed. For CSS styles specific to a component or page, we can store them in a file with the `.razor.css` extension. The filename should correspond to the `.razor` file in the same folder. For instance, on our login page, we can copy the `sign-in.css` file from the Bootstrap example to `Login.razor.css`, making minor adjustments as demonstrated in *Listing 8.8*:

```css
div {
    display: flex;
    align-items: center;
    background-color: #f5f5f5;
}
.form-signin {
    width: 100%;
    max-width: 330px;
    padding: 15px;
    margin: auto;
}
.form-signin .checkbox {
    font-weight: 400;
}
.form-signin .form-floating:focus-within {
    z-index: 2;
}
.form-signin input[type="email"] {
    margin-bottom: -1px;
    border-bottom-right-radius: 0;
    border-bottom-left-radius: 0;
}
.form-signin input[type="password"] {
    margin-bottom: 10px;
    border-top-left-radius: 0;
    border-top-right-radius: 0;
}
#first {
    margin-top: 3em;
}
```

Listing 8.8: Login.razor.css *(https://epa.ms/Login8-8)*

The styles defined in `Login.razor.css` are only applied to the rendered output of the `Login` component. Finally, let's look at this new login UI in Blazor:

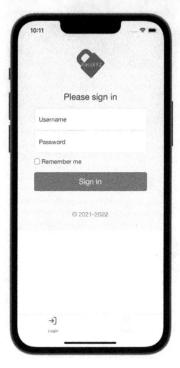

Figure 8.8: Sign in page

In *Figure 8.8*, from left to right, we can see the login page on Windows, iOS, and Android. We observe that the look and feel of this new UI closely resemble the Bootstrap sign-in example, with the exception of a modified icon. The login functionality remains unchanged; however, we employed Blazor to develop a new UI.

As the Blazor UI is constructed using web technologies, the appearance and user experience are consistent across different platforms. For instance, in the Android screenshot, you can see an overlap of the input fields with the placeholders upon entering the username and password. This behavior aligns with what you would encounter on all three platforms. Though this issue isn't present on the desktop browser, BlazorWebView's behavior does present some discrepancies compared with traditional desktop browsers. Therefore, while the Blazor UI maintains consistency across various platforms, it may behave differently when accessed through different browsers.

Upon logging in using this Razor page, the subsequent programming logic continues to align with what was demonstrated in *Chapter 6*, *Software Design with Dependency Injection*. After the login process, the UI framework reverts to XAML as no other modifications have been made thus far.

The code in this chapter illustrates the potential to combine a Blazor UI and XAML-based UI within a single application. However, it is advisable to avoid this approach unless there are no other alternatives available. As depicted in *Figure 8.8*, Blazor and XAML UIs employ different technologies, which can present unique challenges during development. By mixing them, we essentially inherit the issues from both types of UI. This could introduce unforeseen complications in the design and development process of the UI.

Summary

In this chapter, we explored Blazor and how to develop a Blazor Hybrid app. Blazor serves as an alternative solution for UI design within .NET MAUI. The primary distinction between Blazor and XAML lies in their appearance: while the XAML UI closely resembles the native interface, the Blazor UI adopts the aesthetics of a web app. Functionality-wise, both offer similar capabilities. Moreover, it is possible to integrate Blazor and XAML within a single app and utilize the MVVM pattern in both.

An advantage of using Blazor is the ability to share UI code between the Blazor Hybrid app and a web app. If you seek a solution compatible with both native and web apps, .NET MAUI Blazor could be an ideal choice.

In the upcoming chapter, we will transition to using Blazor for all UIs within our app. Additionally, we will discuss the initial UI design using layout and routing techniques.

Further reading

- ASP.NET Core updates in .NET 8 Preview 2: `https://devblogs.microsoft.com/dotnet/asp-net-core-updates-in-dotnet-8-preview-2/#improved-blazor-webassembly-performance-with-the-jiterpreter`

- ASP.NET Core updates in .NET 8 Preview 7: `https://devblogs.microsoft.com/dotnet/asp-net-core-updates-in-dotnet-8-preview-7/#auto-render-mode`

- What's new in ASP.NET Core 8.0: `https://learn.microsoft.com/en-us/aspnet/core/release-notes/aspnetcore-8.0?view=aspnetcore-8.0`

- ASP.NET Core Blazor hosting models: `https://learn.microsoft.com/en-us/aspnet/core/blazor/hosting-models?view=aspnetcore-8.0`

- ASP.NET Core Blazor render modes: `https://learn.microsoft.com/en-us/aspnet/core/blazor/components/render-modes?view=aspnetcore-8.0`

Learn more on Discord

Join our community's Discord space for discussions with the author and other readers:

`https://packt.link/cross-platform-app`

9

Understanding Blazor Routing and Layout

In the previous chapter, we explored the process of designing a login page using Blazor. Although the app layout and navigation hierarchy remain XAML-based, our app utilizes a hybrid UI implementation that combines both Blazor and XAML. Blazor offers an alternative approach to UI design for .NET MAUI apps. In this second part of the book, we will reconstruct the entire UI using Blazor exclusively. Since the initial step of UI design typically involves the implementation of layout and navigation, this chapter will introduce the concepts of layout and routing within Blazor.

We will cover the following topics in this chapter:

- Client-side Blazor routing
- Using Blazor layout components
- Implementing navigation elements

Technical requirements

To test and debug the source code in this chapter, you need to have Visual Studio 2022 installed on your PC or Mac. Please refer to the *Development environment setup* section in *Chapter 1, Getting Started with .NET MAUI*, for the details.

The source code for this chapter is available in the following GitHub repository: `https://github.com/PacktPublishing/.NET-MAUI-Cross-Platform-Application-Development-Second-edition/tree/main/2nd/chapter09`.

To check out the source code of this chapter, we can use this command:

```
$ git clone -b 2nd/chapter09 https://github.com/PacktPublishing/.NET-MAUI-
Cross-Platform-Application-Development-Second-edition.git PassXYZ.Vault2
```

To find out more about the source code in this book, please refer to the *Managing the source code in this book* section in *Chapter 2, Building Our First .NET MAUI App*.

Understanding client-side routing

The routing and layout of Blazor bear similarities to the concepts of Shell and navigation in the XAML realm. In *Chapter 5, Navigation Using .NET MAUI Shell and NavigationPage*, we introduced navigation and Shell while discussing the routing strategy of Shell. Shell offers a URI-based navigation experience that relies on routes to navigate to designated pages. The routing of Blazor closely resembles this approach.

Blazor routing allows for seamless transitions between Razor pages. Rendering Razor pages in `BlazorWebView` is akin to web apps operating in a browser.

In traditional web applications, loading an HTML page in a browser fetches the page from the web server. Selecting a different route subsequently retrieves a new page from the server. However, the process varies slightly for **single-page applications (SPAs)**.

Blazor WebAssembly applications fall under the category of SPAs. When launching an app, it is loaded into the browser, and any subsequent page navigation occurs solely on the client side. This approach is known as client-side routing, which is also employed by Blazor Hybrid apps.

Setting up BlazorWebView

To implement client-side routing, the router must be installed during the application's startup. In .NET MAUI apps, both XAML and Blazor entry points are configured in App.xaml.cs. To switch the UI implementation from XAML to Blazor, refer to the modifications made to App.xaml.cs within the provided code.

A Blazor Hybrid app operates within `BlazorWebView`. To initiate the Blazor Hybrid app, it is necessary to establish an instance of `BlazorWebView` first. In the previous chapter, we accomplished this setup in `LoginPage` and successfully navigated back to Shell after logging in.

To configure a `BlazorWebView` instance for the entire application, it is necessary to replace the instance assigned to the `MainPage` property within the `App` class. To achieve this, we modified the constructor of the `App` class (found in App.xaml.cs) as follows:

```
public App()
{
  InitializeComponent();
#if MAUI_BLAZOR
  MainPage = new MainPage();                                    //(1)
#else
  Routing.RegisterRoute(nameof(ItemsPage),
      typeof(ItemsPage));
  Routing.RegisterRoute(nameof(ItemDetailPage),
    typeof(ItemDetailPage));
  Routing.RegisterRoute(nameof(NewItemPage),
      typeof(NewItemPage));
  MainPage = new AppShell();
#endif
}
```

We can use a symbol, `MAUI_BLAZOR`, to facilitate conditional compilation, enabling the ability to switch between XAML and the Blazor UI during the build process. To utilize the Blazor UI, we assign the `MainPage` property to a `MainPage` instance **(1)**. Within the `MainPage` class, we define the `BlazorWebView` control as follows:

```
<BlazorWebView HostPage="wwwroot/index.html">
  <BlazorWebView.RootComponents>
    <RootComponent Selector="#app" ComponentType="{x:Type
        local:Main}" />
  </BlazorWebView.RootComponents>
</BlazorWebView>
```

Within `BlazorWebView`, an HTML page (`index.html`) is loaded to initiate the Blazor UI setup. Let's examine how the router configuration operates.

Setting up the Router component

The Blazor UI employs an HTML page-based design, resembling the structure of an SPA that originates from a static HTML page. Within `BlazorWebView`, the initial HTML page to be loaded is `index.html`. This closely resembles the `login.html` page we discussed in the previous chapter.

The top-level Razor component, loaded in `RootComponent`, appears as the `Main` component, which can be viewed here:

```
<Router AppAssembly="@typeof(Main).Assembly">                //(1)
  <Found Context="routeData">                                //(2)
    <RouteView RouteData="@routeData"
      DefaultLayout="@typeof(MainLayout)" />
      <FocusOnNavigate RouteData="@routeData" Selector="h1" />
  </Found>
  <NotFound>                                                  //(3)
    <LayoutView Layout="@typeof(MainLayout)">
      <p role="alert">Sorry, there's nothing at this
         address.</p>
    </LayoutView>
  </NotFound>
</Router>
```

Listing 9.1: `Main.razor` *(https://epa.ms/Main9-1)*

As we can see in *Listing 9.1*, we set up the `Router` component, **(1)**, in `Main.razor`.

The `Router` component employs reflection to scan all page components and construct a routing table. The `AppAssembly` parameter determines which assemblies will be scanned. Upon encountering a navigation event, the router consults the routing table for a corresponding route. The `Router` component is, in essence, a templated component, which we will explore further in the next chapter. When a matching route is identified, the `Found` template is utilized. Conversely, if no matching routes are present, the `NotFound` template comes into play.

The `Found` template, **(2)**, employs a `RouteView` component to render the chosen component alongside its layout. The layout is specified in the `DefaultLayout` attribute, which we will examine in the upcoming section. Additionally, the new page to be loaded, as well as any route parameters, is passed using an instance of the `RouteData` class.

If a match cannot be found, the `NotFound` template, **(3)**, is rendered. This template utilizes a `LayoutView` component to display error messages. The layout employed by `LayoutView` is designated via a `Layout` attribute.

Defining routes

After setting up the router, we can proceed to create pages and define route templates within those pages. The router will then scan the route templates defined in the pages to construct a routing table.

At the top level of our app, the navigation hierarchy and route templates can be established by referring to *Figure 9.1*:

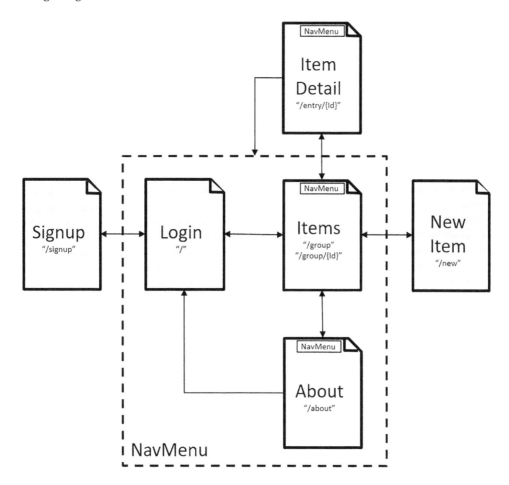

Figure 9.1: Navigation hierarchy of Razor pages

We presented the primary pages of our app in *Figure 9.1*. Each page possesses a name, which corresponds to the class name of a Razor page. Located beneath the name is the route template. For instance, for the About page, the route template can be declared as follows:

```
@page "/about"
```

The @page directive comprises two components – the directive name and the route template. In this example, the route template is /about, which must be enclosed in quotes and always begin with a forward slash (/). Given that a Razor page's final output is an HTML page, navigation to a Razor page can be treated like navigating to a web page using an anchor tag, <a>, as demonstrated here:

```
<a href="/about">About</a>
```

Passing data using route parameters

When navigating to a page using a route template, data can be passed to the page through route parameters. If we recall the process of passing data with query parameters in Shell, the use of route parameters is quite similar.

As depicted in *Figure 9.1*, after successfully logging in, the Items page appears, displaying a list of items in the root group, as shown in *Figure 9.2*. On this page, clicking on an item allows navigation based on the item type. To identify the selected item, an item Id value is passed to the new page as a parameter.

Figure 9.2: Items page in a Blazor Hybrid app

In the Items page, we have the following route templates defined:

```
@page "/group"
@page "/group/{SelectedItemId}"
```

The first route template is employed when displaying the root page, while the second comes into play upon selecting a group. The group Id value is transmitted to the Items page using the SelectedItemId route parameter. To designate the type of route parameter, we can incorporate constraints tied to the data type, as demonstrated here:

```
@page "/user/{Id:int}"
```

In the preceding page directive, we define the data type of Id as an integer. For more information about route constraints, please refer to the relevant Microsoft documentation. You can access the pertinent document here: https://learn.microsoft.com/en-us/aspnet/core/blazor/fundamentals/routing?view=aspnetcore-8.0#route-constraints.

Navigating with NavigationManager

In a Razor page, navigation to another page typically involves using an <a> anchor tag. However, under certain circumstances, it may be necessary to perform the action via code. One such instance is when handling an event, where redirection to a page occurs within the event handler. This is precisely the situation on our Login page. Let's explore how to navigate to the Items page using NavigationManager once a successful login has been achieved.

In our app, after logging in, we must redirect users to the Items page to display the root group. The user interface for the Login page remains unchanged from the previous chapter; however, we have modified the event handler in Login.razor.cs as shown below:

```
namespace PassXYZ.Vault.Pages;
public partial class Login : ComponentBase {
  [Inject]
  private IUserService<User> userService { get; set; } =
      default!;
  [Inject]
  private IDataStore<Item> dataStore { get; set; } =
      default!;
  [Inject]
  private NavigationManager navigationManager {get; set;} //(1)
  private LoginService currentUser { get; set; } =
      default!;
  private async void OnLogin(MouseEventArgs e) {
    bool status = await userService.LoginAsync
        (currentUser);
    if (status) {
```

```
        navigationManager.NavigateTo("/group");              //(2)
      }
    }
  }
```

We obtain an instance of `NavigationManager` through dependency injection **(1)**.

Then, we invoke the `NavigateTo("/group")` method of `NavigationManager` to facilitate navigation to the `Items` page **(2)**.

In this section, we explored routing and navigation. As a next step, we can implement a navigation
hierarchy akin to that of Shell navigation within the Blazor UI.

The top level of the HTML page navigation hierarchy encompasses a header, toolbar, menu, and
footer. We can design this layout using a Blazor layout component, which shares similarities
with the flyout and menu items in Shell. We previously introduced these concepts in *Chapter 5,
Navigation Using .NET MAUI Shell and NavigationPage.*

Using Blazor layout components

Most web pages typically feature fixed elements such as headers, footers, or menus. By designing
a page with a layout combined with its content, we can minimize redundant code. The page itself
displays the content intended for users, while the layout assists in constructing visual styles and
providing navigational methods.

Blazor layout components are classes derived from `LayoutComponentBase`. Any functionality
applicable to regular Razor components can also be applied to layout components.

In *Listing 9.1*, we observe that `MainLayout` serves as the default layout for the pages. Its definition
can be found in *Listing 9.2*, as shown below:

```
@inherits LayoutComponentBase                                //(1)
<div class="page">
  <div class="sidebar">
    <NavMenu />                                              //(2)
  </div>
  <main>
    @Body                                                    //(3)
  </main>
</div>
```

Listing 9.2: `MainLayout.razor` *(https://epa.ms/MainLayout9-2)*

The **MainLayout** component **(1)** inherits from the LayoutComponentBase class. The component features a **NavMenu (2)** to outline the navigation menu. Within the <main> tag **(3)**, the @Body Razor syntax designates the location in the layout markup for rendering content.

It is essential to thoroughly examine the NavMenu component, as it serves as the primary navigation method within the app. Please refer to *Figure 9.3* for a visual representation of the **NavMenu** interface before reviewing the code. **NavMenu** comprises three menu items: **Home**, **About**, and **Logout**.

Figure 9.3: NavMenu

NavMenu is a Razor component responsible for defining the links used in navigation. The source code for NavMenu can be found in *Listing 9.3*, as shown here:

```
<div class="top-row ps-3 navbar navbar-dark">                    //(1)
  <div class="container-fluid">
    <a class="navbar-brand" href="">PassXYZ.Vault</a>
<button title="Navigation menu" class="navbar-toggler"
  @onclick="ToggleNavMenu">                                      //(2)
      <span class="navbar-toggler-icon"></span>
    </button>
  </div>
</div>
<div class="@NavMenuCssClass" @onclick="ToggleNavMenu">
  <nav class="flex-column">
    <div class="nav-item px-3">                                  //(3)
      <NavLink class="nav-link" href="/group">                   //(4)
        <span class="oi oi-home" aria-hidden="true"></span>
            Home
      </NavLink>
    </div>
    <div class="nav-item px-3">
      <NavLink class="nav-link" href="/about">
        <span class="oi oi-plus" aria-hidden="true"></span>
            About
      </NavLink>
    </div>
    <div class="nav-item px-3">
      <NavLink class="nav-link" href="" Match=
          "NavLinkMatch.All">
        <span class="oi oi-list-rich" aria-hidden="true">
            </span>
        Logout
      </NavLink>
    </div>
  </nav>
</div>
@code {
  private bool collapseNavMenu = true;
  private string NavMenuCssClass => collapseNavMenu ?
```

```
        "collapse" : null;
    private void ToggleNavMenu() {
      collapseNavMenu = !collapseNavMenu;
    }
  }
```

Listing 9.3: NavMenu.razor *(*https://epa.ms/NavMenu9-3*)*

In the source code of the NavMenu component, we can observe that it consists of a Bootstrap navBar component accompanied by some C# logic within the code block. The NavBar is defined using a navbar Bootstrap class in the following <div> tag **(1)**:

```
<div class="top-row ps-3 navbar navbar-dark">
```

As illustrated in *Figure 9.3*, a hamburger icon, **(2)**, is positioned at the top right of the screen, utilizing a <button> tag to toggle NavMenu. The hamburger button UI is implemented using the Bootstrap class, navbar-toggler, as detailed below:

```
<button title="Navigation menu" class="navbar-toggler"
  @onclick="ToggleNavMenu">
  <span class="navbar-toggler-icon"></span>
</button>
```

Three links are defined as menu items, utilizing the nav-item Bootstrap class **(3)**. Instead of employing the anchor tag, <a>, NavLink is used **(4)**. The NavLink component functions similarly to <a>. However, it toggles an active CSS class, contingent on whether its href matches the current URL, as demonstrated below:

```
<div class="nav-item px-3">
  <NavLink class="nav-link" href="/group">
    <span class="oi oi-home" aria-hidden="true"></span>
        Home
  </NavLink>
</div>
```

We previously discussed MainLayout, which serves as the default layout in our app. Now, let's examine how to apply this layout to a component.

Applying a layout to a component

MainLayout serves as the default layout component, applying to all pages unless an alternative layout is specified. In certain scenarios, we may need to use a unique layout rather than the default one.

For instance, within our app, we employ a distinct layout component for the Login page instead of the default layout (refer to *Listing 9.4*). MainLayout incorporates a NavMenu component, which we do not wish to display on the Login page since users should not access other content before logging in. Let's examine the alterations made to the Login page after applying a specific layout, as shown in *Listing 9.4*:

```
@page "/"
@layout LogoutLayout                                          //(1)
@namespace PassXYZ.Vault.Pages
<div class="text-center">
  <main class="form-signin">
    <form>
      <img id="first" class="mb-4" src=
          "passxyz-blue.svg"...>
      <h1 class="h3 mb-3 fw-normal">Please sign in</h1>
      <div class="form-floating">
        <label for="floatingInput">Username</label>
        <input type="text"
            @bind="@currentUser.Username"...>
      </div>
      <div class="form-floating">
        <label for="floatingPassword">Password</label>
        <input type="password" @bind=
            "@currentUser.Password"...>
      </div>
      <div class="checkbox mb-3">
        <label>
          <input type="checkbox" value="remember-me">
              Remember me
        </label>
      </div>
      <button...>Sign in</button>
      <p class="mt-5 mb-3 text-muted">&copy; 2021-2022</p>
    </form>
  </main>
</div>
```

Listing 9.4: Login.razor *(https://epa.ms/Login9-4)*

To apply a specific layout, we can utilize the @layout Razor directive **(1)**. On the Login page, we implement the LogoutLayout. The code for LogoutLayout is presented in *Listing 9.5*, as follows:

```
@inherits LayoutComponentBase
<div class="page">
  <main>
    <div class="top-row px-4">
      <a href="#" target="_blank">Sign-in</a>
    </div>
    <article class="content px-4">
      @Body
    </article>
  </main>
</div>
```

Listing 9.5: LogoutLayout.razor *(https://epa.ms/LogoutLayout9-5)*

In LogoutLayout, we eliminated the NavMenu element and incorporated a sign-in link, enabling new users to register for an account.

Nesting layouts

Layout components can be nested as well. In MainLayout, we did not specify any margin for the content. While this layout is suitable for content list views on items pages or item details pages, it may not be visually appealing for content pages like the About page. To improve this, we can employ a distinct layout for the About page that is nested within MainLayout. Let's call it PageLayout, and its implementation can be found in *Listing 9.6*:

```
@inherits LayoutComponentBase
@layout MainLayout
<article class="content px-4">
  @Body
</article>
```

Listing 9.6: PageLayout.razor *(https://epa.ms/PageLayout9-6)*

PageLayout is a layout component that utilizes MainLayout. It places @Body inside an <article> tag with the "content px-4" style applied, thereby enabling the content to adopt a style that is appropriate for a paragraph of text.

On the About page, we can designate the layout as PageLayout in the following manner:

```
@page "/about"
@layout PageLayout
```

We have now covered the basics of routing and layout in Blazor. Armed with this knowledge, we can proceed to implement the navigation elements within our app.

Implementing navigation elements

In *Chapter 5, Navigation Using .NET MAUI Shell and NavigationPage*, we introduced the concepts of absolute and relative routes within Shell. Absolute routes can be defined in a visual navigation hierarchy, while relative routes are navigable using query parameters.

This navigation approach closely resembles the strategy employed in the Blazor version of our app. As illustrated in *Figure 9.4*, we implement Blazor UI elements in a manner similar to the XAML version.

Figure 9.4: Navigation elements

The Items page serves as the main page of our app after login. On this page, which displays a list of items, the following UI elements are related to navigation:

- **A list view** – Users can navigate the list and select an item.
- **Context menu** – Associated with each item in the list view, enabling users to edit or delete items.
- **Back button** – Allows users to navigate back.
- **Add button** – Enables users to add new items.

In this section, we will leverage the knowledge we have acquired to implement the aforementioned navigation elements.

Implementing a list view

In the XAML version, our navigation begins with a list of items once the user logs in to the app. The list view is implemented using a .NET MAUI ListView control, which leverages platform-specific UI components for a consistent look and feel across platforms. In the Blazor version, we utilize a web-based UI, ensuring a uniform appearance on different platforms.

When it comes to implementing a list view with a web UI, we have numerous options to choose from. Throughout this book, we adhere to the Bootstrap framework. Our methodology, as demonstrated in the previous chapter, involves reusing UI designs from Bootstrap examples. Since we're employing Bootstrap 5.1 in this book, we can reference the list group example depicted in *Figure 9.5*.

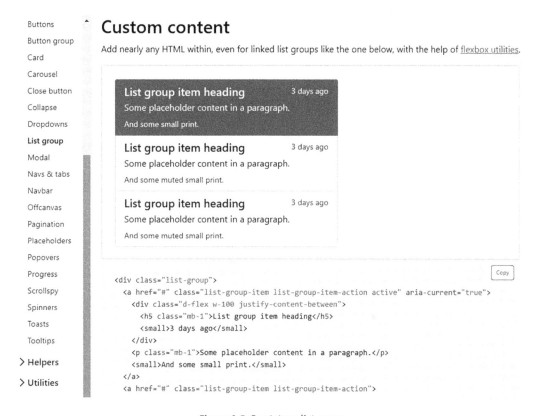

Figure 9.5: Bootstrap list group

The preceding example can be accessed via this URL: https://getbootstrap.com/docs/5.1/components/list-group/.

A Bootstrap list group can be employed to construct a UI component similar to the ListView in XAML. To achieve this, we can apply the CSS class "list-group" to HTML tags, such as <ul> or <div>, to create a list group. Within the list group, the "list-group-item" CSS class is applied to individual list items in the group.

In the XAML version, we facilitated CRUD operations using the context menu. However, the Bootstrap list group does not feature a built-in context menu, so we have to implement one ourselves. To create a context menu within the list group, we can utilize the Bootstrap dropdown component.

In order to employ the dropdown component, it is necessary to include the JavaScript dependency in `index.html`, as demonstrated below:

```
<script src="_framework/blazor.webview.js"
  autostart="false"></script>
<script src="css/bootstrap/bootstrap.bundle.min.js">
  </script>
```

We included a JavaScript file, `bootstrap.bundle.min.js`, following `blazor.webview.js`. The `bootstrap.bundle.min.js` file is a component of the Bootstrap release package.

To create a new Razor component called `Items`, simply right-click on the **Pages** folder in Visual Studio and choose **Add -> Razor Component...**. After this, insert the code provided in *Listing 9.7* and name the Razor file `Items.razor`:

```
@page "/group"
@page "/group/{SelectedItemId}"
<!-- Back button and title -->
<div class="container">...
<!-- List view with context menu -->
<div class="list-group">                                //(1)
  @foreach (var item in items) {
    <div class="dropdown list-group-item
      list-group-item-action...>                         //(2)
      <img src="@item.GetIcon()"...>
      <a href="@item.GetActionLink()"
          class="list-group-item...>
        <div class="d-flex">
          <div>
            <h6 class="mb-0">@item.Name</h6>
            <p class="mb-0 opacity-75">@item.Description
            </p>
          </div>
        </div>
```

```
          </a>
          <button class="opacity-50 btn btn-light
              dropdown-toggle"
            type="button" id="itemsContextMenu"
            data-bs-toggle="dropdown" aria-expanded="false">
            <span class="oi oi-menu" aria-hidden="true"></span>
          </button>                                        //(3)
          <ul class="dropdown-menu"
            aria-labelledby="itemsContextMenu">            //(4)
            <li>
              <button class="dropdown-item"
                  data-bs-toggle="modal"
                data-bs-target="#editModel"> Edit </button>
            </li>
            <li>
              <button class="dropdown-item"
                  data-bs-toggle="modal"
                data-bs-target="#deleteModel"> Delete </button>
            </li>
          </ul>
        </div>
    }
</div>
<!-- Editing Modal -->
<div class="modal fade" id="editModel" tabindex="-1"
  aria-labelledby="editModelLabel" aria-hidden="true">...
<!-- Deleting Modal -->
<div class="modal fade" id="deleteModel" tabindex="-1"
  aria-labelledby="deleteModelLabel" aria-hidden="true">...
<!-- New Modal -->
<div class="modal fade" id="newItemModel" tabindex="-1" aria-
labelledby="newItemModelLabel" aria-hidden="true">...
```

Listing 9.7: `Items.razor` *(https://epa.ms/Items9-7)*

In `Items.razor` **(1)**, we can copy the Bootstrap list group sample code that utilizes the `<div>` tag with the `list-group` CSS class applied to it.

We customize the list group item to meet our requirements **(2)**, as demonstrated in *Figure 9.6*. The list group item is created within a `foreach` loop using the `<div>` tag, containing an icon, a name, a description, and a context menu:

```
<div class="dropdown list-group-item list-group-item-action...">
```

We apply the `dropdown`, `list-group-item`, and `list-group-item-action` CSS classes to the `<div>` tag, transforming it into a list group item that incorporates a context menu using a dropdown.

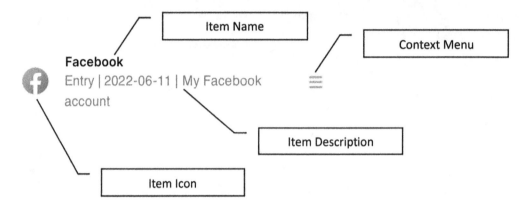

Figure 9.6: List group item

Within the list group item, we utilize an `<img>` tag to display the item's icon:

```
<img src="@item.GetIcon()"...>
```

We can obtain the icon source by using an extension method called `GetIcon` from the `Item` class. To create this extension method, we need to add a new class file under the `Shared` folder and name it `ItemEx.cs`, as demonstrated in *Listing 9.8*.

An `<a>` anchor tag is utilized to display the item's name and description. The name and description are defined within the `<a>` tag like this:

```
<a href="@item.GetActionLink()" class=
    "list-group-item...">
  <div class="d-flex">
    <div>
      <h6 class="mb-0">@item.Name</h6>
      <p class="mb-0 opacity-75">@item.Description
      </p>
    </div>
```

```
        </div>
    </a>
```

The item's link can be obtained using the `GetActionLink` extension method, which is also defined in *Listing 9.8*.

The context menu is a Bootstrap dropdown component that comprises a `<button>` tag **(3)** and an unordered list created with the `<ul>` tag **(4)**. Utilizing the Open Iconic icons, this button appears as a hamburger icon.

Open Iconic icons

In Blazor UI design, we utilize Open Iconic icons. Open Iconic is an open-source icon set featuring 223 icons in SVG, web font, and raster formats. For XAML design, FontAwesome is used, which can also be implemented in Blazor alongside Bootstrap. However, additional configuration is required prior to its use. Open Iconic comes bundled with the Blazor template and is included with Bootstrap. As a result, we can use it directly without any extra configuration. For instance, to display a hamburger icon in the context menu, the following HTML tag can be employed:

```
<span class="oi oi-menu" aria-hidden="true"></span>
```

In the drop-down menu, there are two context action buttons: `Edit` and `Delete`. We apply the `dropdown-item` CSS class to these buttons. The context action button triggers a dialog box to perform CRUD operations, hence the inclusion of two Bootstrap modal CSS attributes, `data-bs-toggle` and `data-bs-target`. We will discuss handling CRUD operations in the next chapter.

Now, let's review the extension methods of `Item` that we will use to support a list view UI, as shown in *Listing 9.8*:

```
using KeePassLib;
using KPCLib;
using PassXYZLib;
namespace PassXYZ.Vault.Shared {
  public static class ItemEx {
    public static string GetIcon(this Item item) {          //(1)
      if(item.IsGroup) {
        // Group
```

```
      if(item is PwGroup group) {
        if(group.CustomData.Exists(
          PxDefs.PxCustomDataIconName)) {
          return $"/images/{group.CustomData.Get
              (PxDefs.PxCustomDataIconName)}";
        }
      }
    }
    else {
      // Entry
      if(item is PwEntry entry) {
        if(entry.CustomData.Exists
          (PxDefs.PxCustomDataIconName)) {
          return $"/images/{entry.CustomData.Get
              (PxDefs.PxCustomDataIconName)}";
        }
      }
    }
    // 2. Get custom icon
    return item.GetCustomIcon();
}
/// <summary>
/// Get the action link of an item.
/// </summary>
public static string GetActionLink(this Item
    item, string? action = default) {                        //(2)
  string itemType = (item.IsGroup) ?
      PxConstants.Group : PxConstants.Entry;
  return (action == null) ? $"/{itemType}/{item.Id}" :
      $"/{itemType}/{action}/{item.Id}";
}
/// <summary>
/// Get the parent link of an item.
/// </summary>
public static string? GetParentLink(this Item item) {        //(3)
  Item? parent = default;
  if (item == null) return null;
```

```
      if(item.IsGroup) {
        PwGroup group = (PwGroup)item;
        if (group.ParentGroup == null) return null;
        parent = group.ParentGroup;
      }
      else {
        PwEntry entry = (PwEntry)item;
        if (entry.ParentGroup == null) return null;
        parent = entry.ParentGroup;
      }
      return $"/{PxConstants.Group}/{parent.Id}";
    }
  }
}
```

Listing 9.8: ItemEx.cs *(https://epa.ms/ItemEx9-8)*

In *Listing 9.8*, we create a static class called ItemEx to implement extension methods for the **Item** class. Within this class, we define three extension methods to obtain the necessary URL for navigation:

- GetIcon **(1)** – Returns the icon image's URL
- GetActionLink **(2)** – Returns the URL of a selected item based on its type
- GetParentLink **(3)** – Returns the URL of the parent item

In the previous implementation of the list view UI, we created a list comprising both password entries and groups. When an item is selected, an anchor tag, <a>, is actually clicked. The href property of <a> is set to the return value of the GetActionLink method. This return value follows a "/{itemType}/{item.Id}" route template format, enabling navigation to the desired item. Additionally, a context menu button is situated to the right of each item. Upon clicking it, a list of context actions appears, allowing users to select an action for editing or deleting the current item.

We have now managed to handle most of the navigation actions; however, two actions are still lacking. We are unable to navigate back after entering a child group and cannot add a new item. In the following section, we will address these two functionalities.

Adding a new item and navigating back

To facilitate navigation back to the previous page and the addition of new items, we can incorporate a Back button and an Add button in the title bar. This simulates the navigation page of the XAML version, as demonstrated in *Figure 9.7*:

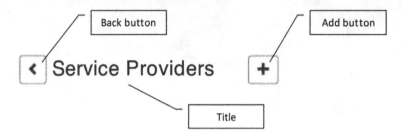

Figure 9.7: The title bar of the Items page

As observed in the title bar, three UI elements are included:

- **Title** – Representing the current item group's title
- **Back** button – Facilitating navigation back; however, it remains hidden when there is no parent group
- **Add** button – Enabling the addition of a new item

To examine the implementation, let's expand the code for the Back button and the Title section in *Listing 9.7*, as demonstrated below:

```
<!-- Back button and title -->
<div class="container">
  <div class="row">
    <div class="col-12">
      <h1>
        @if (selectedItem!.GetParentLink() != null) {
          <a class="btn btn-outline-dark" href=
            "@selectedItem!.GetParentLink()"><span
              class="oi oi-chevron-left"
                aria-hidden="true"></span></a>           //(1)
        }
        @(" " + Title)
        <button type="button" class="btn btn-outline-dark
          float-end" data-bs-toggle="modal" data-bs-
```

```
            target="#newItemModel"><span class="oi
            oi-plus" aria-hidden="true"></span></button>                //(2)
      </h1>
    </div>
  </div>
</div>
```

The **Back button (1)** is implemented using an anchor tag, `<a>`. The `href` attribute of this anchor tag is set to the return value of the `Item` extension method, `GetParentLink`. This function returns the parent item's link in the route template format, enabling navigation back through this link. If there is no parent group, such as a root group, the `Back` button remains invisible.

The **Add button (2)** is implemented using a `<button>` tag and is displayed on the right-hand side of the title bar. To position the button on the right side of the screen, we can utilize the Bootstrap class, `float-end`. When a user clicks on this button, a new item dialog box appears. This dialog box is configured using the following attributes:

```
data-bs-toggle="modal" data-bs-target="#newItemModel"
```

In `Items.razor`, as depicted in *Listing 9.7*, three Bootstrap modal dialogs are utilized:

```
<!-- Editing Modal -->
<div class="modal fade" id="editModel" tabindex="-1"
  aria-labelledby="editModelLabel" aria-hidden="true">...
<!-- Deleting Modal -->
<div class="modal fade" id="deleteModel" tabindex="-1"
  aria-labelledby="deleteModelLabel" aria-hidden="true">...
<!-- New Modal -->
<div class="modal fade" id="newItemModel" tabindex="-1" aria-
labelledby="newItemModelLabel" aria-hidden="true">...
```

These dialogs are utilized to perform CRUD operations. To implement them, we also reuse code from Bootstrap. While this approach is relatively straightforward, it does involve a significant amount of duplicated code. To conserve space, the details have been collapsed in *Listing 9.7*. In the subsequent chapter, we will delve into the implementation of modal dialogs and demonstrate how to transform the code into reusable Razor components.

Summary

In this chapter, we explored the routing and layout of Blazor, which are essential components for constructing the navigation hierarchy of our application. By the end of this chapter, we are now capable of executing basic navigation, similar to the functionality offered by the XAML version of our app.

Throughout the UI construction process in this chapter, we observed that the UI design technique of Blazor aligns with conventional web UI design practices. This allows for the reuse of code from existing frameworks, such as Bootstrap.

When creating a custom UI, it is often beneficial to design the initial layout in a playground first. Once satisfied with the UI design, the HTML and CSS code can be copied into a Razor file to construct a Razor component. Several playgrounds popular among frontend developers can also be utilized by Blazor developers, including CodePen, JSFiddle, CodeSandbox, and StackBlitz.

In this chapter, we utilized Bootstrap examples to construct our UIs. Although this approach offers a simple method for implementing a web UI, it results in a significant amount of duplicated code. In the upcoming chapter, we will streamline our code and transform it into reusable Razor components. By employing these Razor components, we will carry out CRUD operations to add, edit, and delete items.

Learn more on Discord

Join our community's Discord space for discussions with the author and other readers:

```
https://packt.link/cross-platform-app
```

10

Implementing Razor Components

In the previous chapter, we explored Blazor routing and layout and, subsequently, built a navigation framework by establishing our app's routing and layout. Upon setting up the navigation framework, we crafted top-level pages. The implementation of Razor pages allows for password database navigation, akin to the XAML version. While Razor pages are indeed Razor components, they are not reusable. In this chapter, we will introduce the creation of reusable Razor components. Furthermore, we will delve into data binding and the Razor component lifecycle to foster a comprehensive understanding of these aspects. Armed with this knowledge, we will optimize our code by converting duplicate code into reusable Razor components. Ultimately, we will use the Razor components to implement CRUD operations within our app.

We will cover the following topics in this chapter:

- Understanding Razor components
- Creating a Razor class library
- Creating reusable Razor components
- Understanding the Razor component lifecycle
- Refactoring Razor components
- Using templated components

Technical requirements

To test and debug the source code in this chapter, you need to have Visual Studio 2022 installed on your PC or Mac. Please refer to the *Development environment setup* section in *Chapter 1, Getting Started with .NET MAUI*, for details.

The source code for this chapter is available in the following GitHub repository: `https://github.com/PacktPublishing/.NET-MAUI-Cross-Platform-Application-Development-Second-edition/tree/main/2nd/chapter10`.

To check out the source code of this chapter, you can use the below command:

```
$ git clone -b 2nd/chapter10 https://github.com/PacktPublishing/.NET-MAUI-
Cross-Platform-Application-Development-Second-edition.git PassXYZ.Vault2
```

To find out more about the source code in this book, please refer to the *Managing the source code* section in this book, in *Chapter 2, Building Our First .NET MAUI App*.

Understanding Razor components

Although we developed and utilized Razor components in the previous two chapters, we have not yet delved deeply into them. In this section, we will continue refining the app from the last chapter while exploring Razor components more thoroughly, thereby gaining a better understanding of key concepts surrounding these components.

Blazor apps are constructed using Razor components. The first Razor component in our app is `Main`, and it is defined in `Main.razor`, as illustrated below:

```
<Router AppAssembly="@typeof(Main).Assembly">
  <Found Context="routeData">
    <RouteView RouteData="@routeData"
      DefaultLayout="@typeof(MainLayout)" />
    <FocusOnNavigate RouteData="@routeData" Selector="h1" />
  </Found>
  <NotFound>
    <LayoutView Layout="@typeof(MainLayout)">
      <p role="alert">
        Sorry, there's nothing at this address.
      </p>
    </LayoutView>
  </NotFound>
</Router>
```

The Router component, which is installed within the Main component, takes care of routing pages and selecting the default layout component. All other Razor pages are managed by the Router components. These Razor pages, loaded by the Router, have route templates defined and serve to display the user interface. In our project, Razor pages can be found in the Pages folder.

To understand the startup sequence of the Blazor Hybrid app, we can refer to *Figure 10.1* below:

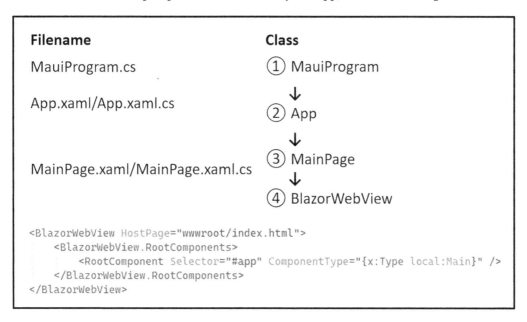

Figure 10.1: Startup of the Blazor Hybrid app

As a .NET MAUI application, the starting point of the Blazor Hybrid app is also the MauiProgram class **(1)**. Within the MauiProgram class, an instance of the App class **(2)** is constructed. The first XAML page to be loaded into this is the MainPage **(3)** class. This MainPage includes an instance of BlazorWebView **(4)** that hosts the Blazor pages. For further information on how the Razor component Main is loaded into BlazorWebView, please refer to *Chapter 8, Introducing Blazor Hybrid App Development*. Once the Main component is loaded into BlazorWebView, it exhibits the root of the navigation stack. In this particular scenario, the root page of the navigation stack is the Login page.

Additionally, there are reusable Razor components that act as the building blocks of Razor pages. These Razor components are stored in the Shared folder.

Essentially, each file possessing a `.razor` file extension represents a Razor component, which is compiled into a C# class upon execution. The filename serves as the class name, while the folder name contributes to the namespace. For instance, the `Login` Razor component resides in the `Pages` folder, so the folder name `Pages` is included as part of the namespace. Thus, the complete name of the `Login` class is `PassXYZ.Vault.Pages.Login`.

Razor components can be written either in a single file or divided into a Razor file (`.razor`) and a code-behind C# file (`.cs`). The code-behind C# file defines a partial class containing all the programming logic. This approach was employed when we created the `Login` component in *Chapter 8, Introducing Blazor Hybrid App Development.*

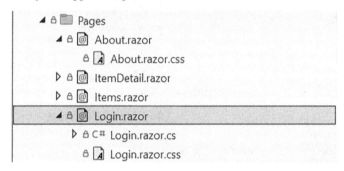

Figure 10.2: Razor component naming convention

As shown in *Figure 10.2*, when creating the `Login` component, we incorporated the Bootstrap CSS style for styling purposes. Razor components offer CSS isolation, which simplifies CSS usage and prevents collisions with other components or libraries. Moreover, Razor components can include their own CSS style in a `.razor.css` file.

Inheritance

As a Razor component is a C# class, it encompasses all features inherent to a C# class. Consequently, a Razor component can serve as a child class of another Razor component. In *Chapter 9, Understanding Blazor Layout and Routing*, we observed that all layout components are derived classes of `LayoutComponentBase` when creating layout components. As illustrated in the `MainLayout.razor` code below, we employ the `@inherits` directive to specify the `LayoutComponentBase` as the base class:

```
@inherits LayoutComponentBase
<div class="page">
  <div class="sidebar"><NavMenu/></div>
  <main>@Body</main>
</div>
```

Every Razor component is derived from the `ComponentBase` class. As a result, it is feasible to create a Razor component derived from the `ComponentBase` class using a C# file, without requiring a Razor markup file. For instance, we can create an `AppName` Razor component within a C# class, demonstrated as follows:

```
using Microsoft.AspNetCore.Components;
using Microsoft.AspNetCore.Components.Rendering;
namespace PassXYZ.Vault.Pages;
public class AppName : ComponentBase
{
  protected override void BuildRenderTree
    (RenderTreeBuilder builder)
  {
    base.BuildRenderTree(builder);
    builder.OpenElement(0, "div");
    builder.AddContent(1, "PassXYZ.Vault");
    builder.CloseElement();
  }
}
```

`AppName` is a Razor component that is designed without a Razor markup file (`.razor`); however, it functions identically to other Razor components, as demonstrated here:

```
...
<AppName/>
...
```

The above example is used to demonstrate how to create a Razor component in C# code. However, it's generally recommended to create UI components utilizing Razor markup instead of C# code.

In this section, we introduced Razor components. We can place reusable Razor components in a shared folder to ensure that they are accessible throughout the project. Additionally, a Razor class library can be created to share Razor components across multiple projects. In the subsequent section, we will delve into the process of packaging these Razor components into a library.

Creating a Razor class library

In our project, we create reusable components and store them in the `Shared` folder. These components can be utilized by other components, such as layout components or `NavMenu`. Additionally, we can encapsulate Razor components within the Razor class library, making them accessible for use across various projects.

The components in the Razor class library are not specific to a single project, making them suitable for use in any Blazor project, whether it be Blazor Hybrid, Blazor WebAssembly, or Blazor Server apps.

In this book, we construct Razor components utilizing Bootstrap. Numerous open-source Razor class libraries built on top of Bootstrap can be found on GitHub. Several of these libraries are sufficiently robust for commercial product development. Below are a few examples:

- `BootstrapBlazor:` `https://github.com/dotnetcore/BootstrapBlazor`
- `Blazorise:` `https://github.com/Megabit/Blazorise`
- `Havit.Blazor:` `https://github.com/havit/Havit.Blazor/`

These open-source projects are constructed as Razor class libraries, enabling their reuse in a manner analogous to other .NET libraries. Razor class libraries can be published as `NuGet` packages, allowing for seamless integration into our Blazor projects. For example, the `BootstrapBlazor` library can be found at this link: `https://www.nuget.org/packages/BootstrapBlazor/`.

In this section, we will develop a Razor class library similar to the aforementioned open-source projects. We will incorporate reusable Razor components within our Razor class library. This library can then be published as a NuGet package. We have the option to create a Razor class library using either Visual Studio or the .NET command line.

To create a Razor class library using Visual Studio, we can add a new project to our solution, as illustrated in *Figure 10.3*, by following these steps:

1. Search for and select **Razor Class Library** from the project templates.
2. Click **Next**, and name the project **PassXYZ.BlazorUI**.
3. On the subsequent screen, click **Create** to establish the library.

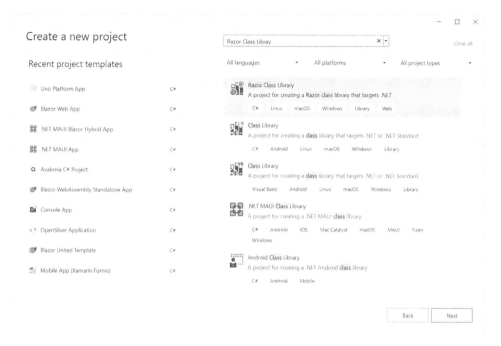

Figure 10.3: Creating a Razor class library

To create the project using a dotnet command line, we can navigate to the solution folder and execute the following command in the Command Prompt:

```
dotnet new razorclasslib -n PassXYZ.BlazorUI
```

The dotnet new command creates a new project utilizing the razorclasslib template, naming the project PassXYZ.BlazorUI. In order to include the project in the solution, we can execute the following command:

```
dotnet sln add PassXYZ.BlazorUI\PassXYZ.BlazorUI.csproj
```

In order to create our Razor components using this skeleton project, we must remove the unused Component1.* and ExampleJsInterop.cs files from the PassXYZ.BlazorUI project.

To utilize Razor components in the `PassXYZ.BlazorUI` project, we must include the project reference within the `PassXYZ.Vault` project. To do so, we can simply right-click the project node in Visual Studio and select `Add -> Project Reference`. Alternatively, we can directly modify the `PassXYZ.Vault.csproj` project file by adding the following line:

```
<ItemGroup>
  <ProjectReference
    Include="..\PassXYZ.BlazorUI\PassXYZ.BlazorUI.csproj"
      />
</ItemGroup>
```

In order to create a new Razor component utilizing this library, we must update the `PassXYZ.Vault\_Imports.razor` file by adding the following line:

```
@using PassXYZ.BlazorUI
```

Using static assets in the Razor class library

We employ Bootstrap within our Razor components, so it's necessary to include Bootstrap CSS and JavaScript files in the Razor class library. From the perspective of a Blazor app, we can place these static assets in either the project's `wwwroot` folder or the component library's `wwwroot` folder. Taking the Bootstrap CSS file as an example, if we store it in the project's `wwwroot` directory, we can reference it in `index.html` using the following path:

```
<script src="css/bootstrap/bootstrap.bundle.min.js"/>
```

If we opt to store it in the component library's `wwwroot` folder, we can reference it using the following path:

```
<script src="_content/PassXYZ.BlazorUI/css/bootstrap/
  bootstrap.bundle.min.js"/>
```

The distinction lies in the necessity to reference the URL in the component library, which should begin with `_content/{LibraryProjectName}`.

Once we have established a Razor class library project, we can proceed to include additional components in it.

Creating reusable Razor components

In this section, we will refactor our code to develop reusable components. This process will enable us to gain a deeper understanding of the features of Razor components and learn how to optimize them to improve reusability.

In *Chapter 8, Introducing Blazor Hybrid App Development*, we created the Blazor Hybrid version of our app. Additionally, we incorporated layout and routing functionalities in *Chapter 9, Understanding Blazor Routing and Layout*. As a result, our app can now browse and update the password database. However, we have not yet implemented the majority of CRUD operations. After refining the Razor components in this chapter, we will proceed to add these functionalities.

To navigate the password database, we developed two Razor components – Items and ItemDetail. The Items class is employed to exhibit a list of password entries and groups within the current group, while the ItemDetail class is utilized for presenting the content of an individual password entry.

Upon examining the layout of Items and ItemDetail, as illustrated in *Figure 10.4*, we can observe that both pages possess a similarity in terms of their appearance and overall design.

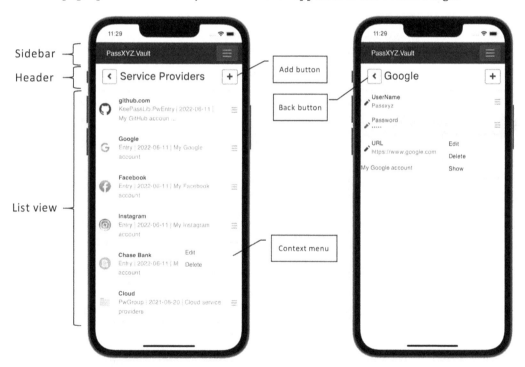

Figure 10.4: UI layout of Items and ItemDetail

The layout of both pages features a sidebar, a header, and a list view. The sidebar is defined in the layout component, while the header and list view are implemented in both Items and ItemDetail with partially duplicated code. In this chapter, we will optimize our code by abstracting the duplicated portions into reusable components.

There are two buttons in the header: Add and Back. The Back button allows for navigation back to the parent group, while the Add button enables the user to add a new item or field.

In the list view item, we can utilize the context menu to execute item-level operations, such as editing or deleting. The context menu comprises menu items designated for specific actions related to the selected item or field. When performing edit or delete CRUD operations, upon selecting a menu item, a modal dialog relevant to the chosen action will appear.

In the present implementation, both Items and ItemDetail incorporate all UI elements within a single Razor markup. We will begin to streamline the code by breaking it down into smaller, reusable components, which will result in a cleaner implementation.

In this chapter, we will transform modal dialogs, headers, and list views into Razor components. Let's begin with modal dialogs. To facilitate adding, editing, and deleting operations, we require two types of dialog boxes:

- Editor dialog: for adding or editing items or fields
- Confirmation dialog: for confirmation prior to deleting an item or a field

In *Chapter 9, Understanding Blazor Routing and Layout*, we implemented modal dialogs by utilizing HTML and CSS code from Bootstrap examples. However, we have not examined these elements thoroughly, as our markup files appear lengthy and intricate. In this chapter, we will dissect the code and convert it into Razor components.

Creating a base modal dialog component

To improve the editor and confirmation dialogs, we can first construct a base modal dialog. By leveraging this base modal dialog, we can create either editor or confirmation dialogs as needed.

To create a new Razor component in the PassXYZ.BlazorUI project, right-click on the project node and select Add -> New Item... -> Razor Component from the project template. Name the Razor component ModalDialog, and create a C# code-behind file for it. Next, enter the code shown in *Listing 10.1* into ModalDialog.razor and the code in *Listing 10.2* into ModalDialog.razor.cs.

The UI code is derived from the Items and ItemDetail code found in *Chapter 9, Understanding Blazor Routing and Layout*, as depicted in *Listing 10.1*:

```
<div class="modal fade" id=@Id tabindex="-1"
    aria-labelledby="ModelLabel" aria-hidden="true">
  <div class="modal-dialog"><div class="modal-content">
    <div class="modal-header">                                      //(1)
      <h5 class="modal-title" id="ModelLabel">@Title</h5>           //(2)
      <button type="button" class="btn-close"                      //(3)
        data-bs-dismiss="modal" aria-label="Close"/>
    </div>
    <div class="modal-body">                                        //(4)
      <form class="row gx-2 gy-3">
        @ChildContent                                              //(5)
        <div class="col-12">
          <button type="button" class="btn btn-secondary"
            data-bs-dismiss="modal" @onclick=
              "OnClickClose">
          @CloseButtonText                                         //(6)
          </button>
            <button type="submit" class="btn btn-primary"
              data-bs-dismiss="modal" @onclick=
                "OnClickSave">
            @SaveButtonText                                        //(7)
            </button>
        </div>
      </form>
    </div>
  </div></div>
</div>
```

Listing 10.1: `ModalDialog.razor` (https://epa.ms/ModalDialog10-1)

In the markup code displayed in *Listing 10.1*, we observe a typical HTML code snippet with Bootstrap styling. We have incorporated C# variables within the HTML to construct the component UI.

This base dialog UI comprises a header **(1)** and a body **(4)**. Within the header, there is a title **(2)** and a close button **(3)**. The body contains a child content area **(5)** and two buttons (**Close (6)**/ **Save (7)**).

For a visual representation of the layout of this base modal dialog, please refer to *Figure 10.5:*

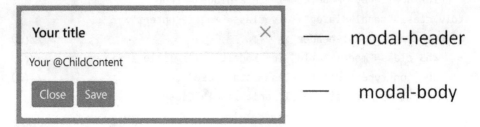

Figure 10.5: Base dialog

Although the HTML and CSS code closely resemble the Bootstrap example, we have substituted all hardcoded content with C# variables. If we were to use this modal dialog component to construct a new component, the following would serve as an example:

```
<ModalDialog Id=@id Title="Please confirm"
  OnSaveAsync=@OnSaveClicked
  SaveButtonText="Save" CloseButtonText="Close">
    Do you want to delete UserName?
</ModalDialog>

<button class="dropdown-item" data-bs-toggle="modal"
  data-bs-target="#@Id">Please confirm</button>
```

In the above markup code, we define the modal dialog using the `<ModalDialog>` component tag. Each modal dialog is assigned a unique ID for identification purposes. We can display the dialog box by clicking a button, wherein the modal dialog ID is provided to facilitate its identification.

Within the `<ModalDialog>` component tag, we have assigned values to multiple attributes defined in the `ModalDialog` component, including the ID, `title`, `button text`, `event handler`, and more.

Data binding

Rather than directly assigning a string or data to the attribute of an HTML element, we have the option to assign a variable to it. This capability is the data binding feature provided by Razor components. In this section, we will explore how to use data binding effectively. In data binding, assigning a variable to the attribute of a DOM element results in data flow from Razor components to DOM elements. Conversely, responding to a DOM event causes data to flow from DOM elements to Razor components.

Since we can use a Razor component in the same way as a DOM element, the data flow between child and parent Razor components resembles the data exchange between Razor components and DOM elements.

For instance, we can bind the id variable to the Id attribute of ModalDialog, managing the button click event using the OnSaveClicked event handler:

```
<ModalDialog Id=@id Title="Please confirm"
  OnSaveAsync=@OnSaveClicked
  SaveButtonText="Save" CloseButtonText="Close">
```

In the previous example, the data flows from the id variable to the Id attribute of ModalDialog. When the OnSaveClicked event handler is invoked, the data flows back from ModalDialog to the current context. The ModalDialog attributes, Id and OnSaveAsync, are defined in the C# code-behind file. In the following section, let's examine the C# code-behind file of ModalDialog.

Component parameters

Razor components' attributes can be defined using component parameters. To establish component parameters, we need to create public properties adorned with the [Parameter] attribute.

In the ModalDialog class, illustrated in *Listing 10.2*, we declare seven component parameters: Id, Title, ChildContent, OnClose, OnSaveAsync, CloseButtonText, and SaveButtonText. These component parameters can be utilized in data binding:

```
using Microsoft.AspNetCore.Components;
using System.Diagnostics;
using System.Diagnostics.CodeAnalysis;
namespace PassXYZ.BlazorUI;
public partial class ModalDialog : IDisposable
{
  [Parameter]
  public string? Id { get; set; }                            //(1)
  [Parameter]
  public string? Title { get; set; }                         //(2)
  [Parameter]
  public RenderFragment ChildContent { get; set; }           //(3)
  [Parameter]
  public Func<Task>? OnClose { get; set; }                   //(4)
```

```
[Parameter]
public Func<Task<bool>>? OnSaveAsync { get; set; }                //(5)
[Parameter]
[NotNull]
public string? CloseButtonText { get; set; }                     //(6)
[Parameter]
[NotNull]
public string? SaveButtonText { get; set; }                      //(7)
private async Task OnClickClose() {
   if (OnClose != null) { await OnClose(); }
}
private async Task OnClickSave() {
   if (OnSaveAsync != null) { await OnSaveAsync(); }
}
void IDisposable.Dispose() {
    GC.SuppressFinalize(this);
}
}
```

Listing 10.2: `ModalDialog.razor.cs` *(*`https://epa.ms/ModalDialog10-2`*)*

The parameters of the `ModalDialog` component are defined as follows:

- `Id` **(1)**: This identifier is used to distinguish a modal dialog.
- `Title` **(2)**: This represents the title of the modal dialog.
- `ChildContent` **(3)**: This is designated for the insertion of the child component's content. The data type that we're referring to is a `RenderFragment` delegate, which represents a segment of UI content. For more details, please refer to the following Microsoft document. We'll dive deeper into this topic in *Chapter 11*: `https://learn.microsoft.com/ en-us/aspnet/core/blazor/performance?view=aspnetcore-8.0#define-reusable- renderfragments-in-code`.

Two event handlers – `OnClose` **(4)** and `OnSaveAsync` **(5)** – are defined to manage button click actions. We can customize the text on both buttons using `CloseButtonText` **(6)** and `SaveButtonText` **(7)**.

We can handle component parameters similarly to HTML attributes. A C# field, property, or method return value can be assigned to the component parameter of `ModalDialog`. Once we create the base `ModalDialog` component, we can then develop `Editor` and `Confirmation` dialog components using it.

Let's create a new modal dialog, ConfirmDialog, which will prompt the user to confirm the deletion of an item. To create a new ConfirmDialog component within the PassXYZ.BlazorUI project, you can right-click on the project node and select Add -> New Item... -> Razor Component from the project template. We can name the Razor component ConfirmDialog and input the following code provided in *Listing 10.3*:

```
<ModalDialog Id=@Id Title=@($w"Deleting {Title}")
  OnSaveAsync=@OnSave
  SaveButtonText="Confirm" CloseButtonText="Cancel">
  Please confirm to delete @Title?
</ModalDialog>
@code {
  [CascadingParameter(Name = "Id")]
  public string Id { get; set; } = "confirmDialog";              //(1)
  [Parameter]
  public string? Title { get; set; }                             //(2)
  [Parameter]
  public Action? OnConfirmClick { get; set; }
  async Task<bool> OnSave() {
    OnConfirmClick?.Invoke();
    return await Task.FromResult(true);
  }
}
```

Listing 10.3: ConfirmDialog.razor *(https://epa.ms/ConfirmDialog10-3)*

We define the Id **(1)** and Title **(2)** component parameters in the ConfirmDialog and pass their values to the base class using data binding. Additionally, we subscribe to the OnSaveAsync event by utilizing the OnSave event handler. We also define our own event handler, OnConfirmClick, as a component parameter, allowing other components to subscribe to it.

In the ConfirmDialog, we actually bind parameters using nested components. In this scenario, the data flow should follow the suggested directions:

- Change notifications should move upward through the hierarchy.
- New parameter values should flow downward through the hierarchy.

The values for the Id and Title attributes are assigned by the components that utilize ConfirmDialog, and their values cascade down to ModalDialog. The Save or Close button events are initiated within the ModalDialog component and subsequently propagate upwards through the chain to ConfirmDialog and higher-level components. Using the Save button as an example, the event follows the upward direction illustrated here:

```
onclick (DOM) -> OnSaveAsync (ModalDialog) -> OnConfirmClick
(ConfirmDialog)
```

The process begins with the onclick event in the DOM. ModalDialog defines its own event, OnSaveAsync, which is activated by the onclick event handler. ConfirmDialog, on the other hand, establishes its own event called OnConfirmClick, which is initiated by the OnSaveAsync event handler.

Nested components

ConfirmDialog serves as an example of nested components. As demonstrated, we can embed components within other components by declaring them using HTML syntax. The embedded components appear as HTML tags, with the tag name corresponding to the component type. For instance, we can utilize ModalDialog inside ConfirmDialog, as illustrated here:

```
<ModalDialog ...>Please confirm to delete @Title?</ModalDialog>
```

Nested components serve as a means to construct a component hierarchy in Blazor. In object-oriented programming languages, inheritance and composition are two methods for extending and reusing a class. In Blazor, composition is employed within nested components to enhance functionalities. Inheritance represents an 'is-a' relationship, whereas composition signifies a 'has-a' relationship. In the case of nested components, the parent component encompasses a child component.

In Microsoft Blazor and ASP.NET Core documents, the terms "ancestor" and "descendant" or "parent" and "child" are utilized to describe the relationship between nested components. In this context, the parent and child relationship is not one of inheritance but of composition. A more suitable term could be "outer component" or "inner component." However, to maintain consistency with Microsoft documentation, I will not opt for alternative terms in our discussion. Please be mindful that when we discuss nested components and data binding, the ancestor and descendant relationship represents a "has-a" relationship or a composition.

In our previous example, the `ConfirmDialog` component serves as the outer component, while the `ModalDialog` acts as the inner component. The relationship between them is such that the `ConfirmDialog` contains the `ModalDialog` within it.

Child content rendering

When building nested components, there are often scenarios where one component sets the content of another component. The outer component supplies the content situated between the inner component's opening and closing tags. In the case of `ConfirmDialog`, the content of `ModalDialog` is configured as follows:

```
<ModalDialog Id=@Id Title=@($"Deleting {Title}")
  OnSaveAsync=@OnSave
    SaveButtonText="Confirm" CloseButtonText="Cancel">
    Please confirm to delete @Title?
</ModalDialog>
```

This is accomplished by employing a unique component parameter called `ChildContent`, which is of the `RenderFragment` type. In the previous code, the `"Please confirm to delete @Title?"` string is assigned to the `ChildContent` parameter of `ModalDialog`.

The `ConfirmDialog` represents a relatively simple example of nested components. Let's consider another example, `EditorDialog`, to further examine the features of Razor components. As previously mentioned, we require two dialog boxes to manage add, edit, and delete actions. The `ConfirmDialog` serves to seek user confirmation before deleting an item or a field. In order to add or edit an item or a field, we need a dialog box equipped with editing capabilities.

We can follow the same procedure to create a new component, `EditorDialog`. After selecting Add -> New Item… -> Razor Component in the project template, we can assign the name `EditorDialog` to the Razor component and create a corresponding C# code-behind file. Subsequently, we can input the code from *Listing 10.4* into `EditorDialog.razor` and the code from *Listing 10.5* into `EditorDialog.razor.cs`.

Let us examine the Razor markup code of `EditorDialog`, as displayed in *Listing 10.4*:

```
<ModalDialog Id=@Id Title=@Key OnSaveAsync=@OnSaveClicked
  SaveButtonText ="Save" CloseButtonText="Close">
  @if (IsKeyEditingEnable) {                                //(1)
    <input type="text" class="form-control" id="keyField"
```

```
        @bind="Key" placeholder=@KeyPlaceHolder required>                  //(2)
    }
    @ChildContent
    <div>
      <textarea class="form-control" id="valueField"
        style="height: 100px"
        placeholder=@ValuePlaceHolder
        @bind="Value" required />                                          //(3)
    </div>
  </ModalDialog>
```

Listing 10.4: `EditorDialog.razor` *(https://epa.ms/EditorDialog10-4)*

The `EditorDialog`, built using `ModalDialog`, is designed for editing key-value pairs. There are two use cases we aim to support with this component: creating a new key-value pair, where both the key and value are editable, and modifying an existing key-value pair, where only the value field may need alteration.

To facilitate these scenarios, we use a component parameter called `IsKeyEditingEnabled` **(1)** to detect the conditions. To create a new key-value pair, the key input is rendered as an `<input>` element **(2)**, while to edit an existing key-value pair, the key is displayed as the title in the header area. In both cases, the value can be edited using a `<textarea>` element **(3)**. This constitutes the core functionality of our `EditorDialog` component.

As shown in *Figure 10.6*, the UI depicts two different dialogs. On the left-hand side, a dialog appears when we intend to add a new field, requiring us to input the field name and content. Meanwhile, on the right-hand side, a dialog is displayed when we aim to edit an existing URL field. The field name is presented in the title, and the content can be modified in the `<textarea>` element.

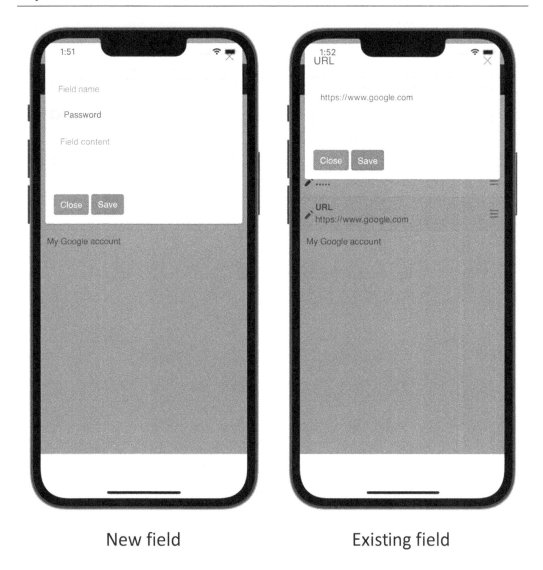

New field   Existing field

Figure 10.6: Editing a field

In the EditorDialog component, when we edit the key and value using the <input> and <textarea> HTML elements, the initial value is displayed. This initial value is set from the Razor component to the DOM. Once we make changes, the data flows from the DOM back to the Razor component, exemplifying two-way data binding.

Two-way data binding

Two-way data binding can be established using the @bind Razor directive attribute. This syntax enables an HTML element attribute to bind to a field, property, expression value, or the result of a method. In *Listing 10.4*, the value of the <input> element is bound to the Key property within the EditorDialog component:

```
<input type="text" class="form-control" id="keyField"
    @bind="Key" placeholder=@KeyPlaceHolder required>
```

In the case of two-way data binding, the DOM element <input> value is updated whenever the Key property undergoes a change. Similarly, when the user modifies the <input> value in the DOM, the Key property is updated accordingly.

In the previous example, we have the option to replace the @bind directive attribute with two one-way data bindings, as demonstrated in the following code:

```
<input type="text" class="form-control" id="keyField"
  value="@Key"
  @onchange="@((ChangeEventArgs e) => Key = e?.Value?
    .ToString())"
  placeholder=@KeyPlaceHolder required>
```

Upon rendering our EditorDialog component, the value of the <input> element is derived from the Key property. As the user inputs a value into the textbox and shifts the element focus, the onchange event is triggered, subsequently updating the Key property with the modified value.

For the <input> element, the default event of the @bind directive attribute is the onchange event. We can modify the event using the @bind:event="{event}" attribute. The {event} placeholder should represent a DOM event. For instance, we can replace the onchange event with the oninput event using the following code snippet:

```
<input type="text" class="form-control" id="keyField"
  @bind="Key" @bind:event="oninput" placeholder=@KeyPlaceHolder required>
```

Binding with component parameters

In the previous section, we explored two-way data binding between a Razor component and a DOM element. As Razor components can function similarly to DOM elements, it is also possible to establish two-way data binding between two Razor components. This often occurs when there is a need for communication between parent and child components.

We can bind a component parameter of an inner component to the property of an outer component using the @bind-{PROPERTY} syntax. In this case, {PROPERTY} refers to the property to be bound. We have explained that the @bind directive attribute can be replaced by two one-way data binding setups, which involve assigning a variable to the <input> value attribute and assigning an event handler to the onchange event. While the compiler can automatically add the event handler for @bind, it cannot do so for @bind-{PROPERTY}. Therefore, we need to define our own event of the EventCallback<TValue> type to bind with component parameters. The event name must follow the {PARAMETER NAME}Changed format. To illustrate the @bind-{PROPERTY} directive attribute's usage, let's use our EditorDialog component as an example.

In our code, we utilize the EditorDialog in the ItemDetail component to edit a field, or similarly, in the Items component to edit an item. Let's examine field editing as an example:

```
<EditorDialog Id=@_dialogEditId
  @bind-Key="listGroupField.Key"                          //(1)
  @bind-Value="listGroupField.Value"                      //(2)
  IsKeyEditingEnable=@_isNewField
  OnSave="UpdateFieldAsync"
  KeyPlaceHolder="Field name"
  ValuePlaceHolder="Field content">
  @if (_isNewField) {
    <div class="form-check">
      <input class="form-check-input" type="checkbox"
        @bind="listGroupField.IsProtected"
          id="flexCheckDefault">
      <label class="form-check-label"
        for="flexCheckDefault">
        Password
      </label>
    </div>
  }
</EditorDialog>
```

In the previous code of the ItemDetail component, we can create data binding for Key **(1)** and Value **(2)** to the listGroupField of the Field type. We need to implement the {PARAMETER NAME} Changed events in the C# code-behind for EditorDialog, as demonstrated in *Listing 10.5*:

```
namespace PassXYZ.BlazorUI;
public partial class EditorDialog {
```

```
[Parameter]
public string? Id { get; set; }
bool _isKeyEditingEnable = false;
[Parameter]
public bool IsKeyEditingEnable ...
[Parameter]
public EventCallback<bool>? IsKeyEditingEnableChanged {
  get; set; }
string _key = string.Empty;
[Parameter]
public string Key {                                            //(1)
  get => _key;
  set {
    if(_key != value) {
      _key = value;
      KeyChanged?.InvokeAsync(_key);                            //(3)
    }
  }
}
[Parameter]
public EventCallback<string>? KeyChanged { get; set; }          //(2)
[Parameter]
public string? KeyPlaceHolder { get; set; }
string _value = string.Empty;
[Parameter]
public string Value ...
[Parameter]
public EventCallback<string>? ValueChanged { get; set; }
[Parameter]
public string? ValuePlaceHolder { get; set; }
[Parameter]
public RenderFragment ChildContent { get; set; } =
  default!;
[Parameter]
public Action<string, string>? OnSave { get; set; }
async Task<bool> OnSaveClicked() {
    OnSave?.Invoke(Key, Value);
```

```
        return true;
    }
}
```

Listing 10.5: `EditorDialog.razor.cs` *(https://epa.ms/EditorDialog10-5)*

In *Listing 10.5*, we utilize the Key property as an example to illustrate the component parameter binding process. The Key property is defined as a component parameter with the [Parameter] attribute. An associated event, KeyChanged, is defined as an EventCallback<TValue> type. When the text input is modified by the user and the element focus shifts, the Key property setter is invoked. Within the setter of the Key property, the KeyChanged event is triggered, which notifies the outer ItemDetail component. Consequently, the linked variable listGroupField.Key is updated.

Communicating with cascading values and parameters

We can utilize data binding to transfer data between parent and child components. Data binding is effective when passing data to intermediate child components. However, there may be instances where we need to pass data to components located several levels deep. In such situations, utilizing data binding requires creating multiple levels of chained data binding – subsequently increasing the complexity as the chained levels expand. For instance, when passing data from Items to ModalDialog, we first need to establish a data binding with ConfirmDialog. Then, another level of data binding must be created between ConfirmDialog and ModalDialog.

In the Items component, we need to pass the Id of the dialog to ModalDialog. An Id is necessary to identify the specific dialog instance we wish to display. As demonstrated below, we define ConfirmDialog within the Items component. The Id is defined within Items and passed to ConfirmDialog through the use of component parameters:

```
<ConfirmDialog Id="@_dialogDeleteId"
    Title=@listGroupItem.Name
    OnConfirmClick="DeleteItemAsync" />
```

Then, ConfirmDialog must pass the Id to ModalDialog:

```
<ModalDialog Id=@Id Title=@($"Deleting {Title}")
    OnSaveAsync=@OnSave
    SaveButtonText="Confirm" CloseButtonText="Cancel">
    Please confirm to delete @Title?
</ModalDialog>
```

In `ModalDialog`, `Id` is used as an attribute of the `<div>` element:

```
<div class="modal fade" id=@Id tabindex="-1"
  aria-labelledby="ModelLabel" aria-hidden="true"> ...
```

In order to prevent numerous levels of data binding, we can employ cascading values and parameters as a technique to facilitate data flow through a component hierarchy.

`CascadingValue` is a component within the Blazor framework. The outer component supplies a cascading value by using `CascadingValue`, while the inner component can obtain it by employing the `[CascadingParameter]` attribute. To demonstrate its usage, we can modify the `Items` component's code as follows:

```
<CascadingValue Value="@_dialogDeleteId" Name="Id">
  <ConfirmDialog Title=@listGroupItem.Name
    OnConfirmClick="DeleteItemAsync" />
</CascadingValue>
```

We utilize cascading values with the `<CascadingValue>` tag. Within the `<CascadingValue>` tag, we assign the `_dialogDeleteId` variable to the `Value` attribute and the `Id` string to the `Name` attribute. As this `Id` is not directly employed by `ConfirmDialog`, the `Id` component parameter can be safely removed from `ConfirmDialog`.

In the `ModalDialog`, we modify the `Id` property to be a parameter by utilizing the `[CascadingParameter]` attribute instead of a component parameter:

```
[CascadingParameter(Name = "Id")]
public string Id { get; set; } = default!;
```

When working with just one cascading value, specifying its name is not mandatory, as the compiler can locate it by data type. However, to prevent ambiguities, we can assign a name to the cascading value using the `Name` attribute. Next, we will examine the final modifications in the `Items` component, which employs cascading values for both `ConfirmDialog` and `EditorDialog`:

```
<CascadingValue Value="@_dialogEditId" Name="Id">
  <EditorDialog @bind-Key="listGroupItem.Name"
      @bind-Value="listGroupItem.Notes"
      IsKeyEditingEnable=true
      OnSave="UpdateItemAsync" KeyPlaceHolder="Item name"
      ValuePlaceHolder="Please provide a description">
    @if (_isNewItem) {
```

```
        <select @bind="newItem.SubType" class="form-select"
          aria-label="Group">
          <option selected value=@ItemSubType.Group>
            @ItemSubType.Group</option>
          <option value=@ItemSubType.Entry>
            @ItemSubType.Entry</option>
          <option value=@ItemSubType.PxEntry>
            @ItemSubType.PxEntry</option>
          <option value=@ItemSubType.Notes>
            @ItemSubType.Notes</option>
        </select>
      }
    </EditorDialog>
  </CascadingValue>
  <CascadingValue Value="@_dialogDeleteId" Name="Id">
    <ConfirmDialog Title=@listGroupItem.Name
      OnConfirmClick="DeleteItemAsync" />
  </CascadingValue>
```

As demonstrated, after implementing a cascading value, `ConfirmDialog` and `EditorDialog` no longer need to handle the `Id` field directly. Consequently, the code is more compact compared to the previous version.

In this section, we explored the creation of reusable components. Some Razor components might rely on data or network services, necessitating additional steps during their creation or destruction. We can accomplish these actions as part of the lifecycle management of Razor components.

In the following section, let us examine the lifecycle of Razor components in greater detail.

Understanding the Razor component lifecycle

A Razor component, like any other object, possesses a lifecycle. It consists of a series of synchronous and asynchronous lifecycle methods that developers can override to perform additional operations during component initialization and rendering.

Refer to *Figure 10.7* for an overview of the Razor component lifecycle:

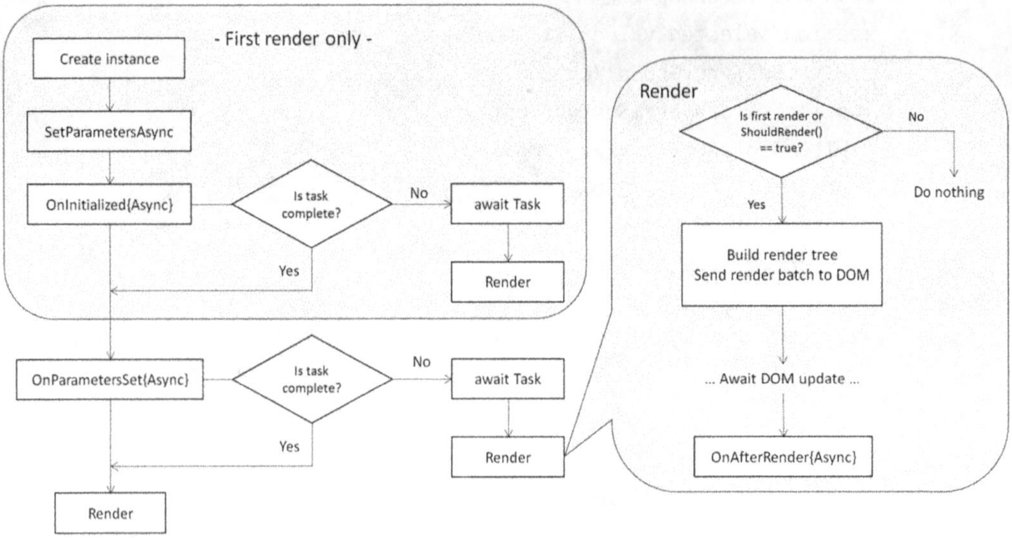

Figure 10.7: Razor component lifecycle

In *Figure 10.7*, it is evident that we have the ability to add hooks during both the initialization and rendering phases. The methods listed below can be overridden to capture initialization events:

- `SetParametersAsync`
- `OnInitialized` and `OnInitializedAsync`
- `OnParametersSet` and `OnParametersSetAsync`

`SetParametersAsync` and `OnInitializedAsync` are invoked only in the first render. `OnParametersSetAsync` is called every time a parameter is changed.

The following methods can be overridden to customize rendering:

- `ShouldRender`
- `OnAfterRender` and `OnAfterRenderAsync`

We will examine these lifecycle methods in detail and demonstrate how they can be utilized in our code.

SetParametersAsync

`SetParametersAsync` is the first hook after the object is created and it has the following signature:

```
public override Task SetParametersAsync(ParameterView parameters)
```

The `ParameterView` parameter encompasses component parameters or cascading parameter values. `SetParametersAsync` assigns values to each property with either the [`Parameter`] or [`CascadingParameter`] attribute. This function can be overridden to incorporate any logic that must be executed before setting the parameters. The subsequent hook following `SetParametersAsync` is `OnInitializedAsync`.

OnInitialized and OnInitializedAsync

`OnInitialized` and `OnInitializedAsync` are invoked when the component is initialized. They have the following signatures, respectively:

```
protected override void OnInitialized()
protected override async Task OnInitializedAsync()
```

By overriding these two functions, we can incorporate logic to initialize our component at this stage. However, keep in mind that these functions are called only once, immediately following the component's creation. For resource-intensive initialization tasks, asynchronous methods can be employed, such as downloading data via RESTful API calls. As illustrated in *Figure 10.7*, once an asynchronous method is completed, the DOM necessitates re-rendering.

OnParametersSet and OnParametersSetAsync

When component parameters are set or modified, `OnParametersSet` and `OnParametersSetAsync` are invoked. We observe that there are two versions to accommodate both synchronous and asynchronous scenarios. The asynchronous version, `OnParametersSetAsync`, can be employed to manage time-consuming tasks. Upon completion of the asynchronous task, the DOM must be re-rendered to display any updates.

The methods have the following signatures, respectively:

```
protected override void OnParametersSet()
protected override async Task OnParametersSetAsync()
```

These two methods are invoked whenever component parameters or cascading parameters change and may be called multiple times. In contrast, `OnInitializedAsync` is called only once.

As illustrated in *Figure 10.7*, the DOM can undergo multiple renderings during the initialization phase, resulting in the invocation of asynchronous calls. The methods involved in this rendering process include `ShouldRender` and `OnAfterRenderAsync`.

ShouldRender

The ShouldRender method returns a Boolean value, indicating whether the component ought to be rendered. As illustrated in *Figure 10.7*, the first render disregards this method. Consequently, a component must be rendered at least once. This method possesses the following signature:

```
protected override bool ShouldRender()
```

OnAfterRender and OnAfterRenderAsync

OnAfterRender and OnAfterRenderAsync are invoked after a component has completed its rendering process. Their respective signatures are as follows:

```
protected override void OnAfterRender(bool firstRender)
protected override async Task OnAfterRenderAsync(bool
  firstRender)
```

These methods can be utilized to execute supplementary initialization tasks with the rendered content, such as invoking JavaScript code in the component. This method features a Boolean firstRender parameter, enabling us to attach JavaScript event handlers only once. Although there is an asynchronous version of this method, the framework does not schedule another render cycle upon the completion of the asynchronous task.

To examine the impact of lifecycle methods, we can conduct a test by incorporating all lifecycle methods into the ConfirmDialog component, as demonstrated below:

```
public ConfirmDialog()
{
  Debug.WriteLine($"ConfirmDialog-{Id}: is created");
}
public override Task SetParametersAsync
  (ParameterView parameters)
{
  Debug.WriteLine($"ConfirmDialog-{Id}:
    SetParametersAsync called");
  return base.SetParametersAsync(parameters);
}
protected override void OnInitialized()
  => Debug.WriteLine($"ConfirmDialog-{Id}: OnInitialized
    called - {Title}");
protected override async Task OnInitializedAsync() =>
```

```
  await Task.Run(() => {
    Debug.WriteLine($"ConfirmDialog-{Id}: OnInitializedAsync
      called - {Title}");
});
protected override void OnParametersSet()
  => Debug.WriteLine($"ConfirmDialog-{Id}: OnParametersSet
    called - {Title}");
protected override async Task OnParametersSetAsync() =>
  await Task.Run(() => {
Debug.WriteLine($"ConfirmDialog-{Id}:
  OnParametersSetAsync called - {Title}");
});
protected override void OnAfterRender(bool firstRender)
  => Debug.WriteLine($"ConfirmDialog-{Id}: OnAfterRender
    called with firstRender = {firstRender}");
protected override async Task OnAfterRenderAsync(bool
  firstRender) => await Task.Run(() => {
    Debug.WriteLine($"ConfirmDialog-{Id}:
      OnAfterRenderAsync called - {Title}");
});
protected override bool ShouldRender() {
  Debug.WriteLine($"ConfirmDialog-{Id}: ShouldRender called
    - {Title}");
  return true;
}
```

We have overridden all lifecycle methods in `ConfirmDialog` and added debug output to display the progress. Upon launching our app, we can observe the following output:

```
ConfirmDialog-: is created
ConfirmDialog-: SetParametersAsync called
ConfirmDialog-deleteModel: OnInitialized called -
ConfirmDialog-deleteModel: OnInitializedAsync called -
ConfirmDialog-deleteModel: OnParametersSet called -
ConfirmDialog-deleteModel: OnParametersSetAsync called -
ConfirmDialog-deleteModel: ShouldRender called -
ConfirmDialog-deleteModel: ShouldRender called -
ConfirmDialog-deleteModel: OnAfterRender called with
```

```
    firstRender = True
ConfirmDialog-deleteModel: OnAfterRenderAsync called -
ConfirmDialog-deleteModel: OnAfterRender called with
    firstRender = False
ConfirmDialog-deleteModel: OnAfterRenderAsync called -
ConfirmDialog-deleteModel: OnAfterRender called with
    firstRender = False
ConfirmDialog-deleteModel: OnAfterRenderAsync called -
```

The previous output is displayed when we first launch our app and the Items page appears. We can observe that the Id cascading parameter is not set before the SetParametersAsync method is called. Since we have overridden the asynchronous methods, multiple render cycles are scheduled to occur simultaneously. As a result, the ShouldRender and OnAfterRenderAsync methods are invoked multiple times due to parallel rendering.

Now, let's consider another case, which occurs when we click on the context menu on the Items page. Upon clicking on the context menu of an item, such as a Google icon, the ConfirmDialog is initialized once more. The resulting output is as follows:

```
ConfirmDialog-deleteModel: SetParametersAsync called
ConfirmDialog-deleteModel: OnParametersSet called - Google
ConfirmDialog-deleteModel: ShouldRender called - Google
ConfirmDialog-deleteModel: OnParametersSetAsync called -
    Google
ConfirmDialog-deleteModel: ShouldRender called - Google
ConfirmDialog-deleteModel: OnAfterRender called with
    firstRender = False
ConfirmDialog-deleteModel: OnAfterRenderAsync called -
    Google
ConfirmDialog-deleteModel: OnAfterRender called with
    firstRender = False
ConfirmDialog-deleteModel: OnAfterRenderAsync called -
    Google
```

The SetParametersAsync method is called again, since the Title component parameter has been changed. In the subsequent calls, we can observe that the Title component parameter is set to Google.

In our code, we use OnParametersSet to load the list of items in Items.razor.cs, as well as to load a list of fields in ItemDetail.razor.cs. Let's examine OnParametersSet in ItemDetail.razor.cs:

```
protected override void OnParametersSet() {
  base.OnParametersSet();
  if (SelectedItemId == null) {                             //(1)
    throw new InvalidOperationException(
    "ItemDetail: SelectedItemId is null");
  }
  selectedItem = DataStore.GetItem(SelectedItemId, true);   //(2)
  if (selectedItem == null) {
    throw new InvalidOperationException(
  "ItemDetail: entry cannot be found with SelectedItemId");
  }
  else {
    if (selectedItem.IsGroup) {
      throw new InvalidOperationException(
        "ItemDetail: SelectedItemId should not be a group
          here.");
    }
    fields.Clear();
    List<Field> tmpFields = selectedItem.GetFields();       //(3)
    foreach (Field field in tmpFields) {
      fields.Add(field);
    }
    notes = selectedItem.GetNotesInHtml();
  }
}
```

(1) In OnParametersSet, we check whether the SelectedItemId component parameter is null. This represents the ID of the selected item. **(2)** If it is not null, we can locate the item by calling the IDataStore method named GetItem. **(3)** Once we obtain the instance of the selected item, we can retrieve a list of fields by invoking the GetFields method.

The implementation of OnParametersSet in Items.razor.cs is quite similar to this. For more details, you can refer to the following GitHub link: https://epa.ms/Items10-6.

Thus far, we have developed a near-complete password manager app, with its UI built using Blazor. We have established reusable modal dialog components to accommodate the context menu, enabling us to perform CRUD operations. The final component we need to address is the actual implementation of these CRUD operations.

Implementing CRUD operations

After preparing the modal dialogs for CRUD operations, as discussed in the previous sections, we can now proceed to implement these CRUD operations in this section.

CRUD operations of items

To add or update an item, we can utilize the `UpdateItemAsync` method in `Items.razor.cs` to accommodate both scenarios. To distinguish between creating a new item and updating an existing one, we define a private `_isNewItem` field as follows:

```
bool _isNewItem = false;
```

Next, we'll see how to add or edit an item.

Adding a new item

To add a new item, simply click the + button located in the header of the `Items` page, as depicted in *Figure 10.8*:

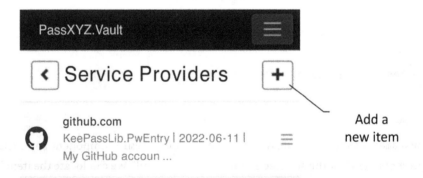

Figure 10.8: Adding a new item

The Razor markup of this page header can be reviewed here:

```
<div class="container"><div class="row">
  <div class="col-12"><h1>
    @if (selectedItem?.GetParentLink() != null) {
```

```
      <a class="btn btn-outline-dark"
        href="@selectedItem?.GetParentLink()">
        <span class="oi oi-chevron-left"
          aria-hidden="true"></span></a>                          //(1)
    }
    @(" " + Title)                                                //(2)
  <button type="button"
    class="btn btn-outline-dark float-end"
        data-bs-toggle="modal"
        data-bs-target="#@_dialogEditId"
        @onclick="@(() => _isNewItem=true)">
        <span class="oi oi-plus" aria-hidden="true">
      </span></button>                                            //(3)
    </h1></div>
  </div></div>
```

The page header features the Back button **(1)**, the Title **(2)**, and the Add button **(3)**. The Back button is displayed only when there is an existing parent link.

Upon clicking the Add button, a modal dialog with an Id defined in the _dialogEditId variable will be displayed. The onclick event handler sets _isNewItem to true, allowing the modal dialog event handler to recognize that the action is intended to add a new item.

Editing or deleting an item

To edit or delete an item, click on the context menu found on the item, as demonstrated in *Figure 10.9*:

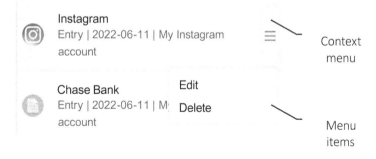

Figure 10.9: Editing or deleting an item

Upon clicking the context menu button, a list of menu items will be displayed. Let's examine the markup for the context menu found in `Items.razor`:

```
<div class="list-group">
  @foreach (var item in items) {
<div class="dropdown list-group-item list-group-item-action
  d-flex gap-1 py-2" aria-current="true">
      <img src="@item.GetIcon()" alt="twbs" width="32"
        height="32"
          class="rounded-circle flex-shrink-0 float-start">
      <a href="@item.GetActionLink()" class="..."> ...
      <button class="opacity-50 btn btn-light
          dropdown-toggle" type="button"
            id="itemsContextMenu"
          data-bs-toggle="dropdown" aria-expanded="false"
          @onclick="@(() => listGroupItem=item)">                      //(1)
        <span class="oi oi-menu" aria-hidden="true"></span>
      </button>
      <ul class="dropdown-menu" aria-labelledby=
        "itemsContextMenu">
        <li><button class="dropdown-item"
          data-bs-toggle="modal"
            data-bs-target="#@_dialogEditId"
            @onclick="@(() => _isNewItem=false)">                      //(2)
            Edit</button></li>
        <li><button class="dropdown-item"
          data-bs-toggle="modal"
            data-bs-target="#@_dialogDeleteId">                        //(3)
            Delete</button></li>
      </ul>
    </div>
  }
</div>
```

In the preceding markup code, a context menu button **(1)** is defined. Upon clicking this button, two menu items, `Edit` **(2)** and `Delete` **(3)**, will appear. As the context menu markup code runs within a `foreach` loop, we need to obtain a reference to the selected item for editing or deletion. In the C# code-behind logic, the `listGroupItem` variable is employed to reference the selected item.

We can capture this reference through the onclick event handler of the context menu button.

Upon selecting the Edit menu item, it is crucial to set the _isNewItem variable to false. This adjustment allows the event handler of the modal dialog to discern that we are modifying an existing item.

Having completed all the previous setup, it's time to examine the event handler in modal dialogs. First, let's take a look at the UpdateItemAsync event handler within Items.razor.cs:

```
private async void UpdateItemAsync(string key, string value) {
    if (listGroupItem == null) { return; }
    if (string.IsNullOrEmpty(key) || string.IsNullOrEmpty(value))
    { return; }
    listGroupItem.Name = key;
    listGroupItem.Notes = value;
    if (_isNewItem) {                                          //(1)
        // Add new item
      if (listGroupItem is NewItem aNewItem) {
        Item? newItem = DataStore.CreateNewItem
          (aNewItem.SubType);
        if (newItem != null) {
          newItem.Name = aNewItem.Name;
          newItem.Notes = aNewItem.Notes;
          items.Add(newItem);
          await DataStore.AddItemAsync(newItem);
        }
      }
    }
    else {
      // Update the current item
      await DataStore.UpdateItemAsync(listGroupItem);
    }
}
```

The UpdateItemAsync event handler can manage both adding and editing an item. It checks the _isNewItem variable (1) to determine whether we aim to add or edit an item. Subsequently, it calls IDataStore methods to perform either addition or update actions.

Now, let's examine the event handler for deleting an item:

```
private async void DeleteItemAsync() {
  if (listGroupItem == null) return;
  if (items.Remove(listGroupItem)) {
      _ = await DataStore.DeleteItemAsync
        (listGroupItem.Id);
  }
}
```

In the `DeleteItemAsync` event handler, the item is simply removed from the list, and the `IDataStore` methods are called to execute the delete action.

CRUD operations of fields

The CRUD operations for fields resemble those we implemented for items. To add or update a field, we can employ the `UpdateFieldAsync` method in `ItemDetail.razor.cs` to manage both scenarios. To determine whether we aim to create a new field or update an existing one, we define a private `_isNewField` field as follows:

```
bool _isNewField = false;
```

The UI for CRUD operations also bears similarity to what we discussed in the previous section. To view the Add button and context menu items, please refer to *Figure 10.10*.

Figure 10.10: Add, edit, or delete a field

We can examine the Razor markup code for the page header found in ItemDetail.razor as follows:

```
<div class="container">
  <div class="row"><div class="col-12">
    <h1>
      @if (selectedItem?.GetParentLink() != null) {
        <a class="btn btn-outline-dark"
          href="@selectedItem?.GetParentLink()">
        <span class="oi oi-chevron-left"
          aria-hidden="true"></span></a>
      }
      @(" " + selectedItem!.Name)
      <button type="button" class="btn btn-outline-dark
        float-end"
        data-bs-toggle="modal" data-bs-
          target="#@_dialogEditId"
        @onclick="@(() => _isNewField=true)">
          <span class="oi oi-plus"
            aria-hidden="true"></span></button>
    </h1>
  </div></div>
</div>
```

As we can observe, the preceding source code is quite similar to the one found in Items.razor, with the exception of replacing the _isNewItem variable with _isNewField. We can consider refining this page header into a reusable component later on.

Similar to the previous section, let's now examine the source code for the list group and context menu:

```
<div class="list-group">
  @foreach (var field in fields) {
    @if(field.ShowContextAction == null) {
      <div class="dropdown list-group-item ...
        aria-current="true">
        <span class="oi oi-pencil" aria-hidden="true">
         </span>
        <div class="d-flex gap-2 w-100
          justify-content-between"> ...
```

```
            <button class="opacity-50 btn btn-light
              dropdown-toggle" type="button"
              id="itemDetailContextMenu"
              data-bs-toggle="dropdown" aria-expanded="false"
              @onclick="@(() => listGroupField=field)">          //(1)
                <span class="oi oi-menu" aria-hidden="true">
                </span>
            </button>
            <ul class="dropdown-menu"
              aria-labelledby="itemDetailContextMenu">
              <li><button class="dropdown-item"
                data-bs-toggle="modal"
                data-bs-target="#@_dialogEditId"
                @onclick="@(() => _isNewField=false)">          //(2)
                    Edit
              </button></li>
              <li><button class="dropdown-item"
                data-bs-toggle="modal"
                data-bs-target="#@_dialogDeleteId">          //(3)
                    Delete
              </button></li>
              @if (field.IsProtected) {
                <li><button class="dropdown-item"
                  @onclick="OnToggleShowPassword">          //(4)
                    @if (field.IsHide) { <span>Show</span> }
                    else { <span>Hide</span> }
                </button></li>
              }
            </ul>
          </div>
        }
      }
</div>
```

The preceding source code of ItemDetail.razor features a context **Menu** button **(1)** and three buttons for the **Add (2)**, **Edit (3)**, and **Show (4)** menu items. You may have noticed that the source code is quite similar to that in Items.razor, encompassing a list group and a context menu.

We will further develop this into a reusable component later in this chapter. The variation in the context menu lies in the addition of a menu item that displays or conceals a field, if it is a protected field such as a password. We utilize the `onclick` event handler, `OnToggleShowPassword`, to set the `IsHide` field property, thereby toggling the visibility of the password field.

Finally, let's examine the event handlers for modal dialogs in `ItemDetail.razor.cs`:

```
private async void UpdateFieldAsync(string key, string
  value) {
  if (selectedItem == null || listGroupField == null) {
      throw new NullReferenceException("Selected item is
        null");
  }
  if (string.IsNullOrEmpty(key) ||
      string.IsNullOrEmpty(value)) { return; }
  listGroupField.Key = key;
  listGroupField.Value = value;
  if (_isNewField) {
    // Add a new field
    Field newField = selectedItem.AddField
      (listGroupField.Key,
      ((listGroupField.IsProtected) ?
        listGroupField.EditValue : listGroupField.Value),
          listGroupField.IsProtected);
    fields.Add(newField);
  }
  else {
    // Update the current field
    var newData = (listGroupField.IsProtected) ?
      listGroupField.EditValue : listGroupField.Value;
    selectedItem.UpdateField(listGroupField.Key, newData,
      listGroupField.IsProtected);
  }
  await DataStore.UpdateItemAsync(selectedItem);
}
```

The UpdateFieldAsync event handler manages both the addition and editing of a field. It receives two parameters – key and value – which are passed from the modal dialog and are used to set the field of listGroupField. By examining the _isNewField variable, the handler determines whether the intent is to add or edit a field. Subsequently, it calls IDataStore methods to execute the add or update actions.

To remove a field, the DeleteFieldAsync event handler below is triggered:

```
private async void DeleteFieldAsync() {
  if (listGroupField == null || selectedItem == null) {
    throw new NullReferenceException(
      "Selected item or field is null");
  }
  listGroupField.ShowContextAction = listGroupField;
  selectedItem.DeleteField(listGroupField);
  await DataStore.UpdateItemAsync(selectedItem);
}
```

In the DeleteFieldAsync event handler, we simply remove the field from the selected item and invoke the IDataStore method to update the database.

Having implemented CRUD operations, we have now successfully completed the implementation of password manager features. We have developed a new version of the password manager app utilizing Blazor UI. The distinction between this version and the one described in *Part 1* of this book lies in our use of Blazor to construct all user interfaces. The appearance and functionality of the Blazor UI closely resemble web apps, while the XAML UI maintains the characteristics of native apps.

Although we have successfully implemented all the required functionalities, we can observe some duplicated code in our current implementation. To resolve this issue, we can refactor our code, transforming the duplicate sections into Razor components.

Refactoring Razor components

In the current implementation, we can observe that most of the duplicated code is found in the Items and ItemDetail pages. Throughout the remainder of this chapter, we will transform this duplicated code into Razor components.

We will create the following components:

- `Navbar`: This component displays a navigation bar.
- `Dropdown`: This component supports a context menu.
- `ListView`: This component displays a list of items.

The `ListView` component is the most complex one, so we will address it at the end of this section. For now, let's focus on the `Navbar` and `Dropdown` components first.

Creating the Navbar component

Let's examine the navigation bar UI in *Figure 10.11*. We can observe that the navigation bar features a **Back** button, a **Title**, and an **Add** button:

Figure 10.11: Navigation bar

The following paragraph presents the current code of the navigation bar. This code snippet appears on both the `Items` and `ItemDetail` pages, resulting in a duplication:

```
<div class="container">
  <div class="row">
    <div class="col-12">
      <h1>
        @if (selectedItem?.GetParentLink() != null) {           //(1)
          <a class="btn btn-outline-dark"
             href="@selectedItem?.GetParentLink()">
            <span class="oi oi-chevron-left"
```

```
                   aria-hidden="true"></span></a>                    //(2)
            }
        @(" " + Title)                                               //(3)
        <button type="button"
          class="btn btn-outline-dark float-end"
          data-bs-toggle="modal"
          data-bs-target="#@_dialogEditId"
          @onclick="@(() => _isNewItem=true)">                       //(4)
          <span class="oi oi-plus" aria-hidden="true">
          </span>
        </button>
      </h1>
    </div>
  </div>
</div>
```

In the preceding code, **(1)** the Back button is displayed when a parent link is present. **(2)** The Back button is implemented using an `<a>` tag. **(3)** The Title, as a string, appears within the `<h1>` tag. **(4)** The Add button is implemented using a `<button>` tag. The styling of both the Back and Add buttons employs Bootstrap formatting.

To transform the preceding code into a Razor component, we can generate a new Razor component in the PassXYZ.BlazorUI project and name it Navbar. The Navbar component will display the UI elements illustrated in *Figure 10.11*, including a Back button, a title, and an Add button. In order to separate the UI and logic, we will create both a Navbar.razor.cs C# code-behind file and the Razor markup, Navbar.razor. We will define component parameters and event handlers in the C# code-behind file, as demonstrated in *Listing 10.6*:

```
public partial class Navbar
{
  [Parameter]
  public string? ParentLink { get; set; }                          //(1)
  [Parameter]
  public string? DialogId { get; set; }                            //(2)
  [Parameter]
  public string? Title { get; set; }                               //(3)
  [Parameter]
  public EventCallback<MouseEventArgs> OnAddClick { get;
```

```
    set; }                                                    //(4)
    private void OnClickClose(MouseEventArgs e) {
        OnAddClick.InvokeAsync();
    }
}
```

Listing 10.6: Navbar.razor.cs *(*https://epa.ms/Navbar10-7*)*

In Navbar, there are four component parameters and an event handler defined. We can assign the parent link for the Back button using the ParentLink parameter **(1)**. The value of Title is set according to the Title parameter **(3)**. For the Add button, it is necessary to provide an Id and an event handler for the dialog box; hence, the DialogId **(2)** and OnAddClick **(4)** parameters are utilized.

Now, let us examine the Razor file of Navbar, presented in *Listing 10.7*:

```
@namespace PassXYZ.BlazorUI
<div class="container">
  <div class="row">
    <div class="col-12">
      <h1>
        @if (ParentLink != null) {                            //(1)
          <a class="btn btn-outline-dark"
            href="@ParentLink">                               //(1)
            <span class="oi oi-chevron-left"
              aria-hidden="true"></span>
          </a>
        }
        @(" " + Title)                                        //(3)
        <button type="button"
          class="btn btn-outline-dark float-end"
          data-bs-toggle="modal"
          data-bs-target="#@DialogId"                         //(2)
          @onclick="OnClickClose">                            //(4)
          <span class="oi oi-plus" aria-hidden="true">
          </span>
        </button>
      </h1>
    </div>
  </div>
```

```
    </div>
  </div>
```

We can observe that the code closely resembles the code used in `Items` and `ItemDetail`. The key difference is that we have substituted hardcoded values with component parameters (`ParentLink` **(1)**, `DialogId` **(2)**, `Title` **(3)**, and `OnClickClose` **(4)**). With the integration of this new `Navbar` component, we can modify the code in `Items` by employing the `Navbar` component, as demonstrated below:

```
<Navbar ParentLink="@selectedItem?.GetParentLink()"
  Title="@Title" DialogId="@_dialogEditId"
  OnAddClick="@(() => {_isNewItem=true;})" />
```

We can then proceed to replace the code in `ItemDetail` as follows:

```
<Navbar ParentLink="@selectedItem?.GetParentLink()"
  Title="@selectedItem?.Name" DialogId="@_dialogEditId"
  OnAddClick="@(() => {_isNewField=true;})" />
```

As observed, we have streamlined the code by eliminating duplications, resulting in a more elegant and concise presentation.

Having completed the work for the Navbar, let us now shift our focus to the Dropdown component.

Creating a Dropdown component for the context menu

To develop a component akin to the context menu, we can reuse the Bootstrap Dropdown component. As illustrated in *Figure 10.12*, a context menu comprises a context menu button and a list of menu items. Upon clicking the context menu button, users are presented with a display of menu items.

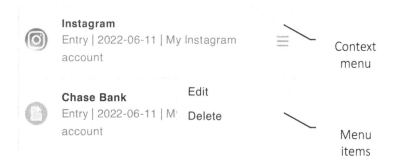

Figure 10.12: Context menu

The present code for the context menu is replicated in both the Items and ItemDetail pages, as demonstrated below:

```
<button class="opacity-50 btn btn-light dropdown-toggle"
  type="button" id="itemsContextMenu"
  data-bs-toggle="dropdown"
  aria-expanded="false"
  @onclick="@(() => listGroupItem=item)">
    <span class="oi oi-menu" aria-hidden="true"></span>
</button>
<ul class="dropdown-menu"
  aria-labelledby="itemsContextMenu">
  <li><button class="dropdown-item" data-bs-toggle="modal"
        data-bs-target="#@_dialogEditId"
        @onclick="@(() => _isNewItem=false)">
        Edit
  </button></li>
  <li><button class="dropdown-item" data-bs-toggle="modal"
        data-bs-target="#@_dialogDeleteId">
      Delete
  </button></li>
</ul>
```

The Dropdown component of Bootstrap comprises a button and an unordered list. We must define an event handler for the button to perform the necessary action. In the previous code, we set the item variable to listGroupItem. Regarding the menu items, each is implemented as a <button> tag and accepts a dialog ID and an event handler as parameters. When a menu item is clicked, the corresponding modal dialog will be displayed.

We can create two new Razor components in the PassXYZ.BlazorUI project, named Dropdown and MenuItem. To separate the UI and logic, we can implement them in the C# code-behind file (*Listing 10.9*) and the Razor file (*Listing 10.8*), which we will demonstrate now.

Let's first examine the Dropdown component UI in Listing 10.8:

```
@namespace PassXYZ.BlazorUI
<button class="opacity-50 btn btn-light dropdown-toggle"
  type="button" id="itemDetailContextMenu"
  data-bs-toggle="dropdown"
```

```
    aria-expanded="false" @onclick="OnClick">
    <span class="oi oi-menu" aria-hidden="true"></span>
  </button>                                                      //(1)
  <ul class="dropdown-menu"
    aria-labelledby="itemDetailContextMenu">
    @ChildContent
  </ul>                                                          //(2)
```

Listing 10.8: Dropdown.razor *(https://epa.ms/Dropdown10-9)*

In the Dropdown component, we define a button **(1)** and an unordered list **(2)**. The button's click event is set up as an OnClick event handler. The items within the unordered list appear as child content of the Dropdown component. The component parameters can be found in the C# Dropdown.razor.cs code-behind file, as shown in *Listing 10.9*:

```
namespace PassXYZ.BlazorUI;
public partial class Dropdown
{
  [Parameter]
  public EventCallback<MouseEventArgs> OnClick {get;set;}       //(1)
  [Parameter]
  public RenderFragment ChildContent { get; set; }             //(2)
}
```

Listing 10.9: Dropdown.razor.cs *(https://epa.ms/Dropdown10-10)*

In Dropdown.razor.cs, two component parameters OnClick **(1)** and ChildContent **(2)** are defined. The MenuItem component can be presented as the child content of the Dropdown component. The UI code for MenuItem can be observed in *Listing 10.10*:

```
@namespace PassXYZ.BlazorUI
<li>
  <button class="dropdown-item" data-bs-toggle="modal"
    data-bs-target="#@Id" @onclick="OnClick">
    @ChildContent
  </button>
</li>
```

Listing 10.10: MenuItem.razor *(https://epa.ms/MenuItem10-11)*

The MenuItem component specifies three component parameters: Id, OnClick, and ChildContent. These parameters are defined within MenuItem.razor.cs, as demonstrated in *Listing 10.11*:

```
namespace PassXYZ.BlazorUI;
public partial class MenuItem
{
  [Parameter]
  public string? Id { get; set; }                          //(1)
  [Parameter]
  public EventCallback<MouseEventArgs> OnClick {get; set;}  //(2)
  [Parameter]
  public RenderFragment ChildContent { get; set; }          //(3)
}
```

Listing 10.11: MenuItem.razor.cs *(https://epa.ms/MenuItem10-12)*

(1) The Id parameter is employed to designate the dialog ID when a menu item is clicked. **(2)** OnClick is utilized to register an event handler for a button click event. **(3)** ChildContent serves to display child content, such as the name of the menu item.

We have successfully implemented the components for the context menu. Now, we can replace the redundant code in the Items and ItemDetail pages with these context menu components. The implementation of the context menu on the Items page proceeds as follows:

```
<Dropdown OnClick="@(() => currentItem.Data=listGroupItem=item)">
  <MenuItem Id="@_dialogEditId"
    OnClick="@(() => _isNewItem=false)">Edit</MenuItem>
  <MenuItem Id="@_dialogDeleteId">Delete</MenuItem>
</Dropdown>
```

On the ItemDetail page, the context menu is implemented as follows:

```
<Dropdown OnClick="@(() = >
  {currentField.Data=listGroupField=field;})">
  <MenuItem Id="@_dialogEditId"
    OnClick="@(() => _isNewField=false)">Edit</MenuItem>
  <MenuItem Id="@_dialogDeleteId">Delete</MenuItem>
  @if (field.IsProtected) {
    <MenuItem OnClick="OnToggleShowPassword">
      @(field.IsHide ? "Show":"Hide")
    </MenuItem>
```

```
    }
</Dropdown>
```

Following the refinement of the code for the Items and ItemDetail pages, we have implemented modal dialogs, navigation bars, and context menu components. Consequently, the code appears significantly more elegant and concise. Nevertheless, there is still potential for further refinement. The main UI logic in both the Items and ItemDetail pages revolves around a list view. We can optimize this part of the code by implementing a ListView component. In order to create a ListView component, we will need to utilize an advanced feature known as templated components.

Using templated components

In constructing a Razor component, component parameters serve as the communication channels between parent and child components. While discussing nested components, we brought attention to a special ChildContent component parameter of the RenderFragment type. This parameter enables the parent component to set the content of the child component. For instance, the content of MenuItem in the following code can be assigned an HTML string:

```
<MenuItem Id="@_dialogDeleteId">
    <strong>Delete</strong>
</MenuItem>
```

We are able to achieve this as MenuItem defines the following component parameter, which can be observed in *Listing 10.11*:

```
[Parameter]
public RenderFragment ChildContent { get; set; }
```

If we want to explicitly specify the ChildContent parameter, we can achieve this as follows:

```
<MenuItem Id="@_dialogDeleteId">
    <ChildContent>
        <strong>Delete</strong>
    </ChildContent>
</MenuItem>
```

ChildContent is a unique component parameter that can be implicitly used in markup language. To utilize ChildContent, we create a component capable of accepting a UI template of the RenderFragment type as its parameter. Furthermore, we can define multiple UI templates as parameters when developing a new component. Components of this nature are referred to as templated components.

A render fragment, of the `RenderFragment` type, signifies a portion of the UI designated for rendering. Furthermore, there is a generic version, `RenderFragment<TValue>`, which accepts a type parameter. A specific type can be provided when invoking `RenderFragment`.

Creating a ListView component

To create a `ListView`, we need to utilize multiple UI templates as component parameters. We can create a new Razor component within the `PassXYZ.BlazorUI` project and name it `ListView`. Similar to what we did for `Navbar` and the context menu, we can separate the UI and code into a Razor file (*Listing 10.12*) and a C# code-behind file (*Listing 10.13*):

```
@namespace PassXYZ.BlazorUI
@typeparam TItem
<div class="list-group">
  @if (Header != null) {
      @Header                                                    //(1)
  }
  @if (Row != null && Items != null) {
    @foreach (var item in Items) {
       <div class="dropdown list-group-item
          list-group-item-action
          d-flex gap-1 py-2" style="border: none"
          aria-current="true">
            @Row.Invoke(item)                                    //(2)
       </div>
    }
  }
  @if (Footer != null) {
      <div class="container">
        <article>@Footer</article>
      </div>                                                     //(3)
  }
</div>
```

Listing 10.12: `ListView.razor` *(https://epa.ms/ListView10-13)*

In the `ListView` Razor file, we define three UI templates, `Header` **(1)**, `Row` **(2)**, and `Footer` **(3)**. We render the `Header` and `Footer` similarly to `ChildContent`, but the `Row` component parameter appears distinct. The rendering process for the `Row` component is as follows:

```
@Row(item)
```

Alternatively, we can render it like this:

```
@Row.Invoke(item)
```

We render it with an `item` argument. The type of `Row` is `RenderFragment<TValue>`, as we demonstrate in *Listing 10.13*:

```
namespace PassXYZ.BlazorUI;
public partial class ListView<TItem>
{
  [Parameter]
  public RenderFragment? Header { get; set; }                        //(1)
  [Parameter]
  public RenderFragment<TItem>? Row { get; set; }                    //(2)
  [Parameter]
  public IEnumerable<TItem>? Items { get; set; }                     //(3)
  [Parameter]
  public RenderFragment? Footer { get; set; }                        //(4)
}
```

Listing 10.13: `ListView.razor.cs` *(https://epa.ms/ListView10-14)*

We define the `ListView` as a generic `ListView<TItem>` type with the `TItem` type parameter. In the `ListView` component, we can specify a list view header, using the `Header` (1) parameter, and a footer, using the `Footer` (4) parameter. The `ListView` can be bound to any data collection of the `IEnumerable<TItem>` type via the `Items` parameter (3). The `Row` (2) parameter can be employed to establish the UI template for an individual item within the `foreach` loop.

Using the ListView component

At this point, let's examine the usage of the `ListView` component in the `Items` and `ItemDetail` pages. We will use the `ItemDetail` page as an example for our discussion:

```
<ListView Items="fields">                                            //(1)
  <Row Context="field">                                              //(2)
    @if (field.ShowContextAction == null) {
      <span class="oi oi-pencil" aria-hidden="true"></span>
      <div class="d-flex gap-2 w-100
        justify-content-between">
        <div>
          <h6 class="mb-0">@field.Key</h6>
```

```
                <p class="mb-0">@field.Value</p>
            </div>
        </div>
        <Dropdown
         OnClick="@(() =>
         {currentField.Data=listGroupField=field;})">
            <MenuItem Id="@_dialogEditId"
              OnClick="@(() => _isNewField=false)">
              Edit
            </MenuItem>
            <MenuItem Id="@_dialogDeleteId">Delete</MenuItem>
          @if (field.IsProtected) {
            <MenuItem OnClick="OnToggleShowPassword">
              @(field.IsHide ? "Show":"Hide")
            </MenuItem>
          }
        </Dropdown>
      }
    </Row>
    <Footer>
      @((MarkupString)notes)
    </Footer>
  </ListView>
```

As we have defined Header, Row, and Footer as optional parameters, there is no obligation to specify all of them. In the ItemDetail page, we utilize Row and Footer. **(1)** First, we need to pass the list of fields to the Items parameter. **(2)** In the foreach loop, each field is passed to the ListView as an argument for the Row, which is defined as follows:

```
<Row Context="field">
```

The "field" value of the Context property is employed to specify the argument for Row. Within the UI template of Row, we showcase the key value of field and establish a context menu using the Dropdown and MenuItem components, which were implemented in the previous section.

By utilizing the ListView component, we have significantly enhanced the implementation of the ItemDetail page. This improvement was achieved through the creation of our own Razor components.

Having completed the refactoring of our code, we have concluded the introduction of the .NET MAUI Blazor Hybrid app. In Part 2, we recreated our app using Blazor while maintaining the same functionalities.

If you have experience in Blazor web app development, you may not see too much difference between the Blazor Hybrid app and the Blazor web app. This is precisely the advantage of the Blazor Hybrid app. You may now be wondering, how do we access a native API in a Blazor Hybrid app? Let's have a brief overview in the next section.

Accessing a native API from Blazor Hybrid apps

When it comes to accessing native APIs, there isn't a significant difference between .NET MAUI apps and Blazor Hybrid apps. As we learned in *Chapter 7, Using Platform-Specific Features*, it's vital to always create an abstract layer that encapsulates native access at the platform layer. Hence, we're not directly accessing native APIs from cross-platform code in .NET MAUI or Blazor Hybrid apps. In our app, while we do need to access native APIs, we will access a native API through an abstract layer.

Access to platform APIs from .NET has seen significant evolution over time, transitioning from Xamarin plugins to the unified NuGet dependency presented by Xamarin.Essentials. As discussed in *Chapter 7, Using Platform-Specific Features*, Xamarin.Essentials aimed to standardize all native access within a single library. Initially, the plan with .NET MAUI was to migrate everything as .NET MAUI Essentials. However, the .NET MAUI team later realized that breaking it down into more logically granular namespaces, such as Microsoft.Maui.Storage or Microsoft.Maui.Devices, and so on, made more sense.

In our app, we access platform-level APIs in the classes defined in the Services folder, such as LoginService.cs. For example, we defined a property, IsPrivacyNoticeAccepted, in LoginService to store whether the user has accepted the privacy notice or not. We use a Preferences API to store the data in platform-specific persistent storage. Preferences APIs are defined in the Microsoft.Maui.Storage namespace, as we can see from the following code:

```
Public static bool IsPrivacyNoticeAccepted
{
get => Preferences.Get(PrivacyNotice, false);

set => Preferences.Set(PrivacyNotice, value);
}
```

APIs such as Preferences are provided by Microsoft as part of .NET MAUI libraries. If we find something that is not supported by Microsoft APIs, we have to create our own plugins or use plugins provided by the community. Please refer to *Chapter 7* about how to create and use .NET MAUI plugins.

Summary

In this chapter, we explained the process of creating Razor components. We covered topics such as data binding and the component lifecycle. Subsequently, we developed a set of modal dialog components to optimize our code. By utilizing Razor components, we can eliminate duplicate code and enhance the UI design. We incorporated CRUD operations within the event handlers of modal dialogs. As a result, we now have a new version of the password manager app.

In the subsequent chapter, we will transition to *Part 3* of this book. In *Part 3*, we will introduce the implementation of unit tests and the process of publishing a .NET MAUI application to app stores.

Leave a review!

Enjoying this book? Help readers like you by leaving an Amazon review. Scan the QR code below for a 40% discount code.

*Limited Offer

Part 3

Testing and Deployment

In *Part 1* of this book, we delved into .NET MAUI app development, while in *Part 2*, we explored .NET MAUI Blazor Hybrid app development. As a result, we now have two different versions of the password management app from *Part 1* and *Part 2*. Both the XAML and Blazor Hybrid apps utilize the MVVM pattern in their design. While introducing the MVVM pattern, we highlighted the ability to test the view model and model independently. So, after the initial two parts of this book, we have thorough practice in app development.

In *Part 3* of this book, we will turn our attention to other important aspects of software development, namely unit testing in .NET MAUI and the deployment process for .NET MAUI apps. By learning how to create mock components in unit tests, you will learn how to examine software modules within an isolated environment.

Part 3 includes the following chapters:

- *Chapter 11, Developing Unit Tests*
- *Chapter 12, Deploying and Publishing in App Stores*

11

Developing Unit Tests

Testing plays a crucial role in ensuring software quality in contemporary software development. Various types of testing are involved in the software development lifecycle, including unit testing, integration testing, and system testing. Unit testing is employed to examine software modules or components within an isolated environment and is typically carried out by developers. With a well-devised unit test strategy, programming issues can be detected at the earliest stage of the software development lifecycle, rendering unit testing the most efficient and cost-effective approach to guaranteeing software quality.

In .NET MAUI app development, we can utilize existing unit test frameworks or libraries present in the .NET ecosystem. By employing a test framework or library, we can expedite unit test development. An effective test framework is generally designed for seamless integration with a **continuous integration (CI)** and **continuous deployment (CD)** environment. In this chapter, we will demonstrate how to set up unit testing and execute unit test cases as part of the .NET MAUI app development lifecycle.

We will cover the following topics in this chapter:

- Unit testing in .NET
- Mock .NET MAUI components
- Razor component testing using bUnit

Technical requirements

To test and debug the source code from this chapter, you need to have a .NET 8 environment set up. You can install .NET 8 by following the instructions provided at the Microsoft link below on Windows, macOS, or Linux: https://dotnet.microsoft.com/en-us/download/dotnet/8.0.

Unit tests can be executed from the command line using the dotnet command, or via the Test Explorer in Visual Studio if you're using Windows.

To set up Visual Studio 2022, please refer to the *Development environment setup* section in *Chapter 1, Getting Started with .NET MAUI*, for the details.

The source code for this chapter is available in the following GitHub repository: `https://github.com/PacktPublishing/.NET-MAUI-Cross-Platform-Application-Development-Second-edition/tree/main/2nd/chapter11`.

To check out the source code of this chapter, we can use the below command:

```
$ git clone -b 2nd/chapter11 https://github.com/PacktPublishing/.NET-MAUI-
Cross-Platform-Application-Development-Second-edition.git PassXYZ.Vault2
```

To find out more about the source code in this book, please refer to the section *Managing the source code in this book* in *Chapter 2, Building Our First .NET MAUI App*.

Unit testing in .NET

To develop unit test cases, it is common to utilize a unit test framework to enhance efficiency. There are several unit test frameworks available in the .NET environment, which are as follows:

- **Microsoft Test Framework (MSTest)** comes bundled with Visual Studio. The initial version of MSTest (V1) was not an open-source product, and it first appeared alongside the release of Visual Studio 2005. For more information about MSTest (V1), please refer to the book Microsoft Visual Studio 2005 Unleashed by Lars Powers and Mike Snell. Later, Microsoft made the MSTest (V2) open-source, hosting it on GitHub, with the first release becoming available around 2017.

- **NUnit** is an open-source testing framework ported from JUnit. It was the inaugural unit test framework for .NET, with its earliest releases hosted on SourceForge in 2004. For more information on version 2.0, please refer to the release notes in the *Further reading* section. The latest releases have since been moved to GitHub.

- **xUnit** is a modern and extensible framework developed by Jim Newkirk and Brad Wilson, the creators of NUnit. They made significant improvements to this new test framework compared to NUnit. To find out more about these enhancements, please refer to Jim's blog, *Why Did we Build xUnit 1.0?* The first stable release of xUnit was available around 2015.

All of these frameworks are quite popular and can be selected according to the project's requirements. In this chapter, we will utilize xUnit to develop unit test cases, as it is a more recent framework that offers numerous enhancements compared to NUnit.

Regardless of the unit test framework you select, the process of developing unit tests is rather consistent. Even if you employ a different framework for your project, this chapter's content remains applicable. Unit test cases are designed to run exclusively on cross-platform target frameworks instead of platform-specific ones. In this book, we utilize .NET 8.0; therefore, the target framework for unit testing is net8.0, as opposed to net8.0-android or net8.0-ios.

In this chapter, we will first develop unit tests for the model layer, which is common to both XAML and Blazor. Subsequently, we will introduce unit test development for Blazor apps using bUnit. bUnit is a versatile testing library compatible with all three test frameworks: xUnit, NUnit, and MSTest.

Setting up the unit test project

To gain some practical experience, let's create a unit test project. We can create a xUnit project using either Visual Studio or the .NET command line:

1. To start with Visual Studio, we can add a new project to our current solution, as shown in *Figure 11.1*:

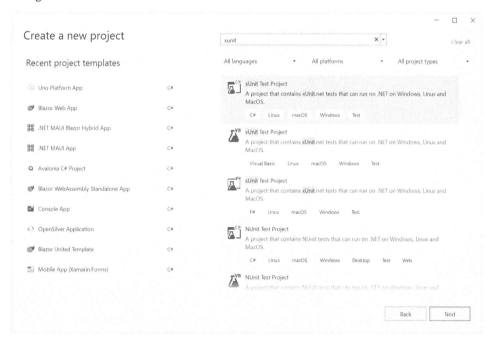

Figure 11.1 – Creating an xUnit project using Visual Studio

2. To begin, type xunit into the search box and select **xUnit Test Project** for C#.

3. On the following screen, name the project PassXYZ.Vault.Tests and click **Next**.

4. Subsequently, set the framework to .NET 8.0 and click **Create**.

If you're using Visual Studio Code, the first step is to install the .NET MAUI extension in your environment. Once the extension is installed, you can navigate through your project using Solution Explorer, akin to how you would in Visual Studio. Please be aware that the .NET MAUI extension is still in the preview stage as of March 2024.

To create an xUnit project, click the + button located in the solution. This action will reveal a list of project templates, as demonstrated below:

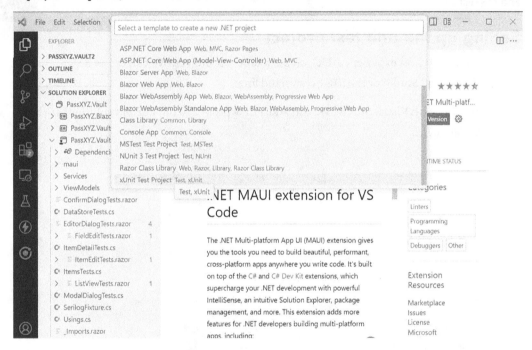

Figure 11.1a – Creating an xUnit project using Visual Studio Code

To create the project using a command line, we should first create the folder and then utilize a .NET command to establish the project, as demonstrated below:

```
mkdir PassXYZ.Vault.Tests
cd PassXYZ.Vault.Tests
dotnet new xunit
dotnet test
```

After creating the project, we can utilize the dotnet test command to run the test cases. The default test case in the template will be executed, and we will proceed to add more test cases to this project. Our test targets incorporate components from both the PassXYZ.Vault and PassXYZ.BlazorUI projects, hence requiring us to include these two projects as reference projects. The target framework of PassXYZ.BlazorUI is net8.0, allowing us to add it directly. However, as the target frameworks of PassXYZ.Vault are platform-specific, we must implement some modifications before incorporating them as references in PassXYZ.Vault.Tests.

As we need to build the unit test against the target framework net8.0, it is necessary to modify the PassXYZ.Vault.csproj file to include net8.0 as one of the target frameworks:

```
<TargetFrameworks>net8.0;net8.0-android;net8.0-ios;net8.0-
  maccatalyst</TargetFrameworks>
```

When building the PassXYZ.Vault project on supported platforms, we anticipate an executable, as it is an app. However, when building PassXYZ.Vault for the net8.0 target framework, we aim to test it. PassXYZ.Vault should be generated as a library so that the test framework can utilize it to run test cases. In this instance, we expect to build a file with a .dll extension instead of .exe, which necessitates the following modification:

```
<OutputType Condition="'$(TargetFramework)'!='net8.0'">
  Exe</OutputType>
```

In the preceding build setup, a condition has been added to verify the target framework for the output type. If the target framework is not net8.0, the build output will be generated as an executable. Conversely, if the target framework is set to net8.0, a library will be generated.

After making these changes, we can add reference projects to PassXYZ.Vault.Tests by either right-clicking on the solution node and selecting **Add -> Project Reference**, or by editing the project file for PassXYZ.Vault.Tests to include these lines:

```
<ItemGroup>
  <ProjectReference
    Include="..\PassXYZ.BlazorUI\PassXYZ.BlazorUI.csproj" />
  <ProjectReference
    Include="..\PassXYZ.Vault\PassXYZ.Vault.csproj" />
</ItemGroup>
```

In order to test the MAUI project, it is also necessary to add the following configuration to the PassXYZ.Vault.Tests project:

```
<UseMaui>true</UseMaui>
```

We have now successfully set up the xUnit project. Next, let's proceed to add our test cases.

Developing test cases for the model

We use xUnit as a unit testing tool for our app. It provides a comprehensive and efficient way to run tests sequentially in isolation from each other, supporting both desktop and mobile applications.

Two fundamental concepts in xUnit are Fact and Theory.

Fact in xUnit refers to a parameterless test method that confirms the correctness of certain conditions in code. It states that something should always be true. A "fact" test always runs every time the test suite runs as they are supposed to be invariant conditions, regardless of the data state at the execution time.

On the other hand, Theory allows parameterized tests to be conducted. It allows developers to run a single test method multiple times with different sets of data, reducing code redundancy while enhancing coverage. It is based on the idea that if the test method's contract is true for a specific dataset, it should be true for all datasets.

We will begin by adding test cases to examine the model layer, as the test case setup for the model layer is identical in both the XAML and Blazor versions of our app.

In the model layer, the primary implementation resides within the PassXYZLib library. For more information on the unit test cases at the model layer, please refer to the PassXYZLib source code: https://github.com/shugaoye/PassXYZLib.

In our app, IDataStore is the interface used to export PassXYZLib. Therefore, let's incorporate test cases to test this interface, IDataStore. To assess the IDataStore interface, we can establish a new test class, DataStoreTest, within the PassXYZ.Vault.Tests project. We can add a new test case by testing "the addition of an item" as follows:

```
public class DataStoreTests
{
    [Fact]                                                    //(1)
    public async void Add_Item()
    {
```

```
        // Arrange                                              //(2)
        IDataStore<Item> datastore = new MockDataStore();
        ItemSubType itemSubType = ItemSubType.Entry;
        // Act                                                  //(3)
        var newItem = datastore.CreateNewItem(itemSubType);
        newItem.Name = $"{itemSubType.ToString()}01";
        await datastore.AddItemAsync(newItem);
        var item = datastore.GetItem(newItem.Id);
        // Assert                                               //(4)
        Assert.Equal(newItem.Id, item.Id);
    }
}
```

xUnit employs attributes to inform the framework about test case configurations. In this test case, we utilize the [Fact] attribute **(1)** to designate this method as a test case. To define a test case, we can follow a common pattern – Arrange, Act, and Assert:

- Arrange **(2)** – We will prepare all necessary setup for the test. To add an item, we need to initialize the IDataStore interface first, and then we will define a variable to hold the item type.

- Act **(3)** – We execute the methods that we want to test, which are CreateNewItem and AddItemAsync.

- Assert **(4)** – We check the result that we expected. In our case, we try to retrieve the new item using item.Id. After that, we check to ensure that the item ID retrieved is the same as what we expected.

As you may have noticed, we tested the Entry type in the previous test case. The Entry type is only one of the item types – we have many. To test all of them, we need to create many test cases. xUnit supports another test case type, [Theory], which helps us to test different scenarios with one test case.

We can use the "delete an item" test case to demonstrate how to test different scenarios in one test case with the [Theory] attribute. In this test case, we can delete an item in different item types in one test case:

```
public class DataStoreTests
{
  ...
  [Theory]                                                     //(1)
```

```
    [InlineData(ItemSubType.Entry)]                                    //(2)
    [InlineData(ItemSubType.Group)]
    [InlineData(ItemSubType.Notes)]
    [InlineData(ItemSubType.PxEntry)]
    public async void Delete_Item(ItemSubType itemSubType)
    {
        // Arrange
        IDataStore<Item> datastore = new MockDataStore();
        var newItem = datastore.CreateNewItem(itemSubType);            //(3)
        newItem.Name = $"{itemSubType.ToString()}01";
        await datastore.AddItemAsync(newItem);
        // Act
        bool result = await
          datastore.DeleteItemAsync(newItem.Id);                       //(4)
        Debug.WriteLine($"Delete_Item: {newItem.Name}");
        // Assert
        Assert.True(result);                                           //(5)
    }
    ...
}
```

When we create a test case using the [Theory] attribute, **(1)**, we can pass different item types using the itemSubType parameter. The value of the itemSubType argument is defined using the [InlineData] attribute, **(2)**.

To arrange test data, we create a new item using the itemSubType argument, **(3)**. Then, we execute the DeleteItemAsync method, **(4)**, which is the one that we want to test.

Finally, we check the return value, **(5)**. If the item is deleted successfully, the result is true. Otherwise, the result is false.

We have learned the process of creating a test case using the [Fact] attribute, as well as how to address different scenarios with the [Theory] attribute. In the next section, we will delve into further topics related to test case development.

Sharing context between tests

In our previous test cases, we created a new IDataStore instance for each test. Is it possible to share one IDataStore instance, instead of repeatedly creating the same instance for every test? By sharing the test setup among a group of test cases in xUnit, we can minimize duplication.

There are three methods for sharing setup and cleanup code between tests in xUnit:

- **Constructor** and **Dispose**: We can use a class constructor to share the setup and cleanup code without sharing instances.

- **Class Fixture**: We can use a fixture to share object instances in a single class.

- **Collection Fixtures**: We can use collection fixtures to share object instances in multiple test classes.

Sharing using a constructor

To remove the duplicated setup code from the previous tests, we can move the creation of the IDataStore instance to the constructor of the DataStoreTests test class as follows:

```
public class DataStoreTests
{
  IDataStore<Item> datastore;
  public DataStoreTests()
  {
    datastore = new MockDataStore();
    Debug.WriteLine("DataStoreTests: Created");
  }
  ...
}
```

In this code, we added a private member variable, datastore, and created an instance of IDataStore in the constructor of DataStoreTests. We also added a debug output so we can monitor the creation of the IDataStore interface. Let us debug the execution of the DataStoreTests class so we can see the debug output here:

```
DataStoreTests: Created
Delete_Item: Entry01
DataStoreTests: Created
Delete_Item: Group01
DataStoreTests: Created
Delete_Item: PxEntry01
DataStoreTests: Created
Delete_Item: Notes01
DataStoreTests: Created
Create_Item: PxEntry
DataStoreTests: Created
```

```
Create_Item: Group
DataStoreTests: Created
Create_Item: Entry
DataStoreTests: Created
Create_Item: Notes
DataStoreTests: Created
Add_Item: Done
```

We can see from the debug output that a DataStoreTests class is created for each test case. There is no difference whether we create the instance of IDataStore inside the test method or in the constructor. All the test cases are still isolated from each other. When we use the [Theory] attribute to test different scenarios with one method, each of them looks like a separate test case at runtime. To understand this better, we can use the dotnet command to list all the defined tests:

```
dotnet test -t
  Determining projects to restore...
  All projects are up-to-date for restore.
Microsoft (R) Test Execution Command Line Tool Version 17.3.0
  (x64)
Copyright (c) Microsoft Corporation.  All rights reserved.
The following Tests are available:
    PassXYZ.Vault.Tests.DataStoreTests.Add_Item
    PassXYZ.Vault.Tests.DataStoreTests.Delete_Item(itemSubType:
      Entry)
    PassXYZ.Vault.Tests.DataStoreTests.Delete_Item(itemSubType:
      Group)
    PassXYZ.Vault.Tests.DataStoreTests.Delete_Item(itemSubType:
      Notes)
    PassXYZ.Vault.Tests.DataStoreTests.Delete_Item(itemSubType:
      PxEntry)
    PassXYZ.Vault.Tests.DataStoreTests.Create_Item(itemSubType:
      Entry)
    PassXYZ.Vault.Tests.DataStoreTests.Create_Item(itemSubType:
      Group)
    PassXYZ.Vault.Tests.DataStoreTests.Create_Item(itemSubType:
      Notes)
   PassXYZ.Vault.Tests.DataStoreTests.Create_Item(itemSubType:
      PxEntry)
```

We can see that each parameter defined by the [InlineData] attribute is shown as a separate test case. They are all isolated test cases at runtime.

After we list all the tests, we can selectively execute them using the dotnet command.

If we want to run all the tests in the DataStoreTests class, we can use this command:

```
dotnet test --filter DataStoreTests
```

If we want to run Add_Item tests only, we can use this command:

```
dotnet test --filter DataStoreTests.Add_Item
```

As we can see from the debug output, even though we created an instance of IDataStore in the constructor, the instance is re-created for each test. The instances created in the test class constructor won't be shared across tests. Even though the effect is still the same, the code looks more concise.

However, in certain scenarios, we may want to share instances across multiple tests. To achieve this, we can utilize class fixtures. In the following section, we will examine these specific cases.

Sharing using class fixtures

When utilizing a tool across all test cases, it can be more efficient to share the setup among them rather than creating the same one each time. Let's use a logging function as an example to illustrate this approach.

To generate a test report, we aim to create a test log that monitors the execution of unit tests. The Serilog library is the one which can be used for this purpose. Serilog enables us to log messages to different channels. In order to use Serilog, we must first set it up and then clean it up after all the tests have been executed. In this scenario, we prefer to share a single instance of Serilog between all the tests instead of creating one for each test. This setup allows us to produce a consolidated log file for all the tests rather than generating multiple log files for each individual test.

To incorporate Serilog, we need to add the Serilog package to the project. This can be accomplished by executing the following dotnet commands in the project's PassXYZ.Vault.Tests folder:

```
dotnet add package Serilog
dotnet add package Serilog.Sinks.File
```

Having added the `Serilog` libraries to the project, we can now create a class fixture, `SerilogFixture`, for demonstration purposes:

```
public class SerilogFixture : IDisposable {                        //(1)
  public ILogger Logger { get; private set; }
  public SerilogFixture() {
    Logger = new LoggerConfiguration()                             //(2)
        .MinimumLevel.Debug()
        .WriteTo.File(@"logs\xunit_log.txt")
        .CreateLogger();
    Logger.Debug("SerilogFixture: initialized");
  }
  public void Dispose() {
    Logger.Debug("SerilogFixture: closed");
    Log.CloseAndFlush();                                           //(3)
  }
}
public class IDataStoreTests : IClassFixture<SerilogFixture> {     //(4)
  IDataStore<Item> datastore;
  SerilogFixture serilogFixture;
  public DataStoreTests(SerilogFixture fixture) {                  //(5)
      serilogFixture = fixture;                                    //(6)
      datastore = new MockDataStore();
      serilogFixture.Logger.Debug("DataStoreTests: Created");
  }
  [Fact]
  public async void Add_Item() ...
  ...
}
```

If we want to use class fixtures, we can create them using the following steps:

- We can create a new class as the fixture class and add the setup code to the constructor. Here, we created a fixture class, `SerilogFixture`, **(1)**, and initialized the `ILogger` interface, **(2)**, in the constructor.

- Because we need to clean up the setup after the test case execution, we need to implement the `IDisposable` interface for the fixture class and put the cleanup code in the `Dispose` method. We implemented `IDisposable` in `SerilogFixture` and called the `Serilog` function, `Log.CloseAndFlush`, **(3)**, in the `Dispose` method.

- To use the fixture, the test case needs to implement the `IClassFixture<T>` interface. We implemented this in the `DataStoreTests` test class, **(4)**.

- To access the fixture instance, we can add it as a constructor argument and it will be provided automatically. In the constructor of `DataStoreTests`, **(5)**, we assign the argument to the private member variable, `serilogFixture`, **(6)**. In test cases, we can access `Serilog` using this variable.

To verify this setup, we replaced all our debug output with `Serilog Debug`. After executing the tests in `DataStoreTests`, we can see the log messages here in the `xunit_log.txt` log file:

```
2022-08-28 10:25:39.273 +08:00 [DBG] SerilogFixture: initialized
2022-08-28 10:25:39.332 +08:00 [DBG] DataStoreTests: Created
2022-08-28 10:25:39.350 +08:00 [DBG] Delete_Item: Entry01
2022-08-28 10:25:39.355 +08:00 [DBG] DataStoreTests: Created
2022-08-28 10:25:39.355 +08:00 [DBG] Delete_Item: Group01
2022-08-28 10:25:39.356 +08:00 [DBG] DataStoreTests: Created
2022-08-28 10:25:39.357 +08:00 [DBG] Delete_Item: PxEntry01
2022-08-28 10:25:39.358 +08:00 [DBG] DataStoreTests: Created
2022-08-28 10:25:39.358 +08:00 [DBG] Delete_Item: Notes01
2022-08-28 10:25:39.359 +08:00 [DBG] DataStoreTests: Created
2022-08-28 10:25:39.359 +08:00 [DBG] Create_Item: PxEntry
2022-08-28 10:25:39.360 +08:00 [DBG] DataStoreTests: Created
2022-08-28 10:25:39.360 +08:00 [DBG] Create_Item: Group
2022-08-28 10:25:39.361 +08:00 [DBG] DataStoreTests: Created
2022-08-28 10:25:39.361 +08:00 [DBG] Create_Item: Entry
2022-08-28 10:25:39.362 +08:00 [DBG] DataStoreTests: Created
2022-08-28 10:25:39.362 +08:00 [DBG] Create_Item: Notes
2022-08-28 10:25:39.362 +08:00 [DBG] DataStoreTests: Created
2022-08-28 10:25:39.364 +08:00 [DBG] Add_Item: Done
2022-08-28 10:25:39.367 +08:00 [DBG] SerilogFixture: closed
```

As anticipated, the `SerilogFixture` class is initialized only once, allowing its instance to be utilized in all tests within `DataStoreTests`. This is in contrast to the `IDataStore` interface, which is initialized for each individual test.

Sharing using collection fixtures

Utilizing class fixtures, as demonstrated in the previous section, allows us to share the test setup context within a single test class. However, there may be instances where we need to share the test setup across multiple test classes. In such cases, we can employ collection fixtures to achieve this.

In the case of Serilog, we can utilize it across multiple test classes, allowing us to view all log messages in a single log file. To achieve a unified Serilog setup for all test classes, we can implement collection fixtures in our project. By employing collection fixtures, we can create two new classes, SerilogFixture and SerilogCollection, within the PassXYZ.Vault.Tests project, as demonstrated in *Listing 11.1*:

```
namespace PassXYZ.Vault.Tests;
public class SerilogFixture : IDisposable {
  public ILogger Logger { get; private set; }
  public SerilogFixture() {
      Logger = new LoggerConfiguration()
          .MinimumLevel.Debug()
          .WriteTo.File(@"logs\xunit_log.txt")
          .CreateLogger();
      Logger.Debug("SerilogFixture: initialized");
  }
  public void Dispose() {
      Logger.Debug("SerilogFixture: closed");
      Log.CloseAndFlush();
  }
}
[CollectionDefinition("Serilog collection")]                                    //(1)
public class SerilogCollection:ICollectionFixture<SerilogFixture>
{
}                                                                               //(2)
```

Listing 11.1: SerilogFixture.cs *(https://epa.ms/SerilogFixture11-1)*

To implement collection fixtures, we can follow the steps outlined below:

*   Create a new class file, SerilogFixture.cs, that houses both the SerilogFixture and SerilogCollection classes.

*   Decorate the collection definition class, SerilogCollection, with the [CollectionDefinition] attribute **(1)** and assign it a unique name to help identify the test collection.

*   Ensure that the collection definition class, SerilogCollection, implements the ICollectionFixture<T> interface **(2)**.

To utilize a collection fixture, we can implement the following modifications to our test classes:

- We can attach the [Collection] attribute to all test classes that will be incorporated into the collection. We designate Serilog collection as the name for the test collection definition within the attribute. In our case, as displayed in *Listing 11.2*, we append a [Collection("Serilog collection")] attribute **(1)** to the DataStoreTests class.

- To access the fixture instance, we can follow the same approach as in the previous section with class fixtures by including it as a constructor argument. It will then be provided automatically. In the DataStoreTests constructor, we assign a fixture argument to the serilogFixture variable **(2)**.

- In order to save space, the full code is not provided in *Listing 11.2*. The absent parts are indicated with the "..." symbol. The Add_Item test case was constructed using Fact to examine the creation of an entry. The Create_Item and Delete_Item test cases both employ Theory, enabling us to test a variety of items.

```
namespace PassXYZ.Vault.Tests;
[Collection("Serilog collection")]                                      //(1)
public class DataStoreTests {
  IDataStore<Item> datastore;
  SerilogFixture serilogFixture;
  public DataStoreTests(SerilogFixture fixture) {
    datastore = new MockDataStore();
    serilogFixture = fixture;                                           //(2)
    serilogFixture.Logger.Debug("DataStoreTests
      initialized");
  }
  [Fact]
  public async void Add_Item() {
    // Arrange
    ItemSubType itemSubType = ItemSubType.Entry;
    // Act
    var newItem = datastore.CreateNewItem(itemSubType);
    newItem.Name = $"{itemSubType.ToString()}01";
    await datastore.AddItemAsync(newItem);
    var item = datastore.GetItem(newItem.Id);
    // Assert
    Assert.Equal(newItem.Id, item.Id);
```

```
        serilogFixture.Logger.Debug("Add_Item done");
    }
    [Theory]
    [InlineData(ItemSubType.Entry)]
    [InlineData(ItemSubType.Group)]
    [InlineData(ItemSubType.Notes)]
    [InlineData(ItemSubType.PxEntry)]
    public async void Delete_Item(ItemSubType itemSubType)...
    [Theory]
    [InlineData(ItemSubType.Entry)]
    [InlineData(ItemSubType.Group)]
    [InlineData(ItemSubType.Notes)]
    [InlineData(ItemSubType.PxEntry)]
    public void Create_Item(ItemSubType itemSubType) ...
}
```

Listing 11.2: DataStoreTests.cs *(*https://epa.ms/DataStoreTests11-2*)*

Through these examples, we have demonstrated how to create unit tests in the model layer. The knowledge we have acquired thus far can also be applied to unit testing in other .NET applications.

Having concluded the introduction to the model layer unit testing, we will proceed to explore the Razor component unit testing using the bUnit library in the next part of this chapter.

Mock .NET MAUI components

In developing unit tests for .NET MAUI, we will present test case development for both XAML-based and Blazor-based apps. In both instances, we will incorporate the MVVM pattern in the design. The unit test cases at the model layer are identical for both; however, testing the view and the view model differs significantly. Developing unit test cases for the view and the view model in a XAML-based app can be quite complex. To test the view model, it is necessary to resolve the dependencies of XAML components. For instance, in the XAML version of our app, we need to invoke Shell navigation methods within the view model, as demonstrated in the following code:

```
await Shell.Current.GoToAsync(
    $"{nameof(ItemsPage)}?{nameof(ItemsViewModel.ItemId)}={item
    .Id}");
```

To address dependencies in Xamarin.Forms, an open-source project, Xamarin.Forms.Mocks, is available to help mock Xamarin.Forms components. In the case of .NET MAUI XAML apps, we require a similar solution for developing unit test cases for the view model, but currently, an equivalent does not seem to exist. Furthermore, there is a native user interface test framework, Xamarin.UITest, specifically for Android and iOS. However, it is not yet compatible with .NET MAUI. Additionally, since Xamarin.UITest is not a cross-platform solution, it will not be discussed in this book.

To partially address the dependency issue related to the view model test in this book, we can reference the .NET MAUI source code directly. Found at https://github.com/dotnet/maui, this source code includes the original unit test code containing mock .NET MAUI components.

I have incorporated some elements from the .NET MAUI source code into the unit test project PassXYZ.Vault.Tests. To resolve the Shell navigation issue in the view model, the following code from PassXYZ.Vault.Tests/maui/ShellTestBase.cs is included:

- In the NewItemViewModel tests, we can incorporate the ShellTestBase class with the following namespace:

  ```
  using Microsoft.Maui.Controls.Core.UnitTests;
  ```

- After implementing the namespace above, a mock Shell can be created using the following code:

  ```
  TestShell shell = new TestShell();
  ```

- Once we have a mock Shell instance, we can use this mock Shell instance in the following test case:

  ```
  [Fact]
  public async void CancelNewItem()  {
  NewItemViewModel vm = new(dataStore, logger);
  await shell.GoToAsync("//About/Maui/");
  vm.CancelCommand.Execute(null);
  Assert.Equal("//About/Maui/content", Shell.Current.CurrentState.
  Location.ToString());
  }
  ```

For a Blazor Hybrid app, we don't have the above issue. We have access to a reliable testing library called bUnit, which can be utilized for testing Razor components. This allows us to develop unit test cases for the view, view model, and model layers for Blazor apps.

Razor component testing using bUnit

In .NET MAUI development, we cannot create unit test cases for all view and view model layers in XAML-based UI components; however, this is possible with Blazor. bUnit is an exceptional test library that can be employed for developing unit tests for Razor components. The bUnit library facilitates the creation of unit test cases for Razor components using xUnit, NUnit, or MSTest. Throughout the remainder of this chapter, we will utilize xUnit in conjunction with bUnit. The structure of unit test cases using bUnit bears similarity to the xUnit test cases we discussed in the previous section.

In the remainder of this chapter, we will focus on testing the following Razor components, which were created in the second part of this book:

- Razor components in the `PassXYZ.BlazorUI` project
- Razor components in the `PassXYZ.Vault` project

To test Razor components using bUnit, it is necessary to modify the project configuration of `PassXYZ.Vault.Tests`.

Changing the project configuration for bUnit

To establish the test environment, we must add the bUnit and Moq packages, as well as updating the SDK type. The following modifications can be made to the xUnit `PassXYZ.Vault.Tests` testing project:

1. Add bUnit to the project.

    To incorporate the bUnit library into the project, first navigate to the project folder, then execute the following command from a console:

    ```
    cd PassXYZ.Vault.Tests
    dotnet add package bunit
    ```

    Additionally, we need to include the Moq package, which is a mocking library that will be utilized during the test setup process.

    ```
    dotnet add package Moq
    ```

2. Change the project configuration.

    To test the Razor components, we also need to change the project's SDK to `Microsoft.NET.Sdk.Razor`.

In the `PassXYZ.Vault.Tests.csproj` project file, we need to replace the following line:

```
<Project Sdk="Microsoft.NET.Sdk">
```

with

```
<Project Sdk="Microsoft.NET.Sdk.Razor">
```

Once we have the project configuration ready, we can create a simple unit test case using bUnit to test our Razor components.

Creating a bUnit test case

In our PassXYZ.Vault app, there are two types of Razor components that can be tested. The shared Razor components are located in the `PassXYZ.BlazorUI` project and serve as generic Razor components, which can be utilized across different projects. The second set of Razor components can be found in the `Pages` folder of the `PassXYZ.Vault` project. These components are specific to the `PassXYZ.Vault` app and make use of shared components from the `PassXYZ.BlazorUI` project.

To test the Razor components within the `PassXYZ.BlazorUI` project, we can examine each component individually. These test cases are unit test cases. The Razor components located in the `Pages` folder of the `PassXYZ.Vault` project serve as UI pages. Since these pages utilize UI components from other packages, they possess more dependencies. Consequently, these test cases can be regarded as integration test cases.

To begin, let's first create a test case for the `ModalDialog` Razor component in the `PassXYZ.BlazorUI` project. To test `ModalDialog`, we can generate an xUnit test class called `ModalDialogTests`, as illustrated in *Listing 11.3*:

```
namespace PassXYZ.Vault.Tests {
  [Collection("Serilog collection")]
  public class ModalDialogTests : TestContext {               //(1)
    SerilogFixture serilogFixture;
    public ModalDialogTests(SerilogFixture serilogFixture) {
      this.serilogFixture = serilogFixture;
    }
    [Fact]
    public void ModalDialogInitTest() {
      string title = "ModalDialog Test";                      //(2)
      var cut = RenderComponent<ModalDialog>(                 //(3)
        parameters => parameters.Add(p => p.Title, title)     //(4)
```

```
        .Add(p => p.CloseButtonText, "Close")
        .Add(p => p.SaveButtonText, "Save"));
    cut.Find("h5").TextContent.MarkupMatches(title);                    //(5)
    serilogFixture.Logger.Debug("ModalDialogInitTest:
      done");
  }
  ...

  }
}
```

Listing 11.3: `ModalDialogTests.cs` (https://epa.ms/ModalDialogTests11-3)

As seen in the `ModalDialogTests` unit test class, it bears a strong resemblance to the unit test class created for the model layer. We reuse the collection fixture established earlier and initialize it in the constructor. In the `ModalDialogInitTest` test case, we continue to employ the `Arrange`, `Act`, and `Assert` pattern for the implementation of the test case.

All bUnit test classes inherit from `TestContext` **(1)**. During the `Arrange` phase, we initialize a local `title` variable, **(2)**, with a predefined string. In the `Act` phase, we call a generic method, `RenderComponent<T>`, **(3)**, and use the `ModalDialog` type as the type parameter. We pass the `title` variable, **(4)**, as the component parameter. The outcome of `RenderComponent<T>` is stored in the `cut` variable. In the `Assert` phase, we confirm that the title text after rendering is consistent with the argument we pass, utilizing the bUnit method `Find` **(5)**. The bUnit method `Find` can be used to find any HTML tag. In `ModalDialog`, the title is rendered as an `<h5>` HTML tag.

In the `ModalDialogInitTest` test case, we observe the structure of the bUnit tests. For bUnit tests, we first render the component being tested. The rendering outcome is stored in the `cut` variable, **(3)** which is an instance of the `IRenderedComponent` interface. To verify the result, we can refer to the properties or invoke the methods of the `IRenderedComponent` instance.

When Razor components are rendered in the `TestContext`, they exhibit the same lifecycle as any other Razor component. We can pass parameters to the components being tested, and they can generate output akin to their behavior in a browser.

In the preceding example, when rendering the `ModalDialog` component, we can pass component parameters to it using the `Add` method, which belongs to the parameter builder of the `ComponentParameterCollectionBuilder<TComponent>` type.

Rendering simple components using C# code may not pose a problem. However, when passing multiple parameters to a component, using C# code can be inconvenient. By employing bUnit, we can develop test cases in Razor files, which significantly improves the experience of unit test development.

Creating test cases in Razor files

To create tests directly in Razor markup files, we can declare components using Razor markup, similar to how we utilize them within a Razor page. This approach eliminates the need to call Razor components in the C# code or pass parameters using function calls. For a Razor page, we can render Razor components using **Razor templates**.

We can illustrate the process of creating tests in Razor markup files by developing test cases for a more complex `EditorDialog` component. We previously created the `EditorDialog` component in *Chapter 10, Implementing Razor Components*. In *Listing 11.4*, we will examine the unit tests for this component:

```
@inherits TestContext                                    //(1)
<h3>EditorDialogTests</h3>
@code {
  bool _isOnCloseClicked = false;
  string _key = string.Empty;
  string _value = string.Empty;
  string updated_key = "key updated";
  string updated_value = "value udpated";
  void OnSaveClicked(string key, string value) {
    _key = key; _value = value;
  }
  void OnCloseHandler() {
    _isOnCloseClicked = true;
  }
  [Fact]
  public void EditorDialog_Init_WithoutArgument() ...
  [Fact]
  public void Edit_OnClose_Clicked() {

    var cut = Render(@<EditorDialog Key="@_key"
                                    Value="@_value"
                                    OnSave=@OnSaveClicked
```

```
                                        OnClose=@OnCloseHandler>
                        </EditorDialog>);                                   //(2)
    cut.Find("button[class='btn btn-secondary']").Click();                  //(3)
    Assert.True(_isOnCloseClicked);                                         //(4)
  }
  [Fact]
  public void Edit_With_KeyEditingEnabled() {                               //(5)
    var cut = Render(@<EditorDialog Key="@_key"
                                    Value="@_value"
                                    IsKeyEditingEnable="true"
                                    OnSave=@OnSaveClicked>
                        </EditorDialog>);
    cut.Find("input").Change(updated_key);
    cut.Find("textarea").Change(updated_value);
    cut.Find("button[type=submit]").Click();
    Assert.Equal(_key, updated_key);
    Assert.Equal(_value, updated_value);
  }
  [Fact]
  public void Edit_With_KeyEditingDisabled() ...
}
```

Listing 11.4: `EditorDialogTests.razor` (https://epa.ms/EditorDialogTests11-4)

We can develop a new Razor component, called `EditorDialogTests`, within the `PassXYZ.Vault.Tests` project. As it serves as a bUnit test class, it is a child class of `TestContext` **(1)**. Within this class, we generate test cases in a code block by utilizing **Razor templates**.

Let's first examine the `Edit_OnClose_Clicked` test case. In this scenario, we initially render the `EditorDialog` component and then proceed to test the close button.

To render the `EditorDialog` component, we invoke the `Render` method **(2)** of `TestContext`. Compared to the previous example, in this case, we can render the Razor markup directly rather than calling the C# function. The Razor markup utilized here is referred to as **Razor templates**. For more information about Razor templates, refer to the following Microsoft documentation: https://learn.microsoft.com/en-us/aspnet/core/blazor/components/?view=aspnetcore-5.0#razor-templates-1.

`Razor templates` can be defined in the following format:

```
@<{HTML tag}>…</{HTML tag}>
```

It consists of an @ symbol and a pair of open and closed HTML tags. Razor templates can be used in the code block of the Razor file. They cannot be used in a C# or C# code-behind file.

Employing this format, we can designate a snippet of Razor markup as the parameter for a C# function. This Razor markup snippet represents a Razor template, and its data type is either RenderFragment or RenderFragment<TValue>. In *Listing 11.4*, we use Razor templates to pass parameters to the EditorDialog, as demonstrated in the subsequent code:

```
var cut = Render(@<EditorDialog Key="@_key"
Value="@_value" OnSave=@OnSaveClicked
OnClose=@OnCloseHandler>
                </EditorDialog>);
```

After EditorDialog is rendered, we can find the close button and simulate the click action, **(3)**:

```
cut.Find("button[class='btn btn-secondary']").Click();
```

In the OnCloseHandler event handler, the _isOnCloseClicked variable, **(4)**, is set to true so that we can assert the result.

In the Edit_With_KeyEditingEnabled test case, **(5)**, after the component is rendered, we can simulate user interactions to set the key and value fields in the component. After that, we can simulate clicking on the save button as we can see here:

```
cut.Find("input").Change(updated_key);
cut.Find("textarea").Change(updated_value);
cut.Find("button[type=submit]").Click();
```

Upon clicking the button, the event handler is triggered. Within the OnSaveClicked event handler, we receive the modified key and value, enabling us to assert the result.

```
Assert.Equal(_key, updated_key);
Assert.Equal(_value, updated_value);
```

As evidenced by these two test cases, designing bUnit tests becomes more straightforward when creating tests within a Razor file. By utilizing Razor templates, we can render components and also simulate various user interactions, enabling us to test the components interactively.

Razor templates serve as an excellent tool for combining Razor markup and C# code, allowing us to benefit from the strengths of both approaches. However, there are certain limitations when using Razor templates. In the next section, we will explore how to overcome these constraints.

Using the RenderFragment delegate

Although Razor templates can help to simplify test setups, they have their limitations, especially in complex test case scenarios. With intricate test cases, Razor templates can become quite lengthy. If we intend to reuse the same Razor templates in another test case, we would need to copy them, potentially resulting in a significant amount of duplicated code. This is one of the main drawbacks of using Razor templates.

In this case, we can use a RenderFragment delegate. As its name indicates, it is the delegate type of RenderFragment or RenderFragment<TValue>. The data type of Razor templates is RenderFragment or RenderFragment<TValue>. A RenderFragment delegate is the delegate type for Razor templates.

You can find more information about the RenderFragment delegate in the following Microsoft document: https://learn.microsoft.com/en-us/aspnet/core/blazor/performance?view=aspnetcore-3.1#define-reusable-renderfragments-in-code-2.

To demonstrate how to use the RenderFragment delegate, let's set up a more complex test for the EditorDialog component. EditorDialog can be used to edit either Item or Field. We can use an item-editing case to show how to use the RenderFragment delegate.

We have the option to create a new test class, ItemEditTests, within the PassXYZ.Vault.Tests project. To differentiate the Razor markup and C# code, we can divide the ItemEditTests test class into a Razor file (ItemEditTests.razor) and a C# code-behind file (ItemEditTests.razor.cs). The markup designated for testing can be declared in the Razor file, as demonstrated in *Listing 11.5*:

```
@inherits TestContext
@namespace PassXYZ.Vault.Tests
<h3>ItemEditTests</h3>
@code {
  private RenderFragment _editorDialog => __builder =>
  {
    <CascadingValue Value="@_dialogId" Name="Id">
    <EditorDialog IsKeyEditingEnable=@isNewItem
    OnSave=@OnSaveClicked Key=@testItem.Name
    Value=@testItem.Notes>
      @if (isNewItem) {
        <select id="itemType" @bind="testItem.ItemType"
          class="form-select" aria-label="Group">
            <option selected value="Group">Group</option>
            <option value="Entry">Entry</option>
```

```
                    <option value="PxEntry">PxEntry</option>
                    <option value="Notes">Notes</option>
            </select>
            }
        </EditorDialog>
        </CascadingValue>
    };
}
```

Listing 11.5: ItemEditTests.razor *(*https://epa.ms/ItemEditTests11-5*)*

We define a RenderFragment delegate, _editorDialog, in the @code block of ItemEditTests.razor. The RenderFragment delegate must accept a parameter called __builder of the RenderTreeBuilder type. In the markup code, we can access the variables defined in the test class.

Now let's look at the usage of _editorDialog in the C# code-behind file in *Listing 11.6*:

```
namespace PassXYZ.Vault.Tests;
[Collection("Serilog collection")]
public partial class ItemEditTests : TestContext {
    readonly SerilogFixture serilogFixture;
    bool isNewItem { get; set; } = false;
    NewItem testItem { get; set; }
    string _dialogId = "editItem";
    string updated_key = "Updated item";
    string updated_value = "This item is updated.";

    public ItemEditTests(SerilogFixture fixture) {
        testItem = new() {
            Name = "New item",
            Notes = "This is a new item."
        };
        serilogFixture = fixture;
    }

    void OnSaveClicked(string key, string value) {
        testItem.Name = key; testItem.Notes = value;
    }
```

```
[Fact]
public void Edit_New_Item() {
  isNewItem = true;
  var cut = Render(_editorDialog);                                    //(1)
  cut.Find("#itemType").Change("Entry");
  cut.Find("input").Change(updated_key);
  cut.Find("textarea").Change(updated_value);
  cut.Find("button[type=submit]").Click();
  Assert.Equal(updated_key, testItem.Name);
  Assert.Equal(updated_value, testItem.Notes);
}


[Fact]
public void Edit_Existing_Item() {
  isNewItem = false;                                                  //(3)
  var cut = Render(_editorDialog);                                    //(1)
  var ex = Assert.Throws<ElementNotFoundException>(() =>
    cut.Find("#itemType").Change("Entry"));                          //(2)
  Assert.Equal("No elements were found that matches the
    selector '#itemType'", ex.Message);                              //(4)
  cut.Find("textarea").Change(updated_value);
  cut.Find("button[type=submit]").Click();
  Assert.Equal(updated_value, testItem.Notes);
  }
}
```

Listing 11.6: `ItemEditTests.razor.cs` (https://epa.ms/ItemEditTests11-6)

Since `_editorDialog` defines the `Item` editing, we can develop multiple test cases for it. We can see that we render `_editorDialog`, **(1)**, for multiple test cases, such as `Edit_New_Item` and `Edit_Existing_Item`. By employing the `RenderFragment` delegate, our testing code appears more elegant and streamlined. Without taking this approach, we would need to replicate lengthy mark-up code in multiple locations. Directly using C# code may result in even more duplication of code.

In both test cases, we employ a similar process to test the `EditorDialog` by setting values and then clicking the Save button. In the markup code, we have a `<select>` tag defined. We can change the option, **(2)**, of the `<select>` tag within the test code. This `<select>` tag is conditionally rendered based on the value of the `isNewItem` variable.

In the `Edit_Existing_Item` test, we can also examine the negative case when the `isNewItem` variable, **(3)**, is set to `false`. In this instance, an exception is raised since the `<select>` tag is not rendered. We can observe that bUnit can also be utilized to test negative cases by verifying the content of the exception, **(4)**.

In the previous examples, we developed bUnit tests for the shared components in the `PassXYZ.BlazorUI` project. As these shared components serve as reusable building blocks for a high-level UI, many of them declare numerous component parameters. Utilizing the `RenderFragment` delegate or **Razor templates** can aid in simplifying the test setup process.

Upon examining the Razor pages within the `Pages` folder of the `PassXYZ.Vault` project, we find that `Items`, `ItemDetail`, and `Login` also function as Razor components. However, they are not designed for reuse. These Razor pages feature defined route templates and lack an extensive range of component parameters. The component parameters present in these Razor pages serve routing purposes. When designing test cases for these Razor pages, it is advisable to implement tests in a C# class instead of Razor files.

Testing Razor pages

During the development testing of Razor pages, we will become familiar with some highly beneficial bUnit features. Since it is not possible to review all the tests of Razor pages in our app, we will use `ItemDetail` as an example. `ItemDetail` is a Razor page designed to display the contents of a password entry, and it has a defined route.

```
@page "/entry/{SelectedItemId}"
```

When we want to display the `ItemDetail` page, we need to pass the `Id` info for an `Item` instance to it, and this instance cannot be a group. The initialization of the `ItemDetail` page is done in the `OnParametersSet()` lifecycle method, as we can see here:

```
protected override void OnParametersSet() {
  base.OnParametersSet();
  if (SelectedItemId != null) {
    selectedItem = DataStore.GetItem(SelectedItemId, true);
    if (selectedItem == null) {
        throw new InvalidOperationException(                    //(2)
    "ItemDetail: entry cannot be found with SelectedItemId");
    }
    else {
      if (selectedItem.IsGroup) {
```

```
            throw new InvalidOperationException(            //(3)
    "ItemDetail: SelectedItemId should not be group here.");
        }
        else {                                              //(4)
            fields.Clear();
            List<Field> tmpFields = selectedItem.GetFields();
            foreach (Field field in tmpFields) {
                fields.Add(field);
            }
            notes = selectedItem.GetNotesInHtml();
        }
      }
    }
    else {
      throw new InvalidOperationException(                  //(1)
        "ItemDetail: SelectedItemId is null");
    }
  }
}
```

We will develop an `ItemDetailTests` test class to cover all the execution paths in `OnParametersSet()`. To cover all the execution paths, we can find the following test cases:

- Test case 1: Initialize the `ItemDetail` instance without a selected item Id. We will get an `InvalidOperationException` exception, **(1)**, in this case.

- Test case 2: Initialize the `ItemDetail` instance with the wrong item Id. In this case, we will get an `InvalidOperationException` exception, **(2)**.

- Test case 3: Initialize the `ItemDetail` instance with a valid item Id, but the item type as a group. In this case, we will get an `InvalidOperationException` exception, **(3)**.

- Test case 4: Initialize the `ItemDetail` instance with a valid item Id and the item type is an entry, **(4)**.

We can implement these test cases in an `ItemDetailTests` bUnit test class, as shown here in *Listing 11.7*:

```
namespace PassXYZ.Vault.Tests;
[Collection("Serilog collection")]
public class ItemDetailTests : TestContext {
  SerilogFixture serilogFixture;
```

```
Mock<IDataStore<Item>> dataStore;
public ItemDetailTests(SerilogFixture fixture) {
    serilogFixture = fixture;
    dataStore = new Mock<IDataStore<Item>>();          //(1)
    Services.AddSingleton<IDataStore<Item>>
      (dataStore.Object);                              //(2)
}


[Fact]
public void Init_Empty_ItemDetail() {                  //(3)
    var ex = Assert.Throws<InvalidOperationException>(
      () => RenderComponent<ItemDetail>());
    Assert.Equal(
      "ItemDetail: SelectedItemId is null", ex.Message);
}


[Fact]
public void Load_ItemDetail_WithWrongId() {
  var ex = Assert.Throws<InvalidOperationException>(() =>
    RenderComponent<ItemDetail>(parameters =>
    parameters.Add(p => p.SelectedItemId, "Wrong Id")));
  Assert.Equal("ItemDetail: entry cannot be found with
      SelectedItemId", ex.Message);
}


[Fact]
public void Load_ItemDetail_WithGroup() {
  Item testGroup = new PwGroup(true, true) {
    Name = "Default Group",
    Notes = "This is a group in ItemDetailTests."
  };
  dataStore.Setup(x => x.GetItem(It.IsAny<string>(),
    It.IsAny<bool>())).Returns(testGroup);
  var ex = Assert.Throws<InvalidOperationException>(() =>
    RenderComponent<ItemDetail>(parameters =>
   parameters.Add(p => p.SelectedItemId, testGroup.Id)));
  Assert.Equal("ItemDetail: SelectedItemId should not be
```

```
      group here.", ex.Message);
  }


  [Fact]
  public void Load_ItemDetail_WithEmptyFieldList() {
    Item testEntry = new PwEntry(true, true) {
      Name = "Default Entry",
      Notes = "This is an entry with empty field list."
    };
    dataStore.Setup(x => x.GetItem(It.IsAny<string>(),
        It.IsAny<bool>())).Returns(testEntry);
    var cut = RenderComponent<ItemDetail>(parameters =>
      parameters.Add(p => p.SelectedItemId, testEntry.Id));
    cut.Find("article").MarkupMatches(
      $"<article><p>{testEntry.Notes}</p></article>");
  }
}
```

Listing 11.7: `ItemDetailTests.cs` *(https://epa.ms/ItemDetailTests11-7)*

The first test case is implemented in `Init_Empty_ItemDetail` **(3)**. During the test setup, we attempt to render the `ItemDetail` component directly without providing a selected item Id. We anticipate encountering an `InvalidOperationException` exception as a result.

Before executing the test case, we must first address the `IDataStore` dependency. `ItemDetail` relies on the `IDataStore<Item>` interface, and we can resolve this through dependency injection. In our app, this dependency is registered within the `MauiProgram.cs` file.

With bUnit, dependency injection is supported using `TestContext`. We can register the dependency using `AddSingleton`, **(2)**. To isolate the test, we use the `Moq` mocking framework, **(1)**, to replace the actual implementation of `IDataStore`, so we can reduce the complexity of the test setup.

Using `Moq`, we only need to fake the method or property that we need in our test setup. It can help to isolate our tests from their dependencies. To use the `Moq` framework, we can create a `Moq` object using the interface or class that we need as a type parameter. Later, we can define the behavior of the target interface or class when we use it. In the constructor, we create a `Mock` object and register the `IDataStore<Item>` interface using `dataStore.Object`:

```
dataStore = new Mock<IDataStore<Item>>();
Services.AddSingleton<IDataStore<Item>>(
  dataStore.Object);
```

After we register IDataStore in the constructor, we can execute the first test case again. This time, we can get the exception and verify the message is what we expect:

```
[Fact]
public void Init_Empty_ItemDetail() {
  var ex = Assert.Throws<InvalidOperationException>(
    () => RenderComponent<ItemDetail>());
  Assert.Equal("ItemDetail: SelectedItemId is null",
    ex.Message);
}
```

Next, let us look at the second test case. In the second test case, we pass an invalid Id to ItemDetail and try to render it:

```
[Fact]
public void Load_ItemDetail_WithWrongId() {
  var ex = Assert.Throws<InvalidOperationException>(() =>
    RenderComponent<ItemDetail>(parameters =>
    parameters.Add(p => p.SelectedItemId, "Wrong Id")));
    Assert.Equal("ItemDetail: entry cannot be found with
      SelectedItemId", ex.Message);
}
```

In this case, we also get an expected exception, and we can verify its content using Assert.Equal.

In the third test case, we provide a valid Id to ItemDetail, but the item is of a group type. This is a scenario that may be challenging to reproduce during an integration or user acceptance test. However, in a unit test, it is relatively simple to verify, as demonstrated here:

```
[Fact]
public void Load_ItemDetail_WithGroup() {
  Item testGroup = new PwGroup(true, true) {
    Name = "Default Group",
    Notes = "This is a group in ItemDetailTests."
  };
```

```
dataStore.Setup(x => x.GetItem(It.IsAny<string>(),
    It.IsAny<bool>())).Returns(testGroup);
var ex = Assert.Throws<InvalidOperationException>(() =>
    RenderComponent<ItemDetail>(parameters =>
    parameters.Add(p => p.SelectedItemId, testGroup.Id)));
    Assert.Equal("ItemDetail: SelectedItemId should not be
    group here.", ex.Message);
}
```

To test this, we need to create a group and assign it to a testGroup variable. In this test case, we must call the GetItem method of IDataStore. Since we mocked IDataStore in our setup, we also need to mock the GetItem method here. The Moq method returns testGroup when called. Once the test setup is prepared, we can render ItemDetail with testGroup.Id. The expected outcome of this test is the exception that we anticipate.

In the final test case, we will pass a valid Item Id and the item type is an entry:

```
[Fact]
public void Load_ItemDetail_WithEmptyFieldList() {
  Item testEntry = new PwEntry(true, true) {
    Name = "Default Entry",
    Notes = "This is an entry with empty field list."
  };
  dataStore.Setup(x => x.GetItem(It.IsAny<string>(),
    It.IsAny<bool>())).Returns(testEntry);
  var cut = RenderComponent<ItemDetail>(parameters =>
    parameters.Add(p => p.SelectedItemId, testEntry.Id));
  cut.Find("article").MarkupMatches(
    $"<article><p>{testEntry.Notes}</p></article>");
  Debug.WriteLine($"{cut.Markup}");
}
```

This test case is similar to the third test case, except we can create an entry and assign it to the testEntry variable. After we render ItemDetail with testEntry.Id, we can verify that the <article> rendered HTML tag is the one that we expect.

Thus far, we have explored testing Razor components using bUnit. It is evident that we can attain an impressively high level of test coverage with bUnit. This serves as one of the advantages of Blazor UI design.

We have now addressed all the topics related to unit test development with .NET MAUI in this chapter that we intended to explore.

Summary

In this chapter, we discussed unit test development for .NET MAUI apps. Although multiple test frameworks are available, we selected xUnit as our framework for this chapter. In the MVVM pattern, unit testing of the model layer is consistent with any other .NET application. We developed test cases for the `IDataStore` interface to evaluate our model layer. For unit testing the view and view model, we concentrated on the Blazor Hybrid app utilizing the bUnit test library. By combining the xUnit framework and bUnit library, we can develop end-to-end unit tests for a Blazor Hybrid app. With bUnit, we addressed topics such as Razor templates, the `RenderFragment` delegate, dependency injection, and the Moq framework.

With the understanding of unit testing acquired in this chapter, you should now be capable of developing your own unit tests. For more information on .NET unit test development, please refer to the *Further reading* section.

Unit testing can be integrated into a CI/CD pipeline. This setup allows unit tests to be executed automatically during the development process. We will explore this topic in greater detail in the upcoming chapter.

Further reading

- *Microsoft Visual Studio 2005 Unleashed* by Lars Powers and Mike Snell: `https://www.amazon.com/Microsoft-Visual-Studio-2005-Unleashed/dp/0672328194`

- MSTest: `https://github.com/microsoft/testfx`

- *Strengthening Visual Studio Unit Tests* by John Robbins: `https://learn.microsoft.com/en-us/archive/msdn-magazine/2006/march/bugslayer-strengthening-visual-studio-unit-tests`

- *NUnit Pocket Reference* by Bill Hamilton: `https://www.amazon.com/NUnit-Pocket-Reference-Running-OReilly/dp/0596007396`

- NUnit Releases at SourceForge: `https://sourceforge.net/projects/nunit/`

- *Why Did we Build xUnit 1.0:* `https://xunit.net/docs/why-did-we-build-xunit-1.0`

- xUnit documentation: `https://xunit.net/`

- xUnit.NET 2.0 release note: `https://xunit.net/releases/2.0`

Learn more on Discord

Join our community's Discord space for discussions with the author and other readers:

`https://packt.link/cross-platform-app`

12

Deploying and Publishing in App Stores

After completing the development work, our aim is to publish our app on various app stores. Since .NET MAUI is a cross-platform framework, we can build the same source code for Android, iOS, macOS, and Windows. While it's possible to deploy our app to a repository such as GitHub, most users on these platforms rely on app stores. As a result, we need to understand how to prepare our app for different app stores. That is the focus of this chapter. In this chapter, we will discuss the steps required to prepare the application packages before publishing.

We will cover the following topics in this chapter:

- Preparing application packages for publishing
- Automating the build process using GitHub Actions

Technical requirements

To test and debug the source code in this chapter, we need to install .NET MAUI on Windows and macOS. For complete details about environment setup, please refer to the *Development environment setup* section in *Chapter 1, Getting Started with .NET MAUI.*

We will build Windows and Android packages using Windows, while iOS and macOS packages will be built using macOS.

The source code for this chapter can be found at the following GitHub repository: `https://github.com/PacktPublishing/.NET-MAUI-Cross-Platform-Application-Development-Second-edition/tree/main/2nd/chapter12`.

To check out the source code for this chapter, use the command below:

```
$ git clone -b 2nd/chapter12 https://github.com/PacktPublishing/.NET-MAUI-
Cross-Platform-Application-Development-Second-edition.git PassXYZ.Vault2
```

For more information about the source code in this book, please refer to the *Managing the source code in this book* section in *Chapter 2, Building Our First .NET MAUI App.*

Preparing application packages for publishing

In previous chapters, minimal platform-specific knowledge was required for .NET MAUI development. However, when preparing to publish our app to individual app stores, we cannot avoid addressing platform-specific information. In this chapter, we will discuss the necessary steps to prepare the app for publishing, and then we will show how to automate the process using GitHub Actions.

There are numerous CI/CD tools available for automating the build and deployment process. For .NET MAUI, both GitHub Actions and Azure DevOps are viable options. You can refer to the *Further reading* section for more details about other alternatives. However, in this chapter, our primary emphasis will be on employing GitHub Actions as a build and deployment instrument.

Preparing for publishing

To prepare for publishing, we will focus on the tasks that need to be completed before submitting the package to an app store. For information about the actual publishing process, please refer to the documentation provided by each app store.

During the preparation for publishing, we aim to answer the following questions:

- How is an app identified in the app store?
- How are the app developers identified?
- Which devices can the app support?

Building and signing application packages on different platforms require platform-specific configurations. In .NET MAUI, the platform-specific information is included in the Visual Studio project file and the platform-specific configuration file. Conditional compilation is used in the Visual Studio project file to specify platform-specific information. Refer to *Table 12.1* for an overview of the necessary changes for each platform.

Item	Android	Windows	iOS	macOS
Package format	`.apk/.aab`	`.msix`	`.ipa`	`.app/.pkg`
Signing	`Keystore`	Signing certificate `Package.StoreAssociation.xml`	Distrubution certificate Distribution profile	

ApplicationId	`package="com.passxyz.vault2"`	`Publisher="CN=F81DB 4B-AF4A-473E-ADEA-A55EE7432C05"`	`<key>CFBundleIdentifier</key>`
			
			`<string>com.passxyz.vault2</string>`	

ApplicationVersion	`android:versionCode="1"`	`Version="0.3.8.0"`	`<key>CFBundleVersion</key>`
			
			`<string>2</string>`	

Configuration file	`AndroidManifest.xml`	`Package.appxmanifest`	`Info.plist`	

Table 12.1: The build configuration

Table 12.1 outlines how to identify an app using the `ApplicationId` and `ApplicationVersion` variables defined in the Visual Studio project file. For each platform, a specific platform configuration file is used.

For Android distribution, either a `.apk` file or `.aab` file is generated. The `.apk` file is the original Android package format used to install app packages on devices or emulators, while the `.aab` file is used for submission to Google Play Store. Before submission, we need to sign the package using a Keystore. `ApplicationId` and `ApplicationVersion` are mapped to a package ID and version code in the Android configuration file `AndroidManifest.xml`.

For iOS or macOS distribution, a `.ipa` file is generated for iOS, and either a `.app` or `.pkg` file is generated for macOS. To sign an iOS or macOS package, we need a distribution certificate and a distribution profile. The `ApplicationId` is mapped to the bundle ID, and `ApplicationVersion` is mapped to the bundle version in `Info.plist`.

For Windows distribution, the MSIX package format is used, and the package is built with the `.msix` file extension. Windows employs a **universally unique identifier** (**UUID**) as the `ApplicationId`, which is generated as `ApplicationGuid`.

The `ApplicationVersion` is mapped to the `Version` attribute of the `Identity` tag in `Package.appxmanifest`.

What is MSIX?

MSIX is a modern Windows app package format designed for all Windows apps. It aims to provide a more reliable and secure installation process, along with enhanced system resource usage and simplified updates. MSIX allows developers to package and distribute their applications through various channels, including Microsoft Store, web, or third-party platforms.

For more information on MSIX, please refer to the Microsoft documentation: `https://learn.microsoft.com/en-us/windows/msix/overview`.

In the following sections, we will explain how to generate release packages for each platform. We will build Windows and Android packages on Windows, while iOS and macOS packages will be built on macOS. We will demonstrate how to accomplish this using both Visual Studio and the command line.

Publishing to Microsoft Store

We can build a `.msix` package for Microsoft Store using either Visual Studio or the command line on Windows.

In Visual Studio, we need to set the target framework as `net8.0-windows10.0.19041.0` and set the build type to `Release`.

After that, we can right-click on the project node and select the `Publish...` menu item.

A window will appear with the **Select distribution method** option (*Figure 12.1*). Here, select **Microsoft Store under a new app name** and click the **Next** button:

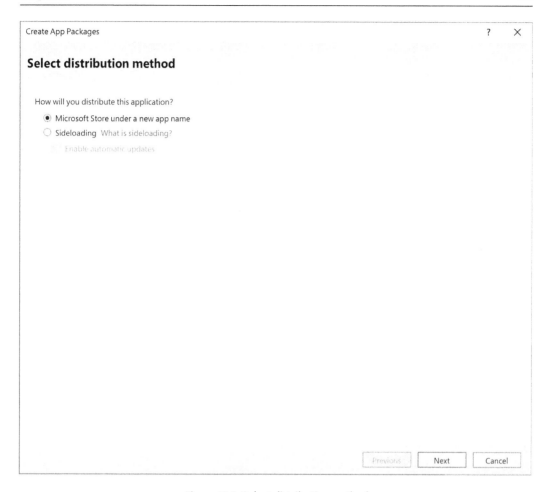

Figure 12.1: Select distribution method

Before proceeding to the next step, as shown in *Figure 12.2*, we need to have an app name ready.

To create a new app name, follow these steps:

1. Visit **Microsoft Store Developer Dashboard** at the following URL: `https://partner.microsoft.com/en-us/dashboard/`.

2. Register and create a new app name.

Once we have an app name, we can associate it with our app, as shown in *Figure 12.2*:

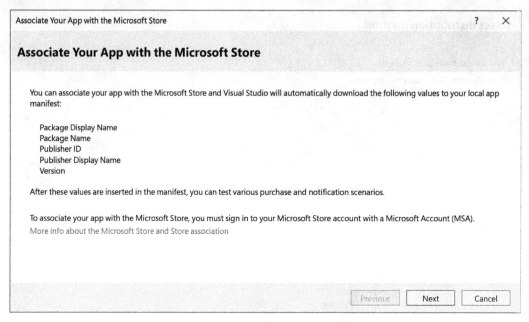

Figure 12.2: Associating your app with Microsoft Store

After clicking the **Next** button, Visual Studio will search for the app name in Microsoft Store. The app name created in Microsoft Store, as shown in *Figure 12.3*, will be retrieved for you to continue the publishing process:

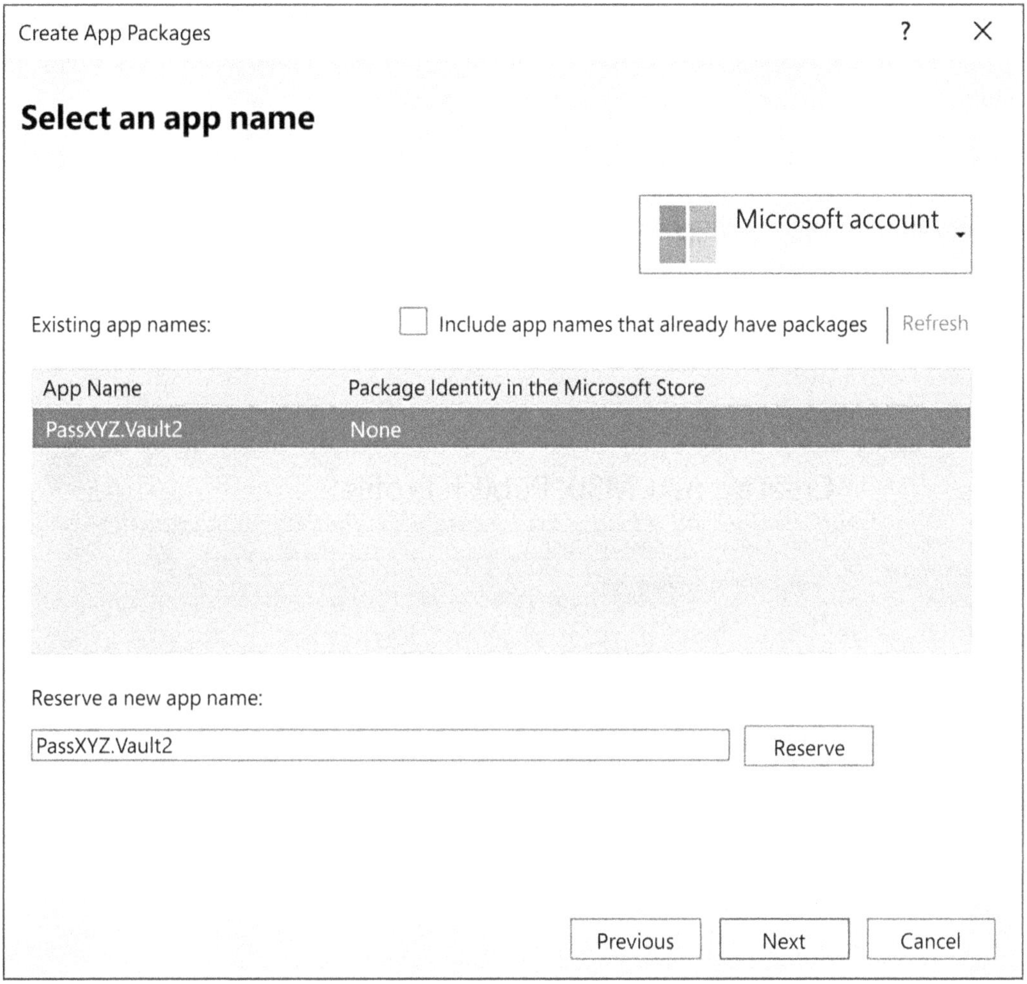

Create App Packages ? ✕

Select an app name

| | Microsoft account ▾ |

Existing app names: ☐ Include app names that already have packages │ Refresh

App Name	Package Identity in the Microsoft Store
PassXYZ.Vault2	None

Reserve a new app name:

| PassXYZ.Vault2 | Reserve |

Previous   Next   Cancel

Figure 12.3: Selecting an app name

After selecting the app name, click the **Next** button. A screen to select and configure packages will appear, as shown in *Figure 12.4*. Here, we can choose the packages for our app and configure additional settings before proceeding with the publication process.

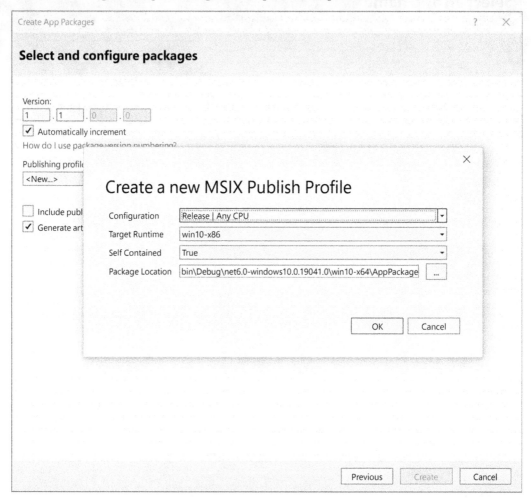

Figure 12.4: Selecting and configuring packages

To continue the process, we need to create a publish profile here. To create an MSIX publish profile, follow these steps:

1. Click on the drop-down menu under **Publishing profile**. A dialog will be displayed, as shown in *Figure 12.4*.

2. Clicking the **OK** button in the dialog box to create a new MSIX publish profile.

Once we have a publish profile, click on the **Create** button (which will now be active) to create the package. The build and package creation process may take some time. Upon completion, we will see a screen similar to the one depicted in *Figure 12.5*, indicating that the MSIX package is ready for submission.

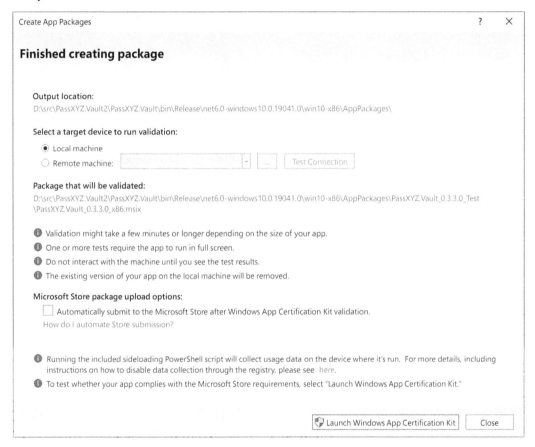

Figure 12.5: An MSIX package

The location of the new package is shown in *Figure 12.5*. There is an option to verify the package by running the **Windows App Certification Kit.**

In the preceding steps, two files related to the app's publication will have been created in the project folder:

- `Package.StoreAssociation.xml`: this file associates the app with Microsoft Store.
- `Properties\PublishProfiles\MSIX-win10-x86.pubxml`: this is the publish profile.

Both files may contain sensitive information, so they should not be checked into the Git repository.

To integrate the build process in the CI/CD environment, we need to execute the build process using the command line. To build a `.msix` package using the command line, execute the following command from the project folder:

```
dotnet publish PassXYZ.Vault/PassXYZ.Vault.csproj -c Release -f net8.0-
windows10.0.19041.0
```

Once the `.msix` package is built, we can upload it to Microsoft Store in the `Packages` section of the app submission.

Publishing to Google Play Store

To prepare for submission to Google Play Store, you need to create a new app in the Google Play Console. A Google account is required to create a new app in the Google Play Console.

Every Android app has a unique application ID or package ID, which is defined in the configuration file, `AndroidManifest.xml`. This configuration file is generated by Visual Studio from the project file and can be found at `Platforms/Android/AndroidManifest.xml`. Let's review the `AndroidManifest.xml` of our app in *Listing 12.1*:

```
<?xml version="1.0" encoding="utf-8"?>
<manifest
  xmlns:android="http://schemas.android.com/apk/res/android"
  package="com.passxyz.vault2"                                    //(1)
  android:installLocation="auto"
  android:versionCode="1">                                        //(2)
  <application
    android:allowBackup="true"
    android:icon="@mipmap/appicon"
    android:roundIcon="@mipmap/appicon_round"
```

```
      android:supportsRtl="true"></application>
  <uses-permission
    android:name="android.permission.ACCESS_NETWORK_STATE" />
  <uses-permission android:name=
    "android.permission.INTERNET" />
</manifest>
```

Listing 12.1: AndroidManifest.xml *(https://epa.ms/AndroidManifest12-1)*

In our app, the application ID is "com.passxyz.vault2" **(1)**, which is generated from ApplicationId, and the version is the value of android:versionCode **(2)**, which is generated from ApplicationVersion.

The declaration of the app identifier and version can be found in the PassXYZ.Vault.csproj project file:

```
<!-- App Identifier -->
<ApplicationId>com.passxyz.vault2</ApplicationId>
<ApplicationIdGuid>8606B3B5-C03C-41D7-825F-B33718CF791C
  </ApplicationIdGuid>
<!-- Versions -->
<ApplicationDisplayVersion>1.0</ApplicationDisplayVersion>
<ApplicationVersion>1</ApplicationVersion>
```

To sign an Android package, we need to create a Keystore file. For information on creating a Keystore file and signing an Android app, refer to the following Android documentation: https://developer.android.com/studio/publish/app-signing.

Once we have a Keystore file and have prepared the required configuration, follow these steps in Visual Studio:

1. Set the target framework as net8.0-android and the build type as Release.
2. Right-click the project node and select **Publish…**.

After completing these steps, the build will start, and an archive will be created, as shown in *Figure 12.6*:

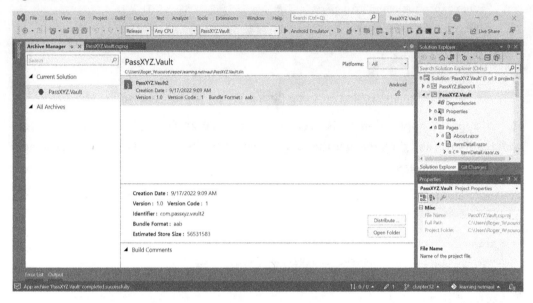

Figure 12.6: Creating an archive for Android

After the package is created, we can sign it by clicking the **Distribute...** button. Then, we will need to choose a distribution channel, as shown in *Figure 12.7*:

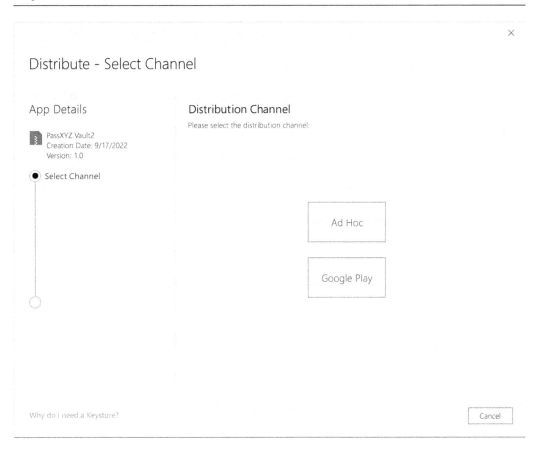

Figure 12.7: Selecting a channel

Although it is possible to sign and submit the package by selecting **Google Play**, we will choose **Ad Hoc** for signing. We will manually submit the signed package to Google Play later.

Upon selecting Ad Hoc, we will be presented with a different screen, as shown in *Figure 12.8*, where we can proceed with the process of signing our Android package:

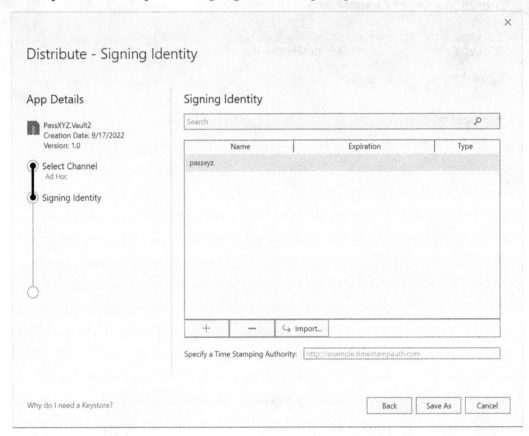

Figure 12.8: Signing Identity using a Keystore file

As shown in *Figure 12.8*, click the + button to add a Keystore file. After adding the Keystore file, click the **Save As** button to sign the package.

The signed .aab file can be submitted to Google Play Store through the Google Play Console.

If you don't have an existing Keystore file, you can follow the guide mentioned earlier to create a new one. The default location of Keystore files is %USERPROFILE%\AppData\Local\Xamarin\ Mono for Android\Keystore\.

It's critical to securely store your keystore file and password, as they will be required again when you submit an updated version of your application to the App Store.

If you select the **Google Play** option in *Figure 12.7*, the screen displayed is as shown in *Figure 12.9*. You will then need to access the Google Play API using your **Client Id** and **Client Secret**. Despite the **Google Play** and **Ad Hoc** options sharing strong similarities, selecting **Google Play** allows you to automatically submit the build result to Google Play Store:

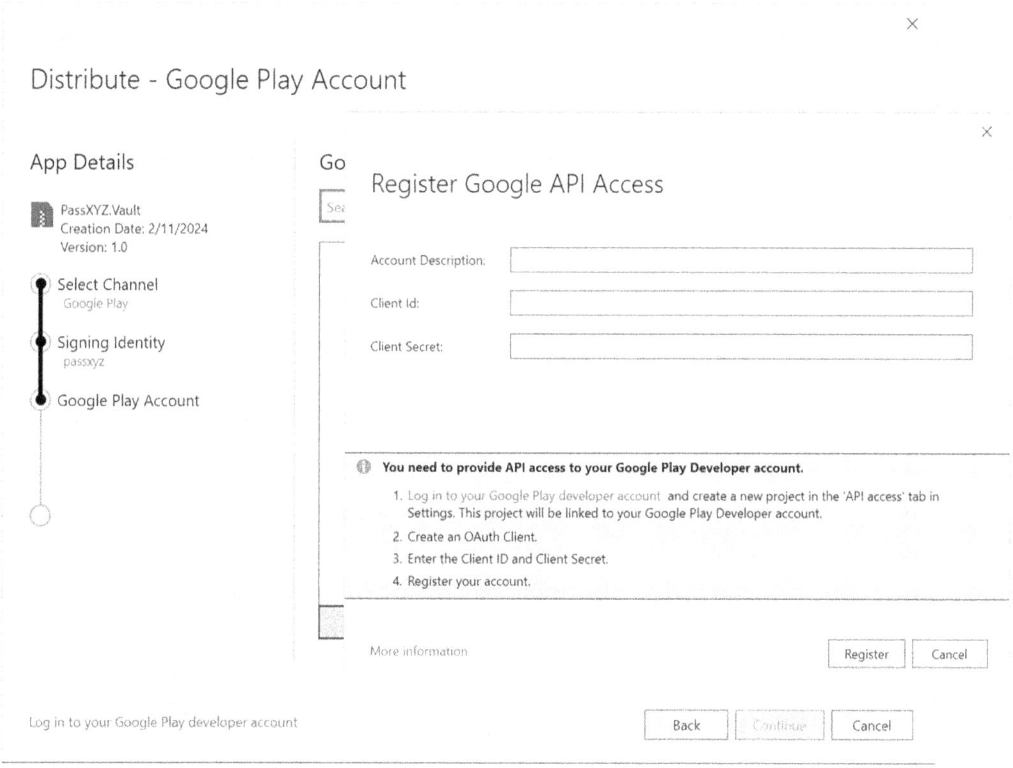

Figure 12.9: Connect to Google Play Store using your Client ID and Client Secret

To create the package from the command line, execute the following command in the project folder:

```
dotnet publish PassXYZ.Vault/PassXYZ.Vault.csproj -c Release -f net8.0-
android
```

To learn how to upload a signed Android app bundle to Google Play Store, please refer to the following Android document: `https://developer.android.com/studio/publish/upload-bundle`.

Publishing to Apple's App Store

We can discuss the submission of an iOS or macOS app to the App Store simultaneously, since they share many similarities.

In this section, we will be discussing the process of building, signing, and deploying .NET MAUI apps for iOS and macOS using a macOS environment.

Building, signing, and deploying .NET MAUI apps for iOS or macOS requires specific tooling and environments, due to Apple's requirements. Here's what you need:

- **macOS**: Because of Apple's restrictions, you must build iOS and macOS applications on a Mac. This can be a local machine, or you could use a cloud macOS environment like GitHub Actions or Azure Pipelines, which offers hosted macOS agents.

- **Xcode**: Install the latest stable version of Xcode. This is required for iOS SDKs and simulators.

- **.NET 8**: .NET MAUI is built on .NET 8, so you will need the .NET 8 SDK installed.

- **MAUI**: Install the latest stable version of .NET MAUI, including the .NET MAUI workload and templates.

- **Apple Developer account**: To sign and deploy an app to the App Store, you will need an Apple Developer account. This requires an annual subscription fee but is necessary to distribute your apps to users.

- **Provisioning profiles and certificates**: To sign your app, you will need a provisioning profile and a matching distribution certificate. You can create and manage these in the Apple Developer portal or automatically manage them through Xcode. For details on how to create a signing certificate and a provisioning profile, refer to the following document: https://learn.microsoft.com/en-us/dotnet/maui/ios/deployment/provision.

To simultaneously fulfill the needs of Xamarin and .NET MAUI builds, you might have multiple Xcode installations on your macOS. You can check for all Xcode installations on your Mac with the following command:

```
% ls /Applications | grep 'Xcode'
Xcode.app
Xcode_14.3.1.app
Xcode_15.2.app
```

To check the currently selected Xcode, you can use this command:

```
% xcrun xcode-select-print-path
/Applications/Xcode_15.2.app/Contents/Developer
```

If you need to choose a specific Xcode version, the following command can be used:

```
% sudo xcode-select -s /Applications/Xcode.app
```

Once these tools are installed and set up, you can build, sign, and deploy your .NET MAUI apps for iOS or macOS using the .NET CLI for command-line builds and deployments.

In iOS or macOS apps, the bundler identifier and bundler version are used to identify an app. This information is stored in the `Info.plist` configuration file. The bundler identifier is generated from `ApplicationId`, and the bundler version is generated from `ApplicationVersion` in the Visual Studio project file.

iOS apps can be distributed exclusively through the App Store. The package for submission is a file with the `.ipa` extension. Although macOS apps can also be distributed through the App Store, their packages can be installed directly.

Although some publishing steps can be performed in a Windows environment, you still need to connect to a network-accessible macOS computer. To reduce the complexity, we use a macOS environment to build both iOS and macOS apps. Before building the packages, we need to update the Visual Studio project file to configure our own signing certificate and distribution profile:

```
<PropertyGroup Condition="$(TargetFramework.Contains('-ios')) and
'$(Configuration)' == 'Release'">
  <RuntimeIdentifier>ios-arm64</RuntimeIdentifier>
  <CodesignKey>iPhone Distribution: Shugao Ye (W9WL9WPD24)
  </CodesignKey>
  <CodesignProvision>passxyz_2023</CodesignProvision>
</PropertyGroup>
<PropertyGroup Condition="$(TargetFramework.Contains('-
  maccatalyst')) and '$(Configuration)' == 'Release'">
  <CodesignEntitlement>Entitlements.plist
  </CodesignEntitlement>
  <CodesignKey>
    3rd Party Mac Developer Application: Shugao Ye
      (W9WL9WPD24)
  </CodesignKey>
  <CodesignProvision>passxyz.maccatalyst</CodesignProvision>
</PropertyGroup>
```

As shown, you can use conditional configuration for both iOS and macOS builds. Different signing certificates and distribution profiles are used for iOS and macOS.

If you are not sure whether the settings are correct, you can verify them using Xcode. Creating an app in Xcode involves using the same `"com.passxyz.vault2"` bundler ID as our app. After that, check the configuration of **Signing**, as shown in *Figure 12.10*. This process allows you to compare the signing configurations between your Visual Studio project and the equivalent in Xcode, helping to identify any discrepancies or issues with the setup.

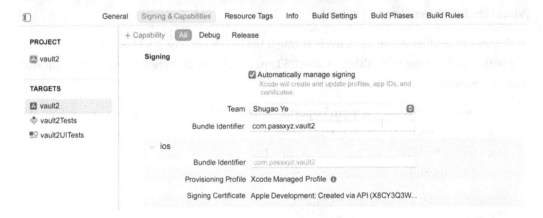

Figure 12.10: The iOS signing settings in Xcode

If there are any issues with the signing certificate or provisioning profile, error messages will be reported by Xcode. Once the settings are correct in Xcode, the same settings can be used in the Visual Studio project without any issues.

With all the configurations ready, we can build the `.ipa` file in the project folder using the following command:

```
dotnet publish PassXYZ.Vault/PassXYZ.Vault.csproj -c Release -f net8.0-ios
/p:CreatePackage=true /p:ArchiveOnBuild=True
```

Once the command executes successfully, an `.ipa` file is generated. We can submit this file to the App Store. There are three methods that can be used to upload a package to the App Store. For more details, please refer to the following documentation: `https://developer.apple.com/help/app-store-connect/manage-builds/upload-builds`.

From the documentation, we know that we can use **Xcode**, **altool**, or **Transporter** to upload a package.

As we are not directly utilizing Xcode to construct the .NET MAUI app, we will not employ Xcode to upload the build to Apple Store. If the goal is to establish a comprehensive CI/CD solution, **altool** can be used to upload the build to Apple Store.

However, in this chapter, our primary focus is on **Continuous Integration (CI)**, leaving **Continuous Delivery (CD)** for you to delve into independently. The setup for CD often requires more account-specific configurations.

We will use the Transporter app here. After signing in to the Transporter app, we can upload the package to the App Store, as shown in *Figure 12.11*:

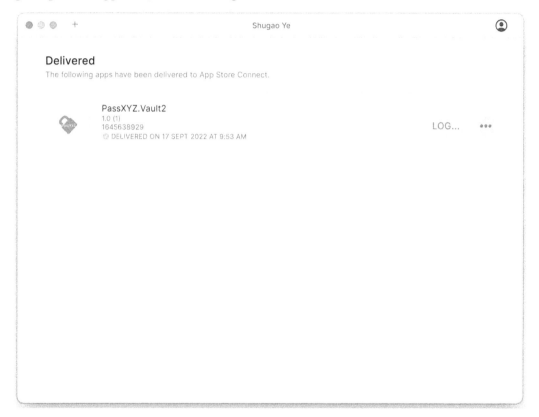

Figure 12.11: Uploading a package using the Transporter app

The building and uploading processes of a macOS package are similar to those for an iOS app. There are three different frameworks (AppKit, Mac Catalyst, and SwiftUI) that can be employed to build macOS apps. In .NET MAUI, Mac Catalyst is used for platform-specific implementation.

By default, App Sandbox is not enabled in Mac Catalyst apps, so we need to enable it. To enable it in the macOS app, we need to add an `Entitlements.plist` file to the build configuration.

We can review the `Entitlements.plist` file in *Listing 12.2*:

```
<?xml version="1.0" encoding="UTF-8"?>
<!DOCTYPE plist PUBLIC "-//Apple//DTD PLIST 1.0//EN"
  "http://www.apple.com/DTDs/PropertyList-1.0.dtd">
<plist version="1.0">
<dict>
  <key>com.apple.security.app-sandbox</key>
  <true/>
  <key>com.apple.security.files.user-selected.read-only
    </key>
  <true/>
  <key>com.apple.security.network.client</key>
  <true/>
</dict>
</plist>
```

Listing 12.2: `Entitlements.plist` *(https://epa.ms/Entitlements12-2)*

Just like in the iOS build, we can verify the configuration for the macOS build in Xcode, as shown in *Figure 12.12*. By doing this, you ensure that the proper signing and provisioning setup is in place for our macOS app, before building and submitting it to the App Store.

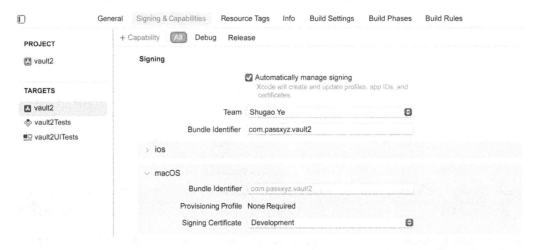

Figure 12.12: The macOS app's Signing settings in Xcode

With all configurations ready, we can build the package in our project folder using the following command:

```
dotnet publish PassXYZ.Vault/PassXYZ.Vault.csproj -c Release -f net8.0-
  maccatalyst  /p:CreatePackage=true /p:EnablePackageSigning=true"
```

After successfully building the package, we can upload the `.pkg` file to the App Store using the Transporter app, as shown in *Figure 12.13*. This will demonstrate that both iOS and macOS packages have been successfully uploaded to the App Store. You can then proceed to App Store Connect to complete the rest of the submission process.

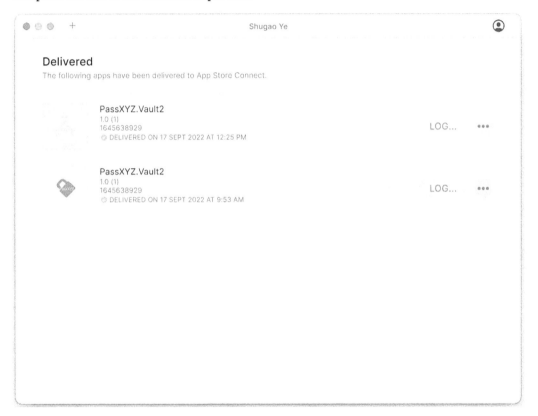

Figure 12.13: Uploading the macOS app using the Transporter app

After uploading packages to Microsoft Store, Google Play Store, and Apple App Store, we can test the uploaded packages before the final release using the testing tools provided by the stores:

- **Apple App Store: TestFlight** can be used to test iOS/macOS apps before the production release
- **Google Play Store**: Alpha or beta testing can be set up before the production release
- **Microsoft Store**: Package flights can be used on Microsoft Store to test uploaded packages

Now that we have learned the basic steps of preparing application packages for supported platforms, we can explore setting up the automated build of .NET MAUI app in a CI/CD environment, such as GitHub Actions or Azure DevOps. Implementing CI/CD can streamline the development and deployment process, ensuring that your app is continuously tested, built, and ready for release as you make updates and improvements.

GitHub Actions

Since our source code is hosted on GitHub, let's use GitHub Actions as an example to introduce you to how to set up CI workflows for .NET MAUI development. GitHub Actions is an automation platform that can help streamline and automate essential tasks related to your project, like building, testing, and deploying code updates. This powerful feature ensures that your code remains verified and ready for deployment at any time, allowing developers to focus on writing new features and fixing bugs while maintaining quality assurance.

Understanding GitHub Actions

For .NET MAUI app development, our target is to build, test, and deploy our apps to app stores or specified publishing channels. In this section, we will focus on CI using GitHub Actions rather than both CI and CD. To deploy apps to various stores, there are many account-specific setup steps; please refer to the .NET MAUI document for the details: `https://learn.microsoft.com/en-us/dotnet/maui/deployment/`.

A GitHub Actions workflow is a process that automatically builds and deploys the deliverables from a project. The workflow usually starts from an event such as a `push` or `pull_request` event, or when an issue is submitted. Once a workflow is triggered, the defined jobs will start to perform certain tasks inside a runner. Each job consists of one or more steps that either run a script or an action.

In summary, GitHub Actions includes events, runners, jobs/steps, actions, and runners. These components work together to automate various tasks in your development and deployment process, making it more efficient and less error prone.

Workflows

GitHub Actions workflows are defined by a YAML file in the `.github/workflows` directory. YAML is a superset of JSON and provides a more human-readable language. A repository can have one or multiple workflows to perform different jobs. Refer to *Figure 12.14* to understand the workflow defined in the `PassXYZ.Vault` project.

Figure 12.14: The workflow of Windows runner

As seen in *Figure 12.14*, this example illustrates how a workflow performs Android and Windows builds. A workflow is triggered by a push or pull_request event, or manually. It runs inside a Windows runner to perform the builds. When the workflow is triggered, two jobs, **Android Build** and **Windows Build**, begin execution. Each job includes four steps to perform the build, as depicted in *Figure 12.14*.

In our project, we defined the two following workflows:

- passxyz-ci-macos.yml: This is a workflow to build iOS and macOS on a macOS runner.
- passxyz-ci-windows.yml: This is a workflow to build Android and Windows on a Windows runner.

We can see the YAML files in *Listing 12.3* and *Listing 12.4*:

```
name: PassXYZ.Vault CI Build (Windows)
on:                                                  //(1)
  push:                                              //(2)
    branches: [ chapter12 ]
    paths-ignore:
      - '**/*.md'
      - '**/*.gitignore'
      - '**/*.gitattributes'
  pull_request:                                      //(3)
    branches: [ chapter12 ]
  workflow_dispatch:                                 //(4)
permissions:
  contents: read
env:
  DOTNET_NOLOGO: true
```

```
    DOTNET_SKIP_FIRST_TIME_EXPERIENCE: true
    DOTNET_CLI_TELEMETRY_OPTOUT: true
    DOTNETVERSION: 8.0.x
    DOTNETSDK: 'net8.0'
    PROJECT_NAME: PassXYZ.Vault
jobs:                                                            //(5)
# MAUI Android Build
  build-android:                                                 //(6)
    runs-on: windows-latest                                      //(7)
    name: Android Build
    steps:                                                       //(8)
      - name: Checkout
        uses: actions/checkout@v3                                //(9)
      - name: Setup .NET
        uses: actions/setup-dotnet@v2
        with:
          dotnet-version: ${{env.DOTNETVERSION}}
      - name: Install MAUI workload
        run: dotnet workload install maui
      - name: Restore Dependencies
        run: dotnet restore ${{env.PROJECT_NAME}}/$
          {{env.PROJECT_NAME}}.csproj
      - name: Build MAUI Android
        run: dotnet publish ${{env.PROJECT_NAME}}/$
          {{env.PROJECT_NAME}}.csproj -c Release -f ${{env.DOTNETSDK}}-
android --no-restore
      - name: Upload Android Artifact
        uses: actions/upload-artifact@v3
        with:
          name: passxyz-android-ci-build
          path: ${{env.PROJECT_NAME}}/bin/Release/
${{env.DOTNETSDK}}-android/*Signed.a*

# MAUI Windows Build
  build-windows:
    runs-on: windows-latest
    name: Windows Build
```

```
steps:
  - name: Checkout
    uses: actions/checkout@v3
  - name: Setup .NET
    uses: actions/setup-dotnet@v2
    with:
      dotnet-version: ${{env.DOTNETVERSION}}
  - name: Install MAUI workload
    run: dotnet workload install maui
  - name: Restore Dependencies
    run: dotnet restore ${{env.PROJECT_NAME}}
      /${{env.PROJECT_NAME}}.csproj
  - name: Build MAUI Windows
    run: dotnet publish ${{env.PROJECT_NAME}}/
${{env.PROJECT_NAME}}.csproj -c Release -f ${{env.DOTNETSDK}}-
windows10.0.19041.0
  - name: Upload Windows Artifact
    uses: actions/upload-artifact@v3
    with:
      name: passxyz-windows-ci-build
      path: ${{env.PROJECT_NAME}}/...
```

Listing 12.3: `passxyz-ci-windows.yml` *(https://epa.ms/passxyz-ci-windows12-3)*

These workflow files define the steps necessary to automate the build process for different target platforms, helping ensure that our .NET MAUI app is always ready for deployment.

In the following sessions, we will now analyze it in detail, providing insights into how these workflows help automate the build process for your .NET MAUI app. Understanding the structure and functionality of these workflow files will enable you to customize and enhance your development pipeline, ensuring that your app is always ready for deployment and matches your specific requirements.

Events

Events are crucial in triggering the workflow, and they are defined after the on: keyword **(1)**. In the previous workflow, we defined the push **(2)**, pull_request **(3)** and workflow_dispatch **(4)** events. For both push and pull_request events, we monitor the activities on the main branch, and we also don't ignore any build-related commits such as markdown files or configuration files.

For more information on events that can be used to trigger workflows, please refer to the following GitHub documentation: `https://docs.github.com/en/actions/using-workflows/events-that-trigger-workflows`.

Understanding the events triggering workflows enables you to customize when specific actions should be executed in response to changes in your project. This helps maintain your app's quality while accommodating the unique needs of your development process.

Jobs

When a workflow is triggered, it initiates the execution of the defined jobs. Jobs are defined after the `jobs:` **(5)** keyword. One or more jobs can be defined within a workflow, each identified by a job ID, such as `build-android` **(6)**. In *Listing 12.3*, there are two jobs, `build-android` and `build-windows`. Each job can define a name, a runner, and multiple steps.

Jobs are the core components of a workflow, containing a sequence of tasks that need to be executed when certain events occur. By defining jobs specific to your app's development needs, you can ensure that the correct actions are taken during the build process, leading to a smoother and more efficient development pipeline.

Runners

A runner is the type of platform that runs the job. In our configuration, both Android and Windows jobs are executed using Windows runners. The runner is defined after the `runs-on:` **(7)** keyword. For more information on the configuration of runners, please refer to the GitHub Actions documentation. The runner that we use is `windows-latest`, which is the label of the runner image.

Choosing the right runner for your jobs is essential for ensuring that your app builds correctly and efficiently. By understanding the available runner options and their pre-installed tools, you can better tailor your development pipeline to the unique needs of your .NET MAUI app.

Steps

Multiple steps can be defined within a job, and they are defined after the `steps:` **(8)** keyword. In both Android and Windows builds, there are multiple steps: *checkout, install .NET MAUI workload, restore dependencies, build,* and *upload*. Each step can run a script or an action. In the checkout step, a `checkout` action is used after the `uses:` **(9)** keyword. An action is a custom application in the GitHub Actions platform to perform a complex but frequent repeated task. Using actions allows for code reuse, similar to how components function in object-oriented programming. To use an action, simply specify the action name with an optional version number. In our script, we can specify the checkout action as `actions/checkout@v3`.

The source code of the checkout action is hosted on GitHub and can be found at the following site: https://github.com/actions/checkout.

Once the source code is checked out, we need to install the .NET MAUI workload using the following command after the run: syntax:

```
dotnet workload install maui
```

In the restore and build steps, we can run the following dotnet command after the run: syntax:

```
dotnet restore ${{env.PROJECT_NAME}}/${{env.PROJECT_NAME}}.csproj
```

After the build is completed, we can upload the artifact using another upload-artifact action.

We have introduced the passxyz-ci-windows.yml workflow, which performs Android and Windows builds. Now, let's review the passxyz-ci-macos.yml workflow, which performs iOS and macOS builds, in *Listing 12.4*:

```
name: PassXYZ.Vault CI Build (MacOS)
on:
  push:
    branches: [ chapter12 ]
    paths-ignore:
      - '**/*.md'
      - '**/*.gitignore'
      - '**/*.gitattributes'
  pull_request:
    branches: [ chapter12 ]
  workflow_dispatch:

permissions:
  contents: read

env:
  DOTNET_NOLOGO: true
  DOTNET_SKIP_FIRST_TIME_EXPERIENCE: true
  DOTNET_CLI_TELEMETRY_OPTOUT: true
  DOTNETVERSION: 8.0.x
  DOTNETSDK: 'net8.0'
  PROJECT_NAME: PassXYZ.Vault
```

```
jobs:
# MAUI iOS Build
  build-ios:
    runs-on: macos-14                                              //(1)
    name: iOS Build
    steps:
      - name: Setup Xcode
        run: sudo xcode-select -s /Applications/Xcode_15.1.0.app
      - name: Checkout
        uses: actions/checkout@v3
      - name: Setup .NET
        uses: actions/setup-dotnet@v2
        with:
          dotnet-version: ${{env.DOTNETVERSION}}
      - name: Install MAUI workload
        run: dotnet workload install maui
      - name: Restore Dependencies
        run: dotnet restore ${{env.PROJECT_NAME}}
          /${{env.PROJECT_NAME}}.csproj
      - name: Build MAUI iOS
        run: dotnet build ${{env.PROJECT_NAME}}
          /${{env.PROJECT_NAME}}.csproj -c Release -f
${{env.DOTNETSDK}}-ios --no-restore /p:buildForSimulator=True
/p:packageApp=True /p:ArchiveOnBuild=False
      - name: Upload iOS Artifact
        uses: actions/upload-artifact@v3
        with:
          name: passxyz-ios-ci-build
          path: ${{env.PROJECT_NAME}}/bin/Release/
${{env.DOTNETSDK}}-ios/iossimulator-x64/**/*.app
# MAUI MacCatalyst Build
```

```
build-mac:
  runs-on: macos-14
  name: MacCatalyst Build
  steps:
    - name: Checkout
      uses: actions/checkout@v3
    - name: Setup .NET
      uses: actions/setup-dotnet@v2
      with:
        dotnet-version: ${{env.DOTNETVERSION}}
    - name: Install MAUI workload
      run: dotnet workload install maui
    - name: Restore Dependencies
      run: dotnet restore ${{env.PROJECT_NAME}}
        /${{env.PROJECT_NAME}}.csproj
    - name: Build MAUI MacCatalyst
      run: dotnet publish ${{env.PROJECT_NAME}}
        /${{env.PROJECT_NAME}}.csproj -c Release
  -f${{env.DOTNETSDK}}-maccatalyst --no-restore -p:BuildIpa=True
    - name: Upload MacCatalyst Artifact
      uses: actions/upload-artifact@v3
      with:
        name: passxyz-macos-ci-build
        path: ${{env.PROJECT_NAME}}/bin/Release/${{env.DOTNETSDK}}-
          maccatalyst/maccatalyst-x64/publish/*.pkg
```

Listing 12.4: `passxyz-ci-macos.yml` *(https://epa.ms/passxyz-ci-macos12-4)*

This workflow follows similar principles and includes steps to restore, install, build, and upload artifacts for the iOS and macOS versions of our .NET MAUI app. The difference here is that the `macos-14` **(1)** runner is used. The rest of the steps are similar to a Windows or Android build.

We have now introduced the configuration of all builds in GitHub Actions. You can check the build status on GitHub to see how the app builds will progress and succeed in our .NET MAUI project. Monitoring build statuses can help you identify any potential issues with your app during the development process and maintain the quality of your code.

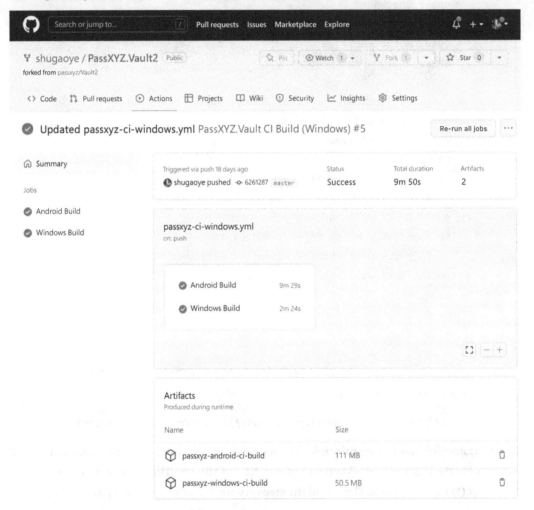

Figure 12.15: The Android and Windows build status

As seen in *Figure 12.15*, both the Android and Windows builds are completed successfully. The build artifacts can be downloaded from GitHub after the build is finished. This ensures you have access to the latest app builds, making it easier to distribute them for testing or deployment.

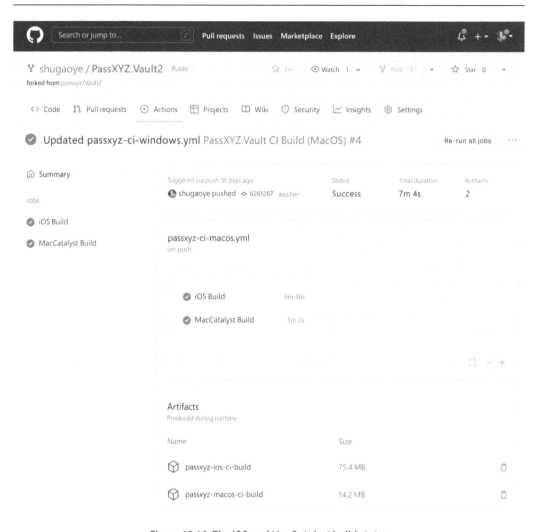

Figure 12.16: The iOS and MacCatalyst build status

As seen in *Figure 12.16*, both the iOS and Mac Catalyst builds completed successfully.

By successfully configuring GitHub Actions for your .NET MAUI project, you can maintain a CI process that ensures the quality of your code and streamlines development. Furthermore, this automated workflow simplifies the management of app builds and allows developers to focus on feature development and bug fixing.

We have now concluded the introduction to packaging our app for app store submissions and automating the build process using GitHub Actions. With these techniques in place, you can ensure a smoother and more efficient development pipeline for your .NET MAUI app, resulting in higher quality code and quicker deployments to the app stores.

Summary

CI/CD are common practices in today's development process. In this chapter, we introduced how to prepare a build so that the resulting packages can be used for the submission to various app stores. The process after the submission of build packages is not covered, since they are platform- and account-specific topics. Please refer to the *Further reading* section to find out more about how to publish applications to Google Play, Apple Store, and Microsoft Store.

After discussing the build process of each platform, we demonstrated how to automate the process using GitHub Actions.

With all the skills that you've learned from this book, you should be able to develop your own .NET MAUI applications and be ready to submit your apps to supported app stores. As you continue to grow as a developer, remember to explore new techniques and refine your understanding of .NET MAUI to create even better applications and streamline your development process.

Here are some online resources to learn .NET MAUI and stay up to date with the latest trends and news:

- **Official .NET Blog**: The Microsoft .NET team frequently posts updates and tutorials on .NET MAUI.

- **.NET MAUI GitHub repository**: This is the official repository of .NET MAUI. You can find the latest code, issues, and discussions about .NET MAUI here.

- **Microsoft docs**: This is the official documentation by Microsoft, and it provides a comprehensive guide to learning .NET MAUI.

- **Microsoft Learn**: Platform to find various learning paths and modules. You can find resources for .NET and possibly future content about .NET MAUI.

- **.NET Community Standups**: Regular community standups hosted by Microsoft engineers, where they discuss the latest trends and updates to .NET MAUI.

- **Stack Overflow**: A question and answer site for professional and enthusiast programmers.

- **.NET MAUI YouTube tutorials**: You can learn .NET MAUI by watching step-by-step tutorials on YouTube. For example, the Xamarin Developers YouTube channel posts tutorials and discussions about .NET MAUI.

- **Twitter**: Follow the official .NET account (@dotnet) and other Microsoft developers for the latest updates and developments.

Further reading

- Getting Started with DevOps and .NET MAUI: `https://devblogs.microsoft.com/dotnet/devops-for-dotnet-maui/`

- Upload your app to the Play Console: `https://developer.android.com/studio/publish/upload-bundle`

- Publish a .NET MAUI iOS app: `https://learn.microsoft.com/en-us/dotnet/maui/ios/deployment/?view=net-maui-8.0`

- Publish a .NET MAUI Mac Catalyst app: `https://learn.microsoft.com/en-us/dotnet/maui/mac-catalyst/deployment/?view=net-maui-8.0`

- Publish a .NET MAUI app for Android: `https://learn.microsoft.com/en-us/dotnet/maui/android/deployment/overview?view=net-maui-8.0`

- Publish a .NET MAUI app for Windows: `https://learn.microsoft.com/en-us/dotnet/maui/windows/deployment/overview?view=net-maui-8.0`

- Upload iOS builds to Apple Store: `https://developer.apple.com/help/app-store-connect/manage-builds/upload-builds`

Leave a review!

Enjoyed this book? Help readers like you by leaving an Amazon review. Scan the QR code below for a 40% discount code.

*Limited Offer

`packt.com`

Subscribe to our online digital library for full access to over 7,000 books and videos, as well as industry leading tools to help you plan your personal development and advance your career. For more information, please visit our website.

Why subscribe?

- Spend less time learning and more time coding with practical eBooks and Videos from over 4,000 industry professionals
- Improve your learning with Skill Plans built especially for you
- Get a free eBook or video every month
- Fully searchable for easy access to vital information
- Copy and paste, print, and bookmark content

At `www.packt.com`, you can also read a collection of free technical articles, sign up for a range of free newsletters, and receive exclusive discounts and offers on Packt books and eBooks.

Other Books You May Enjoy

If you enjoyed this book, you may be interested in these other books by Packt:

.NET MAUI Projects, Third Edition

Daniel Hindrikes

Johan Karlsson

Michael Cummings

ISBN: 9781837634910

- Set up .NET MAUI to build native apps for multiple platforms using its single project capabilities
- Understand the core aspects of developing a mobile app, such as layout, UX, and rendering
- Use custom handlers for platform-specific access
- Discover how to create custom layouts for your apps with .NET MAUI Shell

- Implement serverless services in your .NET MAUI apps using Azure SignalR
- Create a .NET MAUI Blazor application leveraging the power of web technologies
- Build and train machine learning models using ML.NET and Azure Cognitive Services

.NET MAUI for C# Developers

Jesse Liberty

Rodrigo Juarez

ISBN: 9781837631698

- Explore the fundamentals of creating .NET MAUI apps with Visual Studio
- Understand XAML as the key tool for building your user interface
- Obtain and display data using layout and controls
- Discover the MVVM pattern to create robust apps
- Acquire the skills for storing and retrieving persistent data
- Use unit testing to ensure your app is solid and reliable

C# 12 and .NET 8 – Modern Cross-Platform Development Fundamentals, Eighth Edition

Mark Price

ISBN: 9781837635870

- Discover C# 12's new features, including aliasing any type and primary constructors
- Try out the native AOT publish capability for ASP.NET Core 8 Minimal APIs web services
- Build rich web experiences using Blazor Full Stack, Razor Pages, and other ASP.NET Core features
- Integrate and update databases in your apps using Entity Framework Core models
- Query and manipulate data using LINQ
- Build and consume powerful services using Web API and Minimal API

Apps and Services with .NET 8, Second Edition

Mark Price

ISBN: 9781837637133

- Familiarize yourself with a variety of technologies to implement services, such as gRPC and GraphQL

- Store and manage data locally and cloud-natively with SQL Server and Cosmos DB

- Use ADO.NET SqlClient to implement web services with native AOT publish support

- Leverage Dapper for improved performance over EF Core

- Implement popular third-party libraries such as Serilog, FluentValidation, Humanizer, and Noda Time

- Explore the new unified hosting model of Blazor Full Stack

Packt is searching for authors like you

If you're interested in becoming an author for Packt, please visit authors.packtpub.com and apply today. We have worked with thousands of developers and tech professionals, just like you, to help them share their insight with the global tech community. You can make a general application, apply for a specific hot topic that we are recruiting an author for, or submit your own idea.

Share your thoughts

Now you've finished *.NET MAUI Cross-Platform Application Development, Second Edition,* we'd love to hear your thoughts! Scan the QR code below to go straight to the Amazon review page for this book and share your feedback or leave a review on the site that you purchased it from.

https://packt.link/r/1835080596

Your review is important to us and the tech community and will help us make sure we're delivering excellent quality content.

Index

Download a free PDF copy of this book

Thanks for purchasing this book!

Do you like to read on the go but are unable to carry your print books everywhere?

Is your eBook purchase not compatible with the device of your choice?

Don't worry, now with every Packt book you get a DRM-free PDF version of that book at no cost.

Read anywhere, any place, on any device. Search, copy, and paste code from your favorite technical books directly into your application.

The perks don't stop there, you can get exclusive access to discounts, newsletters, and great free content in your inbox daily

Follow these simple steps to get the benefits:

1. Scan the QR code or visit the link below

https://packt.link/free-ebook/9781835080597

2. Submit your proof of purchase
3. That's it! We'll send your free PDF and other benefits to your email directly

www.ingramcontent.com/pod-product-compliance
Lightning Source LLC
Chambersburg PA
CBHW060641060326
40690CB00020B/4480

9781835080597